D1131090

Olga Rudge and Ezra Pound

Anne Conover

Olga Rudge and Ezra Pound

"What Thou Lovest Well . . ."

Yale University Press   New Haven & London

Excerpt from *Shakespeare and Company*, © 1959 by Sylvia Beach and renewed 1987 by Frederic Beach Dennis, reprinted by permission of Harcourt, Inc.

Excerpts from *A Serious Character: The Life of Ezra Pound* by Humphrey Carpenter, © 1988 by Humphrey Carpenter, reprinted by permission of Houghton Mifflin Company.

Excerpts from *Discretions* by Mary de Rachewiltz, © 1971, reprinted by permission of Little, Brown and Company.

Unpublished letters of Ezra Pound: © 2001 by Mary de Rachewiltz and Omar S. Pound, used by permission of New Directions Publishing Corporation.

Unpublished letters of Olga Rudge: © 2001 by Mary de Rachewiltz, used by permission of Mary de Rachewiltz.

Unpublished letters of Dorothy S. Pound: © 2001 by Omar S. Pound, used by permission of Omar S. Pound.

The Cantos, by Ezra Pound: © 1934, 1937, 1940, 1948, 1956, 1959, 1962, 1963, 1966, 1968 by Ezra Pound.

Selected Letters, 1907–1941: © 1950 by Ezra Pound.

Copyright © 2001 by Anne Conover Carson. All rights reserved.
This book may not be reproduced, in whole or in part, including illustrations, in any form (beyond that copying permitted by Sections 107 and 108 of the U.S. Copyright Law and except by reviewers for the public press), without written permission from the publishers.

Designed by Rebecca Gibb. Set in Fournier type by Keystone Typesetting, Inc., Orwigsburg, Pennsylvania. Printed in the United States of America by R. R. Donnelley & Sons, Harrisonburg, Virginia.

Library of Congress Cataloging-in-Publication Data

3 1172 04682 2375

Carson, Anne Conover, 1937–
Olga Rudge and Ezra Pound : "What thou lovest well— " / Anne Conover.
    p.   cm.
Includes bibliographical references (p.   ) and index.
ISBN 0-300-08703-9 (alk. paper)
1. Rudge, Olga, 1895–1996. 2. Violinists—Biography. 3. Pound, Ezra, 1885–1972. I. Title.
ML418.R83 C37 2001
811'.52—dc21
2001001527

A catalog record for this book is available from the British Library.

The paper in this book meets the guidelines for permanence and durability of the Committee on Production Guidelines for Book Longevity of the Council on Library Resources.

10 9 8 7 6 5 4 3 2 1

JUN 2002

What thou lovest well remains,
                    the rest is dross
What thou lov'st well shall not be reft from thee
What thou lov'st well is thy true heritage

                              —*Canto LXXXI*

Contents

Preface

That her acts
>*Olga's acts*
>>*of beauty*
>>*be remembered.*

Her name was Courage
& is written Olga.

These lines are for the
>*ultimate* CANTO

Whatever I may write
>*in the interim.*

—*Ezra Pound*
The Cantos *(fragment 1966)*

In his seventy-first year, Ezra Pound wrote this tribute to his companion of half a century: "There is more courage in Olga's little finger than in the whole of my carcass . . . she kept me alive for ten years, for which no-one will thank her. The true story will not be told until *her* version is known." Olga Rudge's commitment to the poet may be viewed as the sacrifice of her considerable talents on the altar of his genius, since Pound incorporated the persona of the "trim-coiffed goddess" into his early Cantos, and Olga was the muse who inspired him to finish his epic work.

Olga was a distinguished concert violinist before she met Pound, and her legacy to the world of music was considerable, for she researched and brought to light many works of the long-neglected early-eighteenth-century composer Antonio Vivaldi. Her life is worth recording, not only in the supporting role of companion to a literary titan, but as a brilliant woman on her own, a woman ahead of her time who measured values by her own yardstick and defied conventions to concentrate on the two elements most important to her—music, and the man she loved.

She accepted the challenge of maintaining a lasting relationship with difficult, highly creative Ezra Pound—an American original. William

Cody, a psychiatrist who studied Pound, observed that Ezra acted like his own definition of the Vortex, "sucking everything and everyone into his omnivorous intellect. He used people . . . but the manipulation was sometimes unperceived by either side in the drama." The evidence suggests that Olga would not have been sucked into Ezra's Vortex had she not wanted to be.

In her eighties, Rudge wrote to Faber & Faber, Pound's British publisher, to propose "A Story of the Days," a collage of family records, letters, and memorabilia—in her words, "all very Henry Jamesy." But she never completed the project, and she refused to consider herself a proper subject for biography when cornered in her mountain retreat. "Write about Pound," she said.

In art as in life, Pound was a Victorian struggling to become a modern. As a student at the University of Pennsylvania, he immersed himself in medieval and Renaissance poetry, later writing *The Spirit of Romance* about the troubadours and courtly love. In the first years of the new century, he was indisputably a moving force in the creation of the Modernist movement. The Great War hastened the transition to a new age.

"Make it new," Pound said, and his influence on the next generation of poets and writers was both far-reaching and lasting. T. S. Eliot dedicated *The Waste Land* to Pound, "il miglior fabbro." "But for him," wrote James Joyce, "I should still be the unknown drudge he discovered."

Thomas Carlyle has said, "Next to possessing genius one's self is the power of appreciating it in others." Olga was the keeper of the flame who preserved Pound's legacy for posterity.

In this work, I have let Olga and Ezra speak for themselves through their correspondence and her diaries, without correcting errors of style and syntax. Some are written in the imperfect Italian of two people whose mother tongue was English. All reveal a spirited battle of the sexes between two highly intelligent and articulate human beings.

Acknowledgments

Poet Desmond O'Grady of County Cork, Ireland, suggested Olga Rudge—the woman who had the last word in *The Cantos* and in Pound's personal life—as a subject worthy of a biography. I first met Olga at the Fourteenth International Ezra Pound Conference at Schloss Brunnenburg, surrounded by grand- and great-grandchildren and the memorabilia of a fascinating life: programs of concerts in the leading halls of Europe; photos of world figures such as Pablo Casals, Adlai Stevenson, even the belligerent Il Duce, Benito Mussolini, playing with two lion cubs; a small silver bird studded with bright stones, the gift of World War I poet-hero Gabriele d'Annunzio. Her long-term memory was still sharp, offering glimpses of early childhood and her outstanding career as a concert violinist. Her daughter, Mary de Rachewiltz, allowed me to sort through memorabilia stored in old steamer trunks; Mary's son Siegfried Walter de Rachewiltz shared memories of his grandparents. Later, Mary visited my home in Washington and assured me of her family's cooperation.

In May 1993, de Rachewiltz lifted the restriction on the Olga Rudge Papers held by the Beinecke Library at Yale University. Rudge, who early believed in Pound's genius, had saved every scrap of paper, from the first blue *pneumatique* messages in Paris in the 1920s to the almost daily (sometimes twice daily) correspondence of half a century. After Pound's death, Olga continued to record her memories, thoughts, and activities in daily notebooks. I was the first scholar to gain access to these treasures. Grateful acknowledgment is given to the Yale Collection of American Literature, Beinecke Rare Book and Manuscript Library, for permission to publish excerpts from the Olga Rudge–Ezra Pound correspondence and manuscript materials, and other materials cited as "1996 addition," the Ezra Pound Collection, and EPAnnex.

I especially wish to thank Patricia C. Willis, Curator of American Literature at the Beinecke Library, and her accommodating assistants at the reference desk, Stephen C. Jones, Al Mueller, Rick Hart, Lori Misura, Dorothea Reading, and William Hemmig. Diane J. Ducharme, who sorted and cataloged, guided me through the maze of the Olga Rudge Papers. Also at Yale, Pound's bibliographer, the late Donald Gallup, was supportive of my work, as was Dr. Leonard Doob, professor of anthropology, a friend of Mary and the de Rachewiltz family. Charles Grench, then editor-in-chief of Yale University Press, recognized the contribution of the Olga Rudge Papers to the study of Pound and the Modernist poets, encouraged me to write the biography, and shepherded the manuscript through the Committee on Publications. Lawrence Rainey of the University of York reviewed the manuscript for the Press and offered many very helpful suggestions. At the Press, editor Lara Heimert saw the manuscript safely through submission to hardcover publication; and Philip King edited it with meticulous care and sensitivity.

Carroll F. Terrell, editor of *Paideuma*, the journal of Pound scholarship at the University of Maine in Orono, also shared my enthusiasm for Olga Rudge—"one of the miracle women of all time"—and first published Chapter 2 as "The Young Olga."

Among the many scholars who made pilgrimages to the Pound conferences as far afield as Beijing (where the Eighteenth International Ezra Pound Conference met in the summer of 1999) and who offered their support and encouragement were William Pratt, Miami University (Ohio); Zhaoming Qian, University of New Orleans; William McNaughton, City Polytechnic University of Hong Kong; Walter Baumann, Londonderry,

Northern Ireland; Richard Taylor, University of Bayreuth; Wendy Stallard Flory, Purdue University; Emily Mitchell Wallace of Philadelphia; Philip Grover, St. Front-sur-Nizonne, France; Hugh Witemeyer, University of New Mexico; Thomas Heffernan, Kagoshima Prefectural College, Japan; Lesley Hatcher, University of Georgia; Ghayyam Singh, University of Belfast; Peter Dale Scott, University of California, Berkeley; Timothy Redman, University of Texas at Dallas, Pound's next biographer. A. David Moody of the University of York contributed excerpts from his obituary of Olga Rudge published in the *Manchester Guardian* in March 1996. Others who made significant contributions were James J. Wilhelm, Rutgers University, author of a three-volume biography of Pound; and Daniel Hoffman, University of Pennsylvania, who first put me in touch with the Poundians.

Mary Jane Phillips-Matz of New York and Bussetto, Italy, biographer of Giuseppe Verdi and Olga's neighbor on the calle Querini, gave helpful insights into Olga's personality and character. Harriet and Lawrence Gay provided memories of Olga in Venice and San Francisco. Of the many others who contributed to this work, I would especially like to thank: in Venice, sculptor Joan Fitzgerald and Christopher and Mary Cooley; in Rapallo, Giuseppe Bacigalupo, Pound's friend and tennis partner, son of his medical doctor, and Giuseppe's son, Massimo Bacigalupo, professor at the University of Genoa; in Rome, John Drummond and Gabriele Stocchi; in Siena, Dr. Guido Burchi, who provided unpublished Chigi–Rudge correspondence from the collection of the Accademia Musicale Chigiana; Simonetta Lippi of Siena and Rome, who offered memorabilia and photos from her private collection. The late James Laughlin, Pound's publisher (New Directions), a self-described graduate of the "Ezuversity," granted a rare interview at his home in Norfolk, Connecticut. Caroline Smith Warren of Chapel Hill, North Carolina, offered correspondence of her cousin Olga with family friends Esther and Priscilla Heacock of Wyncote, Pennsylvania. In Youngstown, Ohio, Olga's birthplace, her cousins Dorothy Herschel and Sister Isabel Rudge of the Ursuline Mother House provided valuable footnotes to the Rudge history, as did Dr. Richard Murray, a friend of the Rudge family. Diane Speis Shagha of the Mahoning Valley (Ohio) Historical Society was my guide in the museum and library archives there. Peter Rudge, Olga's only surviving nephew (her brother Teddy's son), in Norfolk, England, cooperated through correspondence.

Dr. William Cody, a psychiatrist who observed Pound during his confinement at St. Elizabeth's Hospital in Washington, provided valuable clues to Ezra's relationships with women. Dr. E. Fuller Torrey, a research psychiatrist who analyzed Pound's personality in *The Roots of Treason: Ezra Pound and the Secrets of St. Elizabeth's,* was my guide at the hospital where Pound was incarcerated for thirteen years after World War II; the late Julien Cornell, lawyer for the defense and author of *The Trial of Ezra Pound,* offered helpful suggestions. Transcripts of taped interviews provided valuable clues to Olga's character and personality: five full hours of conversation between Olga and Peter Dale Scott at the University of California, Berkeley (1985); a three-hour interview with Christopher Winner in Venice (1977), intended for a *Newsweek* profile (excerpts of which were published in Rome in 1992). *Ezra Pound: An American Odyssey,* a documentary directed by Lawrence Pitkethly for the New York Center for Visual History (1981), captured Olga and Ezra on film in later years. I am deeply indebted to Robert Hughes, former conductor of the Oakland Symphony, and to his companion Margaret Fisher for memories of Olga in San Francisco overseeing the concert version of Pound's opera, *Le Testament de Villon.* Hughes offered professional advice on the presentation of the original concert version of *Le Testament* at the Sixteenth International Ezra Pound Conference in Brantôme, France (1995).

Among the valuable archival resources are the Ronald Duncan–Olga Rudge correspondence, held by the Harry Ransom Humanities Research Center at the University of Texas, Austin; the Noel Stock–James Laughlin correspondence, held by the Ward M. Canaday Center at the University of Toledo, Ohio; the Caresse Crosby correspondence, held by the Morris Library, Southern Illinois University; and the materials relating to Olga's musical career and Antonio Vivaldi research held by the music division of the Library of Congress.

During Pound's lifetime, Olga preferred to keep a low profile; hence little biographical material about her has been published. Mary de Rachewiltz's *Discretions* provided a portrait of her mother during the years from Mary's birth in 1925 until World War II. Of the many works about Pound, the most useful were J. J. Wilhelm's *Ezra Pound in London and Paris, 1908–1925;* Humphrey Carpenter's *A Serious Character: The Life of Ezra Pound;* Noel Stock's *The Life of Ezra Pound,* the first full-length study; John Tytell's *Ezra Pound: The Solitary Volcano; The Letters of Ezra Pound,* edited by D. D. Paige; and *Ezra Pound and Music,* edited with commentary by R. Murray Schafer.

My grateful acknowledgment for permission to quote heretofore unpublished letters and other writings of Ezra Pound, copyright 1999 by Mary de Rachewiltz and Omar Pound, used by permission of New Directions Publishing Corporation, agent for the copyright holders, and for permission to quote from *The Cantos of Ezra Pound,* copyright 1989. My thanks also to: J. Martin Cornell for permission to quote from the unpublished correspondence of Julien Cornell and James Laughlin; the Society of Authors, as literary representative for the estate of Compton Mackenzie, for permission to quote a brief extract from *Extraordinary Women;* Mary Jane Phillips-Matz, for permission to quote from "The Muse Who Was Ezra's Eyes," published in the *Manchester Guardian,* April 6, 1996; the Hemingway Foundation and its vice president, J. Gerald Kennedy of Louisiana State University, for permission to quote an unpublished letter from Ernest Hemingway to Olga Rudge; Richard Ardinger, editor of Limberlost Press, for permission to quote brief excerpts from *What Thou Lovest Well Remains: One Hundred Years of Ezra Pound;* the estate of Richard Aldington for permission to quote from *Soft Answers;* Noel Stock, for permission to quote from the unpublished correspondence of James Laughlin and Noel Stock, held by the Ward M. Canaday Center at the University of Toledo; Deirdre Levi, acting for the Cyril Connolly estate, for permission to quote unpublished correspondence of Olga Rudge and Cyril Connolly; Horst Tappe, for permission to reprint the photo of Ezra Pound and Olga Rudge in Venice (1962); Jane S. Sargeant, for permission to quote excerpts from "Torna! Torna!" Winthrop Sargeant's profile of Count Chigi Saracini in the September 3, 1960, *New Yorker;* and Meryle Secrest, for permission to quote brief excerpts from *Between Me and My Life: A Biography of Romaine Brooks.*

Also, profound gratitude to my early teacher and mentor, Dr. Frances R. Brown, who inspired me to explore the subtleties of the English language and directed my early archival research; to Elizabeth Courtner and her staff at the Palisades Branch Public Library of the District of Columbia for diligently locating local sources, and to the Washington (D.C.) Biographers, my loyal support group, and our leader, Marc Pachter, who unfailingly gave guidance and encouragement; to Cathya Wing Stephenson, who introduced me to valuable contacts at Yale and Pound's "other" family at Brunnenburg and assisted with the French translations; to her mother, the late Mrs. Charlotte Wing, who sponsored me at the Graduate Club in New Haven, where Sandra Gervais and her staff provided hospitality (and memorable home-baked muffins); to Moira Byrne, translator of the Chigi–Rudge correspondence and other materials in Italian; to my good friend Dottore Liborio Lamagna of the University of Siena, who corrected inaccuracies in the Italian transcriptions; to the late Alan D. Williams, who edited the first draft with a keen eye for inconsistencies; to Norman MacAfee, who contributed his great insight into Pound's poetry, knowledge of music, editorial skills, and good judgment in shaping and pruning the final manuscript; to Alexandre Manfull, my mentor in mastering the mysteries of the computer; to my daughter, Nathalie Ambrose, for encouragement and assistance in ways I cannot count. Last but by no means least, I am most grateful to Thomas B. Carson, my husband and companion on many rewarding voyages of discovery, without whose loyalty, enthusiasm, and support I could never have undertaken this work, who has lived for too many years in a literary ménage à trois with Olga and me but never admitted to being bored with either of us.

I

Olga and Ezra in Paris

1922–1923

Olga Rudge had nothing to gain by an alliance with Ezra Pound. Her reputation as a concert violinist was firmly established, her social position secure. She was living in her late mother's tastefully furnished flat near the Bois de Boulogne on the fashionable Right Bank; her only contact with the bohemian side of the Seine was the atelier of the Grande Chaumière, where her brother Teddy had studied landscape painting before the Great War. As Olga remembered the Americans on the Left Bank: "They stayed to themselves; they did not know the *French* as we did."

Ezra Pound was Left Bank. When he met Olga in the fall of 1922 he was undertaking a translation of Rémy de Gourmont's *Physique de l'Amour* for the American publisher Boni & Liveright. Gourmont's theory that "civilized man endures monogamy only when he can leave it and return at will" was shared by the poet. He was also exploring the connection between creativity and sexuality, and in the translator's preface he suggested "there must be some correlation between complete and profound copulation and cerebral development. . . . The brain itself . . . is a sort of great clot of genital fluid held in suspense." The woman's role was to be the passive receptacle for man's sperm; a secondary role in the creative process, but an essential one nonetheless. But not just any woman would serve as the receptacle for this poet's creativity; only an artistic and accomplished woman would do for a permanent liaison, and the high-spirited Olga was an obvious choice—a striking, poised young artist with dark hair bobbed and parted in the middle in the high fashion of the Twenties. Meeting her for the first time, one could not forget her fiercely energetic way of talking and moving about—an "Irish adrenal personality," as one friend described it—that drew into her circle handsome and talented people.

She was wearing a jacket in her preferred shade of red embroidered with gold Chinese dragons the night she met Ezra. Another of Pound's enthusiasms was translating the works of Li Po, a task left unfinished by the late Orientalist Ernest Fenollosa, and the oriental-motif jacket established a point of communication. Olga had inherited the jacket from Judith Gautier, daughter of the esteemed writer and translator of Chinese poetry, Théophile, whose apartment she visited as a child with her mother. There was instant attraction between the poet and the young musician with the violet, or periwinkle blue, eyes he would describe in *The Cantos* as the eyes of Botticelli's Venus. But he left the fête with Mademoiselle Raymonde Collignon, a blonde singer of *ballades,* and soon thereafter departed for the South of France with his wife, Dorothy.

"Paris is where EP and OR met, and everything in my life happened," Olga said later of the chance encounter with Ezra at 20, rue Jacob, in the salon of Natalie Barney. Like Olga, Barney had arrived in the City of Light as the child of an expatriate artist. Her historic townhouse near the boulevard Saint Germain was a refuge for escapees from Puritan mores, and her explicitly lesbian novel, *Idylle Saphique,* contributed to the legend of "the wild girl from Cincinnati." In her youth, Barney wore white flowing gowns by Schiaparelli or Lanvin and presided like a goddess under the domed, stained-glass ceiling of her drawing room—a rich blend of Turkish hassocks, lavish fur throws, tapestries, portraits, and vast mirrors—described by one guest as "hovering between a chapel and a bordello."

The grand piano that Wanda Landowska played in an earlier era premiered the contemporary works of Darius Milhaud and George Antheil in the Twenties. The large hexagonal table in the dining room was always spread with a feast prepared by Madame Berthe, the housekeeper, confidante, and amanuensis known for her chocolate cake, harlequin-colored gateaux, and triangular sandwiches "folded up like damp handkerchiefs." The Duchesse de Clermont-Tonnerre, a grande dame of impeccable lineage, presided over the tea service, though port, gin, and whiskey were more popular with American guests. A green half-light from the garden reflected from the glasses and silver tea urn as from under water. The garden was an unkempt miniature forest, with rambling paths and iron chairs balanced precariously near a marble fountain long choked with weeds and the Temple à l'Amitié, a copy of the Temple of the Vestal Virgins in Rome.

Barney, some twenty years Olga's senior, was the leader of a freedom-loving and bohemian group of intellectual women in the early 1900s: Colette, Anna de Noailles, and the spy Mata Hari. Another generation, Olga's contemporaries, succeeded them: English suffragettes, militant feminists and lesbians, tolerant heterosexuals and asexual androgynes. The expatriate American painter Romaine Brooks and the Princesse de Polignac (née Winaretta Singer, heiress to the sewing-machine fortune) were among the favored inner circle.

Musical reputations were established at Barney's salon, and Renata Borgatti, Olga's accompanist, invited her there after the two women returned from a sun-filled vacation on the Isle of Capri. Olga recognized Ezra, the tall American wearing a signature brown velvet jacket, as someone she had seen at a concert in London the year before. He was the last to leave, and she had asked Renata, "Who is that? He looks like an artist."

In an early photograph, Pound appears in front of Hilaire Hiler's Jockey Club wearing the floppy beret, velvet jacket, and flowing tie of artists of an earlier generation. With him are Jean Cocteau, Man Ray, and the notorious Kiki of Montparnasse. Those who knew Ezra in the prime of life testify that photos did not do justice to his charismatic appeal. Margaret Anderson, founder of the *Little Review,* described the poet's robustness, his height, his high color, the mane of wavy red-blond hair. And the eyes: "Cadmium? amber? no, topaz in Chateau Yquem," another of his contemporaries observed.

Anderson remarked that Pound was then somewhat patriarchal in his attitude toward women. If he liked them, he kissed them on the forehead or drew them up on his knee. But there was about Ezra an air of someone confidently living his life in high gear. It was not entirely in jest that he wrote to Francis Picabia in the summer of 1921 that he had been in Paris for three months "without finding a congenial mistress."

Pound and his British wife, Dorothy Shakespear, had crossed the Channel in January 1921 and settled into a *pavillon* at 70 bis, rue Notre Dame des Champs, a first-floor apartment facing an alleyway, the bedrooms above reached by an open stairway. There was a tiny lean-to kitchen, of little interest to Dorothy (in Canto 81, Ezra would write "some cook, some do not cook"). As he described his digs to the wealthy art patron John Quinn: "The rent is MUCH cheaper than the hotel . . . 300 francs a month [about twelve dollars in 1921] . . . and I have built all the furniture except the bed and the stove" (sturdy wood and canvas-back chairs, and a triangular typing table that fit neatly into one corner). The books, manuscripts, and a Dolmetsch clavichord were brought over later from London, and Pound added a Henri Gaudier-Brzeska sculpture and the canvas by Japanese artist Tami Koumé that covered one wall.

At age thirty-six, Ezra still lived on small stipends from reviews and other literary endeavors, supplemented by Dorothy's allowance and contributions from the elder Pounds in Philadelphia. Since the time of Victor Hugo, Notre Dame des Champs, close by the Luxembourg Gardens and the charcuteries and bakeries of the rue Vavin, has been home to improvident writers and artists. Ernest Hemingway, who lived with his wife Hadley above the sawmill at No. 13, wrote that Ezra's studio was "as poor as Gertrude Stein's [on the neighboring rue de Fleurus] was rich." Ezra was not a welcome guest on the rue de Fleurus; during his first audience with Stein, he sat down too heavily on one of her fragile chairs, causing it to collapse. Stein did not find Pound amusing: "he is a village explainer," she famously said, "excellent if you were a village, but if you were not, not."

Pound ignored the Stein circle and joined forces with Barney, another fierce individualist. He had corresponded with Natalie as early as 1913 about the translation of de Gourmont's *Lettres à l'Amazone,* open letters to Barney then appearing in the *Mercure de France,* the sensation of Paris. When Ezra arrived on the scene, Natalie provided introductions to Anatole France, André Gide, Paul Valéry, the distinguished literati of an older generation, and his contemporaries, the Dadaist painter Francis Picabia and the avant-garde poet Jean Cocteau, whom Pound described as "the BEST poet and prose writer in Paris." With such comrades, Ezra often was observed enjoying Parisian nightlife with women other than his reserved wife, whose porcelain skin and ice-blue eyes were, in Pound's words, "a beautiful picture that never came to life." It was Ezra's custom to drop in at odd hours, often midnight, at bistros on the rue du Lappe or the Deux Magots, the Dôme, and other Left Bank cafés where artists and intellectuals gathered.

One of the first friends Ezra called on in Paris was composer and musician Walter Morse Rummel. The son of a German pianist and a daughter of Samuel F. B. Morse, the telegrapher, Rummel crossed over from London to cut a dashing figure in the Parisian music world. Rummel discovered and set to music Provençal poetry, also an enthusiasm of Ezra's. And it was Rummel who introduced the poet to Raymonde Collignon, a young soprano known for her porcelain figure and sleek head set in a basketwork of braids. Wearing a shimmery gold-yellow frock, Raymonde arrived at Barney's Turkish drawing room on Ezra's arm the night that he met Olga.

At their next meeting, Olga recalled that Barney was receiving a select group of friends in her boudoir, and Ezra was acting as *cavaliere servente* to the Marchesa Luisa Casati. (Romaine Brooks's thinly disguised painting of Casati rising nude from the rocks at Capri filled one wall of Barney's bedroom.) Ernest Walsh, the poet and co-editor with Ethel Moorhead of *This Quarter*, later husband to the novelist Kay Boyle, was among the chosen few that evening. As they were leaving, Ezra suggested to Olga that she invite Walsh, another visiting American, to her apartment to give him an insider's glimpse of the Right Bank.

Ezra had not yet visited the rue Chamfort, and when he came, Olga assumed he would be accompanied by Walsh. But when she next saw him Ezra was at her door, alone, holding the score of an opera he had written, *Le Testament de Villon*.

Paris was alive with the new music—Maurice Ravel, Igor Stravinsky, Virgil Thomson, Erik Satie, Francis Poulenc, Darius Milhaud. Ezra, who was already experimenting with new rhythms in poetry, surprised visitors who came unannounced to 70 bis, rue Notre Dame des Champs, in the throes of composing an opera with the assistance of Agnes Bedford, an English pianist and voice coach, on the notation.

Pound's study of music had begun on his mother's piano in Wyncote, Pennsylvania. In 1907, he became enamored with the French troubadours and the works of François Villon, the fifteenth-century vagabond poet, an interest reinforced by long walking tours in Provence. "He sang it [*Le Testament*] to me, with one finger on the piano," Olga remembered. "I discovered the pitch was noted accurately, but not the time. We started to work correcting the time." Looking over Ezra's shoulder, Olga interrupted his "piano whack" to protest that the poet was not playing the *written* score. But Pound, the creative genius, was not easily instructed; he continued to play the music he heard with his inner ear, not the notes on the page before him.

The Rudge–Pound correspondence began on June 21, 1923, with a brief *pneumatique* between the Right and Left Bank. These messages on blue paper transmitted through underground tubes from one post office to another and hand delivered by messengers on bicycles were then the most rapid means of communication. This one was the first of many short notes to make or break appointments: "Me scusi tanto, ma impossible per oggi . . . domani forse da Miss B[arney]?" They were often written in Italian and closed with the pet name he often used for Olga, "una bella figliuola" [beautiful young girl].

Ezra soon introduced Olga to Margaret Anderson's protégé, George Antheil, a young pianist and composer from New Jersey who had arrived in Paris to attend the premiere of Igor Stravinsky's *Les Noces* on June 13. With his Romanian *belle amie* Böski Marcus, he took rooms above Sylvia Beach's landmark Left Bank bookshop, Shakespeare and Company. Short and slight, with clipped blond bangs that made him look even younger than his twenty-three years, Antheil met avant-garde composer Erik Satie and "that Mephistophelian red-bearded gent, Ezra Pound," at a tea honoring Anderson and the actress Georgette Leblanc.

Ezra began to take Antheil to Olga's flat to practice. Olga suggested Pound's initial interest in her was her mother's piano—for Ezra, she insisted, work came first. Antheil soon set to composing a violin sonata for

Olga, determined to make the music, he wrote Ezra, "as wildly strange as she looked, tailored to her special appearance and technique. It is wild, the fiddle of the Tziganes . . . totally new to *written* music . . . barbaric, but I think Olga will like it . . . it gives her more to do and show off with than the other sonatas."

In late summer, while Dorothy was in London to assist her mother, Olivia Shakespear, in caring for her husband during a long illness, Ezra introduced Olga to the land of the troubadours. No written record remains of that summer holiday, or their itinerary, only a fading black-and-white photograph album labeled "August 1923—Dordogne." Olga was the photographer and Ezra often the subject, appearing under gargoyles of the cathedrals in Ussel and Ventadour and other unidentifiable French villages. In her eighties, she reminisced about "the photos EP and I took on our walking tour. . . . 'I sailed never with Cadmus,' " she recalled, referring to a line in Canto 27, "but he took me to Ventadour." On the back of one snapshot she wrote: "note how elegant a gentleman could be, walking 25 kilometers a day with a rucksack—in those days, no hitchhiking."

The Antheil-Rudge collaboration at Olga's flat continued on an almost daily schedule in the fall. Antheil praised Olga's mastery of the violin: "I noticed when we commenced playing a Mozart sonata . . . [she] was a consummate violinist. . . . I have heard none with the superb lower register of the D and G strings that was Olga's exclusively." On October 4 at the Théâtre des Champs-Elysées, the three short Antheil sonatas that premiered as the curtain raiser for opening night of the Ballets Suédois became the most controversial musical event of the season. A correspondent of the *New York Herald* compared the evening to the premiere of Stravinsky's *Sacre du Printemps:* "a riot of enormous dimensions occurred when George Antheil . . . played several piano compositions. . . . Antheil is a new force in music . . . of a sharper and more breath-taking order than Stravinsky." In his autobiography, Antheil recalled:

My piano was wheeled out . . . before the huge [Fernand] Léger cubist curtain, and I commenced playing. . . . Rioting broke out almost immediately. I remember Man Ray punching somebody in the nose in the front row, Marcel Duchamp arguing loudly with somebody in the second. . . . By this time, people in the galleries were pulling up the seats and dropping them down into the orchestra; the police entered and arrested the Surrealists who, liking the music, were punching everybody who objected. . . . Paris hadn't had such a good time since the premiere of . . . *Sacre du Printemps.*

The riot was used later as a film sequence in *L'Inhumaine,* starring Georgette Leblanc.

Pound was then undertaking a transcription of a twelfth-century air by Gaucelm Faidet that he had discovered in the Biblioteca Ambrosiana in Milan, "Plainte pour la mort du Richard Coeur de Lion," and composing an original work, *Sujet pour Violon,* for Olga's concert on December 11 at the *ancien* Salle du Conservatoire. One critic of that concert praised the young violinist as possessing "a very pretty sonority bidding fair to develop into virtuosity. . . . We admire this young artist for having enough courage to sacrifice on the altars of Mr. Antheil's conceited art, personal honors which otherwise might have been hers. Both her enterprise and her playing merit commendation." Pound's pieces won their share of applause: "to those who like to push their musical researches into that kind of thing [they] were extremely interesting."

But the critics' focus in the December concert was on the controversial Antheil sonatas for violin and piano. The Paris *Tribune:* "Can this really be denoted music? . . . No, it is a kind of primitive melopoeia . . . like those bizarre tambourine accompaniments of Arab or Moroccan musicians when in their drinking dens and cafés." Mozart's Concerto in A Major was called a "a heaven-sent beneficent repose for the ears" by one critic, while another dissented: "In his own music, Mr. Antheil may try to 'get away' with whatever he wants to, but he really should beware of composers so refined and subtle as Mozart."

Ezra advised Olga to "practice the Mozart and Bach for a couple of days by themselves. I mean DON'T play the Antheil at all, but concentrate on B[eethoven] and M[ozart], so as to EEEliminate the effects of modern music."

In late December, Ezra checked into the American Hospital in Neuilly with an appendicitis attack. After a discreet visit to the hospital with flowers (one of which she pressed and saved with a card from Charlot, the florist), Olga wrote: "Dolcezza mia, how happy she was to see him . . . la bonne tête . . . les mains . . . maigre, bianchi—bella soi!" In old age, Olga confided that the young Ezra possessed the most beautiful head, the most expressive hands she had ever seen. Her letter reveals a greater degree of intimacy: "be good and lie on your back and don't let the pack slip off that tummy peloso."

Whatever Ezra's complex motivations, soon after the new year of 1924 began he and Dorothy left Paris for Rapallo, a quiet resort on the Riviera di Levante of Italy.

2

Julia and Her Daughter

1895–1909

Meeting Olga in Paris, Ezra's friend Ford Madox Ford was astonished to discover she was an American from Ohio: "I did not know such beautiful flowers blossomed in that desert!"

When Olga visited her birthplace of Youngstown for the first time as an adult, in 1969, it was a pleasant valley town. But in 1895, the year of her birth, the air was polluted with smoke from the mills. In summer, townsfolk escaped to Mill Creek Park on the new open-air trolley line, boat and tub races on the Mahoning River drew large crowds to the water's edge, and excursion tickets on the fastest trains to Atlantic City and Cape May, New Jersey, then cost only twelve dollars. In winter, skating and harvesting ice on the river and Mill Creek were popular activities, and tears would flow after Giacomo Puccini's *The Bohemian Girl* (better known as *La Bohème*) was performed at the Youngstown Opera House.

No record exists of the first meeting of Olga's parents, but we may assume that Julia O'Connell met her future husband after a performance at the Youngstown Opera House. Julia was a classical singer from New York City, and Olga loved to tell a story of the stormy night her mother, dressed in concert finery and flowing cloak, took the ferry to Brooklyn and was late getting to an engagement. When she rushed on stage with her long dress still hiked up through her belt, wearing heavy rain boots, the impresario introduced her as "that mad Irish girl—but *she can sing!*"

Church choirs were Julia's training grounds: the Collegiate Dutch Reformed Church on Fifth Avenue and Forty-eighth Street (the oldest Protestant congregation in North America), and Henry Ward Beecher's Plymouth Congregational Church in Brooklyn. She was principal contralto of the Madison Square Presbyterian Church of Dr. Charles Henry Parkhurst, the distinguished clergyman from Amherst College, who launched the attack that defeated Tammany Hall from his pulpit. Many civic leaders and members of society belonged to these congregations, and Julia carved a solid niche for herself among the grandes dames of Old New York. Many years later, Ezra would remind Olga that his Aunt Frank (Frances Weston) had heard O'Connell sing in Dr. Parkhurst's church.

Early records of the arrival of Olga's maternal grandparents in the New World are sketchy. Theirs was a large Irish-Catholic family with many branches. Julia's father, James O'Connell, a gentleman of means before coming to America, wrote a book about the sport of flycasting that Ezra Pound later quoted in Canto 51:

Hen pheasant's feather does for a fly,
green tail, the wings flat on the body.

According to Olga, her grandfather "took my mother to Boston to be born, but not liking the place, he shook the dust of Boston off his feet, and went up to Quebec to die young." In Montreal, Olga's grandmother O'Connell (née Paige) posed for the official photographer to Her Majesty Queen Victoria, from which it is safe to deduce that they were "lace-curtain Irish." James continued to enjoy sport fishing and thoroughbred horseracing throughout his short life, returning to County Limerick every year during the racing season.

Sadly, he had not invested wisely for his family's future. Music was a serious career for his daughter Julia, not a casual pursuit to fill the idle hours of a well-bred Victorian lady. As Olga wrote: "My mother was a very capable woman. She had to be. Her father died when she was a small child, leaving his wife and three children just enough to exist on. My mother, the eldest, at eighteen commenced to support the others with her music. Her piano playing was good enough for her to get accompanying work, and her voice unusual enough to get a good church position before she had any lessons."

When she could afford it, Julia studied singing with two of the leading vocal coaches in New York. But Europe was the home of classical music. Determined to study voice in London, she gave "a GRAND CONCERT" in Steinway Hall on Friday evening, April 11, 1890, as a benefit to finance her coaching under Alberto Randegger and Sir George Henschel, renowned professors of singing at the Royal Conservatory of Music. Julia made her debut in London in *Il Trovatore*, and a performance with the celebrated Lucille Hill of the D'Oyly Carte Opera accompanied by Isidore de Lara drew praise: "Miss O'Connell sang so well that she was invited to the houses of royalty." She was the soloist at another "grand evening concert" at St. James's Hall under the honorary patronage of Princess Christian of Schleswig-Holstein and the Honorable William E. Gladstone, the British prime minister.

In May 1892, Julia returned from two years of study in London and Paris. She was described then as possessing "beauty of the brunette type with large brown eyes. . . . Her greatest charm is a simple, unaffected manner, which wins friends on every side." At the time of her marriage she was twenty-nine—considered a spinster in that era—but her voice and her charm won John Edgar Rudge's heart.

Photos of Olga's father in his thirties show a handsome man of above average height with impressive gray eyes and a thick handlebar mustache —one of Youngstown's most eligible bachelors. He married Julia in New York's St. Paul the Apostle Roman Catholic Church on Sixtieth Street and Columbus Avenue on August 16, 1893. The bride's sister, Louise Birt O'Connell, and J. Edgar's brother, William Rudge, signed as witnesses.

Their first child, Olga Ludovica (Louise) Rudge, was born two years later on April 13, a birthdate shared with Thomas Jefferson, a fact she mentioned often throughout her long and unconventional life. She sat for a first photo—a plump baby in a lace-trimmed, puff-sleeved dress—on a brocade-upholstered parlor chair in the white-frame Victorian home at

733 Bryson Street, where her father had brought his talented young bride to live.

Olga was proud of the Rudge family history dating back to the reign of King Charles II, in 1664, in the County of Worcestershire, England. *Res non verba* (deeds, not words) is the family motto, of great significance to the young Olga. It was the custom to give the name of the manor house to all who lived on the property surrounding it, and when the grandson of Sir William Courten sold "the rudge" adjoining the Abbey of Kingswood to Edward, Olga's great-great ancestor, the family adopted that surname.

Olga's paternal grandfather, George Rudge of Hereford, married Jane Stock, the youngest of four unmarried sisters from Lintridge in the nearby county of Gloucestershire. There was opposition to the match within the family because the young couple were first cousins, and they soon emigrated to America to join George's brother, James.

The two brothers purchased a valuable piece of property in Boardman, a Youngstown suburb, which they homesteaded. George had brought with him a flock of fine Cotswold sheep, providing the beginning of a profitable business; he is credited with introducing the Long Wool breed into northern Ohio before expanding from farming and stock-raising into other ventures. In time, he became a notary public, secretary of the waterworks, and superintendent of Calvary Cemetery, while earning an ample living in insurance and real estate.

When the Rudges first arrived in the new community, they were members of the Anglican Church of their youth. But their close friendship with Father E. M. O'Callahan, rector of St. Columba's Roman Catholic Church, led them to convert to the Catholic faith. Their union, once considered "unfortunate," was not only happy but blessed with eight children and twenty-two grandchildren. Their conversion had long-lasting consequences in the life of their granddaughter, Olga, who was baptized in the parish of St. Columba's on April 18, 1895.

Despite his success in America, Grandfather Rudge always looked back on his English homeland with nostalgia. On Christmas Day 1904, he wrote to young Olga: "My home . . . was near Ross-on-Wye in Herefordshire. . . . [Alexander] Pope in his poem, 'The Man of Ross,' immortalized the little country town. . . . I fear you and your brothers will grow up and forget." Olga was at a convent school in England when her grand-father died at age eighty-three, but many in the Mahoning Valley mourned his passing. His devoted wife Jane died of pneumonia three days later, after saying: "Wouldn't it be nice if I could go, too?"

In the early years of their marriage, his son John remained in Youngs-town while Julia toured, returning to Ohio between singing engagements. Their love match was held together by their strong Catholic faith; divorce was never contemplated. "My parents did not quarrel in front of the children. They married 'till death us do part,'" Olga wrote. Edgar Marie ("Teddy") Rudge, the second child, was conceived in Ohio but born in Paris, followed a year later by another son, Arthur Edgar (nicknamed "Babs" because of his beautiful long curls).

Arthur was a mischievous lad whose acts of derring-do often necessi-tated an older sister's rescue and excuses for him. As a very young child, he fell down the stairs into the dark cellar of the Youngstown house. In this and other emergencies, Olga exhibited the characteristic that shaped her life (which Ezra immortalized in the ultimate Canto)—a blind courage.

Olga recalled very little of those early years in Ohio. To her eyes, Julia appeared "like a cat dragging kittens by the scruff of their necks from a fire . . . we were saved from Youngstown. . . . Even a woman who married for love and produced three children in three years could not stay put in Ohio," she wrote in the brief autobiography commenced in midlife but never completed. Julia had taught a singing class, "a chorus organized among the miners, the first orchestral concert Youngstown had ever known," Olga said. "[It was] considered a great 'social progress.' . . . The local millionaire got into evening clothes as a great favor to my mother. These seeming triumphs were not sufficient to offset the risks we ran (in her view) in that atmosphere. I was first dragged away from my birthplace to Europe at the age of two months. By my ninth year, I was to cross the ocean seven times."

According to Olga, "Once married, [Julia] saw herself put into the category of wives, and treated accordingly. . . . Money doled out in dribs and drabs, secrecy and ignorance of facts . . . the whole situation galling to the pride and to the nerves. . . . My father thought he was behaving in a usual and proper manner. He was certainly a generous man . . . but such methods are too tyrannous and antiquated to work successfully under modern conditions. I realize the influence this had on my life. If one's mother commences dramatically to implore that she will never live to see you any man's chattel, it makes some impression. . . . [I] was not brought up to consider marriage as a career."

In 1903, Julia and the children settled in New York on the fifth floor of 336 West Ninety-fifth Street on the Upper West Side. Olga remembered sledding in winter and rolling her hoops in summer at the foot of Grant's Tomb. Olga was the oldest, the leader of the pack and its conscience. She remembered a plan to build a hut on a vacant lot on West Ninety-fifth Street for herself and the boys to play house in: "It is curious my wanting a home away from home so early . . . 'castles in Spain.'"

There were quieter pursuits on rainy days. Among Olga's keepsakes from that time is an "advertisement" the children composed and designed for "Julia Rudge, Contralto, soloist for church concerts." On the program were "Olga Rudge, Violinest [*sic*]," and "T. Rudge, pianest [*sic*]." Looking back, when someone mentioned putting his or her cards on the table, it reminded Olga of the card game, Patience, she played with her mother. There were always "suitable books. . . . I knew my Grimm and Perrault." Julia complained that her daughter would ruin her eyesight with the "desultory reading" that became a lifetime compulsion.

"All of my life, I never lacked any of the good things money can*not* buy. . . . We had such a good time, we never felt the need of it. . . . it was often thought of, but only when it was *not there*. Our innocent snobberies were a great salve to our pride. We had no roller skates, but we could all speak French . . . my mother sang on the concert stage and got bouquets. . . . The marvel of it is the *courage* with which she kept to her standards . . . one had the best, or one went without—the viewpoint of the artist."

Among those memories of New York summers before air-conditioning were the stifling heat and the smell of melting asphalt through open windows. In the early 1900s there was still a view and a breath of air from the Hudson River. But the family had no money to escape to a cooler and greener place. On one of the last days of May 1903, Olga observed a well-to-do gentleman questioning the elevator boy. The stranger was looking for a furnished apartment for the summer, "when business calls me to New York." On impulse, Olga piped up: "My mother is renting *our* flat on the fifth floor."

Julia had learned to answer opportunity when it knocked. She sublet the apartment for a serendipitous sum that allowed the family to escape for the summer—in Olga's words, "three of the most glorious months of my life"—to an old farmhouse in the White Mountains, with an unobstructed view of Mount Chocorua. In Canto 74, Pound—writing from his "cage" in Pisa—later compared Mount Chocorua to Tai'chen, the sacred mountain of Confucius, recalling the purity of the air on Chocorua "in the land of maple."

Among memories of that summer were visits to nearby Meriden, New Hampshire, where her mother's sister, Aunt Louise Birt Baynes, lived with Olga's beloved Uncle Harold. Baynes, an early conservationist, was a friend of President Theodore Roosevelt and co-founder of the American Bison Society and the Long Island Bird Club, which met in the drawing room of the Roosevelt home at Oyster Bay. After Roosevelt left the White House, Uncle Harold and his club presented "Sanctuary, a Bird Masque" (an effort to stop the then-widespread use of bird plumage on women's headdresses), under the patronage of Mrs. Woodrow Wilson. He was never too busy lecturing and writing to enchant his favorite niece with stories of Jimmie, the black bear cub, a central character in one of his many books. Until his premature death in 1925, Baynes was a beloved presence in Olga's life.

In September 1904, when Olga was nine, Julia sent the child to England, to provide her with "advantages" she herself never had. She was to board at St. Anthony's Convent, Sherborne, Dorset, under the direction of Madame Anselm, the British head, and Madame Pharaïlde, a Belgian nun (whom Olga credited with her fluency in French). She remembered being left in the charge of the captain of the H.M.S. *New York*. Every morning, a stewardess delivered a fresh letter from her mother (from the packet Julia

placed in her hands before departure). There is no evidence of psycholog-
ical distress suffered by the little girl on her first solo voyage away from
home—or she did a very efficient job of concealing it. She was seasick for
only one day and one night, and appeared to enjoy the whole adventure.
She wrote her mother that she saw a "sea-lion or porpoise jumping out of
the water" and was playing cross-tag before the first bugle call with a little
girl and her brother from San Francisco: "It makes an awful noise, that
bugle does."

Julia wrote often to "Dearest Miss Fluffy" at the school and Olga
preserved her own letters, giving a glimpse of life inside the convent and
her own developing independent personality: "I know Madame [Pha-
raïlde] likes me. . . . I am a universal favorite, but I am not vain about it,
because my goodness and reflectiveness are as easily taken off as put on,
but *I feel I must keep up my reputation*." Olga's mischievous nature erupted
when she played "witch" with a black pinafore over her head to scare the
younger girls.

Madame Pharaïlde reported to Julia that the young Olga was *très sym-
pathique:* "Votre fillette est tout à fait charmante . . . vous pouvez être
tranquille, tout marche très bien, santé et travail. Votre jeune fille m'a
même assuré plusieurs fois qu'elle ne s'ennuyait pas. Nous faisons tout ce
qui vous désirez, promenades chaque jour, lecture, etc." [Your little girl is
utterly charming . . . you can be assured that everything is going very
well, health and work. Your daughter has even assured me several times
that she was not bored. We are doing everything that you desire, walks
each day, reading, etc.]

She was preparing for her first Christmas at the convent, perhaps hiding
tears behind a façade of humor, when she wrote to her mother: "Only
twelve days till the holidays! Yesterday afternoon, Madame Marie-Joseph
asked the little ones to help seed raisins for the Xmas pudding. We asked
riddles and told stories: 'Do you know the difference between the post
office and a load of hay?' 'I do not.' 'Then I won't send you to pick up
letters for me'."

In the dreary days of January and February, Olga's enthusiasm gave
way to her first complaints. Julia replied with some memorable advice,

indicating the closeness of their relationship and the major role she played in Olga's life.

> My darling girlie: Let me tell you out of my own experience that when you feel inclined to find fault with circumstances, that the best thing to do is *work*. I have been through so many years of ennui and disappointment, and if I had only had someone to show me how *to make my conditions or surroundings, instead of letting them make me,* I should have been saved much suffering. *Make your music your first duty.* Concentrate on it and try to love even the drudging of it. Then use it (when you can play even a few bars properly) to drive away the little devils of unrest which are always trying to upset us.

Olga's reply indicated that she had recovered her high spirits and was following her mother's advice: "Could you send me some violin strings? Mine have broken. Madame said I was *glad* they were broken, but . . . I'm not spoilt, am I? All the girls say I am."

Olga made her First Communion at St. Anthony's Convent School on June 29, 1905, and it was of such importance to her that—sometime after her eightieth birthday—she recreated the events of that day in her notebook.

> My mother had made me a dress and sent it from New York: short, long-waisted, with a sash, and with insertions and edging of real lace (she must have bought it in Belgium and treasured it), with fine tucks. [I wore] a white tulle veil under a wreath of white roses from the convent garden. . . .
>
> Madame Anselm came into the room . . . to see me get into my dress, that I was looking forward to with joy—not vanity. [She] suggested it would be a fitting sacrifice if I did not look at myself in the long mahogany-framed swinging mirror, and turned it back to front! So I never enjoyed what my mother had done with such care for me. I have no idea what I looked like, but I took pleasure . . . in *renouncing* vanity.

To anyone raised in a convent school of the era, the nun's action rings of overzealous piety; to today's readers, it would seem unduly harsh, even sadistic. In retrospect, Olga considered it a cultural difference: Madame Anselm was *English;* "Madame Pharaïlde [the Belgian nun] would have *enjoyed* the dress with me." Some years before her relationship with Pound began in the 1920s, Olga had fallen away from the strict practices of the Roman Catholic church, but she saved the First Communion dress for their daughter, Mary, who wore it again at Gais and passed it down to Olga's granddaughter, Patrizia.

Letters to Julia from Olga during her eleventh and twelfth years reveal the personality of a talented first child, the focus of her mother's love and attention. She reassured her mother that she was still practicing to perfect her talent for the violin and had developed an aptitude for writing. Even at this early age, her essays were "mentioned," and her letters in later life were carefully crafted.

Later, Julia—foreseeing the day when her voice would lose its brilliance —moved her residence to London to concentrate her hopes and ambitions on her young daughter. She was invited to assist Gertrude Griswold in organizing the Delle Sedie School of Singing, inspired by the grand tradition of her former voice coach, baritone Enrico Delle Sedie, who had died in Paris in 1907. The opening bulletin noted that "Mrs. J. Edgar Rudge has entire charge of the business details connected with the formation of the School." After praising her fine contralto voice and appearances on the concert stage, it announced that Julia had come to the school "after an early marriage and removal to the West cut short a promising career."

Along with her new position came a rent-free "villa" at one of London's most prestigious addresses, 12 Hill Road in St. John's Wood, to which the three children came home on weekends from their boarding schools: Olga from St. Anthony's, and her young brothers from St. Leonard-on-Sea, a Catholic preparatory school.

Julia soon established herself in the expatriate community, in the American Women's Club founded by Mrs. Whitelaw Reid, the U.S. ambassador's wife, and presided over by Mrs. Curtis Brown, wife of the publisher. Other activities centered on the Episcopal Church, of which Julia—a Roman Catholic—was recording secretary.

It was permanently recorded in the *History of Youngstown* that "Mrs. J. Edgar Rudge is residing in London, superintending the musical education of their daughter, Olga, who inherits a large measure of her talented mother's gift of song. It is the parents' intention to give their daughter every educational advantage. . . . Both Mr. and Mrs. Rudge cross the Atlantic almost yearly."

Olga remembered that their dollars seemed to stretch further because of the favorable exchange rate. "The money didn't come with regularity, it never was to, but the English system of books and bills seemed to ease the strain." They could afford a cook and a manservant, with enough left over to take long summer holidays, sometimes at Easter. There are snapshots of the three (very small) children at St. Helier's in Jersey, the Channel Islands, La Panne Bains on the Belgian seacoast, and "the summer that Teddy fell on the rocks at Lyme Regis." Peace and contentment were the theme of the years at St. John's Wood:

> The first room I ever had of my own was at 12 Hill Road; it looked
> on the back garden, . . . [it was] a lovely house, and my mother had
> made it charming. . . . it had a small conservatory, a small front
> garden, which was very nice for tea outside, but not big enough for
> garden parties. . . . I had a collie pup that cost two guineas and had
> a pedigree. Since it howled when kept outside, I once put on
> moccasins and sneaked down to the kennel and slept with the pup
> 'till it fell asleep. After that, the pup was allowed to sleep in the
> scullery, but mostly managed to get up to my room.

To her granddaughter Patrizia, who visited the neighborhood in the 1980s, Olga wrote: "I used to take my pup (though it was really taking me) to Primrose Hill. . . . it used to have a flock of sheep grazing there when I knew it."

Many leaders in the turn-of-the-century music world lived nearby, among them the composer Sir Edward Elgar and the conductor Sir Thomas Beecham (one block down, on Grove End Road). "In the musical circles in which I grew up in London in the early 1900s . . . my mother was 'at home' on Sunday afternoons," Olga remembered. " 'Little pitchers have big ears,' and I used to sit out of sight and watch who came; the occasion was important if top hats arrived. I could always count on *two*." Olga's brother Teddy, who had a beautiful boy-soprano voice, had won a scholarship to study at the Westminster Cathedral Choir School and was required to wear the school "uniform" with Eton collar and topper on Sunday visits home.

Another perennial Sunday guest was "the little old gentleman with a grey mustache and cherished top hat," her mother's Californian friend, Henry Langdon Flint. Flint had spent the earlier part of his life "in the purlieus of La Scala," and was a connoisseur of bel canto opera. He was always invited to stay to supper (that his worn topper had seen better days perhaps explains Julia's special kindness to him). He reported all the musical gossip and details of the opera diva Maria Felicita Malibran's life— a first marriage annulled by the courts in Paris, her child by the violinist Charles de Beriot—"deplorable," in the eyes of many, but an enlightening treat for the "little pitcher" listening in.

Among her mother's close friends were Etta and Halcott Glover, the latter a nephew and member of the brilliant circle that clustered about the poet Leigh Hunt. Glover was a cousin of Margaret Morris, known for her classic Greek profile and for following the fashion of Isadora Duncan with flowing gowns and bare feet and sandals. Olga also remembered walking along a London street with the Glovers and Julia, catching a glimpse of Henry James with a young woman presumed to be his niece.

She had many happy memories of the London years. Whenever she sipped a cup of tea, she was reminded of Strugnull's, the "beautiful little shop on Duke Street, where Mother used to go for 'Twinings'." In her early teens, she enjoyed memorable performances of "the divine Sarah" Bernhardt in *Phèdre* and *Adriana LeCouvrier*, and dutifully recorded these experiences with the music scales and poems she wrote at Sherborne in a leatherbound diary her father gave her.

With his generous contributions, Julia was able to afford more lasting gifts for Olga, including a ten-volume set of Shakespeare's plays purchased at a little bookshop off Charing Cross Road. The entire set cost only "two-and-six" (two pounds, six shillings) but was worth far more, and Olga always assumed the volumes had been stolen goods. She was fascinated by the curious, old-fashioned script (the *s*'s resembling *f*'s), and kept the cherished volumes through many changes of residence until they came to rest in the Knights' Hall at Brunnenburg, her daughter's castle in the Tyrol.

The most treasured gift Olga received from her mother in those affluent years was her first important violin, "a good Klotz." It was on this Klotz that Olga began to impress audiences with her precocity, which inspired one London critic to write: "[Olga Rudge] is of a serious nature and mature turn of mind, and gifted with much musical feeling and temperament . . . becoming one more member of the great feminine army of successful American artists."

The children were never allowed to accept gifts from outside the family, Olga recalled, gifts they could not repay. "That genteel, old-fashioned idea—payer de sa personne—to pay with the marrow of one's bones and with one's best gray matter has clung to me throughout life."

During this time, a patroness of poets and musicians came into their lives whom Olga was to *payer de sa personne* as long as her good friend lived. Katherine Dalliba-John, mother of the poet Gerda Dalliba, was herself an author of romance novels. Katherine affected the pose of a Middle Eastern princess, wearing oriental shawls bordered by long fringe, her dark hair cut short across the forehead in bangs, Twenties style, many years before it became fashionable. Olga's affectionate name for Dalliba-John was "Ramooh" (more appropriate than Katherine, in Olga's view, for her friend's adopted persona). The Studio Meeting Society that Mrs. John established in her home at 9 Langford Place was a short walk from the Delle Sedie School. She provided food, lodging, and practice rooms for young protégés beginning their careers, some of whom later achieved international prominence, Efrem Zimbalist among them. To Olga, she gave encouragement and financial support during her lifetime and a small legacy.

At that time, an inheritance from Olga's father's side of the family came in sight. Grandmother Rudge's brother, head of the Stock family in Gloucestershire, died young and unmarried. His three old-maid sisters sold their inherited "moated grange . . . occupied by druids" and bought a small house in Malvern, left to Emma when Mary and Harriet died. Julia and her daughter visited this "truly Dickensian old maid" who, according to Olga, "sat in her house like a snail and never went out. . . . A child knew instinctively to sit upright in straight-backed chairs . . . no games or signs of a book in the house, the chocolates Mother brought from London put away until after Lent." There was much talk of leaving the house to Teddy, but when Emma died everything went to the eldest male of that generation, Uncle George Rudge of Ohio—for many years a cause of bad feeling in the family. Olga's unflattering view of these local descendants of sheep farmers who came over with William the Conqueror was that they resembled sheep themselves: "They grazed where they were and stayed put." In spite of which, her brother Teddy, after serving in World War I, "took root in the English Midlands as if Grandfather Rudge had never left for the New World."

Olga and Julia were never inclined to stay put. One constant in their lives was a cottage at Saint Cécile, Pas de Calais, their vacation home for many summers. Olga remembered "only one small hotel and five or six modest summer villas, with an enormous sandy beach behind the dunes. No shops, no cafés, no cars, no telephones, no *foreigners* . . . one railroad station between the two villages, Donne-Camiers and Saint Cécile. . . . We were always joined by Father, coming from the States, and sometimes Auntie Lou Baynes and some English friends invited by Mother." One of her childhood memories was of "going to collect driftwood on the beach for the stove in our chalet." Some twenty years later, Etta Glover would remember Olga, "hopping about the Grand Plage, first on one foot then on the other, then on both together as you used to do."

3

Halcyon Days No More

1910–1918

Soon Julia decided it was time to send her daughter to the Paris Conservatoire to perfect her technique under Maestro León Carambât, first violinist of the Opéra Comique. She resigned her position at the Delle Sedie School and, taking the two young brothers with her, signed a lease beginning September 1910—renewable every two, four, or six years—on a choice apartment in the Sixteenth Arrondissement.

"Mother always insisted that we live in beautiful places," Olga recalled. The Rudges were tenants of the *prémière étage* of 2, rue Chamfort, a graceful six-story building with iron balustrades designed by the contemporary architect M. Blanche. A salon with four large windows faced the quiet courtyard of an Ursuline convent across the way; the spacious dining room and two bedrooms occupied the rest of the floor, with a maid's room above and storage below in the *sous-sol*. The monthly rent of thirty-eight hundred francs (plus charges of six hundred francs) included steam heat, rugs, a lift, and a concierge on duty from 8 A.M. till 10 P.M., amenities quite rare in pre–World War I Paris. The apartment was furnished with handsome old English pieces brought over from Hill Road, Julia's desk and a lacquered oriental cabinet that held bibelots and jewelry she later passed on to her daughter. (A "floating memory" recorded in Olga's notebook was a ring with divided hearts her father had purchased from a gypsy at an Ohio state fair and presented to his sweetheart, Julia.) With a little bit of luck and determination (and the absent father's remittances), Julia and her kittens had landed on both feet again in a most genteel and elegant manner.

Olga spoke fondly of the "rue Chamfort's terrain," where the rue de la Source bordered the avenue Mozart and the rue Jasmin. Even today few *quartiers* of Paris rival the cachet of the *Seizième,* a garden spot between the place Victor Hugo and the Bois de Boulogne. In an earlier era, Colette fled there from the crowds and noise of the city. Olga recalled the quiet oasis of the convent garden with its apple trees heavy with fruit, where young novices in white habits sunned themselves in fair weather. The convent has been razed to make way for a Citroën garage, but the stone wall with an iron cross above the gate remains.

Olga's brother Teddy was removed from the Westminster Choir and enrolled in Mr. Denny's Anglo-Saxon School and painting classes at the Left Bank atelier of Jean-Paul Laurens on the rue de la Grande Chaumière. Arthur, the younger boy, entered the Lycée Janson de Sailley to prepare for the *bachot,* or *baccalauréat* examination. Olga recalls the Janson de Sailley boys sitting on wooden benches on the rue de la Pompe, their uniform pants protected by small squares of carpet held together with leather belt straps that doubled as bookbags.

Arthur's closest friend, two doors down, was Choura Stroumillo, son of a Russian nobleman who would later lose his estates in the Revolution. The boys used the attic room as their study, surrounded by books and reproductions of their favorite paintings. They spent much of their spare time reading and discussing the classics and poetry, when they were not attending sports events or exploring museums. In a memoir written in his late seventies, Choura confided that the close friendship that existed between the two boys was a precursor of later heterosexual relationships: "Our love was living proof of the mythical bond that united us in perfect concord. . . . We did not consider ourselves lovers, yet sex gave an extra dimension to our friendship. The innocence of our emotions was as chaste and transparent as the air we breathed."

Among Olga's early memories of this cosmopolitan neighborhood was a small bookshop on the rue Jasmin where the young girl behind the counter spoke Russian—one of a dozen languages. A colorful character who lived nearby was her mother's friend Martinus Sieveking, a pianist who transcribed Chopin for Olga's violin concerts. His hobby was collecting timepieces, and Olga remembered listening to the *tick-tock-tick-tock* of the several dozen clocks at his flat, chiming to different rhythms.

Julia contributed a colorful narrative to the Youngstown newspaper about Paris between the turn-of-the-century Exposition and the beginning of the Great War: "For the first time in six years, the big lake in the Bois de Boulogne has been open to skaters . . . up in the thousands daily," she wrote. The Horseshoe, always the first to freeze, was reserved exclusively for members of the Paris skating club, and Julia and Olga went there "to study the exquisite 'creations' of the dressmaker, furrier, and milliner. . . . no-one can show a beautiful gown to greater perfection than a graceful skater." Though Mardi Gras was bitterly cold, "it did not dampen the ardor of confetti-throwing crowds. . . . Shakespeare's 'seven ages' were all represented." Later, at the mid-Lent carnival, there would be processions and the crowning of the Queen of Queens.

Julia and Olga also saw lively times in the Latin Quarter. At a fair on the Left Bank, acrobats performed in the open air, "many living in gypsy vans . . . spread the table for their noon meal on the street." The buildings from the Paris Exposition of 1900 were fast disappearing: Belgium's model of the Hotel de Ville at Oudenaarde, the most beautiful, was gone, but the United States' pavilion was still standing. One of their favorite walks was to the Place de la Concorde, where the two large fountains were "in their wintry garb, the water thrown high in the air by the dolphin has . . . frozen into exquisite draperies."

When Olga was not following in her perceptive mother's wake on the boulevards or practicing the violin, she was performing at afternoon teas and soirées, gaining experience before sympathetic audiences. She began to draw more attention than Julia (who accompanied "the clever violinist" on the piano). Madame de Saussine, an aristocratic patron of the arts whose daughter also studied violin at the Conservatoire, provided entrée to the finest drawing rooms of Faubourg Saint-Germain, the realm of

Marcel Proust. "Madame thought it important for me to see Isadora Duncan and her children dance at the Châtelet Theater, an experience that was unforgettable bliss," Olga recalled.

In spite of her ample avoirdupois (gossips called the aristocratic doyenne "Mme. de Saucisson" [Mrs. Sausage]), Madame exhibited supremely good taste in her wardrobe. In Paris, a woman's best-kept secret was her dressmaker, and as proof of their friendship, she invited Julia and Olga to the flat of an exclusive modiste in Montmartre. Mme. Laschenez designed a new wardrobe for her expatriate clients: the indispensable blue *tailleur* with full skirt, and a Saxe-blue satin afternoon dress with *panier* for Julia. For Olga, a beige *tailleur* with tucked crepe-de-chine blouse and a green Empire dress for afternoon; a *velours-du-laine* red Empire dress, full red velvet skirt, and sleeveless dress accented with red tassels for evening, foils for Olga's dark beauty.

Mabel and Ethel de Courcy Duncan were among friends of Julia's circle who asked Olga to play at their apartment on the avenue de La Motte-Piquet. (Julia was first introduced to their mother, Mrs. Arthur Grey, in London by the artist Alice Donleavy, a friend of Grandmother Paige.) The Duncans invited Julia and Olga to the *hôtel* of the Marquis Charles de Pomairol on the rue Saint Dominique with one of the most beautiful gardens in Paris to watch the *14 de juillet* parade and fireworks. At receptions in Madame de Pomairol's salon, young poets recited their works, and artists from the Comédie Française often appeared. "I found the poets en masse tiresome," Olga recalled, "and was deeply disappointed in Pierre Loti, the guest-of-honor at one of the evening parties."

Olga and her mother were always welcome in Parisian society; they rated high on guest lists that included barons and baronnes, comtes and comtesses, and the occasional prince or princess. "My mother would take me to the salon for my education, on the condition that I put my hair up," Olga remembered; "I usually wore it tied back with a large bow." A petite five feet three inches tall, Olga appeared younger than her years. "If I looked too young, other jeunes filles would have to be invited. . . . The only other young girl at the Pomairols was Marie Volsamachi, who recited poetry superbly. . . . I was always happy to play after she recited; my tone seemed better (playing after even fine pianists was to be avoided if possible)." In spite of her self-deprecating manner, Olga was gaining a reputation for individual, fresh readings of contemporary works: "Her really strong point is a flowing cantabile," a contemporary critic noted.

The Duncan sisters also introduced Olga and her mother to members of the literary establishment in Paris: Paul Souday, Charles Clermont-Ganneau, Charles Maurras, and Sisley Huddleston (Paris correspondent for the *Observer*). At Madame de Pomairol's they met Judith Gautier, daughter of the essayist and critic Théophile, and thereafter were invited to the Gautier flat on the rue Washington. On one of those evenings, an elderly man—a smallish dark figure to Olga's eyes—was introduced as the author Joséphin Péladan. (Unknown to Olga at the time, Péladan's *Le Secret des Troubadours* was a great enthusiasm of Ezra's.)

Another venue for Olga's talent was St. Geneviève's Club on the rue Vaugirard in Montparnasse (known to the American colony as Sylvia Beach's father's club). The British group assembled at the Lyceum where Olga, still in her teens, "performed with finish" before the evening was brought to a close with impromptu dancing and enthusiastic renditions of "God Save the King." Through Julia's contacts, Olga also was invited to perform at the *matinées musicales* at the avenue Niel home of Madame Giulia Valda with American soprano Julia Porter, then the star pupil of Madame Valda. The *Musical Courier* applauded the obbligato in the Bach-Gounod arrangement of *Ave Maria* "of that very capable young violinist whose excellent musicianship has been mentioned before."

In that time of peace and prosperity before the Great War, Mabel and Ethel Duncan joined the family group in Italy for a summer holiday. They stopped at the Hotel Saturnia in Venice, and Olga became enamored with that city favored by artists, not knowing that some fifteen years later it would become her permanent home. Teddy was displaying artistic talent, sketching the mosaic of Christ on a white donkey in the piazza of St. Mark's. The travelers continued on to Florence, where Julia took an apartment for the summer in an ancient building with high ceilings facing the tree-shaded Via dei Tintori, a cool refuge in the intense heat. This was a memorable interlude for the impressionable young girl. She fondly recalled hearing the great tenor Benjamino Gigli sing *La Spagnola* (mentioned by Pound in Canto 27).

While in Florence, the Duncans introduced Olga to a young man who would become her first love, the *primo amore* whose letters she treasured for the rest of her life. The Duncans' widowed mother had married Lieutenant Colonel Arthur Grey, a widower with two sons, Temple and Egerton, who stayed on the avenue de La Motte-Piquet when in Paris. Egerton spent his early years in France before leaving for Australia where he graduated in chemistry from the University of Sydney. At twenty-five he returned to London to accept a scholarship at the Lister Institute researching the chemical action of bacteria; he was "an attractive man, with strong but unconventional character, full of enthusiasm for his subject." He met the seventeen-year-old friend of his half-sisters, a *coup-de-foudre* from which he never recovered. From the first evening, when he accompanied them to one of Olga's concerts, Egerton laid siege to her heart with the hyperbolic, poetic language of the era: "favored fairy forms tonight / will stoop to earth to hear your violin / . . . like that Orpheus played / 'ere he descended in the hapless quest of his Euridyce." He continued to woo young Olga while continuing his studies at Cambridge. Writing to a friend from Sant'Ambrogio some fifty years later, Olga recalled this early romance: "You never guessed, did you? that my interest in Cambridge was not inspired by Signora Terracini's Italian Seminar, but by Egerton, then at Emmanuel College? He got me piles of books from the London Library (I mugged up on for the course) and came to see me . . . in the garden at Girton. . . . His letters are a joy to me now which I do not deserve, as I treated him horribly."

There was one obstacle, however, that stood in their way: Egerton's early marriage, which had lasted only a few months and which he was seeking to have annulled. One can imagine the conflict in the psyche of the unawakened young girl, strictly raised by a Catholic mother and educated by the nuns in the Sherborne convent.

With ominous war clouds on the horizon, the halcyon days were drawing to a close. In the summer of 1914, at the onset of the *vacances,* Julia sent the boys ahead to the cottage at Saint Cécile. She and Olga were still planning to join them when she wrote from Paris: "There is no letter from America yet, and I am very anxious . . . this war scare is dreadful. . . . How do you manage about supper? . . . all supplies will go up, people are afraid to be without later on. . . . Do pray that the two nations now squabbling may settle their quarrel without bringing the rest of Europe into it." She cautioned the two young men (soon to be mobilized), "not [to] bathe [swim] . . . too soon after eating, or after you are very warm."

A week later, the inevitable news: "Germany has declared war! I could not sleep at all last night. . . . [A] strong searchlight has been put near the bridge at Issy to keep watch for the Zeppelins . . . the sky almost [like] day . . . heard that British warships are patrolling the French coast, putting searchlights out on the shore."

Now that France was at war, Julia and Olga, as foreign residents, had to seek official permission to leave and to return to Paris: "I have to get the papers signed by the Consul, and afterwards to the prefecture of police. . . . There are not likely to be trains out of Paris . . . all are taken for troops. . . . The money [from Father] came only last night. I thought I could change the American and English money, but . . . everything was crowded and shut at 12 o'clock."

Many other Americans in Paris were stranded without funds. The consulate advanced gold dollars for transportation home to anyone with proof of U.S. citizenship, and many queued up in front of the building. Though her husband strongly urged her to do so, Julia never considered returning home.

Her next letter described a visit to the market with its shortages: "no fruit at all by 12 o'clock. The Germans have asked the Belgians for an armistice of twenty-four hours. English troops are said to have landed two or three days ago . . . mothers everywhere are sending their boys off—in many cases never to return."

Olga and her mother did not travel to Saint Cécile that summer. When the brothers returned to Paris, they spent many evenings trying to decipher the often "incomprehensible noises" on the crystal set rigged up in the attic room, and watched planes flying over the airfield at Issy from the roof. "We could see them in the far distance from the rue Chamfort," Olga recalled. The Rudge brothers were still underage and American, but their neighbors Gilbert and Jack Insall were among the first volunteers in the Royal Flying Corps, to be joined later by their younger brother, Cecil.

Gilbert was the first airman of the war to be awarded the Victoria Cross, after being shot down behind enemy lines and imprisoned by the Germans.

Egerton Grey, also of age, volunteered the first day war was declared and shipped out to the Dardanelles as a second lieutenant in the Royal Fusiliers. He served in one of the earliest and bloodiest battles of the war in Gallipoli. Rupert Brooke, the English poet, wrote of that engagement: "There was a fever of excitement about the 'Constantinople Expedition' among the young men in England. . . . 'Shall I loot mosaics from St. Sophia, and Turkish Delight and carpets? Should we be the Turning Point in History?' I suddenly realized that the ambition of my life has been . . . to go on a military expedition against Constantinople." Egerton, who viewed the horrors of war more realistically, spoke out strongly against the British error in engaging in that battle.

After the first shock of the dreaded war subsided, Parisians went on with their daily routines. The Comédie Française remained open, theatergoing and promenades continued, though wartime shortages were beginning to be felt. Patisseries were open only four days a week, sugar, butter, and flour were scarce, and macaroons and truffles were rare treats at teas and *goûters*. Patches of beans and carrots could be seen sprouting among the chestnut paths of the Luxembourg Gardens. Then came the German Zeppelin raids. At the first alarm, the concierge at 2, rue Chamfort would shinny up the lamppost and turn off the gas lamps, but in those early days there was no damage to Auteuil.

Belgium fell after the "massacre of innocents" at Ypres, and as the war progressed, the wounded evacuated from the battlefields filled Paris hospitals. Teddy, who a short time earlier had been a participant in the rollicking Bal des Quatres Arts with other young artists, interrupted his painting classes to volunteer as a surgeon's assistant. He would leave at dawn on his bicycle for the auxiliary hospital quartered temporarily at the Hotel Continental and stay through supper; on occasional night duty he slept over on a cot.

In London, the teaching colleges and instructors continued to present recitals to show their pupils' progress at the closing of the summer season. In early June 1915, Olga and Julia returned to Dalliba-John's Studio Meeting Society. A reviewer noted Olga's improved technique: "She has

acquired a warmth and vivacity which made her interpretations convinc-
ing. . . . Breadth of treatment, fine tone, and skillful interpretations of the
various works augur well for her future musical career." That an eminent
pianist, Percy B. Kahn, agreed to accompany the young violinist is an
indication of his high regard for Olga's talent.

Egerton Grey was back in London, invalided out of the service with an
eye injury—a serendipitous opportunity for the two lovers to meet. Julia
invited the Insall brothers—in London training for the RFC—to join the
threesome for lunch and the theater, and Jack entertained them with a tale
of a flying accident he escaped without injury.

Before returning to Paris, Olga played three concerts in Dover organized by Doris Digby for "our brave men serving King and country." Julia
accompanied her daughter with vocal renditions of "Mother Macree," "I
Wonder If Love Is a Rose," and "The Pipes of Pan," which brought tears
to the eyes of many before a clever impersonator and comedian, Albert
Richards, "kept the audience in roars of laughter." After, the artists were
invited to a formal dinner party hosted by the officers of the Royal Gar-
rison Artillery in Dover Castle.

Egerton was there. Olga recorded with nostalgia that memorable evening: "Apart from the thrill of being whisked up, in the dark, to what I
thought was the Shakespeare Cliff (Mother, who knew her *King Lear,* told
me), it was my first formal dinner, and I was to leave the room with the
ladies, while the gentlemen took their port. Among the regimental silver
on the table was a figure of a kneeling oriental page, holding a book on his
knees with seven silver pages that turned, each carrying a toast for a day of
the week. Our toast (Thursday) was: "To Wives and Sweethearts, may
they never meet!" (Olga recalled this occasion and its message some thirty
years later in Sant'Ambrogio: "My 'first love' explained that the Chinese
symbol for 'roof' over two women meant 'quarrel.' " It was an ideogram
that would come to symbolize much of her life with Ezra Pound.)

Olga and her mother were rerouted to return by way of Dieppe: Americans and Belgians were no longer permitted to cross the Channel at
Boulogne because Admiral Alfred von Tirpitz and the German Navy had
targeted channel boats. Egerton composed a sentimental poem, ending, "I

dread of all things most . . . that you'll not let / me know you're safe
ashore. . . . Please say to your mother that I.S.M.L. [I send my love]."
(Olga recalled that "his sisters teased him about being in love with my
mother. The idea amused us . . . as [I knew] he was in love with me."

In August, when Julia and the boys left for a summer holiday in Annecy,
visiting the churches in Dijon and the Well of the Prophets in Saint-Pierre-
de-Chartreuse, Olga remained in Paris with the Duncans to be near
Egerton.

Back at the auxiliary hospital in the fall, Teddy assisted with the
wounded arriving from across the Channel. (A German plane had dropped
bombs on the hospital at Dunkirk, forcing the staff to evacuate.) Poison gas
was used for the first time at the second battle of Ypres, and many of the
wounded who came to Teddy's hospital were suffering from asphyxiation.

The boys continued their nightly vigils on the roof, watching as a
biplane caught fire only a hundred meters from the ground. They were
following Rudyard Kipling's eyewitness reports in the *Telegraph* of the
Allies' great offensive: some twenty thousand Germans taken prisoner. In
off-duty hours, Teddy and Arthur attended Corneille's *Le Cid* and Mo-
lière's *Les Précieuses Ridicules* at the Comédie Française, "a splendid performance of both." Ted was beginning a mural at the atelier, "the biggest
oil painting I have yet attempted." Recovered from a brief malaise after
Egerton's departure, Olga volunteered to cheer the troops at the Gare de
Lyon canteen and enrolled at the Ecole Espéciale des Langues Orientales
Vivantes on the rue de Lille.

In June 1916, she and Julia returned to London, where Olga was booked
at Aeolian Hall for a recital of operatic arias. Audiences were sparse in
wartime. Trainloads of wounded were arriving daily at Charing Cross
Station, and rationing and restrictions made daily life more difficult. Older
volunteers and women went to work in the factories, and children were
being evacuated to the country.

In July, Olga was invited to play at one of Isadore de Lara's "All British"
concerts under the honorary patronage of King George, Queen Mary, and
the Queen Mother Alexandra. The Princess of Monaco presided, and
Grand Duke Michael of Russia, Lady Randolph Churchill, Lady Cunard,

and the Princesse de Polignac (who would later sponsor Olga's career) were among the distinguished patrons. Critics noticed Olga Rudge, "a distinctly promising young artist."

Back in Paris, Arthur and Teddy often joined Egerton Grey at the Duncans. After recovering from his wounds at Gallipoli, Egerton volunteered to serve as a surgeon-sub-lieutenant in the Royal Navy and would soon return to the Black Sea. His ship, the H.M.S. *Nereïde,* was taking part in rescue operations of Russian refugees fleeing the Revolution, and his services were valued as an interpreter fluent in both French and German.

The first cases of typhoid erupted at the Lycée, but Arthur was spared. At the hospital, Teddy witnessed his first death and helped to put "poor M." in the bier and carry him to the morgue, saw the coffin enveloped in the Tricolor with the aging Veterans of 1870 giving the final salute. He heard from the brother of a friend at the Anglo-Saxon School that "poor Howilies has been killed—only 19-plus, and a promising career ahead."

Olga and Julia returned to Paris for Christmas. Olga noticed how crowded the boulevards were. Even in wartime, Julia continued the musical teas on the rue Chamfort. Teddy jotted in his diary that "Mother reads *Hamlet* to us in the evenings." He was beginning to study Greek history: "Resolved, to learn as much as possible."

In this longest, coldest winter of the war, many fingers and toes were lost to frostbite. For the first time, Teddy assisted with an amputation: "I held the leg, the foot was cut off. . . . Dr. P. dissected the foot to show how far the rotteness went . . . [then] put the drain in . . . and I held the stump." In off-duty hours, he observed firsthand the gangrenous microbes through a delicate microscope at the Pasteur Institute—and for relief he enjoyed performances of *Le Jongler de Notre Dame* and *Les Amoureux de Katherine* at the Opéra Comique (with Martha Chental in both leading roles).

A letter from Father on Teddy's birthday enclosed a generous check and another plea for the family to return home. In Julia's view, crossing the Atlantic was too dangerous after so many lives had been lost on the *Lusitania.* She optimistically predicted that "the war to end all wars" would soon be over, and her goal was to see Olga firmly established as a major concert artist in Europe.

Olga was booked to play another War Emergency Concert on April 22, Isadore de Lara's "Hour of Music." When Teddy saw his mother and sister off at the Gare du Nord, for the first time U.S. citizens were required to show passports.

Teddy, then entering his twenties, soon followed them to London to volunteer for the Artists' Rifles, a branch of the British Army. He enrolled with "private tuition at a tutorial place" to study math, Latin, English, and history for four and a half hours a week, while awaiting a commission in the O.U.T.C. (Officers' Training Corps). "I have a little bedroom on the 4th floor, with cold bath every morning . . . porrige [*sic*] eggs, bacon, coffee, toast . . . other meals not as good," he wrote his brother in Paris. "[Prime Minister Henry Herbert] Asquith is gone at last—the Lloyd George / Bonar Law contribution will be better," he added, referring to the coalition government and war cabinet of David Lloyd George and Conservative leader Bonar Law. Julia and Olga had taken temporary lodgings on Portman Square. The telephone, then a novelty, was "such a convenience . . . I have a chat with [Teddy] every day."

This was a time of searchlights, air raids, soldiers' sheds, and guns in the park, but Julia focused with single-minded purpose on Olga's career. At twenty-one, Olga was touted as "a young violinist of exceptional brilliance" by T. Arthur Russell of Sackville Street, Piccadilly, who handled her bookings: "[Miss Rudge] played with great distinction at several important functions in that City [Paris] . . . [and] is now available for engagements in England." In the publicity release photo, Olga appears as the quintessential young lady of late Edwardian England in a three-tiered, elaborately pleated silk skirt a fashionable six inches from the floor, with matching tucked, long-sleeved blouse, cinched at the waist by a pleated ribbon belt. Another wide ribbon encircling her head like a wreath is tied over the right ear in a large bow.

At a 1916 concert, Olga introduced the *Pastoral* by Kathleen Richards with the composer playing the piano part, "an imaginative work of a very young composer" according to one critic. This was the beginning of Olga's lifelong friendship with Kathleen and the Richards family.

On November 7, Percy B. Kahn again accompanied Olga at Aeolian

Hall before an audience of some six hundred. A critic noted, "Miss Rudge ... is emphatically a musician. . . . If she were not a violinist, she would . . . make an excellent singer. . . . she sings on her violin." Julia considered her efforts well rewarded. She described the event to Arthur: "The first recital is over and a huge success. The *Morning Post*, *Telegraph*, and *Times* have splendid notices . . . the best-noticed recital of the season. . . . Aunt Emma [Rudge] was delighted with Olga's success." The Duncans and Egerton sent a bouquet of pink roses that was "immense—she had to struggle to get off the stage."

On November 28, Olga introduced a new sonata of great interest to the wartime audience. The composer, Paul Paray, winner of the Prix de Rome in 1911, was then a prisoner of war in Germany. "His [Paray's] musical gifts may or may not . . . soften the hearts of his Teutonic gaolers," one hard-hearted critic suggested, but there was "hardly a bar to stir anyone's pulse or fire anyone's imagination." Olga, however, "played with genuine power. . . . She was accurate, crisp, and—above all—sensitive."

Egerton Grey, forced to remain idle in Paris with an eye injury, found consolation in Olga's letters "from dear London." He had been contemplating "The Hypothesis of the Subconscious Mind": "This comes from staying in one's room for a week with one eye shut and the other on the ceiling, thinking of a thousand things one cannot write. . . . Perhaps when you return to Paris, *if* you do intend returning, we may go into details of this and a thousand other things." Olga, however, appeared to be retreating from her ardent admirer. In old age, she wrote in her notebook: "Egerton's attitude toward 'love' was chivalrous in the extreme. I was wrong to mock him."

She and her mother returned to Paris for the holidays, bringing much-needed gifts for the boys, "lovely shirts, socks, ties, and a mountain of books." It was the last reunion of the family before Teddy was posted to the Western Front with the Artists' Rifles.

On April 6, 1917, the United States declared war on Germany. Young Arthur passed his *bachot* at the Lycée with Special Mention (sixth out of forty in natural history), and after celebrating his eighteenth birthday

May 15, he too traveled to London to join up. Julia had asked Arthur at the age of ten what he wanted to do for his birthday, and he had replied, "Something romantic, Mother!" What could be more romantic for a young lad than to follow the Insall brothers into the Royal Flying Corps?

He wrote to the family that it was difficult to find his way around London—"the streets are irregular and all alike"—but he finally located the police station on Tottenham Court Road to enlist. Later in July, he sent a letter from the Church Army Recreation Hut (Romford, Sussex), with photos enclosed of "me, bayonet-fighting . . . the large field is where the recruits have squad and arm drill. I was section commander before the Colonel this morning, and gave orders to my eight men in an imposing basso profundo. . . . We are waiting for our uniforms . . . had a fitting at Studd & Millington's. . . . hope we go to Oxford, as we shall be billeted in the different colleges."

Commissioned a first lieutenant on August 14, the young officer wrote his mother and Olga about his last leave in London, where he was introduced to Frank Mullings of the Beecham Operatic Company. "I went round to see him at Drury Lane . . . [he offered me] a lovely stall to see *Aida*. Mullings, who sang the role of Radames, "introduced me in his room to Beecham, a funny chap with whiskers." Sir Thomas, he remembered, had been their neighbor in St. John's Wood.

Arthur mentioned a friend who—after only three months' training—was killed at the front, and cautioned his mother: "Do not tire yourself and worry about Ted and me." Soon after, Julia was informed that Teddy was among the first of the Artists' Rifles posted as missing; they next heard that he had been wounded on patrol and was being held as a prisoner of war in a German hospital.

In the fall, Arthur was assigned to the Officers' Mess, Royal Flying Corps, Shawbury, Salop. Inspired by a quotation in his mother's letter—"To master the air, one must first master oneself"—he wrote: "The machine I shall fly in France is a lovely little single-seater scout called the Sopwith Camel . . . awfully fast, carries two synchronized machine guns which fire through the field of the propeller." Arthur was among the first to fly the pursuit plane made famous by Germany's "Red Baron," Manfred von Richthofen, an important aircraft for offensive patrols, escort work, and ground staffing.

In late December, he sent this poignant message: "We had no holiday on Xmas or Boxing Day, so we amused ourselves . . . bombed the Mess with confetti, soot, holly, etc. I dropped Xmas cards to different fellows I knew. . . . On Boxing Day I had to take charge of the funeral party of the fellow who was killed. . . . The walk (slow march) in the cold and the last post and firing were very depressing. . . . had a splendid Xmas dinner but not really jolly, for a good many it was the first away from home."

Julia moved to London while Olga was preparing for her next concert. They sublet an apartment in Belsize Park, near their former home on Hill Road, as a temporary lodging, retaining the rue Chamfort apartment for Olga's concerts in Paris. In London, "aliens" were required to present themselves at the police station at Tottenham Court Road, and Julia resented waiting her turn in a long line with the "enemy," while her sons were fighting with the British forces.

In February 1918, Arthur's squadron was posted to the Veneto, joining the Italian Expeditionary Force at San Pietro near Venice. There he established a friendship with Gabriele D'Annunzio, and in a letter to Julia he enclosed a snapshot of the poet-hero standing by his plane. Olga was engaged to play a benefit concert for the Italian Red Cross at the British Institute in Florence, and went there to stay with Katherine Dalliba-John, hoping to see her brother. But Arthur's squadron was sent back to France before he could arrange leave.

Egerton Grey was angling for a posting in the Mediterranean, and he stopped off in Florence for a day and a night on his way to his next base in Malta. Olga kept no record of Egerton's visit, but the strong emotions of that meeting may have caused her to become careless: she lost her first very fine violin, a Klotz, the gift of her mother. She and Ramooh were en route to a restaurant in one of the old-fashioned open cabs with a "cradle" in back where the cab's canopy was stored when not in use. Olga placed the violin case in the cradle behind her, and when she stepped out, the cab sped away. "I did not tell Mother, alone in London, with so much to worry about with the boys." She temporarily replaced it with Ramooh's gift of fifty pounds, "but I never had [one] as good"—until

1934, when she purchased a numbered copy of the Stradivarius "Messiah" in London.

In March 1918, when the first of the American Expeditionary Forces arrived in France, the Allies had been pushed back toward the Marne, and "Big Bertha" began to shell Paris from the forest only seventy-five miles away. On Good Friday, rockets were flying on all sides, and the Magasins Réunis store was reduced to rubble, along with a six-story apartment building on the boulevard Saint Michel. Gotha bombers continued nightly raids, and streetlights were extinguished. The boulevards were empty at night save for the *hirondelles,* caped policemen on bicycles patrolling the neighborhoods. During the day, a blizzard of papers rained down from the skies on which the Germans had printed "à demain soir," or "à bientôt." Paris all but emptied out by June.

Olga and her mother remained in England. As the war accelerated, food was rationed and Zeppelins were raiding naval installations, in spite of which Olga's concerts continued on schedule. Under a banner headline, "London Applauds Americans' Works," *Musical America* praised Olga's Aeolian Hall recital and the gifted young violinist, whose "charm and musical personality permeates all she does, added to which she has a talent for selecting new and interesting programs." Emile Bernard's *Suite,* Nardini's Concerto in E Minor, and Saint-Saëns's *Habanaise* were followed by "Deep River," a Negro spiritual arranged from Samuel Coleridge-Taylor's transcription by Maud Powell. The final piece was the London premiere of a sonata by John Alden Carpenter, a young Chicago composer, at that time a captain in the U.S. Army. Olga also played a benefit concert at Hamilton Hall for the blinded soldiers and sailors of St. Dunstan's Hospital with thoughts of her absent brothers.

Teddy was then at Romford awaiting discharge. After nine months in the German hospital, he had been sent back to England in an exchange of prisoners as a *grand blessé,* having lost one eye. It first appeared that he might lose an arm, but the wound healed after a long period of recuperation. His wartime experience and suffering reinforced his determination to become a doctor.

Serious aerial combat had begun for Arthur: "This morning on patrol

. . . we were about seven miles over the lines, when we spotted at 14,000 feet below us some Huns. The dive down from that height was tremendous . . . right underneath me was a large Hun two-seater (beautifully camouflaged). I dived at him, but both my guns had stoppages, and I had to zigzag away . . . from the ground, they threw up every possible thing at me; machine-gun fire, tracers, shrapnel, etc. The Hun pilot did not see me at first . . . I opened fire before the observer had time to get his gun to bear on me and fired a burst from 25 yards range. In a second, the nose of his machine dropped and he spun down earthward, out of control, engine full on."

Arthur's close friend from the Lycée, Choura Stroumillo, saved many of Arthur's letters from the front. When he asked Arthur if he mused over the possibility of his own death, Arthur admitted a feeling of curiosity: "Death, for me, lost its metaphysical meaning the day I cracked down after a forced landing on the French coast. . . . I did not think at all . . . like an animal at bay, waiting in desperation for the right moment to jump . . . instincts take over." "There is no need to take death too seriously," he continued; "if one has to die, what a great way to go!"

Not long after this letter, the correspondence stopped. Olga and her mother, as next of kin, received a telegram from the Air Ministry informing them of Arthur's death "in action," giving no details. Choura hurried to the rue Chamfort to find his mother and Olga in deep mourning—"they could hardly speak." A few days later they were informed that Arthur had been shot down in aerial combat over Courrières (near Arras), France, and buried by the German enemy in a country graveyard. Some sixty-five years later, his school friend Choura wrote: "[Arthur] was the hero of my youth . . . [with] all the gifts and beauty of a young god descended from Mt. Olympus . . . his apparent reserve masked his shyness and strong sense of personal integrity. . . . [He had] an astonishing enthusiasm about life. . . . We belonged to a generation of mythmakers." He quoted from Arthur's last letter: "I have a feeling that something greater and more vital will come out of this war . . . there will always be someone to carry on the torch of freedom and enlightenment to the following generations."

Olga recorded only the briefest details of her brother's death, as if it hurt too much to think or to write about, but in her seventies, she privately published Arthur's war letters.

4

Lost Loves

1918–1922

The Armistice was signed by the Allied Powers and Germany on November 11, 1918—too late for Arthur and many of the gifted youth of his generation (as Pound commemorated in Canto 110, "the holiness of their courage forgotten"). A million Parisians filled the streets and public squares, celebrating the end of hostilities. But eight million on all sides had died in the war. Julia returned to Belsize Park to be near Ted, her surviving son, but Arthur's death was a blow from which she never recovered. The pain and disillusionment she suffered are evident in this thinly veiled warning to Olga: "Do not worry about me being alone. . . . It seemed rather awful to look forward to, but now that it has come . . . I see how foolish I have been in so many ways. I have been married twenty-five years, and it has taken me all that time to learn a few necessary lessons. . . . I have thrown away my youth and talent in the struggle. My Paris days, as I look back, were wonderful, though I did not in any sense make the best of them."

Her only consolation was her daughter's growing reputation as a concert violinist. A high point in Olga's career at this time was an invitation to play Premier Prix de Rome winner Lili Boulanger's *Nocturne*, accompanied by Nadia, her more famous sister. Paris critics praised Olga's "virtuosity and style." Her mother's friend Halcott Glover was in the audience: "The performance [was] sheer good work, such as one does not often see. . . . I feel sure that if merit has anything to do with it, you will soon be famous. And what a beautiful dress!"

Paris picked up its tempo after the war, followed by *les années folles*. The cost of living almost quadrupled. A baguette that cost fifty centimes in December 1919 cost ninety a month later. Olga's father had signed a long lease at the prewar rent on the rue Chamfort apartment, where she continued to stay during the concert season. She was touted as "violoniste, de l'Orchestre Symphonique de Londres" in a concert at the Théâtre Caton in February 1920, performing the Debussy *Sonata* with Georges de Lausnay of the Conservatoire.

Back at Belsize Park, Olga was preparing for the premiere performance in London of the new Ildebrando Pizzetti sonata. The date—May 17, 1920—was one she would never forget. Julia had been transposing the violin part from a piano score arranged for pianist Henri Etlin. She was not well, resting in bed, copying the second movement, "Preghiera per gli innocenti, chi soffrano e non sanno il perchè" [Prayer for the innocent, who suffer and know not why]. Suddenly, the emotional stress of the war years took its toll, and the tired heart stopped beating. (In the euphemism of the time, her mother died of "a broken heart"; Olga recorded *crepe cuore* in her notebook). Some sixty years later, at La Fenice in Venice when someone in the audience was stricken, she recalled "the terrible sight— MOTHER!—except that after, she looked peaceful and beautiful."

As she lay dying, Julia had made Olga promise that she would not go away with her first love, Egerton Grey, who was—according to law and in the eyes of God—a married man. (Egerton had not asked her to do this, Olga later insisted; he was waiting for an annulment of his early marriage.) But Olga promised, thinking her sacrifice would placate her dying mother. "My duplicity was the last shock she had after Arthur's death and Teddy's imprisonment. I still have all these things on my heart."

Black-bordered mourning cards were sent out to friends of the family at home and abroad: "Julia O'Connell Rudge, décédée après une courte maladie," in the names of John Edgar Rudge, Edgar Marie Rudge, and Mademoiselle Olga Rudge. "Ted and I were alone at Mother's. We did what *she* wanted, though we had no authority and went against what we knew would have been Father's wishes," she recalled later. Without consulting their father in Youngstown, they had the body cremated, though cremation was a sin in the eyes of the Roman Catholic Church, and John Edgar Rudge was a devout believer. (Later, they would scatter the ashes on Arthur's gravesite near Courrières, France.)

Olga undertook the sad task of emptying out Julia's desk. "My mother left her desk in order. Father asked me about his letters to her—destroyed. A few letters to Auntie Lou [Baynes] were marked 'destroy,' [but] I had curiosity to look at them, nothing of a private nature." (Misunderstandings were covered up in the best of families.) A forgotten find was a copy of *The Elfin Artists and Other Poems,* by Alfred Noyes, a gift from Auntie Lou purchased from the Old Corner Bookstore in Boston. "He [Noyes] said what World War I families were feeling, and [it] must have given comfort to many."

Soon after Julia's death, Olga broke off the relationship with Egerton. The letter she wrote has not survived, but with the perspective of years, Olga considered her actions "too brutal, too abrupt." She preserved the passionate love letters Egerton had sent to her from Emmanuel College, including his reply to her farewell letter:

> I do not believe you do not love me. . . . nights I have prayed to you, and I have never lost faith since first you played to me and I secretly loved you. . . . Seven years of hope, and your brutal, awful answer. . . . The contract [of marriage] I signed years ago—for [which] I have been continuously in torture since I was 25—was a purely legal contract. . . . There never was a religious or sacred significance to the act, it never was . . . a barrier between us in any ethical sense.
>
> You must remember . . . you have vowed to be mine forever and ever. You gave me your soul . . . love itself is immortal, you cannot kill it, even if you will. Your soul is mine, and when this world ends, you will come back to me.

A few weeks later, having received no answer, Egerton wrote: "Some months must still pass before all legal formalities are complied with, after which I shall come to you and ask you to be my wife. . . . You can be with me in public as often as you wish . . . *trust me*. Four years ago I made an irrevocable vow . . . *I would never marry any woman but you*, [a] vow binding till death."

In her journal many years later, Olga confessed: "If I had let my mother know how much [Egerton] meant to me, she would have acted and felt differently. She was right. *I did not care enough*." Thumbing through the pages of *The Cantos*, she turned to the line "Nothing matters save the quality of the affection." Distancing herself from the event, she spoke of herself in the third person: "For eight years, [Egerton] was her one thought, which she brutally, childishly, put from her, thinking that her dramatic gesture of sacrifice would placate the spirit of her mother."

After she stopped communicating with him, Egerton—concerned that Olga was alone in the Belsize Park flat—wrote to Katherine Dalliba-John, who invited her to come to Italy in late May. She traveled to Assisi to seek consolation with her second mother. There she met another woman who would play a very important role in her life, the pianist Renata Borgatti, daughter of Giuseppe Borgatti, the renowned Italian tenor. The composer Pizzetti, a friend of the elder Borgatti then visiting in Assisi, introduced the two young musicians. "[Pizzetti] gave Renata and me coaching in the violin sonata which I was to have played with Henri Etlin in London. The only pianos for public use . . . were those used for training piano tuners at the Institute for the Blind . . . poor uprights in little rooms with no daylight. Pizzetti went there [with us]."

Olga recalled that Etlin had arrived from Paris the night before the scheduled May concert and discovered the performance canceled due to Julia's death. The Sharpe booking agency set a new date at Wigmore Hall for November, but Etlin was not free then to accompany her. "Ramooh, who was as delighted with Renata as I was, said she would pay her expenses to England to play [the Pizzetti sonata] with me."

"She had enough private means to keep her from dependency, but not enough to free her from the necessity of supplementing her income from public concerts," the resident novelist on Capri, Compton MacKenzie, wrote of Cleo Gazay in the novel *Extraordinary Women,* his thinly disguised portrait of Borgatti published in 1928.

> [She] was outwardly Greek of the age of Pericles . . . a marble copy
> of the Apoxymenos of Lysippus. . . . So long as she played Bach,
> she remained this tranquil and marmoreal youth; but when she
> played Wagner . . . she was a valkyrie writhing to be free from the
> marble in which she was confined. . . . Picture her then, with
> straight nose and jutting brows . . . a finely carved chin out-
> thrust . . . without any regard to the fashion of the moment, [she]
> kilts up her draperies to imitate the garb of some early Artemis.

Renata was among a celebrated group of Parisian lesbians who, as Marcel Proust's biographer depicted them, were an "innocent, proud, eccentric indispensable leavening in a monotonous society." They enjoyed freedom, social position, and artistic recognition. MacKenzie attempted to define her bisexual temperament: "[Cleo] had suffered . . . from passions which were not returned. . . . She was enjoying the masculine side of herself . . . and avoided the company of women, despising them as every healthy-minded boy at some period of his development does despise them. And then she would go and fall in love again with some utterly unsuitable person."

At this most vulnerable time, still mourning the deaths of her mother and brother, Olga came into Renata's orbit. After several weeks of practice sessions in Assisi, the two moved to Dalliba-John's flat on the Lungarno Giucciardini near the Scottish Church in Florence.

After more rehearsals in London in the fall, they gave the postponed concert on November 10 at Aeolian Hall. Handel's Sonata in D Major opened the program, followed by Edouard Lalo's *Symphonie Espagnole,* Lili Boulanger's *Nocturne* and *Cortège* (the premiere performance in England), and Pizzetti's fateful Sonata in A that Olga's mother was copying the day she died.

A thirty-five-year-old American poet, Ezra Pound, was in the audience to review the program for *The New Age,* writing under the pen name "William Atheling." Ezra wrote that Olga "charmed one by the delicate firmness of her fiddling, when paired with Hela Ziemska, a very alert and promising young pianist," but he found little to praise in Borgatti's technique: "Miss Rudge . . . committed a serious error in changing partners and was unable to overcome the wooden burden of Mlle. Renata Borgatti's piano whack." (In later years he became more tolerant of Renata's technique and her tempestuous personality.)

In the spring, Olga sublet the rue Chamfort apartment and traveled to Ravello to practice in that quiet place, isolated from traffic by narrow medieval streets. Another wealthy patron, the sister of Lord Grimthorpe, invited her to stay at the Villa Cimbrone, a magnificent medieval-style palace surrounded by gardens, terraces, and belvederes, with a breathtaking view of the rockbound Amalfi coast a thousand feet below.

After leaving Cimbrone, Olga joined Renata and her group on the isle of Capri. Borgatti was staying at the Hotel Subario, in one of her "crises de mysticisme and music," seeing no one and practicing hard, when Olga arrived.

Compton MacKenzie and his wife were among the first to discover the island, arriving before World War I when it was still unspoiled by tourists, souvenir stands, and holiday campers. In those days, one had to pick one's way up the winding, stony path to the village square (there was no funicular) to an unpretentious inn where one could get board and lodging (with wine) and a view of Vesuvius for a few shillings a day. They joined that group of expatriates escaping the respectability of late Victorian society: the Swedish doctor Axel Münthe, novelist W. Somerset Maugham, and Norman Douglas, the scandalous Austrian-born Scot who put Capri on the literary map with his novel *South Wind*. To Douglas, it was Nepenthe, "gleaming with golden rocks and emerald patches of culture."

MacKenzie, who served with the British Army in Gallipoli before being invalided out, also described the island in lyrical terms: "The mountains and the sea, the snowy cloud above Vesuvius . . . the white villas of today, the brown ruins of yesterday . . . all were fused here." His roman à clef, *Extraordinary Women,* attracted considerable attention because of its portrait of the women who came to Capri, their frivolous love affairs, petty backbiting, and intrigues.

MacKenzie's method to avoid libel suits was to "change the background but do nothing to the character." He transformed the artist Romaine Brooks into Olimpia Leigh, a composer and Greek scholar who set Sappho's poetry to music. Poet Rory Freemantal was modeled after Radclyffe Hall, known as "John" to her friends, author of the groundbreaking lesbian novel *The Well of Loneliness*. Mimi Franchetti, daughter of a baron and a famous beauty of the time who had composed several operas, became Rosalba Donsante, the flirt of the island and Olimpia's first conquest. Mimi (Rosalba) was Renata's (Cleo's) love interest one year, Romaine (Olimpia) the next, until—if one is to believe the MacKenzie script —a tantalizing new prospect, "Janet Royle," a violinist, appeared on the scene.

There are enough similarities in the character of Janet Royle to assume she was, at least in part, modeled after Olga. Mrs. Royle, Janet's mother, appears as Julia must have to those who did not know their true circumstances, "a rich American widow who had lived in Europe ever since her daughter was born twenty-eight years ago. . . . They had the best apartment in Rome [read Paris] and knew all the people worth knowing." Julia had always considered her daughter's health "delicate," and warned Olga against overexertion. In the novel, "her daughter was very delicate . . . if she did not insist on playing the violin so passionately, she might be less delicate . . . [and] it may be admitted that she played the violin well. . . . Flowers and music and pictures and friends . . . were always well arranged; and if Janet's life seems a little bloodless, it must be remembered that she had a tendency toward anemia."

Janet's relationship with Cleo "had reached the delicious state of tremulous equipoise. . . . Was she or was she not going to allow herself to fall in love with Cleo? That was the question forever pleasantly at the back of Janet's mind while she was talking with junior members of the diplomatic corps who came to her mother's 'Thursdays'."

The Marchesa Luisa Casati also appeared on the Capri scene. Romaine Brooks's biographer described her as "legendary and self-invented, like a D'Annunzio heroine . . . contemptuously accepting and discarding lovers; living with leopards, monkeys, and snakes; inspiring fads for gold evening capes and wide-brimmed hats with cascading feathers, giving rise to dozens of silent screen beauties with cadaverous skins and eyes like searing coals." (Casati would appear again in Venice on the calle Querini in the 1960s.)

A pictorial record of that summer of 1921 is preserved in a black leather-bound album. Olga, then twenty-six years old, had loosely bound, curly dark hair falling below her shoulders (before the characteristic bob). She appears in a rowboat at the entrance to the Blue Grotto, on the rocks in the conventional two-piece wool bathing costume of the era, on the ramparts of the old fort; with Maria Favai and a Dutch friend eating "olandese repasto"; with her brother Teddy; with a dignified gentleman in a white suit facetiously identified as "Gladstone"; with another male companion dragging an unruly shaggy dog. Renata's classic Greek profile appears often in these photographs: Renata draped in a toga, Renata standing near a giant cactus, Renata wearing a white headband, Renata wearing nothing at all (captioned "à la Sultana"). Several (unidentified) female figures appear spread-eagled on the rocks with bare breasts, or viewed voluptuously from behind.

The question lingers whether Olga's relationship with Renata Borgatti was more than the tantalizing possibility described by MacKenzie in his novel: was it a full-blown lesbian love affair, or a precursor of her later heterosexual love for Ezra?

Ezra once made a veiled reference to that summer with the women of Capri: "There is another possible element, that I had not thought of (at least for a long time) . . . namely, that you may more-or-less belong to the 'isola'; not out-and-out, but that every now and again you treat me come se fosse io la donna [as if I were the woman], and that causes some sort of confusion, possibly in your own head . . . error due to my apparent passivity."

Years later, when Olga was suffering from severe depression after her daughter Mary's birth, Ezra reminded her that she had contemplated suicide on that early visit to Capri. She replied: "When he refers to her suicidal tendencies—re. Renata, etc.—she did not try to kill herself because Renata had cocufied her [Olga's term, derived from the French verb *cocufier,* to cuckold]—or was leaving her—because *neither had happened.* It was because R[enata] was simply not what I thought her."

In the many letters and notebooks Olga preserved in the desire "to set the record straight," there was no direct answer to this puzzling question, but there is strong evidence against it. A friend who knew her well stated that Olga and Renata were lifelong collaborators in music; Olga was happiest with musicians and creative people, and a physical bond between the two women was unlikely considering Olga's Catholic background and propensity for guilt. A remark in a notebook (written some sixty years later) remains open to broad interpretation: "three men—my father, Egerton, and Ezra—who knew about everything, liked Renata." It is unlikely that her father and Egerton Grey, the *primo amore*—who were not informed about Mary's birth—"knew about everything" in Olga's early life.

The faithful Egerton, having temporarily abandoned hope that Olga would reconsider his proposal, accepted a position as head of the Government Medical School in Cairo. He was still hopelessly in love at Christmas 1921: "I [am] still suffering from the fever of these last ten years. . . . I respect and reverence you, as much as I passionately love you." It was impossible to think of a gift he could afford that could not be better purchased in London, he added, but "there is one gift I want dearly to make you . . . a *violin*. I am saving up and if you will let me know as soon as you find one . . . I will arrange it."

As a family friend, he offered advice about Teddy's liaison with his future wife, Jane, whom Olga strongly opposed, considering the girl's background inferior to that of her promising brother. "I thoroughly appreciate your feelings. I have seen the girl," Egerton wrote. "You would, however, be acting unwisely to oppose Teddy . . . opposition is the surest way to hasten a union. . . . Do not call Teddy a fool, you will be worse when you are in love. If Teddy is not to be lifted from Circe's charms, then leave them to it. . . . You ladies make such a fuss about such things, until men begin to think themselves criminals. We make our own tragedies."

In later years, Olga recognized the wisdom of Egerton's words. As Egerton had promised, their love endured beyond the grave. At her request, Olga was buried in the red kimono he had brought back from Japan. "I hope that my mother and Egerton and Ezra have long understood my weakness and duplicity—but wrong or right, *that* led to Ezra, and was the right way for me."

5

A Marriage That Didn't Happen

1924–1926

Ezra was slow to acknowledge Olga's importance in his life. He invited her to Rapallo the middle of February 1924 on the pretense of further collaboration on the Villon opera. He tried first to book a room at the Hotel Splendide but, finding no vacancy there, settled her in the Mignon, where he and Dorothy were temporarily lodged. Angry at Pound's indiscretion, Olga left the scene and climbed to Monte Allegro, a village above Rapallo, where she took a room at the Albergo Fernigotti. When Ezra tried to reach her by telephone, he was told that the signorina was out, or the lines were *guaste* (out of order). When he finally got through, Ezra— blind to the nuances of human behavior—questioned why she sounded so cold, "so *frozen* on the phone?" Before the construction of a funicular, Monte Allegro was accessible only by a narrow, difficult path up the mountainside. Still convalescent from appendicitis, Ezra protested he was too weak to climb: "Have had the miseries for three days, e ti voglio [I want you]. . . . If you can come down one day, wd. feed you tea and toast."

While he was vacillating, Olga received a message forwarded from her *primo amore* in Cairo. When she responded quickly and spontaneously by telegram, Egerton suggested that he might "come to Europe for the summer holiday." He closed with one last fervent plea: "There was only one object in this letter, to tell you I am sorry for the past two years and that I love you still with all my heart and to ask you to marry me. Will you be my wife?" Egerton's letter, however, had come too late, for Ezra had put on his walking shoes and climbed up the hill.

After a week alone in the Rapallo apartment, Dorothy Pound followed her husband to Monte Allegro. "There was no discussion. *I* left for Florence," Olga recorded. She was always welcome as the guest of Katherine Dalliba-John, who provided board, lodging, and practice rooms for young protégés on the Lungarno Giucciardini.

The Pounds returned to Rapallo. Ezra wrote that the British poet Basil Bunting had arrived, and he (Ezra) was composing the drum solo of the *Villon* opera and the connecting link of the *bourré*. Olga must have regretted her hasty departure. She wrote that she would like Ezra to meet Mrs. John; both her daughter and second husband were poets. "Are you coming the 19th? . . . Ramooh [would be] delighted to put you up for the week. Pizzy [Pizzetti] is still in Florence."

After joining Olga, Ezra received news from Philadelphia that his paternal grandmother, Susan Loomis Pound, had died. He sent conventional condolences and suggested that his father might take comfort in the fact that "she ended her life in the fullness of time, with no long illness." He mentioned the new violin suite he was trying to finish in time for Olga's London concert, and that he was staying "in a palazzo with huge rooms and bath . . . musicians [in Florence] are treated better than poets."

Olga left Florence soon after to meet George Antheil in Paris and travel with him to London for his debut concert. While stopping over to arrange for passage and visas, they attended the premiere of Igor Stravinsky's *L'Histoire du Soldat*. "Well done," Olga wrote of this major work, "but we went out after five minutes, and gradually one-by-one the rest of the audience did, too. Don't know the fate of the third piece." (Antheil's First Violin Sonata, written for Olga, was influenced by *L'Histoire du Soldat;* the Second Violin Sonata, also for Olga, is more original.)

She reported the difficulties en route with "Smitty" (her nickname for Antheil, borrowed from a popular comic strip character), when he was sputtering with rage at the passport control officer in Dover who questioned him about his Russian and German visas. His appearance—"slightly Bolshy"—was held against him. In an impeccable British accent acquired at the convent school, Olga explained to the sergeant-major that George was an American composer, *not* a jazz musician. After examining his manuscripts and scores, the officer permitted Antheil to enter the country, and they hopped on the boat train as it was pulling out.

Ezra kept in close touch with his protégés: "Too late to instruct you *how* to play, but as [it] was supposed to be written to suit you . . . the instructions wd. have been, play it to suit yourself."

After the concert at Aeolian Hall, May 10, 1924, Olga was praised as "an enterprising young violinist . . . [who] showed, in a beautiful old French lament by Gaucelm Faidit from 'Five Troubadour Songs' arranged by Agnes Bedford and a Bach Gavotte, that she can produce a lovely warm tone and has sympathetic style." Another reviewer observed that "there was humour and subtlety in the composition of the programme," but found little to praise in the "childlike pieces by the poet Ezra Pound, who is apparently as easily pleased with the monotonous repetition of a few rhythms . . . as an infant who arranges and rearranges his bits of coloured glass." Another noted that Pound "composes rather as he writes . . . his material is used in the rough, and his hearers may make what they can of it." Antheil was not spared: "There were endless repetitions of smashing chords, chords which seemed like musical skeletons . . . with no beauty to clothe them." Another viewed George's music as "essentially commonplace and frequently derivative, as in the unexpected intrusion of Debussy's delightful 'Golliwog's Cakewalk.' . . . [He] contrived to say less in the course of a four-movement work than any other person who ever put pen to paper. . . . After the first movement of the first sonata three people left the hall; after the Andante one retired; and at the conclusion of the Presto, thirty-seven sought the air and did not return."

Olivia Shakespear, who also was in the audience, described the concert to Dorothy and Ezra in Rapallo as "very successful, [but] George isn't satisfied. . . . I think he hoped for a row! The audience was small, some sneaked out in the middle, but those who remained were most enthusias-

tic. Ezra's things . . . were liked by those I spoke to, the first ['Resineux']
really beautiful. . . . I took Olga to lunch with me at the Club. She is a
charming girl, and so pretty."

The admiration was mutual. "I think her fascinating—could easily be
sentimental about her—but then I have a passion for old women," Olga
wrote to Pound. In her view, "The Bach was better than Paris—George's
Sonatas better . . . much cleaner."

A family dinner after the concert with brother Teddy and his bride,
Jane, "stirred up old things." Olga never reconciled herself to her idea that
Teddy, a country doctor with a growing but unprofitable practice near
London, had married beneath his station.

She celebrated the Fourth of July with Ezra in Paris. Pound wrote to his
father: "We have the Salle Pleyel for the 7th July . . . the team is all-
American: Antheil, born in Trenton, New Jersey, and Olga, also from the
U.S." He mentioned for the first time that Olga's Aunt Louise and Uncle
Harold Baynes, the respected naturalist, were neighbors of the elder
Pounds in Wyncote.

Monsieur et Madame Ezra Pound sent formal invitations to a select list:
"à une audition privée de Musique Americaine à 9 heures de soir, 7
juillet." Pound's contribution to the concert was a "XV-century piece I
dug up in Perugia [for] javanese fiddle, Chinese fanfare, violin, and tambourine, to celebrate George's entrance." From the front row Sylvia
Beach, proprietor of the expatriate Left Bank bookstore, commented on
the works of the "two musical conspirators": "Adrienne Monnier and I
were seated with [James] Joyce and his son Giorgio. Joyce had brought
Giorgio along in the hope of converting him to modern music, but
Pound's and Antheil's compositions were hardly the best choice for that
purpose."

The next morning, a reviewer described the Antheil compositions as "a
gargantuan feast of cacophonies," adding that "the throng of supporters
of futurist music . . . looked like the Dôme on a Saturday night . . . many of
the brethren posted to that tavern immediately afterward. Mr. Antheil's
hammer-blows on the piano left the nerves of some in a shaken condition."

Pound's compositions were "by far the most interesting and pleasing numbers on the program," another critic observed, "if one understands the architecture of 'horizontal' music, splendid specimens of which are even found in the works of one J.S. Bach."

Pound elaborated his theory of horizontal music in an essay, later published in Paris by William Bird and the Three Mountains Press as *George Antheil and the Treatise on Harmony*. Technical matters were of great importance to Olga, who noted "what she doesn't understand or disagrees with" in a twelve-page handwritten letter:

> She doesn't honestly think it [*The Treatise*] his chef d'oeuvre,
> or . . . likely to be understood by people . . . interested in opera. . . .
> I beg of him once more to consider the question of notation from
> the *performer's* point of view. . . . If, before criticizing singers, he
> would . . . learn to sing a simple rhythm from notes, he would find
> out *why* the notation of the George mss. is impossible to use . . . if
> he would stop confusing time length and accent! It is perfectly well
> known that a player can play in strict time and be dull and
> worse . . . without the right *accents!* . . . the troubadours found the
> matter easy enough. . . . My dear caro, I should think a bar lasting
> 1 / 4 or 1 / 5 of a second *remarkably* quick—if your watch has a
> second hand, try it!

Olga was not the only trained musician to take exception to Ezra's *Treatise.* Her lifelong friend the pianist Kathleen Richards wrote from London: "I disagree with practically everything therein, and think the *Treatise* the maddest thing ever penned."

In October 1924, Pound and Dorothy left Paris with the intention of making their permanent home in the milder climate of Rapallo. Olga was in Venice at the Conservatorio di Benedetto Marcello. She took a room at the Casa Friollo, a *pensione* on the Zattere, and asked Ezra to join her. He refused, but sent a nostalgic letter with a hand-drawn map of the area near San Trovaso where he had lived in the summer of 1908 and wrote his first published book of poems, *A Lume Spento:* "Xe una bbrrrava ragazza [She's a clever girl]. All right, she GO out and look at Venezia. It will probably improve her playing as much as anything else will. Has she been to San Giorgio Schiavoni and S[an] G[iorgio] dei Graeci, and Sa[nta] M[aria] Miracoli? Also S[an] Marco . . . she guarda la fonte a destra, per i riflessi della tettoia [she should look at the baptismal font on the right, for its reflections off the ceiling]. . . . She stick her head back in and out of the window, and NOT fall into the stern chains of the cargo boat just there under the finestra . . . and DON'T take a rez-de-chaussée at ANY price— especially in Venezia!"

Ezra's mother-in-law, Olivia Shakespear, was vacationing in Rapallo until November 11, after which he proposed a rendezvous in Genoa; they might meet at the monument to Cristoforo Colombo in front of the railroad station, and "perhaps in the afternoon, go together to the hotel? If I don't see you, I'll go to the Hotel de Genes and get a room . . . and leave a note at the desk to tell you what number. . . . I take it that you are now certain of being in Genoa from eve[ning] of 12th 'til morning of 14th?"

Olga kept a daily agenda, marking in red on the calendar five days of major significance: Sunday, Monday, Tuesday, Wednesday, and Thursday, November 9–13. But their well-laid plans went awry. Ezra wrote in frustration: "By the time I got to the 'phone, the communication had been cut . . . the porter of [the] Genes was incoherent, save that you 'parte adesso'." It is certain they met later that month, as Olga jotted in the small agenda: "piantato un figlio." She then traveled back to London, stopping in Monte Carlo, before arriving at Dalliba-John's in St. John's Wood on November 21.

Etta Glover, Olga's mother's friend, offered her flat on the Piazza Margana in Rome for the Christmas holiday, but Ezra was distancing himself from the relationship: "Just telegraphed 'no.' We are here 'til 11th, to get safely out of Italy before Anny Santy [Holy Year] begins on Xmas. . . . Non mi piace Roma—only stop there for work in the library—can't suddenly change one's habits and known predilections. . . . I am much too practical, ma!—ti voglio bene, e tante grazie."

The Pounds went to Sicily for the Christmas holiday, possibly with the idea of another change of residence. But after a brief stay in Palermo, Ezra wrote to his father: "It'll be *Rapallo*. . . . This country is interesting, but not exactly habitable." If Dorothy's aim had been to put more miles between Olga and her husband, she was too late. Olga had conceived a child by him.

In the twilight of her life, Olga confided in her notebook: "OR, as early as 1923, said she would like a child by EP. I would not have made the suggestion except that after ten years of marriage, his wife did not want a child, had never wanted a child, and at her age [forty] it did not seem likely that she would have one."

H.D. (Hilda Doolittle), the friend from Ezra's youth who visited the Pounds in London, said of his marriage: "Yes, Ez is 'married,' but there seems to be a pretty general consensus of opinion that Mrs. E. has not been 'awakened.' . . . She is very English and 'cold' . . . she loathes (she says) children!" Even if one allows for the bias of Ezra's former sweetheart, her words have the ring of truth.

In Olga's view, Ezra should not be deprived of the privilege of having a child, a torchbearer. They had a daughter "by mutual consent," Olga wrote, "but it was *I* who wanted the child, and saw no reason to make him responsible. . . . EP could not have undertaken the child's upbringing, and OR was not counting on it." When she first mentioned the subject, Ezra had turned down the suggestion: the world was no place to bring a child into, he said, especially without economic security.

In studying the *New Freewoman,* Ezra had drawn the distinction between the woman who wanted *a* child for the experience (with indifference about the sire of said child), and the woman who wanted a child by a particular man—that is, *his* child. Olga was obviously one of the latter. But she did not mention the subject again until an unidentified patron of the arts, a friend of both, suggested to Ezra that she would supervise the upbringing of Olga's child and support it financially. With this commitment, Ezra changed his mind and asked Olga if she might change hers.

Though Olga held the mutual friend in high regard, she "did not consider the milieu of the art patron [Natalie Barney?] suitable." With the allowance from her father supplemented by subletting her mother's Paris apartment at a higher rent, she was prepared to assume full responsibility for the child. Whatever the complex motives, she recorded some fifty years later that the child was not a mistake, "be it noted that [I] never contemplated abortion—*ever*."

Toward the end of February 1925, Ezra joined Olga in Rome. Etta Glover, who lent the apartment, was "what would have been called a broad-minded woman" (Ezra's words), given the mores of the time. "Is my nail brush under the bed? If so, preserve for future ref[erence]." Olga wrote after the visit, "mi hai lasciato molto felice [you've left me very happy] . . . she feels that she can go on." Her letter reveals a clear understanding of their relationship: "There was no concert today, so I went to the zoo. You will be pleased to hear that the leopardo has succeeded in getting the separate cage, which must have been what he wanted, as he is now quite calm, $+/-$, before feeding time. . . . his Mrs. is next door, with the door between open, but he leaves her alone, just wanders in occasionally to show that he has a right there, too." Pound described this visit to the Roman zoo in Canto 84: "and the he leopard lay on his back, playing with straw / in sheer boredom."

Olga was hoping to find a quiet place in "Régions des Lacs" to avoid the Roman heat—Salò, Gardone, or Sirmione—for her confinement. She left Rome sometime before March 11, stopping first at the Hotel Metropole at Lago di Garda, where there were "lots of ugly old crocks . . . but she likes it." On the twentieth, she moved on to the Albergo della Pace in Sirmione.

"Sirmione [is the] ideal place—only I take it they wouldn't allow such a thing [the birth] in a hotel, especially by an unaccompanied female. [I] will inquire for any casa di saluti in or near. . . . All she wants is a decent cage with straw to bury in—and quaio to anyone who comes and looks through the bars."

She sent a brochure of the "Sanitorio Civico—Stabilimento di Cura" of Dottore de Guggenberg in her next letter: "I rather think this would do. . . . I could go about April and stop first at the Elefante Hotel . . . 1555 . . . I like that." The venerable Albergo Elefante—so named in homage to Hannibal's crossing of the Alps near the Brenner Pass—was at Bressanone (Brixen), a small town of twelfth-century cloisters celebrated by the troubadours.

Olga had just heard that her favorite uncle, Harold Baynes, had succumbed to stomach cancer at Bailey Island, Maine. "She's unhappy because her uncle's dead, the *animal man*. . . . My father saw it in the paper, and that's all I know," she wrote, enclosing the obituary notice so "he can see how respectable and God-fearing her family iz." Baynes, in one of his articles, had written: "Usually full-grown birds, like thoroughbred people, take their troubles, their dangers, even death itself, with quiet courage and without any fuss."

With the same letter, she enclosed a newspaper clipping about Il Duce (whom she would later meet, and play for, at his private residence): "Muss[olini] is surely a nice man," an impression not unusual for that time, when the majority of Italians approved of the new government. Mussolini's black-shirted Fascists had captured Rome in the bloodless coup of 1922, selected a new cabinet, and presented the list of cabinet members to King Victor Emmanuel III. Ezra's early appraisal of the new premier: "I think extremely well of Mussolini . . . if one compares him to American presidents (the last three) or British premiers, etc. . . . If the intelligentsia don't think well of him, it is because they know nothing about 'the state' and government."

For Ezra, the practical concerns of his daily life always came first. He was moving to an apartment "plumb on [the] roof on [the] sea front" at 12, via Marsala. He warned Olga not to send intimate details about her approaching confinement and, for the sake of appearances, "maybe she'd better have an 'alliance' [wedding ring]. . . . don't know why I had a phobia against getting one in Roma . . . if there isn't one in Salò, do you want me to send?"

Back at the Albergo, Olga had purchased a new pen and black ink to pass the time copying music for future concerts with young "Jawg" (Antheil). She was trying to avoid accidental meetings with acquaintances who might recognize her and gossip about her condition: "This life of an escaping criminal is *too* dull. She hasn't been so bored since she was in her teens and nothing ever seemed to happen."

While Olga impatiently awaited the baby's arrival, Ezra continued his daily activities in the new setting: work, work, work at the typewriter, punctuated by energetic afternoons on the tennis courts and dinners with Dorothy and members of the British colony. He was attempting to sign up singers for a performance of *Le Testament de Villon,* and facetiously suggested that Olga "fish a basso and a contralto out of the lake for him. Ought to be bass in lake." He inquired about birthing customs in that former outpost of the Austro-Hungarian Empire: "I suppose Brixen still has German method?"

In June, as the time for the birth drew near, Olga wrote: "The cappellano came to call again, lent me a book, an English 'sunshine' novel." She sent a series of postcards from the Pia Opera dell'Infanzia, a home for abandoned babies. In the first, *bambini* are lined up for adoption in front of the church; in the second, adoptive *mammes* pose for portraits; in the third, a newborn is received into the waiting arms of a nun. "Caro," the message read, "the R[oman] C[atholic]s don't put them in petticoats as the Wesleyans would have done."

Olga was planning to register the birth with the name of Arthur Rudge, her deceased brother, listed as the child's father. She asked Ezra's advice about the penalty for falsifying a birth certificate. "All you appear to have done is to have declared a marriage that didn't happen . . . *that* can't be a *hanging* offense," he replied. Her daughter later resented Olga's having given her "a dead man's name," but Olga insisted she had done it to spare her child the "N.N." (anonymous) in the blank for the father's name on school registrations and other legal documents; to give her real father's name would have been an embarrassment to Ezra.

Olga also was concerned about excuses to be made to Antheil, whose inquiries she could no longer ignore. Why, Antheil wrote Pound, was Olga reluctant to commit herself to the concert tours he organized at considerable expense of time and effort? "Am writing to Olga in this same post about three concerts in America which *ought* to net her $1,500 and a contract for next year enhancing our reputations."

On Thursday, July 9, a baby girl was delivered prematurely after forty-eight hours of difficult labor. At 4 A.M. the doctor had asked Olga if she would allow a "cut" to remove (as she thought) a son, and she said yes, if it would not injure the child. "It wasn't the Caesarian operation, but a taglio of the peri [taglio del perineo]—something-or-other—with forceps," she informed Pound. The child was officially registered on the birth certificate as Maria Q. C. Rudge. Olga, who had hoped for a boy in his father's image, confessed in her notebook, "I felt as if the boy had died," but added that she soon became reconciled to a baby girl.

Ezra received an *espresso* posted on Sunday, then no communication until Friday the tenth. He was troubled by the news of the difficult birth. "Wot! Feet first through the roof, all same as Hercules and Julius Caesar, or wot-t-ell?? He hopes she really is OK. How long she expect to take recovering?" The next day: "He still in dark re / wot sort of operation and . . . when he ought to come, or ought not to, and WHERE."

Olga was accustomed to sparing Ezra unpleasantness, and years later she wrote: "I did not want E. to see me until well after. . . . women make themselves disgusting on these occasions . . . hence my dislike of women in pregnancy being seen, an old instinct of 'tribal women' who went into the forest alone."

In spite of her courage, it was a lonely time for the young mother without husband, family, or close friend to care for her. The nurses in the clinic spoke only German; later she recorded that "all those Tirolese ganged up against the stranger . . . [they were] suspicious—hard—venal." She was unable to nurse, so the child was removed to a special room with other premature infants.

Some eight days later (July 18) Olga wrote to Ezra: "[The] doctor says I can get up, only . . . I faint all over the place, so it's not much use. But the Kind ist besser—no grinning bear look about it—most solemn—it yawns with an abandon I've only seen equaled by one other person [Ezra]! And it does not make miserable cat wailings—it howls with rage until it gets what it wants, then it shuts up tight—very reasonable. We live in separate cages, so don't see much of it—the little Sister who looks after it is very competent . . . I think I can leave the kid here. I can't, or won't, reappear *anywhere* until I can play *at least* as well as prima."

Ezra was still puzzling over the nature of Olga's operation. While he was researching the life and works of Sigismundo Malatesta, the fifteenth-century military leader and patron of the arts, Manlio Dazzi brought to his attention a "pericolosissima operazione . . . con taglio Cesareo classico" performed by a Dottore Aldo Walluschnig, "who, with the force of his intellect, with art and assiduous care, snatched [the mother] from death by a most perilous operation . . . at the same time saving her son" (Canto 28). Recalling this, Olga wrote in her notebook, "no-one has seen any connection!!" and then underlined it.

Ezra enclosed thirty-eight hundred lire for her confinement in his next letter, the first of very few contributions Olga accepted. He was still avoiding a visit to the clinic, but his conscience prompted him to follow up with another letter: " 'Fraid he hasn't been vurry xpressive of sympathy. . . . He is very pleased she didn't up an' die on him."

In her next letter, Olga asked Ezra to consider possible names to substitute for the Q. and C. on Maria Rudge's birth certificate, something unique, "HERS and nobody else's." They first considered classical names from *The Cantos,* and Ezra's choice, after consulting the classical dictionary, was Polyxena (or Polissena), a daughter of Priam and Hecuba, "who made a hit with Achilles." (In Canto 9, she was noted as the second wife of Sigismundo Malatesta.) "[It] makes a good short name if you take the last part, Xena. . . . whether the Xena in Polyx- is the same root as the word meaning 'foreign' I don't abs[olutely] know? or whether it would mean 'foreign in many ways' or 'foreign to the city'? There is also 'Poluxenos,' meaning very hospitable . . . [or] Polyxa, a priestess of Apollo." From the same Canto, Madame Ginevra (a possible form of Geneviève) was discarded as "being the patron de Paris, too used." After many deliberations, the child kept only the name Maria Rudge.

The baby's survival was still touch and go: "About His coming—she had not expected He was going to . . . [but] if you would like to see the child, you had better—there is very little left of it. It has no definite illness—it just doesn't catch on. The doctor says if I had consented to nurse it, it would be different. I did try the fourth day, but it was too late. It has been going up and down ever since . . . very sensitive to the weather . . . two or three thundery days seemed to finish it."

Olga knew she was considered an unnatural mother by the nurses in this remote Tyrolean village, where babies were always put to breast, but she remembered that she and her two brothers had been bottle fed and all grew to healthy maturity. She felt the problem was due, in part, to the baby's resistance; too late she discovered the wet nurse's peasant trick of putting sugar or honey on the nipple.

Little by little, the child began to improve: "Night before last, [a] thunderstorm cleared the air, so yesterday it was better. . . . I think it will go, if it only gets a start . . . looks very grim and determined—e bionda what there is of it, also eyelashes golden, so think it will probably remain bionda."

"There is a contadina here whose child has died, who can nurse it a few weeks at least. . . . Does he expect her to travel with an infant? She wouldn't *consider it*. The child must remain here until I can find some other place for it, and I can't look after it, having no talent that way."

When the wet nurse, Frau Johanna Marcher, had to return to her farm in the nearby village of Gais, she begged to take the baby home with her. In Olga's view, the frau was a sympathetic woman who, after five stillbirths, would give love as well as abundant mother's milk to Maria. Olga went with her to Gais to see for herself that the Marchers offered a wholesome environment for her child. She inspected the house, the clean kitchen, the low wood-paneled room with vaulted ceiling, with a stable leading off the front entrance. There was another foster child in the house, a beautiful little girl of three, obviously well cared for and in good health.

Olga became convinced that the simple farm atmosphere, fresh air, and country life were healthier for Maria than the itinerant gypsy life of a violinist. Even if she had not felt it necessary to conceal the child's birth ("it was *not* the permissive society"), she was unwilling to endanger the prematurely born infant's life on the concert circuit. At that time, it was common practice for children of well-to-do Italian families to be lodged with a peasant nurse until they were old enough to be sent to a convent school; Renata Borgatti had been raised by a wet nurse, she remembered. "I would have stayed on for a month or two at Brixen, but Frau Marcher couldn't be away from the farm, and obviously the place seemed ideal for a small child. I still think it was," she recorded many years later, "[except for] the *dialect*, [which] became an impossible barrier."

In August, Olga returned to Katherine Dalliba-John's villa in Florence, arising early each morning to exercise with a young physical fitness instructor, formerly of the U.S. Army, to regain her trim figure. She returned to Gais in late October, but Ezra did not accompany her: "La mia leoncina sta benissimo . . . holds its head up for itself, nearly bald, needs bigger clothes—country very fine up there with autumn coloring."

She had received "a vague letter from parent, who speaks of coming over to Italy in February! . . . sends check." She did not confide in her father that she was the mother of a baby girl, and to the end of her life she regretted deceiving him in the matter of Maria's birth, although she still accepted his allowance.

By November, Olga was practicing daily to improve her technique for the first performance since her confinement. Ezra sent a selection of his Cantos that Ernest Walsh and Ethel Moorhead were planning to publish in *This Quarter*. The correspondence reveals how often he relied on Olga's critical judgment: "IF she has any STRONG ideas as to which poems he shd. and shd. NOT put in his collected edtn., she SPEAK."

He was still acting as impresario in the Antheil-Rudge collaboration: "No sense of Olga's going to America at her own expense," he wrote Antheil. "If they pay her, I shall then advise her to go." To Olga, regarding dates that Antheil had booked for her: "She is probably x-cited about concerts in Paris on 30th November . . . in Vienner, Prague, etc."

Olga was in Paris chez Madame Spicer on the rue George Sand through November and early December; the rue Chamfort apartment was sublet for the season. Ezra applauded a November 30 performance from Rapallo: "Natalie [Barney] was under the impression your concert wuz . . . crowded and successful."

In a Christmas letter to his parents in Wyncote, he announced that "D[orothy] is in Cairo; sailed from Genoa Thursday December 17, arrived in Cairo Monday December 21. . . . When last heard from she had been there '24 hours without a flea,' but didn't expect it to last." He added that T. S. Eliot had been in Rapallo for four days, "at last escaped from Lloyd's Bank and more alive than might have been expected from the circumstances and from the damn magazine he edits [*The Criterion*]." He failed to mention that Olga was in Rapallo taking Dorothy's place during one of the rare Christmas holidays the couple spent together, while their child assumed the role of the cherished Baby Jesus in the mountain crèche of the Marchers.

Olga remembered that she went down to "rubberneck" at the arrival of Mussolini in Rapallo. "E.P., who had never seen Muss[olini] or had any contact [with him], was not interested enough to leave his desk and go down to see the procession," she jotted in her notebook in later years, no doubt to camouflage Ezra's alleged support of the Fascist government.

Olga was at Natalie Barney's on New Year's Day, 1926, for the premiere of George Antheil's innovative First String Quartet; she then left for Katherine Dalliba-John's villa—a quiet time, "early to bed with *Napoleon, the Last Phase* by Lord Mosebury, and a hot water bottle." When the lease on the rue Chamfort apartment came up for renewal, she was able to continue for another four years with a generous contribution from her father.

In early March, Edgar Rudge traveled to Europe for a second honeymoon, stopping off in Florence to introduce his wife, Katherine, to Olga. After Julia's death, he had waited six years to marry a young woman from Youngstown, his secretary in the insurance office. Olga had not seen her father since 1921, and she was pleased that he had found a suitable companion. She met the couple at the dock in Naples and hired a *carrozza* to take them along the seafront drive to their hotel.

One incident marred the happy reunion. Her father had urged Julia to return to Ohio with the children before the war, but the submarine menace prevented him from insisting. In retrospect, he blamed Olga for their failure to return and greeted her with the "outrageous" remark: "You should have come back. If you had, Arthur would not have been killed, and your poor mother would have been here today." As Olga recalled the incident: "not given to crying as a rule, I was shocked to tears, and sobbed in the open carriage all along the via Carraciole to the hotel, where I rushed to my room."

Katherine gained Olga's respect by the way she ignored this cri de coeur, and the incident was never referred to again. The three went to Capri for a week and appeared to enjoy the rest of the holiday. The only objection her father, a devout Catholic, voiced about Italy and the Italians was that they ate meat on Friday. This was Olga's last visit with her father; he died in Youngstown in 1935.

In mid-March, she returned to Paris, anticipating that Ezra would join her there, but she was disappointed. "D[orothy] has been half ill ever since she got back [from Egypt], took to her bed this a.m.," Pound wrote. A telegram followed: "Troppo incomodo—sorry." Olga resented this injustice and told him so: " 'Troppo incomodo' is probably the mot juste, [but] she feels he might have found a more polite if less direct way of putting it, this idea of a 'maîtresse convenable,' a 'convenient mistress.' " She was not angry enough to risk an open break, and she apologized for the outburst in her next letter, asking Ezra to recommend a reading list of the classics. Because her formal education had ended after the convent school at Sherborne, Olga had a strong desire to hone her fine mind, one possible explanation for her powerful attraction to Ezra.

Determined to keep the upper hand, Ezra replied with the pedantic tone of one surprised by a woman's intelligence: "She's such a high blue [stocking] anyhow, that she has already read everything except H[enry] James, and Tho[mas] Hardy's *Mayor of Casterbridge*. . . . When he feels like readin', he does Greek with a Latin crib. Fat lot o' good that'll do *her*." Instead, he suggested Laurence Sterne's *Sentimental Journey* and *Tristram Shandy*, Henry Fielding's *Tom Jones*, novels he considered not too challenging.

Antheil was then in Paris, corresponding with Ezra about future bookings. "I've got a new violin sonata I want to give a private but important performance of with Olga here in early July. Where is she? Give me her address. . . . You always forget that when I ask." Ezra had kept Olga's confinement a carefully guarded secret.

She was on the Lungarno Guicciardini with Ramooh in April. Ezra's next letter hints at Olga's depression after the birth of their daughter and his own confusion about the future: "Ch'è il fine del mundo [*sic*] [It is the end of the world]. He plunges into her grief . . . HER affairs don't bear looking at. HIS affairs don't bear looking at. The past is forgotten, the future is ominous, the present is beyond words." There followed several paragraphs of tennis scores, local news, and weather reports, then, "*He* is too g—d— stupid to live. He hasn't brains enough to git on wif his canters . . . or earning a honest living. . . . Gorblezz my zoul . . . two years from last concert . . . HELL an' BLAZES."

On the twenty-sixth, Olga was at the Hotel d'Ingleterre in Rome, preparing for a concert on May 7 with Alfredo Casella at the Sala Sgambati. At the last minute, Ezra sent regrets from Rapallo. His comments about her publicity photo reveal the character of both correspondents: "An HER lookin' so bew-yewteeful, to say nothing of her splendid new clothing with quattrocento finish . . . [yet] so filled with inexpungable sorrows, and with such a distinguished melancholy, just as always when she is puffikly convinced that it is ALL his fault, which he declines to believe." The Paris *Tribune* critic praised Olga's performance and the program, which included contemporary compositions by Erik Satie and Maurice Ravel, Pound's *Hommage à Froissart*, the new Pizzetti sonata, and Fritz Kreisler's arrangement of *Danse Espagnole* by Enrique Granados.

Ezra joined Olga in Paris June 19 for an event that achieved considerable notoriety, the premiere of George Antheil's *Ballet Mécanique*, conducted by Vladimir Golschmann, with an orchestra of eighty-five musicians—eight grand pianos, electric bells, a battery of percussionists, and two airplane propellers. Under the banner headline, "George Antheil's Ballet Stirs Huge Audience to Plaudits and Catcalls," the *Tribune* reported: "The carefully upholstered Théâtre des Champs Elysées vibrated to strange and beautiful sounds yesterday afternoon. . . . [Antheil] was greeted with an applause so uproarious to leave no doubt in his mind that his tonal seed had not fallen upon stoney ground. . . . The audience was divided into two belligerent and opposing camps. . . . 'Silence, imbéciles,' Ezra Pound shouted, with the French inflection, although the audience was anything but French." As Sylvia Beach recalled: "The music was drowned out by yells from all over the house. . . . You saw people punching each other in the face, you heard the yelling, but you didn't hear a note of the *Ballet mécanique*." Eventually the airplane propellers drowned out the catcalls and raised a breeze that—as artist Stuart Gilbert remembered —blew the wig off the head of a man sitting next to him.

Not to be upstaged, Pound premiered his avant-garde opera *Le Testament de Villon* on June 29, 1926, in the old Salle Pleyel on the rue Roche-Chouart, former venue of Chopin and Liszt. The large hall resembling a drawing room with seats in rows facing each other around a square was filled with some three hundred guests, near capacity, a who's who of the expatriate literary and musical circles of Paris—Joyce, Hemingway, and Eliot, among others.

In lieu of a fully staged production (set in a brothel next to a cathedral), Pound settled for an expanded concert version. Villon—wanted for crimes, with a premonition of his own death—reviews the transcience of life and love, followed by the ironic comments of his friend, Thier. The Old Prostitute Heaulmière laments her vanished charms (an aria Ezra called "the fireworks of the piece"); then a foppish Gallant stumbles in to visit one of the girls. The voice of Villon's mother can be heard offstage in the cathedral, praying for his salvation. A priest attempts to enter but is barred by Bozo, the boozy brothel keeper, while a chorus of companions sings the drinking song, "Père Noë." As the opera ends, Villon is arrested and carried off for execution; in the final act he is seen hanging from the gallows as the chorus echoes "Frères humains."

Yves Tinayre, the lead tenor, doubled in the Old Prostitute's role in falsetto with a shawl draped over his head when Pound was unable to enlist a soprano. Robert Maitland, a bass-baritone borrowed from Sir Thomas Beecham's opera season, sang Bozo. A miniature orchestra featured Olga on violin, Jean Dervaux and Edouard Desmoulin on tenor and bass trombones, a clavichord, and a five-foot *cornet de dessus* (medieval horn) played by Tinayre's younger brother, Paul. Constantin Brancusi called the concert "une scandale," but composer Virgil Thomson conceded, "it was not quite a musician's music, though it may well be the finest poet's music since Thomas Campion." To Agnes Bedford in London, who was invited to play the harpsichord but did not appear, Ezra wrote: "Dare say it went fairly well—no riots or departures."

Another concert version of *Le Testament* was presented on Monday afternoon, July 12, at the avenue Fouquet home of Mrs. Christian Gross, a wealthy patron of the arts. Olga accompanied Robert Maitland on the violin in this "premiere audition" of Villon's *Les Neiges d'Antan,* with the often-quoted line "Where are the snows of yesteryear?" On the same program, Olga and Antheil premiered George's Third Sonata for piano and violin, which inspired a critic to comment: "Miss Rudge has developed an entirely new violin technique for the interpretation of the tempestuous and, as classical players would say, 'anti-violinistic,' music of today. . . . She has been obliged to run the risk of damaging her classical technique, acquired by so many years of earnest effort."

Antheil viewed her efforts in a different light. After he escaped to Tunis, he wrote Pound: "Olga is the seventh gate of violin playing, [but] she doesn't take the trouble . . . with *my* violin music that she did ONCT. . . . no use telling people they're doing swell when they're so cockeyed sure they know an old piece that they forget it. . . . you gotta snap 'em back into shape. But don't kid yourself, I know I won't find another fiddler like Olga."

The Pounds stayed on in Paris after the controversial performances. Dorothy, now almost forty, was expecting her first child and wanted to be near the American Hospital for her confinement. When her time came on September 10, 1926, Ernest Hemingway, not Ezra, accompanied her to the hospital. Ezra wrote to the elder Pounds for the first time in six weeks: "next generation (male) arrived. Both D. and it appear to be doing well." They named the boy Omar Pound (four years earlier Ezra had written that "Fitzgerald's trans[lation] of Omar [Khayyam] is the only good poem of [the] Vict[orian] era").

Shortly after Omar's birth, William Butler Yeats wrote to his friend Olivia Shakespear: "I divine that you have already adopted the grandchild." Omar's parents had agreed that he should live with his maternal grandmother, with Dorothy returning from Italy for visits every summer. Pound met the boy for the first time in London after Olivia's death. Omar was then twelve years old.

On September 27, 1926, Pound himself checked into the American Hospital for a week of "taps, tests, analyses, etc . . . completely exhausted," a stress-related illness no doubt aggravated by divided loyalties. (Fifty years later Olga wrote, "I did not appreciate then . . . the physical strain He was under.")

Frau Marcher kept the parents informed about Mary. She wrote in German to Ezra, who forwarded the letters to Olga with his often inaccurate translations. He visited his daughter in late November, when the frau was clipping the child's blond hair, and sent one of the "gee-lorious" curls to Olga with a sprig of mountain edelweiss and a check for the "piccolo leone." In a year-end letter to the senior Pounds, he wrote that he was "doing some wild telegraphing to get [Olga] to Budapest in time for a concert next fortnight . . . possibly Vienna and Berlin," adding that "life is stranger than fiction, and imagination always gets left behind" — a statement of the complicated turn his life was taking.

Olga spent Christmas with her daughter. In midlife, Mary wrote in her autobiography: "Over the chaos, hovers one certainty. I, the child, was wanted. The rest is music and poetry. The young violinist stands beside the poet's chair, playing arie from *Le Nozze* . . . and from now on, whenever the scrupulous biographer will report a concert in Budapest, a performance in Vienna, a trip to Frankfurt, Salzburg, it may be assumed that the journey was interrupted for a few hours or a few days in Bruneck."

6

The Hidden Nest

1927–1928

Ezra was not in Budapest for Olga's January 28 concert at the Music Academy with Antheil and Kosa Gyorgy. An early press notice announced the event, but "what sort of reception the temperamental Budapesters gave them has not yet been told." Ezra sent a telegram of *auguri* (congratulations) to the Hotel Bellevue and wrote to Sisley Huddleston, the Paris critic: "I learned from collateral evidence that OR played exceedingly well (3rd and 1st violin sonatas), and that M. Antheil tried out a new piano concerto"—which caused another riot. Pound believed in "big drum" to publicize the concerts, and Olga's conservative approach brought this outburst: "GOD, CHRIST AND THE BUGGERIN' VIRGIN—WHAT THE HELL DO YOU MEAN BY SENDING ME *only one* program? . . . in the early stages of a CAREER the utility of performance is . . . enhanced by allowing the fact to LEAK OUT—DAMN THE EXPENTZ!"

Olga stopped writing for several weeks, and Ezra attempted to woo her back with a Valentine that arrived with apologies—too late. She was preparing for another concert at the Sala Capizucchi in Rome on February 19 and was not sure if young "Jawg," on the eve of departure for America, would appear.

In spite of Ezra's advance publicity for Antheil's works—"the first . . . American-born musician . . . to write music that couldn't have been written before, interpreting his age"—few critics agreed that the "slabs of sound of the youthful master of musical mechanisms have something akin to genius." The *Herald,* however, published Olga's photo above an enthusiastic review: "That Mr. Antheil's music is known outside Italy is largely due to the untiring interest of Miss Rudge. . . . In striking contrast to the modern half of the program, the exquisite performance of Olga Rudge and Maestro Daniele Amfiteatrow was much applauded."

To further her career, Ezra urged Olga to attend a reception at the American Embassy in Rome on Washington's Birthday, February 22. It was an occasion that marked another important milestone in her life. Lilian Gibson, the *Herald*'s Rome correspondent whom she met there, arranged a private performance for Premier Benito Mussolini at his residence on the via Rasella. After her recital of Beethoven's *Romanza,* Mozart's Sonata, opus 15, and a Veracini sonata, accompanied by Daniele Amfiteatrow, the *Herald* reported:

> Mussolini complimented Miss Rudge on her technique and musical feeling, saying that it was rare to find such depth and precision of tone, 'especially in a woman.' He showed his guests the large assortment of violin music on his desk, including many classical compositions. Five violins were on the table in the center of the room, on the best of which the Duce himself plays every evening. Among his literary treasures was a copy of the musical "Suite" composed in England by an 18th Century ancestor, Cesare Mussolini. After the concert, the Premier offered Miss Rudge a bouquet of magnificent carnations.

In the conversation that followed, Mussolini, who was then thirty-nine, agreed that Antonio Vivaldi was "the greatest composer of all time." A half-century later, Olga recalled that Mussolini "played well for an amateur" and "had the manners of an archbishop."

Back home in Ohio, the *Youngstown Telegram* touted the "unusual honor accorded the daughter of J. Edgar Rudge . . . when Premier

Mussolini invited her to play for him. . . . Miss Rudge has achieved outstanding distinction as a violinist."

Antheil, aboard the Cunard line's *Ascania* en route to New York, wrote Ezra: "Olga and I are now on the peak of financial success—we've long ago passed the artistic one. I want you to make a big effort to push me over, and . . . I'll pull Olga over . . . I liked Olga's private performance of the fiddle sonatas at 2, rue Chamfort, better than most anything in the world."

Olga was booked to play two Mozart sonatas and a Mozart concerto with Ernesto Consolo at the Sala Filarmonica in Florence on March 30, a concert that brought the young artist to the attention of Bernard Berenson, who invited Olga to his villa, I Tatti. Ezra coached Olga before the visit: "Berenson is a very great critic; also has sense of humour. Don't imagine B.B. (pronounced bee-bee) will expect you or anyone to have read his works. . . . I Tatti is a perfectly proper place to spend the night—it would have been ungracious to refuse."

I Tatti nestles below the village of Settignano northeast of Florence with a magnificent view of the nearby valley and its olive-drab trees and golden fields. Standing three stories high, the buff-colored villa is ringed by cypresses and a walled garden. At the time of Olga's visit, each room was painted a distinctive color, Aubusson rugs covered the red tile floors, and the walls were hung with Berenson's collection of Italian Renaissance art.

Unconventional members of the Anglo-American colony congregated at I Tatti, especially on Saturdays, when Berenson held court with his wife, née Mary Smith, sister of Logan Pearsall Smith of a wealthy Philadelphia family and sister-in-law of Bertrand Russell. Mary had been married to Frank Costello, before she left with her two children to join Berenson at I Tatti. Berenson, born Lithuanian and raised in Boston's North End, was a self-taught art critic of exquisite taste. One wonders if he had been informed of Olga's liaison with Pound, for he was quoted as saying, "Can anyone be faithful to anyone? Fidelity belongs to an era of slavery."

Olga herself was gaining international recognition. Her photo appeared on May 15 in New York's *Town and Country* above the roving correspondent's byline:

[The] photograph was sent to me by an internationally famous and controversial literary gentleman, who enclosed the "simulacrum of an active and decorative component of . . . art, music, letters, etc." Since he demands anonymity, it is a pity his whole letter about Miss Rudge cannot be printed, because it . . . says a lot more than I could. . . . She was fiddling on the spot in Budapest when the last riot broke out . . . held Mussolini's attention for two hours in private audience. . . . She appears to play a good deal of Mozart as well as the ultra-moderns.

Olga performed with Gabriele Bianchi at the Sala Benedetto Marcello in Venice on July 15, after spending two and a half hours with Maestro Mainardi perfecting her technique. "He does the Ravel magnificently," she wrote Ezra. "Ravel told him the sonata (form) was an exact copy of one of Mozart's."

Another triumph was a recital with Giorgio Levi at Gabriele d'Annunzio's estate, Vittoriale. After World War I, the war hero–poet moved to the Gardone Riviera to construct his memorial in an old villa that housed a museum, library, and amphitheater where he produced his own plays. A mausoleum that looked like a half-submerged submarine was under construction for the bodies of ten men who had fought with him — and later his own. A quotation from *La Città Morta,* "Io ho quel che ho donato" [I have what I have given away], was placed strategically over the main gateway. In the private rooms, Olga recalled a marble statue of St. Sebastian and a coffin-shaped bed on a dias surrounded by chamois-leather curtains.

D'Annunzio was a short man, somewhat plump, with small shoulders and tiny feet, giving him a somewhat feminine appearance. His morbidly sallow complexion and pock-marked skin made it difficult at first to see why so many women found him irresistible. After an affair with the great actress Eleonora Duse in 1896 during voluntary exile in France, he had formed a liaison with Romaine Brooks, and at the time of Olga's visit, the then sixty-five-year-old's resident mistress was a young Russian, Nathalie de Gouloubeff.

Sitting at his right hand at dinner, Olga noticed a tiny book (of verse?) in the bronze goblet before him, an obvious conversation piece. But she couldn't find words to ask its significance, and the moment was lost. The poet was nonetheless impressed with the young violinist, and at the end of the evening he pressed into her hand a small silver bird wrapped in a silk scarf, a memento she treasured till the end of her life.

Ezra reluctantly arranged to visit his daughter in Bruneck in midsummer. He arrived unexpectedly, when Frau Marcher had just laid out in the *salotti* forty loaves of bread ready to be baked. She had left the child unattended for a short interval, and Pound reported in one of his more expansive letters to Olga: "Have now seen it [Mary] under the WORST . . . circumstances, it seized the moment of my arrival to be 'ik . . . I rushed 'em off to Brunik, the medico said it [Mary] was better and to repeat prescription. . . . I observed it is *not in the least* spotted or flea-bitten, has very nice shoulders . . . does not howl while having hair combed . . . hair thicker than two months ago, è molto bello. . . . Shd. have planned to stay longer, two hrs. just gives it time to get used to one." Frau Marcher commented that she was worried about the brevity of his visits, and Ezra suggested that Olga might stop over on her way to the next concert in Salzburg.

Olga spent two weeks at the Hotel de la Poste with Mary, whose illness was diagnosed as *tosse canina* (whooping cough). Pound wrote he was "deeply relieved that the whoops are passing" and suggested that Mary should be taught "to play the fiddle . . . so it won't be a literary female prematurely . . . am anxious about its musical education."

Frau Marcher was alarmed by the child's contrary behavior, which Pound viewed as evidence of a strong personality: "Waal, I 'spose someone'll have to smack it, but LLord knoze-oo. The kussink and swearink is, as you say, hereditary. If it adds your stubbornness to my kussedness, it will be a remarkable character." He sent thanks for the "bucolic photos . . . no doubt her offspring is very photogenic . . . we sh'd produce a film diva."

In September, Olga returned to Paris for a poignant reunion with Egerton Grey, then visiting his half-sisters, Ethel and Mabel Duncan. In spite of his vow to wait for Olga, the *primo amore* had married a second time and, after that marriage failed, had taken another hasty and ill-considered step, embarking on a new career in Tokyo. He returned to Paris in 1927 to rekindle his young love for Olga and bringing gifts, including the red kimono that she treasured (and requested to be buried in). The couple held hands in the old Palais Garnier during a performance of *Tristan and Isolde,* and Egerton again proposed marriage. Olga could not summon the courage to tell him about her relationship with Ezra. She was on the brink of confessing the birth of her child but the right moment never came, and Egerton left to continue his research at Cambridge.

Ezra treated the news of his rival in his usual patronizing and jocular manner: "He rejoices that she should possess a suitable and befitting and imperial kimono, according with her instincts. Is she going to walk in the via Sacra in black lacquer, playing the shamisan??"

Olga returned to St. John's Wood in October for another reunion with Egerton. She was considering asking him to act as sponsor in the baptism of her child in the Catholic faith. After corresponding with a Jesuit cousin, she felt guilty about Mary's lack of religious education and asked Ezra's advice, to which he answered: "As to her P[rimo] A[more], *he* cannot be expected to be an authority. . . . He [Egerton] might want a duplicate [of Mary], and it really wouldn't produce anything similar."

In November, while Olga was with Kathleen Richards and her parents at Hook Heath, tension was mounting in the relationship. Ezra appeared insensitive to her feelings: "Yes, he sh'd pay some attenshun to her. She had a-niversary, and he forgets it regularly." When he entered the Ospedale Civile in Genoa with a fistula (possibly brought on by stressful complications in his personal life), he cautioned her not to come.

Instead, she returned to the Hotel de la Poste. She wrote Ezra about her day with Mary and the Marchers: "I went in the sled and brought them back here—Leoncina, F. Marcher, and Margherita [the Marcher's foster daughter]. Frau Marcher told a charming story about the child, who disappeared one day and couldn't be found in house or garden. She was discovered sitting on a nest in the hen house. When scolded for not answering her call, Mary said, 'How can I? I am a hen—when I have laid my egg, I will cluck!'" Olga complained that "the Leoncina makes F. Marcher do just what she wants—won't do anything if someone suggests it—*which is like Him.*"

"I grew up like one of them," Mary wrote in her autobiography, meaning her adoptive family the Marchers, the good farmers of the Tyrol who, after a hard day's labor, gathered for *knodl* and *speck*, stories and song. On December 20, Olga observed the colorful procession of St. Sebastian, patron saint of the village: "We hung 'round in the snow for a long time, then a very long trail of men, two-by-two, some with banners, Herr Marcher holding a tassle." Pound must have remembered Olga's description of the saint's day when writing Canto 48:

> and all the mountains were full of fires, and
> we went around through the village . . .
> 2 men and 2 horses
> and then the music and on all sides
> children carrying torches and the
> carroze with the priests . . .
> . . . and the carroze were full of fine flowers.

Olga joined Ezra in Santa Margherita the week after Christmas, before returning to Paris and her world of music. Katherine Ruth Heymann, Ezra's former protegée, and a group of friends were meeting at the Café Voltaire to plan a forthcoming Alexander Scriabin concert. Olga wrote to Pound: "They decided . . . a circus was [the] ideal place, with lights reflected on a huge globe—twelve, high above for constellations, eight below for planets, four for the elements—and K. Heymann somewhere in the middle on a platform, some 2,000 francs needed for the experiment."

Olga was amusing herself with a young "disciple simpatico" who envisioned her as "a dark night with stars," she wrote, to arouse Ezra's jealousy. "The young man had a lot to say about the twelve types of people and twelve tones—listening for *the* tone and one's own tone, etc., etc. . . . *He* [would not] think of delicately flattering her with good old-fashioned metaphors."

The poet rose to the challenge: "Elle est une princesse d'orient avecque [*sic*] des astres occidentaux / avecque des dents de tigre or-i-ental / diminué par des pèlerinages dans les forêts des cieux. / Elle est une aube pré-aubale vaguant aux nuages slaviques pénétrés par des feux glacials aux temps Hittites. / Piétinant le labyrinthe compliqué des sphères concentriques allait de la voie lactée, etc. ZIAO!—elle est trop loin, hélas." [She is an oriental princess under occidental stars / with the teeth of an oriental tiger / diminished by pilgrimages in the forests of the heavens. / She is a dawn before the dawn, wandering in Slavic clouds penetrated by glacial fires at the time of the Hittites / treading the complex labyrinth of concentric spheres of the Milky Way, etc. / she is too far away, alas.]

Since no patron had come forward with two thousand francs, Olga's tenants allowed her to use the salon of the rue Chamfort apartment for the Scriabin concert, but the whole character of the room had changed; her mother's beautiful salon, she wrote, was "like a concierge's loge . . . paper fans and large photographs of the husband and musical comedy celebrities, the most god-dam awful vases of artificial flowers, and the books— spiritualistic propaganda, cheap magazines." Heymann played the sonata she had been practicing for London, and two interesting Russians came, one a composer who had known Scriabin. ("He says Scriabin intended a contrepoint de couleur over the music, not couleur illustrating it.")

In the spring of 1928, Olga again picked up correspondence with Egerton, this time about the purchase of sleigh bells for Mary: "I had the idea of musical toys, to teach 'Moidile' what a musical step was, each step a semitone." After a visit to the Mears and Stainbank Church Bell Foundry, her faithful friend replied: "I think you will agree the sound is rather dismal and not calculated either to inspire the young or solace and tranquilize the aged. Awaiting your further esteemed orders, I am, madam, yours interestingly, Egerton." This would be his last letter to Olga, although she did not know it then. The sleigh bells were still hanging on the banister of the Venice house when she left for the last time in the 1980s.

The Leoncina was never far from Olga's thoughts. In March, she purchased a pinafore printed with lions and giraffes; in April, a whirligig from a beautiful Chinese woman in the street. And Mary was often in her dreams: "All the air went dark, and the Leoncina couldn't understand why, then she said, 'God climbed a tree.'"

She was planning to meet her brother Teddy on the anniversary of their mother's death, to return the ashes to the burial site of their brother Arthur in Courrières, France. "Vienna l'ultimo del mese." Ezra had not yet decided to travel with her to Vienna. He was going to Gais in April. "She hopes it is not his intention to take anyone else with him," Olga wrote, referring to his wife, Dorothy. "She considers that *her* private life, and would very much resent any intrusion."

She asked Ezra to take her gift, a violin, to the child. Mary was then three years old, the age Olga was when Julia placed a violin in her small hands. A violin is a tactile instrument; a child can pick it up as easily as a teddy bear. Olga always felt comfortable with its shape and sound. When she listened to Julia sing, she tried to imitate her voice with her instrument.

Some thirty years later Mary wrote that she was "not particularly happy to receive a violin . . . the tunes were too difficult and alien. . . . I would have asked for a zither or a mouth organ to play gay and simple tunes. Mamile [Olga] showed me how to hold it . . . but as soon as I was left to myself, I banged it hard on the chicken coop."

Antheil was in Vienna in April, corresponding with "Ezzerah" about Olga's forthcoming concerts. "I have touched up my friendship with Paul Hindemith a bit, and he . . . would advise Olga to concentrate on modern music until she gets a slight name in Germany. Modern music concerts pay for themselves, because of the great interest. . . . Please have Olga do nothing . . . but the hardest, most painstaking, backbreaking *technic* . . . spend any money that is to be spent upon a good teacher that will raise hell with her."

An Austrian pianist, Fräulein Kraus, accompanied Olga in Vienna, and after the concert Antheil reported to Ezra: "I went to Miss Kraus . . . the very next day. . . . she doesn't consider Olga her equal at all." Neither did Edward Steuermann, another important pianist with whom Olga played professionally. The Germans — strictly trained in rigorous technique — did not consider her ready for a joint artist's tour, Antheil said. "I shall do my very best, always, for Olga, who has done a lot for me. But when I listened to [her] Mozart, although I admired the warmness of her tone and inter-pretation, it struck me that . . . Mozart needed to be *hard* and *absolute*, with the finest filigree work. . . . Olga can't get the hardness, or the perfection of the filigree. . . . She must do it . . . must work all summer long . . . not on Mozart, but on technic."

Olga urged Ezra to join her and Antheil on the American tour. "Will He take a passage from Genoa or Naples and go to the States with her? Incognito? He could sacrifice his beard for awhile. The idea amuses her, [but] she also thinks it is a *serious* idea . . ."

After the Vienna concert, she returned to the Pensione Seguso in Venice and, liking it very much, wished she could settle there, "in some place where there is not eternally someone in the next room." She was sending Ezra the biography of Daisy Kennedy, another American concert artist: "He ought to know the stuff violinists should be made of . . . I feel I'm not flamboyant enough."

An opportunity to be flamboyant came in July when Lindy Shaw-Paige, a friend with a summer home on Capri, asked her to travel with her in a white Chrysler two-seater convertible ("so much nicer than present-day covered cars," Olga recalled). They drove past Austrian dikes and for-tifications and the train bridge to Venice, had dinner on the boules court of the Stella d'Italia, then on to Bologna for the night. A pause at Vergato near the beautiful *passo della Porretta* the next day, to eat wild strawberries with a picnic lunch. "A contadino came along and asked us what we were selling? never having seen anyone picnic but gypsies." They visited Ramooh in Florence, and stopped next at the Hotel Victoria in Rome: "We had been warned that the via was pericolosa . . . but Lindy managed beautifully." After Rome, it was "very nice all the way, except for Naples . . . one hour driving out of it was more tiring than all [the] rest of [the] trip."

On July 12, they arrived at Lindy's villa on the via Castiglione in Capri, where she instructed Ezra to address mail in care of Mrs. Shaw-Paige. That they had quite different ways of viewing the world was apparent in their correspondence: "She hopes He stop writing about 'tin in his teeth,' and 'reducing his figure.' One would think He was His friends Mr. [James] Joyce and Mr. [Ford Madox] Ford rolled into one! His teeth are bellissimo, also His figure, when He keeps His pants hitched up. He please try to be a bit romantic when He's writing to a lady."

Olga was soon taken up by the exiled Russian community. Princesse Gortchakoff and Madame Tchiliekeff suggested a concert with Ottorino Respighi, "*if* he remembers me—and *if* he would do it."

She was a keen observer of the high life on Capri: "The permanent residents throw themselves on newcomers for news of [the] outside world in [a] perfectly ghoulish and indecent manner." She had been to a *café chantant* with a new young man of Lindy's, Peter Millward, who bought Romaine Brooks's villa. "Good looking—money—and some mysterious relationship to [Otto] Kahn, the collector. Teddie Gerrard was . . . charming and 'come-hitherish,' but she is the 'drunk' of the place."

Olga was still attractive, a young woman with immense vitality, considered exciting by men unaware of her liaison with Pound. A young Italian *architetto* "introduced himself and promised to take my photo. . . . he told Lindy that my eyebrows are the most bellissima and curiosissima he has ever seen," she reported to Ezra. Another of Lindy's young men offered to teach her the latest dance step, "a new turn . . . all done with the knees."

A well-intentioned doctor arranged a dinner party to meet Rhoda Backhaus, the English pianist. "The good doctor shows a distressing admiration for Compton MacKenzie's book [*Extraordinary Women*], and [I] was taken aback when he queried, à propos of nothing, 'Have you ever been *married*, Miss Rudge?' "

Peter London, one of the "pretty boys" on the island, was at the Hotel Paradiso with Ezra's friend Robert McAlmon. McAlmon's marriage to heiress Winifred Ellerman, known as Bryher (a pen name), was a marriage of convenience; she was then living with Ezra's young love, the poet H.D., and Hilda's daughter Perdita. Olga's first impression of McAlmon was "his ugly face . . . Bryher's money does not seem to have been lucky to McAlmon." For his part, London described Olga as "one of those pure frank English girls who show a lot of arms and legs." "Pretty exact," Olga agreed—"a girl, in the English sense, is anything female, up to 45."

Olga swam daily in the sea, and Ezra encouraged her to "get all the sea salt she can. . . . Seems to be a lot of young men abaht . . . all bhuggerasts, or is Lesbos de-peopled? [I] believe firmly in [the] orgiastic life."

She continued to enjoy life on the island—if not the orgiastic life—without Ezra. "The architetto . . . attaches himself to me whenever I appear, mostly in the sea, rows me to [the] most romantic spots. Oggi he took me to the most suitable cave, an opening just large enough to swim through, but inside lighted from above, and shallow enough water to stand in—setting ideal for un'amore marino (which is one of her unfulfilled desires) . . . she might have been excused for forgetting? . . . however, [he had] *the* most profound respect, nearly equalling her primo amore. What would He do about it (if He was her, not if He was there)?"

Ezra replied, "He regrets his absence from the cave. It sounds like a spot built to order . . . no use wasting chef d'oeuvre of nature on the unfit. Let her quench her regrets. . . . More than simple muscular appearance is required. Cheer up, he will keep that cave in mind."

"She hasn't got the young architect's scalp yet," she replied; "with every visible sign of defeat, [he is] still holding out. She feeling really annoyed and not showing it, being sustained by her dignity, which never deserts her, except for Him." The young man had discovered "the bellezza of her caratterre, and his sguardo [gaze] was positively incinerating," she wrote. "He is a bellissimo giovane with the manners of an archangel, and she likes young men with beautiful manners—yeow!"

Ezra was trying to keep the reins firmly in hand. He suggested a meeting in Levanto on the coast near Genoa after Capri, but Olga would not promise to be there until the end of August. "The unforgivable sin, to upset his timetable—yeow! He not treat her as if she were a nuisance—*and* he please receive her more than affectionately, not curse and swear at her. . . . He much too bristly to offer carezze."

In late August, tragic news came from Mabel Duncan, vacationing in Heidelberg: Egerton Grey was dead. His sisters had been expecting him to arrive from Cambridge, planning a happy holiday together. Egerton wrote in his last letter (July 24) from the Biochemical Institute that he had been feverishly working to get his book ready and counted on another week to finish it, then would join his sisters in Germany. "He was taken ill from overwork a little over a week ago, and a few days later, taken to a nursing home, where Temple [his brother] saw him, then left for Warsaw," Mabel wrote. "We were all away when E. died on the 10th, and no news in time for us to be at his funeral. . . . He spoke of you on his last visit to us about the 8th June, and asked your news." One can only imagine Olga's feeling of loss after the one man who had loved her unconditionally was gone. She would appreciate his devotion even more with the passage of time.

Masking the full extent of her grief, she wrote to Ezra: "He not expect her to be very brilliant when He arrives. She has heard news that her primo amore is dead, and is feeling molto giù [down]. . . . She feels that she ought to go and yowl over [his] grave. He seems to have dropped all his ridiculosities—just as my mother dropped her unreasonableness—on dying, and [they] became martyrs."

Olga's father sent a typed letter of condolence under the letterhead of the Commercial Union Assurance Company: "I was very sorry to hear of Egerton Grey's death. The young die as well as the old, so it behooves us to try and be prepared." To raise Olga's spirits (or to lure her home) the elder Rudge offered to finance a professional appearance in the United States. "I expect to get some money in the near future, and am willing to help you if it would do you any good." Aware of the passage of years— Olga was then thirty-three—her father continued: "It is time now for you to be doing something. Think it over and give me an idea of the amount of money you would require." He enclosed an allowance of two thousand francs, a generous sum at the time, and signed the letter as always, "Your affectionate father, J. Edgar Rudge."

As one chapter in Olga's life ended with the death of her *primo amore*, she was considering finding a place where she and Ezra could spend time together with their child, away from the curious eyes of Rapallo and Paris. They both shared fond memories of Venice: Pound had lived near the Ponte San Vio in 1908, when acting as impresario for Katherine Ruth Heymann. Olga first went there to perform at the Conservatorio Benedetto Marcello and became enamored with the historic old city where time seemed to stand still.

In Paris she met Gretchen Green, a former secretary to the Nobel Prize–winning poet Rabindranath Tagore in India. (Ezra also had known Green through the Bengali poet, whose works had been published in English translation with an introduction by W. B. Yeats.) The owner of a tearoom in Venice that offered home-baked muffins and English-language newspapers, Gretchen lived in a charming little house belonging to an

American expatriate, Dorothea Watts (at that time Mrs. Albert Landsburg). She mentioned to Olga that Watts was eager to sell one of three adjoining small houses on a cul-de-sac near the old church of Santa Maria della Salute in Dorsoduro, the quiet "back" of the city.

Watts's cousin, May Dodge, had fallen in love with the house, but Watts offered Olga first chance to buy it. Olga began to consider ways to get together enough money. "It was the house that changed my life, and I got it just for the asking," she remembered. "First, I asked Ramooh if she would she give me what she had promised in her will *now*—to buy a house—and she said, 'Yes.' That was *half.* Then I wrote my father and asked him if he could give me the rest, and if so, to cable 'yes,' and he did. I still feel guilty at not having told my father that I had not *seen* the house (he was in the real estate business). If I had, he might not have acted at once. As it was, he lost his money in the 1929 stock market crash, and I would have been left with nothing but my three-year-old."

"Gretchen is very cockawhoop that you've bought it," Ezra informed her a few days later. At the same time, Green wrote Olga from Venice: "Here am I, established in this casa . . . with plumbers and plasterers . . . making *your* house into a home. . . . You are welcome to the use of [my things], as at present I have neither home nor prospect. . . . Olaf, the sculptor, has definitely bought [the house] at the end, so you will be a square of busy, happy people. Perhaps some friend of yours would rent *this* house, the one you know?"

Olga suggested to Ezra that his young friend Adrian Stokes (author of *The Stones of Rimini*) might be persuaded to buy the second house, so Ezra might keep the studio with an entrance next to hers. "I could put [in] a chattière, and give you double entrance and exit, very convenient for comédie Venetienne." To which he replied: "He think next step after pied-à-terre is really LARGE CAGE. . . . he ain't goin' to have his cage in a cellar, he don't care WOTT it is nex' to . . . however, he will endeavor to visit the Queen of the Adriatic."

Olga's retort: "He doesn't want [a] cage next [to] hers with sliding door in between—very *un*suitable He says. . . . She decided against taking the second house, though I would so like to have a place of my own that didn't have to be let—*ever*."

Olga arrived in Venice in late November 1928. "To call it the smallest house in Venice [is] pretty near the truth ('Holy Ghost' houses, they call them in Philadelphia)," she wrote. Poet Desmond O'Grady remarked, after visiting 252, calle Querini, that it was like "three matchboxes on top of each other." The exterior was indeed unremarkable, with faded, peeling paint when Olga first saw it. Some of the windows faced the gray, crumbling back wall of the Dogana, the old Customs House (in summer and early fall, she kept the shutters closed against the blinding sun). A beamed ground-floor kitchen with a table-high brick hearth was, to Olga's eyes, one of the best features. On the top floor was "a studio contrived out of an attic."

Olga passed December in a flurry of activity: "am having [the] downstairs done gesso a cola [chalk white], i.e., whitewash that doesn't come off on your clothes, and leaving the wood rim to focolare [fireplace] black . . . beams black with white underneath. . . . if He cares to give opinion, [the plasterers] are not likely to do much irreparable damage before [your] answer."

Ezra's reply: "My system of decor is absolootly the cheapest poss[ible] . . . advise bright, clear colors. . . . She'z got the [bas relief of] Isotta [da Rimini], which might be putt in wall *inside* but not where the fire wd. smoakk it." He appeared to be unaware of the cat-and-mouse game he was playing: "I think you'd be happier if you'd get me out of your mind for awhile. . . . I should think there might be something brighter to think of. . . . He wishes her a gran bel nuovo amante . . . it is a rotten idea her sitting round waiting for him to come out of a bloody lethargy that neither he, she, or anyone can affect . . . and he don't propose to . . . present any complaints or excuses, he hasn't any."

Olga, the mother of his child, spent a cold and lonely Christmas at the Pensione Seguso while the plasterers were at work on the calle Querini house. She had no desire for a "gran bel nuovo amante." She and Ezra had been together only one Christmas since Mary was born; she felt that he ought to be with her, and let him know that she thought she deserved better. Many years later, after rereading Ezra's next letter, she scribbled "EXPLOSION!!!" in red ink on the envelope. Nowhere in their correspondence are their differences spelled out more clearly:

No, you God Dam fool, it is your vampirism. Your wanting more. What damn pleasure is there in ANYTHING . . . if someone is always telling you what you OUGHT, what you OWE, what they deserve. . . . The only reason people can live near each other is because they let each other ALONE . . . when the spontaneity goes out of a relationship, l'amour est bien fini.

You have a set of values I don't care a damn for. I do not care a damn about private affairs, private life, personal interests. You do. It is perfectly right that you should, but you can't drag me into it. Yeats wrote a long time ago that an artist could not really have friends save among artists. . . . You want to be the centre of a circle. I can not be in perpetual orbit.

For a long time you have wanted me in a 'role,' or to live up to a set of your ideas. . . . It is quite possible that he also made some effort to make her over according to his pattern—one does instinctively— but the moment he saw that was contra natura, he gave it up.

Between the lines, the letter also outlined his conditions for the relationship to continue. In her reply, Olga expressed her pain—and fury:

She feels that He ought—yes *ought*—to notice the difference between one woman and another before He damns them wholesale. Of what good [is] all his Henry James admiration for [women]— can He only *see* in *print?* Is He too big a dog to notice the minute differences?

She would like to play the violin well. Her playing means [to] him agitating—big drum. He has no idea of just what months of work in peace would mean to her. She cannot practice when she is cold or uncomfortable or in other people's houses—in hotels, mostly—or when she is unhappy. She has tried to adapt herself to other people's situations and *failed.* . . . She is now trying to make circumstances suit *her* needs, but He is not interested . . . the fact of His having once been is no reason why He should continue to be. . . . She shouldn't expect the same repetitions of movements— repeats, da capos, etc—in amore, any more than in music.

7

The Breaking Point

1929–1931

Early in the new year of 1929, the hard work, the uncertainty, the coldest winter in many years—in Venice, the canals froze over—had broken Olga's spirit. In deep depression, she wrote to Ezra, crossing out some of the more painful passages: "I have tried very hard to go on working, but I can't . . . nearly two months since I tried to finish things. You didn't want to keep me—or to give me any reason, except unjust ones. . . . Caro, I beg you, if you can explain or help, to be quick—I am just about finished. I have lost everything."

Ezra failed to offer consolation:

I do not think life is possible if you stop to consider peoples'
personal feelings . . . you obviously don't go out to be nasty or
squash people unnecessarily: *But* if you start gearing up everything
in accordance to whether or not it gives someone else a bellyache I
don't see where you come out. . . . One does one's job, well or
badly, and when it's done, one enjoys oneself. . . . My monde . . . is
made up of people who are doing or trying to do something, when
they can't, they give a 'and to them as does. . . . I can't see . . .

where people get to if they start thinking their moods and emotions are the only thing in life.

The same day, he continued: "She was evidently very tired when she wrote . . . been working too hard . . . an' I'm damned if I see 'lost everything.' Where you got the idea that you don't want a younger man?" He added, "not too conceited, without too many brains, obviously not hideous. . . . I'd like to know why you think you wouldn't be perfectly happy with the above?"

Olga: "Am I supposed to want the younger man without any brains—instead of, or in addition to himself? He means kindly, obviously, but He will never be praised for his insight into the 'uman 'art."

When He first knew her . . . he seemed to consider her of the same species (a very poor or inferior kind of course) as himself. Now he speaks of "me" and "my," "my" world, in contra-distinction to "you"—can he tell her why she is to be kept outside?

The *monde* of "Mr. and Mrs. E.P."—only people who can tell a good anecdote of the 1890s admitted. . . . You should have a nice crowd of Bolcheviks to break up all the smug people you have around, who talk about "artistes." . . . I shall bring the Leoncina up illiterate, let your damn Omar have the '90s.

Ezra: "She fed up with hartists, an' he about fed up with women." In Canto 29, Pound had written: "the female / Is a chaos / an octopus / a biological process." Only in his last years did he pay full homage to Olga's courage, her sacrifice, her importance to him as a poet. At forty-four, he was still exhibiting the characteristics of a spoiled only child, a condition later diagnosed at St. Elizabeth's Hospital as narcissism, an inability to know one's own emotions or to empathize with others, and often an unconscious (or conscious?) need to exploit.

In spite of the emotional impasse with Ezra, Olga was beginning to enjoy the fruits of her labors at 252, calle Querini: "There is no greater joy possible than standing 'round watching other people do what you tell them. . . . She hasn't enjoyed anything so much since she used to tag 'round after the gardener as a child in St. John's Wood and watch the man build the dog kennels." She was following Ezra's advice to enjoy the company of younger men: "The two Adrians [Stokes and Kent] have turned up here . . . A. has lent me his gramaphone and books, and took me to a cinema. I am reading Aldington's [translation of Rémy] de Gourmont, who is a great consolation. . . . altogether she is feeling more pleased."

Olga shrewdly recognized that Ezra had started defining their relationship as *"impresario* and *impressed."* Plans were taking shape for her Berlin debut. "I have been told it is certain," Antheil wrote Pound. "Olga will be given a chance to appear before the most artistic audience in Deutschland." Smitty was going to Italy for a much-needed rest, and Olga encouraged Ezra to finish his opera: "now [that] you have a [Dolmetsch] clavichord and George, you could get the Villon into shape so it could be handed to a conductor."

Olga and Kathleen Richards were booked to perform in London on the same night as Jascha Heifetz. "Our concert would draw quite a different type," Kathleen wrote: "depends very much on what we do ourselves with re. to raking in all our friends and acquaintances. . . . [We] begin at 8:15, allowing those good souls who come from the country to get home in decent time."

The Guardian reviewed the concert favorably: "Miss Olga Rudge and Miss Kathleen [Richards] Dale . . . showed that Mozart can easily stand the strain of a whole program. . . . Miss Rudge handled the solo part with style and a wholesome precision." *Musical Opinion* agreed that "these two very fine artists . . . remind one of the passage about Hermia and Helena in 'Midsummer Night's Dream,' they sang 'both in one key' . . . [with] good tone, clear passages, and . . . beautiful finish, simple and unsophisticated."

In September Olga moved into her new home in Venice, the first and last she would ever own. Ezra arrived for a fortnight's visit, then moved on to Verona, while Olga rendezvoused at the railway station with "the Landosk" (harpsichordist Wanda Landowska). "[She] was telling me some story, interrupted in middle of sentence by friends' arrival and business of getting tickets . . . a quarter of an hour later continues: 'Is it the working with diff[erent] voices in the Fugues?' etc. What makes her able to keep all the threads in her head, separate and distinct, like, in a way, *The Cantos*?"

Landowska was booked for a series of concerts in America, but was sacrificing her fee if they would allow her to play with her pupils: "The fact of its being with Revue Musicale puts it on [a] better footing—no fees for us, but receipts may give us a trifle." Both Olga and Pound appeared unaware of the disastrous nosedive the New York stock market had taken on Black Friday (October 28, 1929), marking the beginning of one of the world's worst economic crises. The *Graf Zeppelin* was circling the globe and construction had just begun on the Empire State Building, the world's tallest skyscraper, when U.S. securities lost some $26 billion in value in one week. In European artistic circles, André Breton's second "Surrealist Manifesto" and Jean Cocteau's *Les Enfants Terribles* caused another kind of memorable tremor.

To augment her income, Olga began trying her hand at writing a novel, "The Blue Spill," in the tradition of British "whodunits," a genre both she and Pound enjoyed for light reading. The setting was Graylands, an estate in Surrey, modeled on the British country houses Olga knew in her youth; the characters included a stereotypical butler and an Inspector Love presiding over the inquest. The paterfamilias, Marshall, was found shot to death in his study, a presumed suicide, though his wife insisted it was murder. Pound cut the work mercilessly, scribbling editorial queries about inconsistencies in the margin in blue pencil. The draft manuscript ended after only 133 pages and—like so many of Olga's enthusiasms—was abandoned before completion.

In a late November letter to Ezra, Olga again revealed ambivalence about her role as mother: "I've got to do *something* about the Leoncina— either to go there, or have her come. . . . I have been putting it off and putting it off. . . . no reason why she should suffer for my complexes. . . . She is of [an] age to understand grown-up conversations, to get it into her head that she is abandoned, different—not healthy ideas to grow up on. . . . *It's a year and a half since anyone has seen the child,* and I have been in Italy most of that time. . . . I only want to be sure in most selfish manner that duty to offspring not going to lose the amante." She complained that she was now middle-aged, soon to be forty.

Ezra: "An' he is damn well forty and more, so it's just as hard on him, an where t'ell does she think there are bella donnas on every bush? The young . . . are mostly so idiotic, won't tolerate them." As a consolation prize: "Orl rite, she arrange it, and when she'z got it arranged, she tell him wot, and he will try to accommodate."

Their reunion with Mary took place in November. "He was very nice to her, she very pleased, and she will go on being *good*," she wrote Ezra at the Hotel Berchielli in Florence, where he was working at "the Biblioteck" to revise the first thirty Cantos, soon to be published.

Homer and Isabel Pound had moved in early fall from their home of some forty years to be near their only child, with Homer's pension from the U.S. Mint in Philadelphia providing a comfortable income. On their first Christmas in Rapallo, Ezra took Homer aside and confessed that he was the father of a four-year-old daughter. He described the encounter to Olga: "Dad [was] duly and properly pleased at nooz of his granddaughter . . . said he hoped when he passed on he would be able to leave something. . . . I suggested that his consort [Isabel Pound] was probably not yet sufficiently Europeanized to appreciate, etc. He gasped and said, 'No, she'd take the next boat back'." Ezra did not identify the child's mother, though in previous correspondence he had mentioned Olga as a young violinist whose career he was sponsoring.

Olga was alone in the rue Chamfort apartment, her home for so many years. Ezra invited her to Italy after Christmas, with "lunch at the Hotel Rapallo—if she wants to see WBY [William Butler Yeats], please note." Olga admitted "mild curiosity and awareness that having seen the man is the kind of thing that gives one a slight advantage in philistine circles." In later years she acknowledged: "It is curious how Yeats—against whom I was so childishly prejudiced—is taking form and size. [I can] see *his* influence on EP, as well as *EP*'s on him."

As the year 1930 began, Olga, like many Americans at home and abroad, was suffering from the effects of the worldwide economic depression. The Youngstown properties her father could save did not bring in enough income to pay mortgages and taxes; her allowance curtailed, she would have to rely on concerts and violin lessons to support herself. Ezra appeared to be pulling back, if not withdrawing entirely, from the relationship, and she was too proud to accept his contributions for anything but the modest needs of their child. (A check for five hundred pounds enclosed in a January 2 letter remains in the archive, uncashed, in its original envelope.) Olga faced the reality that she would have to raise her daughter alone (in her words, with very little talent for motherhood). Not for the first time, she reached the bottom of her despair and considered suicide.

Instead of rushing to her side, Ezra presented a carefully reasoned argument against it: "It is so damned hard for anyone to understand *anything* about what goes on in another head. Only she wd. be perfectly wrong to . . . stop living NOW, now of all times . . . nobody ever does get a strange idea into their heads till they get to [the] *breaking point*. . . . She got rid, as her father said, of her religion. . . . You can't scrap a whole thing like that, pericoloso, pericoloso, unless one has another house to go to—in Ireland, one talks of 'making one's soul.'"

Olga:

She doesn't think that she has "given up" her religion, because she doesn't think that with her character, anything that she had 'had' could slip away as easily as water off a duck's back. . . . As for god, she is probably at a stage of low development. One god permeating everything might as well not exist . . . she wants her god incarnate. . . . She is not tryng to tell him He is a god, but her only feeling of god is in him.

Ezra:

He never said she was more bother than she was worth; he said she had given him more trouble than all the other women on the planet . . . but [that is an] *estimate of value*. . . . She don't seem to understand when she gets inside him, which she did not at first. . . . She knows they haven't stai'd si bene insieme [so good together] since heaven knows when . . . not since they were on a walking tour, since Ussel or Ventadour, [but] she not fall to pieces just when one might be gettin' something or other shaped up. Nobody ever had any sense about suicide. . . . They allus take the wrong moment . . . just before "cheque arrived in the morning post" . . .

Bothered by the severe winter and a persistent cold, Ezra, too, was depressed and cantankerous. He suggested the possibility that "one of them flatchested females been gettin' on her nerves. . . . Wot the HELL!!!! . . . bloody bitches. . . . Damn the wimmen!"

He has been seriously ill a good deal of the time when she has been mal contenta. . . . Da tanti anni he has been balancing things on his nose or his head . . . if she thinks he don't care for her a great deal more now than he did in the primi anni and in a very different way, she is very wrong. . . . Au commencement, he believes *she* had the idea of dropping out, I don't mean dying, but of going off to something else. . . . She get it into her head that *he don't want to go on without her, either.* . . . She was more with him . . . the night after he got her letter than she had been—perhaps ever.

Olga:

[It is] absolutely essential that she continue to balance him on the end of the stick on the end of her nose with all the drums rolling, because it is a very difficult feat, and if He rolls off and hits her in the eye, it will hurt her, besides leaving her nothing to look up to . . .

Considering that she isn't a pushing person . . . his going 'round covered with signs: "Keep Off the Grass," "Don't Touch," "Open 10–12, Closed 12–2," "By Appointment Only," etc. is rude and unnecessary. . . . He has always barged into her life just when He wanted, and if she wasn't ready and waiting, He damn well made her feel she "ought" to have been.

And all this blather about . . . a younger man—I could have had quite a pleasant time [with] Adrian. . . . I wasn't encouraged.

Adrian Stokes, one of "Ezra's young men" whom he met on the tennis courts of Rapallo, became Olga's confidant. He wrote to her: "I have perfect faith in your happiness. You fight tooth and nail if necessary. But I think you already have won what victory you needed. You are necessary to Ezra, of that I am certain. You've only got to hold on."

When Ezra recovered from his lethargy and bronchitis in late January, he climbed the hill to the village of Sant'Ambrogio where he discovered a bright peasant's cottage overlooking the Gulf of Tigullio near the old church of San Pantaleo, a perfect pied-à-terre for Olga to let for a modest seventy-five lire per month.

When Olga went there to stay, the façade of Casa 60 was covered with orange-colored wash and decorated with mock-Ionic columns, Ligurian style. Smooth stone steps, half-hidden with creepers and honeysuckle vines, led up to a green front door. Inside were white walls and red-brick tile floors, pale blue and pink vaulted ceilings painted with morning glory vines "convoluting into bouquets and wreaths," her daughter remembered.

The Pellegrini family, who lived on the ground floor, operated an olive press, and Olga was serenaded by the clunking of the press and the echo of a bucket hitting water as it plunged into the well. "It was *good* olive oil," she said, ignoring the noisy machinery.

Pound would recall the "house of smooth stone" as the "ingle of Circe" in Canto 39; the noise of the olive press became the sound of Circe at work on her loom:

> "thkk, thgk"
> of the loom
"Thgk, thkk" and the sharp sound of a song
> under olives . . .
When I lay in the ingle of Circe
I heard a song of that kind.

Olga furnished the cottage simply, with a long bookcase and mirror near the entrance, a dining table and four cane-bottomed chairs along the walls, one painting—blue sea, a white shell. No clutter, no electricity, only candlelight. In the kitchen was an old-fashioned potbellied stove meant for charcoal, but one guest remembered that Olga preferred to cook with pine cones or a spirit lamp, and used them "with as much success as some people do with gas."

Olga was near enough to descend the footpath to Rapallo and be with Pound in less than an hour. But she was never comfortable with provincial resort life or the tight little world of the British colony that wintered there. William Butler Yeats and his wife Georgie Hydes-Lee, who first visited "in Dorothy and Ezra's charge," were delighted with the town and moved their furniture from Merrion Square in London to 12, via Americhe, in Rapallo, transporting with them their English way of life. Yeats described to Olivia Shakespear, Ezra's mother-in-law, their "first dinner-coated meal" with the couple, where they met the 1912 Nobel Prize winner, Gerhart Hauptmann, "who does not speak a word of English, but is fine to look at, after the fashion of William Morris." Yeats also relayed the news that "George Antheil and his lady-wife might be there, and a certain Basil Bunting, who had got into jail as a pacifist, one of EP's more savage disciples." Peggy Guggenheim, who arrived after the rainy season drove her out of Venice, admitted that, in Rapallo, "we had sun, but we paid for it. What a horrid, dull little town it was!"

To Olga's eyes, the hills above Rapallo were different. Even the dialect of the *contadini* was not the same as the *lingua* of the townspeople. The weather was variable, with clouds hanging over Zoagli for several days, bringing rain in from the sea. But nothing could dim her enthusiasm for the remote cottage where she spent part of each year.

"Those people didn't know I was in Sant'Ambrogio over their heads all the time," Olga said, refusing to recognize how closely *il poeta's* activities were monitored by the gossips of the colony. Ezra, who spent mornings at work in the via Marsala apartment and then stopped off for a set at the Tennis Club, in the afternoon was observed climbing the *salita* to Sant'Ambrogio. If he was too busy or too tired to climb the steep, narrow mule path up the hill, Olga would descend and leave notes for him in the

Café Yolanda. Giuseppe Bacigalupo, son of Pound's doctor and sometime tennis partner, noticed when the poet and Olga were guests for dinner that there was no sign of intimacy between them; she was especially reserved, both were perfectly proper.

Once settled in, Olga dug into the task Pound had set out for her, translating Jean Cocteau's *Mystère Laïc*, a secular mystery play, to be published by the editors of *Hound and Horn*, the Harvard-based literary journal.

Her spirits restored, she returned to the rue Chamfort in April, when people of all ages were in the parks enjoying the spring sunshine; children rolling their hoops reminded Olga of her little brothers so many years ago. On May 25, she joined Ezra in Frankfurt am Main near Munich to attend the world premiere of George Antheil's jazz opera, *Transatlantique*, subtitled *The People's Choice*.

Antheil, then only twenty-eight, went to Vienna with no connections and succeeded in having his composition accepted by Universal Verlag, the largest music-publishing house on the Continent. It was the first time the German State Opera had subsidized an American work, and people came from all over Europe to hear it. The *Herald* critic Waverly Root hailed *Transatlantique*, with its cast of bootleggers, crooks, politicians, and gangsters, as "the dawn of a new era. . . . Antheil has seen the possibilities of modernity, and skyscrapers, transatlantic liners and jingling telephones, newspaper bulletins and cinema screens to provide background for his scene." The Berlin press was unanimous in lauding the work of young Antheil as "full of new charm and rich rhythmic verve." But one dissenter viewed the music as "badly handicapped by a series of conventional phrases. . . . [Antheil] seems to have returned to a simpler scoring than, say, the followers of Wagner and Richard Strauss."

Back in Italy, Olga was beginning to carve out a new life for herself in Venice. Blanche Somers-Cocks, widow of the former British ambassador to the Vatican, invited her to tea and became a devoted friend. Among the guests was a Mr. Carr, an English gentleman who claimed to be the city's oldest inhabitant, remembering conversations with Robert Browning and John Ruskin. (Six decades later, Olga would call herself the oldest resident of Venice.)

She invited Egerton Grey's stepsisters, Ethel and Mabel Duncan, to visit at the end of August. "She hasn't had time to breathe . . . these old ladies!" she wrote Ezra. "She hopes to die youngish and spare her friends the grasshopper talking noises and parrot laughing they make!" (Olga lived to 101, and was never accused of "grasshopper talking noises.")

Old ladies were not her only visitors. Adrian Stokes returned from the Stone House, Pangbourne, Berkshire, "completely undone by England and my family." He presented Olga with a discarded male dressing gown from one of the smart shops in Venice ("I suspect he thought it was a bit effeminate"). "My stay in Venice was vivid, so too my impression of the Young Lioness [Mary], for which I thank you," he wrote after returning to England. Olga remembered Adrian, in those days, as "a beautiful young man, and very charming. He sent me many more letters thanking me for the privilege of meeting my daughter. She was on the new bed that had to be hauled up through the first floor window . . . pretty and pink on pink sheets, with golden hair on a pink pillow, gazing starry-eyed at the most beautiful young man she had ever seen before (or since?). But her dark infant soul held some grudge against the female parent."

Ezra did not join Olga in Venice that fall. "She hasn't any place to attach him to," she wrote him. "He is floating 'round in a most god-like manner . . . please think of her affectionately."

On September 29, a year after the crash, her father sent two drafts for one thousand francs each, with this poignant message: "I will not be able to send more this year. I have never been so hard up in my life. You may do as you wish with the Paris flat and its content. It is too expensive traveling back and forth." Like many suffering from the Depression, the elder Rudge was no longer willing to indulge a daughter who, in his view, was not earning her keep. "Too bad if you cannot make a go of it with your music," he wrote. "You won't stay in one place long enough. When you started to teach in Paris a few years ago, I was in hopes you would soon have enough pupils to keep you busy. There are teachers who have not had the start you had making a living there. . . . You are old enough now to settle down to hard work."

After receiving his letter, Olga wrote Ezra from Paris: "Nothing decided about the flat. Having announced giving it up, I got Renata [Borgatti] and Teddy [Rudge] falling over themselves trying to help me keep it. . . . Teddy sent rent and proposed to repeat doing so. I couldn't allow [it], of course, but it's nice he thought of it. . . . I wish I could get enough to live somewhere near 'the Center of the Universe'."

In November, she let the rue Chamfort flat for thirty-three hundred francs per month to the Princesse de Polignac, the American heiress Winaretta Singer, a music patron. In Olga's words, "the whole idea, which came from her, was to help me over the difficulties." Then Renata Borgatti "bought" Julia's grand piano for five thousand francs and allowed Olga to keep it on loan.

"She plunk in on hi sassiety," Ezra suggested. "She does much better on her own than when encumbered with *him*."

In 1931, in Ezra's words, "the state of murkn [American] industry" was not getting better; 768 companies were missing their dividends. Olga's father had to give up his office in downtown Youngstown and take a larger apartment to include a home office. He had driven to Toledo for the consecration of the new bishop and to visit his brother, Father Eugene. "Mussolini is trying to make trouble for the Pope," he commented. "He had better lay off the Church, for She has drowned hundreds of better men than he is."

Olga's financial situation continued precarious until the Princesse engaged her to play a Bach concerto and Schumann quintet in Venice's Corte del Duca Sforza with Giorgio Levi in January. She returned to the Richards family at Gorse Cottage in February to play Mozart, Strauss, and Schubert with their daughter Kathleen.

Her passport for the years 1930 and 1931 is stamped with eight entries into and out of Italy. After a short visit with Dalliba-John in Florence, she wrote Ezra: "I asked her [Ramooh] to tell my fortune with cards (as a way of keeping her quiet), and she at once turned up the King of Diamonds. 'Mr. Pound . . . What about his opera? I see it here. It's going to be a success—only given once.' I have not mentioned the Villon for years . . . the fact of her remembering you had written an opera was surprising."

Frau Marcher brought the Leoncina to Venice in August for the annual visit. "She [Mary] enquires anxiously about the date of His arrival. I fear she thinks she has been brought on false pretenses." Adrian Stokes had come again, and Olga defended him to Ezra: "I assure you the young man is the most admiring and devoted of your disciples, the only person to whom she can confide her romantic passion for the Serene Highness and find understanding and approval and applause for the Leoncina, enough to satisfy her. Nobody was suggesting He alter his schedule. She is now going to get into a bathing suit and get into the sea." She was photographed — tanned, healthy, smiling — in a modest contemporary tank suit at the glamorous Lido, where William Randolph Hearst was sighted with his mistress, movie actress Marion Davies, and Constance Talmadge, another star of the silent screen.

They were still waiting for Ezra to arrive: "sua figlia professes proper filial feeling (she regrets the gross vater [grandfather] can't come too) . . . [has] been in bathing twice, and not a bit afraid of the water . . . am taking her to a Topolino [Mickey Mouse film] this evening, and Sunday afternoon to Mestre to a grand circo with lions and tigers which [I] consider part of her education." After: "The Leoncina saw Topolino without a smile! . . . she had been through Central Africa first, and Frau M[archer]'s unspoken but audible scandalizedness at the nudities had chilled the air." She asked Ezra to observe the proprieties while Frau Marcher and Mary were present.

Ezra: "All right / DAM it / he will sleep in the house next door until September 1."

It was Ezra's custom to spend late summer and early fall with Olga and Mary in Venice, while Dorothy was in England with her mother and Omar. Mary recorded her first impressions of those visits in her autobiography, *Discretions*. The tiny calle Querini house seemed like a palace to the little girl, her mother Olga "majestic and beautiful like a queen." She was placed on a pile of cushions in a high, dark blue armchair over which they spread a leopard skin in front of the open fire. A monumental dark table was placed against the wall, and a broad bench, painted dark blue, was where her father sat.

The second floor was Olga's sanctuary. Mary first noticed the king-sized pearl-gray velvet sofa and a long, low bookcase on which stood two pairs of strange (to the child's eyes) shoes, one of straw, the other of black wood. She learned later that these were the clogs that Egerton had brought back from Japan, and the exotic dress hanging on her mother's looking-glass door was a kimono. On the wall of the staircase leading up to the top floor was a painting in shades of gray by the Japanese artist Tami Koumé: "chaos, the universe, or the torso of a giant, crucified." The small studio above was Mary's room, with a bed "stifled with a voluminous mosquito net," a long bookcase, desk, and square wooden armchair, Ezra's creations. In the bookcase was a rare, crumbling volume of Ovid, bound with wooden boards. In Canto 76, Ezra would recall,

> the hidden nest, Tami's dream, the great Ovid
> bound in thick boards, the bas-relief of Ixotta.

The days of Mary's yearly visits followed a familiar pattern. Immediately after breakfast, her father (whom she called "Babbo") walked over the bridge to Signora Scarpa's, where he rented a room to work in. Mary did not exactly understand what Babbo called "work"; it wasn't tending the animals or harvesting the crops as the men did in her village. (Babbo said he worked with his *head*. Hard work, much thinking. Everyone must work, either with his hands or with his head, he told her.) His return toward noon was signaled by the tapping of the black malacca cane, a rattle of keys, and a loud, prolonged "Miao." From the floor above, a "Miao" answered back. It was time to go shopping with Babbo, a happy ritual for the child, a walk from San Gregorio to the Salute, or a short *traghetto* ride across the Canal Grande or from Punta della Salute to San Marco. After the errands, there were treats at Moriondo's, the pastry shop, or a stop for an *aranciata* at the American Bar under the clock tower.

When they returned, the sound of Olga practicing the violin: "precise, passionate." Again, "Miao." The music stopped and Olga descended from her room, and mother and daughter prepared a light lunch: often a salad of plum tomatoes and white beans, cheese, artichokes and peaches, slices of freshly baked bread. Olga liked to set an attractive table, and Mary's job was to find a few flowers creeping over the walls from the neighbor's garden to put in the finger bowls.

After lunch, Ezra went back to Signora Scarpa's, and mother and daughter stretched out together on the big velvet sofa. Olga read in

English from a story book. Mary's first language was German, she had not yet mastered Italian, and English she did not understand. Her mother would summarize the stories in Italian, and the child could only try to piece them together from the pictures. Olga stopped often to ask Mary to repeat after her, to improve Mary's fluency in the language, but it was a difficult time for both. "I never felt safe," Mary admitted later. In the late afternoon, Olga would practice again for an hour or so, and the child was left alone on the top floor, sad with the coming dusk, listening to the mournful tolling of the Venetian church bells.

Some afternoons Mary went to the Lido to swim with her father. Late in the season, the beach was almost deserted, and Ezra would rent a *pattino* and row out some distance to swim from the boat. No loafing on the beach: "We were there to swim and to row, and it was done with zest and speed," according to Mary. On one of these outings, Mary confessed that she had *Heimweh*, that she wanted to go "home" to Gais. She was uncomfortable under "Mamile's [Olga's] resentful, disappointed eyes. . . . I was absolutely hopeless in learning English and Italian . . . a clumsy pigheaded peasant, instead of a graceful sprig." When they returned to the calle Querini, there was a whispered conversation in English between her parents, and her mother started to cry. "It was pitiful to see a great goddess cry in anger and hurt pride. Or was she a mortal woman hankering after her child's love?" Mary questioned in later years. In Olga's view, she was trying to teach the simple child from the Tyrol the manners of civilized society. "The differences between Mary and me grew out of the difference of race [that is, nationality, the Germanic temperament] she absorbed with Frau Marcher's milk."

In October, after Frau Marcher and Mary returned to Bruneck, Olga joined Ezra in Sant'Ambrogio. She began to record the details of their daily lives together in a school-exercise notebook, punctuated by frequent XXX's when they engaged in sexual intercourse.

October 2: "According to E., G[eorge] Washington in his diary used to put the names of one or the other of his female slaves—without further comment. Tho' E. objects . . . my 'X' will . . . appear again for my own private satisfaction."

On October 3, Ezra "went on typing with awful explosions of swearing and singing" while writing the Adams Cantos. When his work was completed, they "celebrated in a fitting manner—XXX."

Another evening before dinner, Olga played Mozart, Brahms, Schumann, and Beethoven's "Kreutzer Sonata," and Ezra asked to borrow her "second best fiddle with worst bow, played with unexpected delicacy and none of [the] roughness one might expect. . . . Whenever I play, he never just listens . . . it always sets him off, either composing, or wanting to play himself or discovering some weak point in my playing."

Ezra was composing a new opera, based on the life of the thirteenth-century Italian poet Guido Cavalcanti, whose poetry he had translated. Olga played what he had written, "he interrupting all the while to make me 'try this.'" Afterward, they "went out with the most beautiful night to look for new moon, but couldn't find it—XXX." Together, they had proofread the galleys of Ezra's translations of the Cavalcanti poems, "he reading and spelling out each word, the way he says they proofread telephone directories," while Olga mended his underpants and socks. When Ezra went to collect the post, he came back with "a beautiful new bag for me—black ostrich leather."

He arrived for tea, dripping from a heavy rain, and they worked on a new violin sonata, "my playing over what he had written so he could get the time and phrasing right." She cried when he suggested that Dorothy might use the house when she wasn't there: "He very nice when he saw it upset me—[he has] *curious blank spots!*"

On October 25, they listened to the BBC broadcast from Milan of Ezra's first opera, *Le Testament de Villon,* at the Rapallo home of a young mechanic with a radio. (Olga did not think it proper to be seen there in the company of the married Pound, so she listened through a crack in the door.)

On the twenty-eighth, Ezra was at work again on the violin sonata, "in a fit of rage because the thing [was] not going right." Olga was told to "observe how useful a fit of rage was for starting and keeping one at work." She noted that "E. wants the same unity in music he has achieved in poetry."

On Ezra's forty-sixth birthday (October 30): "I cried in the morning because E. had forgotten. . . . E. returned in the afternoon and corrected more proofs, wandered around naked from his bath while I got tea . . . in very good form, beautiful to see."

A discussion started when Ezra recalled their decision to have a child: "At first, the idea of having a child was as repugnant to him as having a chow [dog] or any other animal," Olga wrote, "but he feels differently about it now, he doesn't regret it. . . . E. only admits a line of conduct— ethics—for himself, not . . . for everybody. His system [is] that of a scientific investigator who experiments in every possible manner until the experiment is perfect." He admitted that from "five to sixteen, he was very sensitive, then he made himself a shell, so things do not hurt him now."

The diary ended with their long-talked-of walk to Monte Allegro: "E. very gay, a large lunch and mezza bottiglia di chianti . . . came down hill singing the drinking song, as it should be sung, from the Villon."

After this idyllic interlude, Olga returned to Paris.

8

Rare and Unforgettable Little Concerts

1931–1936

Back in her world of music, Olga was beginning a flirtation with Arturo Brown, a possible patron from Argentina by way of London and Venice, enjoying elegant dinners à deux. The worldwide economic depression was worsening, and even the wealthy Don Arturo was forced to give up one valet and refused to pay more than a thousand francs daily—in the 1930s a considerable sum—for his hotel suite.

Olga was still seeking translation jobs, hoping to get "something French, old or new," and that Colette might like it well enough to write a foreword. Colette seemed "as if she had known me from birth," Olga said, when they met at Polignac's. "She has lost her money . . . broken her leg, but still has the air of un chic type."

Ezra advised her to stop in to see Caresse Crosby, socialite and patron of the arts, who had published Pound's slim volume of *Imaginary Letters*. Her Black Sun Press was currently bringing out a posthumous edition of Harry Crosby's collected poems, and Ezra agreed to write the introduction to the fourth volume, *The Torchbearers*. He had heard they weren't pleased with the Samuel Putnam version of Cocteau's novel *Les Enfants Terribles,* and suggested Olga might do the translation.

Through Caresse, Olga met the Hungarian illustrator of the Black Sun edition of *Les Liaisons Dangereuses,* Hans Hemming von Voigt (known as Alastair). He had been a friend of the eccentric Harry Crosby, who had died in a suicide pact with a young lover, leaving his widow to preside over the Black Sun Press alone. A talented pianist, Alastair joined Olga and Borgatti in a recital at Versailles, but "excess nervousness made him play, not out of time, but in a curious oblique manner."

Ever mindful of Pound's opera, Olga visited Yves Tinayre to arrange for the Princesse de Polignac to hear excerpts from *Le Testament.* Tinayre spoke fondly of "the little Yehudi Menuhin . . . now fourteen, gone into long pants, as beautiful as people in the Psalms . . . must be dripping with myrrh." Olga herself heard "the miraculous child" perform: "He did the Bach double concerto with [Georges] Enesco, the Mozart *re* major, and the Beethoven—no-one else plays anyway near it." She was invited to meet the little Menuhin girls, who "already speak five languages, and play the piano—nothing like it since the famille Mozart."

Olga was scheduled to play Pound's sonata ("Ghuidonis, pour violon seul") at a teatime concert on December 5 at the avenue de La Motte-Picquet apartment of the Duncan sisters, a program that included works by Respighi, Fritz Kreisler, and Lili Boulanger. The *Figaro* critic praised "la matinée musicale chez Mlle. de Courcy Duncan . . . brillamment interpreté par Mlles. Olga Rudge et Renata Borgatti." According to Olga, as she reported it to Ezra: "Some said they liked it . . . and considering the atmosphere of old ladies, petits-fours, and decayed duchesses, she thinks it went off very well."

In spite of a cup overflowing with social activities often reported in the columns of the Paris *Herald,* Olga was alone on Christmas Eve when Ezra sent this message: "She's 'sposed to git a C.G. [Christmas gift], but that won't come fer at least a quinzaine an' don't seem enuff / along wiff the affections of the seazon." She never complained, except to say "she has a bad cold—yeow!—it's *freezingly* cold." The Duncans had invited her to lunch with Egerton's brother Templeton Grey, in Paris attending a conference on international law, "with talk of the League of Nations."

One can only imagine Olga's thoughts of the *primo amore*—what might have been!

In a New Year's letter to Ezra, Olga explained her situation: "the complication being that she needs a job in default of an income, that she ain't found one, except a shadowy, undefined, but still there in the background, one of—may we say—'geisha' to the noble samurai Arturo [Brown] who, having forked out 5,000 francs, has a right . . . to tea-pouring and kowtowings . . . all vague and not to be counted on. . . . Will He [Pound] still remember her and be glad to see her end of January?"

Ezra was willing to accept more responsibility, but his offer was couched in none too reassuring terms: "wotter baht HIM lookin' fer some lucrative employment—abaht time—seems to have carried bein' artistic a bit too far . . . he better git the nubel [Nobel Prize] that'd give her 2,000 francs a month . . . as fer eatin' / she is welcome to what he actually *earns,* i.e. gate receipts."

Early in the new year, she enrolled in a stenotyping class, hoping to earn the three thousand francs a month she needed to live comfortably and bring Mary up properly. Mabel Duncan did what she could, "provided a hand-me-down tailleur . . . complete with hat, scarf, and petticoat, fresh from [the] cleaners."

Olga was still enjoying social success in the French capital, and was learning to ice skate again, a sport neglected since the early years with Julia. But "*He* gets larger and larger in the distance, and everyone near gets smaller and smaller . . . she is an incorrigible hero-worshipper."

At the end of January, she confessed the birth of Mary to her mother's friend Etta Glover, a woman wise in the ways of the world. Etta was pleased with the news: "You set the seal to my final approval of you when you threw everything to the winds for it and the Leoncina resulted. Let those who will sneer at a grand passion; it's they who know nothing and are in eternal outer darkness. . . . But, my dear, there's another time later on and a very different one for the woman when, if she doesn't consolidate her position, all the past joy and glory will turn to bitterness, and there'll be nothing else to take its place. . . . I'm amused at the stenotyping—a rich man's *secretary?*"

Olga was preparing to apply for a position at an American consulate (in

Genoa, Venice, or Paris) by doing "voluntary work" with Sir Thomas Barclay, who would be useful for a recommendation. She was "trying to get some sort of solid ground under her feet," and hoping to save enough (580 francs) for a twelve-day return train ticket to Rapallo, but "where does the money come from *after* that? She *does not* propose to live by borrowing money from Him. God bless my rich friends."

She was writing to Pound with a new "perpetual" pencil, a gift of the Marquise de Belboeuf (known as "Missy"), a daughter of the Duc de Morny (the illegitimate half-brother of Napoleon III), whom Olga had met through Henri Etlin, "our original pianiste pederaste." The old lady was one of the few women at that time who dared to wear men's clothes in the streets of Paris and was invariably dressed in shirts, pants, and waist-coats. She was "l'amie de Colette in the Year One," Olga recalled. They did a sketch at the Moulin Rouge, Rêve d'Egypt, by Colette's husband, Willy (Henri Gaulthier-Villars), and the women's embrace on stage was so ardent that "all the nobles in Paris were so outraged they rioted . . . the show couldn't go on."

The artist Tami Koumé had accompanied Olga to a Japanese garden party dressed in swallowtail coat and white spats and a "peculiar" top hat, and at the Salle du Conservatoire in the company of Don Arturo—"a tout-Paris house—Sauget's songs were pas méchant, and Poulenc's amusing. . . . They cut out the Bach and replaced [it] with Darius Milhaud's 'Sonata for Clarinet' . . . then all got together and did a comedic ballet of Erik Satie." Olga's comment on the performance of the famed chanteuse Mistinguett: "She is 102 and does acrobatic dancing that doesn't belong to her day at all—and gets away with it."

"Parisian life sounds more divertin' than the squabbles of the Pellegrini family" in Sant'Ambrogio, Ezra commented in his Valentine's Day letter.

On April 27, Mary made her First Communion in Gais, wearing the beautiful lace dress that Julia had designed for Olga, but Olga was not there to see it. Her best-laid plans went "Lord knows where," she wrote Pound. Mary appears in a photo with a large ribbon sash around her waist, beautiful blond hair haloing a wistful face—with white cotton stockings and sensible black oxfords spoiling the effect. Frau Marcher had written that the child asked daily for her parents: "The child cries so much she might even die if they don't come." ("It was enough to break any mother's 'eart," Olga duly reported to the child's father.)

Ezra forwarded a cable from Antheil in New York: "Offer Olga tour next season, $500 guaranteed, boat and rail expenses paid, cable acceptance." George would be back at Le Planestel in Cagnes-sur-Mer in July, and asked her to stop over to discuss the American tour with him. Pound was against Olga's going to America, "but if she could do it in six or seven weeks?" Olga cabled, "With pleasure under guaranty," but admitted doubts about Antheil. "I have noticed his good intentions re. me usually coincide with some service he wants you to render him." Yet the offer seemed the only solution to her financial dilemma.

Wanda Landowska was planning a June 4 concert, the first in a series featuring Olga and a Spanish pianist, with an eye to winning Don Arturo Brown's backing. "But whether that wily bird will be enticed, chi lo sa?" A week later, she reported to Ezra that the musicale had gone very well, with "all the best people" attending. Don Arturo was impressed: "Last night was a wonderful fête, you know how enormously I enjoyed it . . . [but] I fear you think I only enjoyed the music because the public was so gorgeous. Life is not always as easy as it seems." He was awaiting news from his banker in Buenos Aires, but "I fear there is little hope of my staying."

During this era, the poet wrote almost daily to his lady love about his work, his tennis games and scores, his dental problems, his broken reading glasses, his health (recurring head colds), and a newly purchased blue suit. He was in Florence in late May to lecture at the Settimana Internazionale di Cultura in the Palazzo Vecchio, but Katherine Dalliba-John could not put him up; she, like everyone else, was terribly worried about money. "We go nowhere, eat only vegetables at home, I wear my old rags and buy nothing," she wrote, adding a poignant finale: "This world is an inferno, and will soon be finished. We go to another star, where we are happy and *well*—there is no death!"

Olga was visiting Lindy Shaw-Paige in St. Julien–Biot in June when Pound wired: "Meet composers [Tibor] Serly and [Geza] Frid at the Cannes station—IMPORTANT—treat 'em well!" Frid had been Olga's page-turner in Budapest and, in Pound's view, was a "damn fine composer"; he had written a divertimento for orchestra and a violin sonata performed by

Pierre Monteux, Serge Koussevitzky, and others. The artists were stopping in Cannes "solely on yr / account."

"Frid began to show interest when he discovered I, too, had played for Muss[olini]," Olga wrote. After, Antheil drove her to Cannes and with his wife, Böski, hosted a party at their "charming and suitable house." Olga found the couple "much improved and stimulating."

In mid-September, she was invited to the Settimana Musicale Senese, an international music festival held annually at the Accademia Musicale Chigiana in Siena. The inaugural concert directed by Maestro Bernardo Molinari celebrated early Italian music; the second and third, contemporary composers Hindemith, Ravel, Webern, and de Falla; the fourth, Walton's *Façade,* a concert of piano and cello by Maestro Alfredo Casella, and ending with Stravinsky's *Les Noces.* Olga watched the procession of traditional Sienese *contrade* in medieval costume in the Piazza del Campo, and was enchanted by the pageantry of this ancient city, unchanged over centuries. (Among her keepsakes was a program with a note scribbled in red: "*Very important—*first time Siena on my map.")

In October, Ezra joined her at the Hidden Nest in Venice for the fall visit with Mary. Cantos 34 through 37 were ready for Olga to review: "She got any bright ideas for his next?" he asked. Olga's reply: "She hopes all these will be printed soon. . . . Why should posterity get all the thrills?"

At Christmas, Frau Marcher sent a card from "Moidile" (Mary) with two little birds in the snow, and asked for a gift of practical long-sleeved shirts for the little girl. Ezra sent only this message to the child's mother: "Her Xmas present had to be sent back cause it wuzzz wrong, & heaven knows if she will get it at all."

Olga's first letter of 1933 ended with the usual terms of endearment: "ciao, amore, tante belle cose, auguri e carezze." She was then in Florence, helping to put order into Ramooh's affairs, and trying to persuade the Scottish Church to reduce "the excessive rent they have been taking all these years." In Olga's view, Dalliba-John was "dribbling away enormous amounts into the wrong hands . . . lost, strayed, or stolen on monthly accounts." She was preparing for a concert, "in disgrace, because we practiced the Beethoven scherzo with many thumpings over the Church's

Lenten afternoon service." Ramooh, a talented artist, recovered her health and good spirits sufficiently to ask Olga to sit for her portrait.

Olga met Ezra in Milan at the Hotel Angioli e Semproni on March 21 en route to Paris for her next performance. His work on *The Cantos* was progressing, and Olga was "very bucked up being allowed to see a canto [38] again—quite a stiff one for the meanest intelligence." Ezra "wuz pleased to see her lookin' more cheerful before she left."

Frau Marcher sent a *Buona Pasqua* card of two little girls in a meadow, enclosing a snapshot of Leoncina in the new shoes Ezra had purchased. Olga was not with her daughter. She was with the Richardses in Hook Heath, embroiled in family problems—Kathleen's separation and divorce. "The UNSPEAKABLE Dale," Ezra wrote, unaware of his own shortcomings: "[He] is the kind of male pustulence that DOES NOT appeal to MUH [me]!! HOWEVER how th'hell IZ the male to give pleasure to the utterly KANtankerous sex?"

Kathleen, who was "astonishingly fit," played six Beethoven sonatas in concert with Olga, who was herself suffering from another nervous crisis, "past caring . . . in a state of fatigue." She could always rely on the old family friends for sustenance, "being fed on cream and stout and sleeping in feathers and half asleep most of the time, which is probably good for the nerves, the rest of the time she is playing, which is good for morale, so she will probably survive."

Teddy's telephone call from Spondon on her April birthday she considered "kind and brotherly." She had begun to take contract bridge lessons from Mrs. Richards, "worryin' when she gets a good hand, in case it means she is to be 'unlucky in love'."

She and Kathleen "got through all Beethoven, all Brahms, Debussy, and John Ireland, and a new Mozart concerto . . . so time not wasted," she wrote Ezra (though Olga considered *all* time away from Ezra lost time). He again postponed their meeting in Paris because Dorothy was ill with flu. He was passing the time editing the manuscript of Olga's detective story, "The Blue Spill," and reserving her description of a day in London for a Canto.

Olga's "day in London" began at five o'clock in the afternoon, when she left Hook Heath by car with Kathleen and the Richardses to dine at the

Savoy Hotel at a choice table in the window. Then to the first night of *Der Rosenkavalier* at Covent Garden, "where His friend, [Sir Thomas] Beecham conducted marvelously, even if he did . . . leave the singers tailing after." Covent Garden was "jam-packed, and there were a lot of old frumps and a few good-looking young things (female), and *no* good looking males, and old [Isadore] de Lara with one foot in the grave, Lady Colifax, Lady Lowery (looking like the wreck of the Hesperus), the Duchess of York. And if you saw the way the patriotic British female stiffens to attention for the 'God Save the what-you-may-call him,' chest out, hands at sides, just like a Tommy on parade at the mention of [the] holy nime [name] . . . no wonder poor old [King] George leads a pure and virtuous life."

Adrian Stokes turned up, "most shatteringly beautiful," and took Olga to dine in Soho. He had searched out and copied rare texts for the *Cavalcanti* opera, and was the recipient of Pound's encouragement, publicity, and instruction while laboring over the first volume of his masterwork, *Stones of Rimini*.

Inspired by Olga's presence in Rapallo for part of each year, Ezra was organizing a series of concerts fashioned after the string quartets that flourished in the "chambers" of every Italian town during the Renaissance. The idea had come to him when he and Olga attended a concert with Manlio Dazzi in Cesena. Could Rapallo, another small town of some fifteen thousand people—ten thousand of whom were *contadini* who lived in the hills—support such a series with first-rate music?

Long favored by British travelers and the Romantic poets, Rapallo remained a retreat for writers and artists in the 1920s and 1930s. Max Beerbohm's villa was just outside the town, and Expressionist painter Oskar Kokoschka, and Nobel Prize winners Thomas Mann, Gerhart Hauptman, and W. B. Yeats often were seen strolling along the seaside promenade. As Yeats described the *ambiente:* "On the broad pavement by the sea pass Italian peasants or working people . . . a famous German dramatist, the barber's brother looking like an Oxford Don, a British retired skipper, an Italian prince descended from Charlemagne and no richer than the rest of us, and a few tourists seeking tranquility. As there is no great harbor full of yachts, no great yellow strand, no great ballroom, no great casino, the rich carry elsewhere their strenuous lives." Pound envisioned this provincial town as a "laboratory, specializing in works not being done in the heavily moneyed centers." In the Great Depression, many wealthy patrons had withdrawn their support of performing artists, and Pound recognized that "the problem of Rapallo is the problem of raising money." In 1932, he organized the Amici del Tigullio, a local group taking its name from the Gulf surrounding it. The Stagione Musicale did not begin in earnest until a year later. Ezra himself wrote and distributed broadsides and posters, persuaded the editor of the Rapallo newspaper, *Il Mare,* to donate advertising space, and dropped in at hotels to hand out flyers about the recreational advantages of the Riviera di Levante. As an additional lure to tourists, he persuaded the railroads to offer a 20 percent reduction in round-trip excursion fares.

Father Desmond Chute, the resident Anglican priest, recalled: "Fanned by his [Pound's] unflagging enthusiasm, rare and unforgettable little concerts sprang up, according to the frequency and incidence of musicians. . . . The season started under the sign of Mozart, all of whose sonatas were played at least once. One remembers blocks of music." In Ezra's words, "the Mozart fiddle sonatas are possibly the kernel of his whole musical thought. The only way to get a clear concept of Mozart's form is to hear the series all together."

The first concert of the announced Mozart Week took place June 26, 1933, at the Teatro Reale, the local cinema, under the patronage of the Marchesa Solferina Spinola, the Comte de Robilant, Mrs. Ephra Townley, and other prominent members of the expatriate colonies. Olga was joined by a cellist from the nearby town of Chiavari, Marco Ottone, and the part-time conductor of the municipal orchestra, violinist Luigi Sansoni. Pound touted the performance in *Il Mare,* the local newspaper: "The American violinist Olga Rudge showed her mastery of technique with great richness of tone. . . . Judging by last night's audience, music has come to stay in Rapallo." "My only interest in getting these programs together is to get some work for Olga," he wrote Tibor Serly.

At the end of the first concert, after the applause and taking her bows, Olga retired to the little room backstage with a large basket of red roses, the gift of Mercedes de Codina, a friend of the Duncans who lived in a nearby villa. "I could not have carried them up the hill with [the] fiddle, and Father Desmond was near. . . . I remember thinking he looked like the picture of Christ in 'The Light of the World,' knocking on a door and holding a lantern, with a long cloak. . . . [I remember] his gentle manner, holding the basket by the handle. . . . He used to invite me for ensemble music, and paid me, though no arrangement [was] thought of or suggested." This scion of a wealthy Bristol family would remain Olga's most trusted friend and confidant.

After the first season of Rapallo concerts came to a close, Olga returned to Venice and let her house for four months. At Ezra's suggestion, she enrolled in master classes in violin at the prestigious Accademia Musicale Chigiana. Soon after arrival in Siena, it was her good luck to be invited to dine at the Chigi palazzo by a friend, Adriana da Vinci. Since Olga had not brought the proper evening wear, Adriana lent her a crimson gown to complement her newly hennaed hair. Wearing a borrowed dress, Olga caught the eye of another important man in her life.

Count Guido Chigi Saracini, it was said, resembled an El Greco grandee: a tall, lean presence with straight patrician nose and pale blue eyes, courtly and aloof, but happiest in the company of beautiful women. Descended from two of the great banking families of the twelfth century (before the Medicis founded their fortune), Chigi inherited a thirteenth-century palazzo—the ancestral home of Marco Antonio Saracini—from his childless Uncle Fabio. In 1260, from its historic tower, a youth reported the famous Battle of Monteaperti, Siena's decisive victory over the rival Florentines. The Count's early attempts to become a musician himself ended in frustration—he acquired the reputation of being a "piano smasher"—and thereafter he devoted his energies and considerable fortune to furthering the careers of other young talents. He remodeled his inherited palazzo to house a concert hall that Bernard Berenson described as "a view one might get when standing inside a gigantic wedding cake." The Count then filled the palazzo with a collection of valuable instruments and lured some of the world's most renowned musicians to Siena to play them.

Olga charmed him, not only because of her striking good looks but because she had chosen to wear a gown in the same shade of red found in the heraldic arms of the Chigi family. Pound immortalized the evening in Canto 74:

> she did her hair in small ringlets, à la 1880 it might have been
> red, and the dress she wore Drecol or Lanvin
> a great goddess.

The Count invited Olga to remain in Siena, to use her fluent French and Italian, her knowledge of music and musicians, and her talent for organizing, as administrative secretary of the Accademia of which he was Fondatore and Presidente.

When Olga arrived in 1933, the Accademia was just gaining momentum, with two pupils for organ, six or seven for violin, and sixteen or twenty for master classes with Maestro Alfredo Casella. "Siena seems very pleasant, with wonderful air," Olga wrote Ezra, after installing herself in a small apartment overlooking the market. "I don't know how long I am to prova [on trial], but take it is till September. . . . if He would come, she would like to talk things over with Him—He got her here!"

Ezra replied, "If she stuck in Siena, he will as planned come down *when* she thinks it tactful and not detrimental to her interests." He suggested a press notice to publicize the then little known Accademia: "What is needed is some fetchy views of Siena, mentioning the romance of Sienese history, then exposition of how the Acad / Chigi is flowering in them ENchantin' surroundin's."

Olga enjoyed exploring the narrow, curbless streets of the city, with its medieval walls and stone and pink brick façades, overlooking the vineyards of Tuscany. "[One of] the best walks in Siena," she wrote Ezra, "is just back of the Palace, a country road with magnificent view of town and country. . . . [At] a little church on a hill . . . the parrocco . . . took me into the presbitero and treated me to wine and cakes . . . the only really hospitable Tuscan I've found," not to mention her distinguished host. As for the Count, his discourse at dinner was sprinkled with quotations from the classics: he reflected on "the hardness of another's chair" (after Dante), and expounded his philosophy of music. He had little interest in twentieth-century composers, and considered Beethoven too intellectual and mechanical—without *cuore*. "Music without cuore is not music at all."

When Ezra joined Olga, he discovered that the Chigi library had no catalog and urged Olga to take on the job of creating one. "It would keep you occupied fer some time . . . the excuse of making a catalog often serves for a life's job." When Olga rebuked him about a contretemps between himself and Maestro Casella during the visit, he replied, "I beehaved vurry nicely. When I want to insult people there is *no* ambiguity."

In mid-August, the Accademia closed down until after the horse race in medieval costume that takes place every summer in the Piazza del Campo, "to which His Nibs has presented her a place." Count Chigi was then rector-for-life of the magistrates of the *contrade*, and Olga was fortunate to be so honored in this very traditional city. The names of the *contrade* for reasons long forgotten by history are taken from the animal kingdom— Oca (Goose), Civetta (Owl), and La Torre (Elephant, or Tower), and so on. One is born into, and fiercely loyal to, a *contrada*, seldom marrying outside one's own clan or moving away. On the eve of the most important feast day of the year, that of the patron saint, the streets are lighted with *braccialetti* (wall-torches in carved wood), and the whole town is transformed.

The next morning, the piazza is covered with a thick layer of earth, stands are set up around the shell-shaped center of the square, and the *contrade*, wearing colorful costumes and waving banners, head for the cathedral where the procession starts. Once the cortège files around the earthen track and all take their seats on the grandstand in front of the Palazzo Publico, the colorful silken banner is hoisted into position on the judges' stand, the starter gives the signal, and the race is on!

Olga watched the jockeys riding bareback wearing *contrade* colors nudge and jostle each other until one of the horses crossed the finish line. The Palio was handed down from the judges' stand, and the winners pushed their way through the crowds to the cathedral to offer thanks for the victory. Pound later would draw a colorful word-picture of the scene:

"Torre! Torre! Civetta!" . . .
> and the parade and the carrocchio [*sic*] and the flag-play
> and the tossing of the flags of the contrade (Canto 80)

> four fat oxen
> having their arses wiped
> and in general being tidied up to serve god under my window
>> with stoles of Imperial purple
> with tassels, and grooms before the carroccio
> on which carroch six lion heads
>> to receive the wax offering (Canto 43).

In early September, Ezra took Homer to Bolzano to meet his grand-daughter. Early photographs show a striking resemblance between the white-haired *Grossvater* and his towheaded Moidile. "Her figlia has comported herself most nobly," Ezra reported; "Leoncina and I had [a] lovely walk in a porfik day." Olga had suggested that Ezra might bring his father to Venice with Mary for two weeks in October, and in the first letter she ever received from him Homer thanked her cordially but added: "I cannot accept this time, hope all is well with you and *yours*."

After the fall concert week at the Accademia, Olga traveled to Merano to introduce the child to her old friend Renata Borgatti. Mary, then nine years old, was "behaving exceedingly well and making a good impression," she wrote the child's father, "so much so that the hotel owner, who was starting to be annoying about lack of papers, etc., and asking embarrassing questions, decided to let matters be." The old castle where they were paying guests housed a collection of armor and stuffed deer heads that the child described as "spada" and "animale" in a letter to her father. The interlude ended when a letter from the Princesse de Polignac summoned Olga to Venice to rehearse the Schubert and Beethoven trios with Giorgio Levi and Nadia Boulanger.

Ezra was busy promoting the first full season of concerts, beginning October 10. The son of Oscar Chilesotti, the great authority of sixteenth- and seventeenth-century lute music, was discovered living in Rapallo, and handed over to Pound his deceased father's collection of lute tablatures gathered from libraries throughout Europe. Ezra lured pianist Gerhart Münch to Rapallo to arrange the lute music for contemporary instruments. A friend of Tibor Serly, Münch had debuted with the Dresden Orchestra at the age of fourteen. When Olga heard him play Béla Bartók (then considered extremely avant-garde) in a Venice concert with the Hungarian Quartet, she recommended him to Ezra as a major drawing card. Münch arranged and played for the first time in Rapallo the *Canzone degli Uccelli*, "taking the birds in autumn for a model, Jannequin's birds, lost for 300 years until Francesco da Milano brought them back into Italy," in Pound's words. (He later reproduced the original score in Canto 75).

For the next concert, the mayor opened up the Sala del Municipio, a new building with murals and trompe l'oeil designs that seated an audience of some 250 people. Ezra wangled a secondhand Steinway grand from a local patron, and Münch joined Olga, Marco Ottone, and Luigi Sansoni in a program of Corelli, Bach, and Debussy. The Princesse de Polignac heralded her arrival by requesting two tickets, "not too conspicuous, as I shan't have time to dress, after a nine-hour train trip from Rome and no dinner." Pound reminded Münch that "no-one but Olga could have brought the attention of that person [Polignac] so quickly upon your work. I had no idea she was coming." Ezra had met the Princesse in Paris when Olga invited him to sit in the Polignac box for the premiere of his *Concerto*.

The audience in Rapallo that evening included several contessas and marchesas, Father Desmond Chute, and Ezra's newly arrived, disheveled disciple, the poet Basil Bunting. All proceeds went to the performers, save for a few printing expenses and ten lire reserved for the janitor and doorkeeper. Ezra was observed distributing programs, his big slouch hat held out to collect from members of the audience as they entered the hall. He took the collection home after each concert, heaped it on the bed, and divided it up, Dorothy Pound remembered.

After the concerts, Olga insisted on climbing up the *salita* to Sant'Ambrogio in the dark, even when invited by the Bacigalupos and other friends to stay overnight. Mary, who was with her mother on one of these occasions, remembered that they went to look for the pair of old espadrilles

Olga had hidden at the bottom of the mulepath: "That's what all of the peasant women in the hills do when they go to town," Olga said, slinging the violin case over her shoulder so that both hands were free to carry satin shoes and music in one hand and hitch up the long skirt of her evening gown with the other.

When they sat down to rest on a narrow bench halfway up, near the landmark eucalyptus, Olga said: "I always have to sit down here. Gee, I'm tired sometimes." She reminisced about Paris, how beautiful her apartment had been, and added as an afterthought, "It's awful these nights when it rains, the *violin* is so sensitive." Only this, Mary commented, after endless practicing, the long walk down to the hall, the climb back up in the dark. "I knew exactly what Babbo meant when he said, 'The *real* artist in the family is your mother.'"

That winter was unseasonably cold in Rapallo, with a great deal of snow. In November, Olga and Münch appeared at the Istituto Fascista di Cultura in Genoa, a program featuring fifteenth- and sixteenth-century compositions from the Chilesotti collection, Bach, Mozart, and Debussy sonatas, and as an encore two movements of Purcell's "Golden" Sonata.

Olga, spending another white Christmas with the Richardses in Hook Heath, considered her life there "pretty ghastly after Sant'Ambrogio . . . incredibly boring . . . if she didn't get some oxygen pumped in from outside, she will suffocate." She was pulling herself together to enjoy "an English fambly Xmas . . . more fuss and yatter about the getting ready of houses than is conceivable. . . . they are like dogs turning round and round before they lie down—then they *don't!*" The old couple had tactfully invited "a Mrs. Hanys and a Miss Stella Fife for some mild quartette playing, with interruptions from grandma for 'little Tony' to turn the pages."

Ezra admitted "feeling very solitary and Dickensian." He enclosed a Christmas card forwarded from Frau Marcher with a message from Leoncina. Their gift of a new coat "arrived in time and pleases." He asked Olga to search in London for "the spare parts of [the] William Young," a sixteenth-century composer he wanted to present at the Rapallo concerts. These works—written five years before the birth of Purcell by the court musician to Charles II—were the first published English sonatas for the violin, edited by Gillies Whittaker, head of the Scottish Academy of Music.

Olga had been shopping for a new "fiddle," and Ezra offered twenty-five hundred lire "lying there in the bank, doing no particular good. . . . It is all lire she has paid back to him at one time or another."

Olga: "It [is] all very noble of Him and his 2,500, but she has already planted the Leoncina on Him and all sorts of expenses."

Ezra: "All he thinks is that she git a good one. What is a few quid one way or the other. . . . As soon as she gets [the] fiddle / he announces matinee with 3 Wm / Young fer 2 fiddles."

Olga saved an invoice dated February 20, 1934, from William Hill & Sons, Makers & Sellers of Violins & Bows on New Bond Street, "official violin maker to His Majesty the King of England, the King of Italy and the Queen of Holland." It was the finest violin she would own in her lifetime, No. 295 in the style of "Le Messie" Stradivarius. The purchase price of some fifty pounds was a considerable sum in the Depression year of 1934.

She returned to Rapallo for the March 13 concert to play the works of William Young on the new violin. An enthusiastic letter from Lindy Shaw-Paige cheered her on: "Awfully pleased about your concerts at Rapallo. As for EP, what a Man!!! I love people who are a law unto themselves."

Early April was Music Festival Week in Florence, and Olga met there the acclaimed Spanish guitarist Andres Segovia, who would soon join Maestro Casella and Ildebrando Pizzetti at the Accademia. Her friends from Venice, Giorgio and Alice Levi, were also in Florence, but Count Chigi, who disliked travel, received the delegates in Siena. The Count was "very down," Olga said, because his mother had died a month before.

She returned to Rapallo to play a series of Mozart sonatas—composed in 1778, 1781, 1784, and 1787, at important stages of the boy genius's development—accompanied by Borgatti. The audience was "DEElighted wiff [the] concert, so her violin wuzn't wasted."

Olga commenced another diary that summer, providing a brief picture of her life with the poet, beginning with a concert in Chiavari on June 20, after Dorothy's departure for England.

"This year [I] am not allowed in the [via Marsala] flat, [we] dine at the Albergo Rapallo and then up here [Sant'Ambrogio], at 3 or 4:30 . . . not

such a convenient system. Ma che! He showing such noble firmness coming up and down hill."

July 16: "Reward for virtue—invited to dine with Max Beerbohm, the
impeccable. His wife didn't come, recovering from Rome heat, so had
[the] luxury of EP and MB solo." Beerbohm was in good form, telling
stories of Henry James at George Meredith's memorial service, "looking
more imposing than Hardy," of meeting James "on a cold corner on the
way to a jolly corner," a euphemism for a rendezvous with his (male)
partner. He then amused them with anecdotes of Edward VII at "Con-
suelo's" (Vanderbilt's), and of d'Annunzio's lugubrious death chamber at
Il Vittoriale, which Olga remembered.

August 30: "Leave for Venice con lui. He goes up to Gais and brings
down Leoncina, who stayed ten days. . . . takes her out bathing every day,
she very good. Münchs arrive the 14th, stay at Signora Scarpa's for a week.
Lui, they and self dine at Palazzo Polignac and play the Chilesotti. . . .
[Vladimir] Horowitz' remark on hearing M[ünch] practice chez moi: 'ce
pianiste joue aussi bien que moi.' Thé for the Congrès Musicale chez
Princesse. Present: EP, R[ichard] Strauss, Alban Berg, etc. End of month,
Horowitz and Princesse to play Lili Boulanger, Bach. He leaves 24th. I stay
on. P'sse. hurts hand, but before end of month, is well enough to play Lili
Boulanger, Bach etc."

After this memorable week of concerts, the Princesse rewarded Olga
and the pianist Dame Clara Haskell with a motor trip to Brescia, Vicenza,
Bergamo, and Gardone. Olga remarked on the superb *truite saumonée* in
Gardone at the "12 Apostoli," and "wished He was at it." (Ezra mentioned
the "Trattoria degli [*sic*] Apostoli [dodici]" in Canto 74.)

She was back in Rapallo in time for his birthday on October 30, "which
properly celebrated—XXX."

In November, young James Laughlin, the twenty-four-year-old scion
of the Jones & Laughlin Steel Corporation of Pittsburgh and on leave
from Harvard, arrived to sit at the feet of the master. "Jaz," as he liked
to be called, had studied at Choate Academy under Dudley Fitts, where
he read Pound and Eliot and won an Atlantic Monthly prize before coming
to Rapallo to study at the "Ezuversity." Impressively tall (six feet three
inches), Laughlin was a personable young man with an earnest manner,

a stubborn jaw, and much practical business sense. Encouraged by Ezra, he later founded the New Directions press on his uncle's estate near Norfolk, Connecticut, to publish the works of Pound and other Modernist writers.

The fragmentary diary abruptly ended when Olga returned to Paris via Turin on November 20, then crossed the Channel to perform at the American and British Women Composers' Club on Grosvenor Street December 1. A concert of works by Americans featured pianist Jessie Hall (Mrs. Thompson) with Olga, "the U.S.A. guest," playing a sonata by Gena Branscombe, the last selection on the program—an honor reserved for the most accomplished artists.

London was preparing for a royal wedding, and Olga was taken down Bond Street to see the decorations "at a local gathering, got up by the young Balfour girl" (the earl's daughter), and with the elder Richards followed the wedding procession. Her generous friends produced a check for ten pounds for a new gown for her Saturday afternoon concert, but conservative Olga "didn't blow 10 pounds, only 4 pounds 14 on an afternoon dress . . . useful generally."

Homer and Isabel Pound had moved to the Villa Raggio, up the hill on the opposite side of Rapallo, Ezra wrote. "He wd/ like to give her a merrier Xmas," but the only gift suggested was his old typewriter—if Olga would purchase a new one for him in London!

To revive Ezra's waning interest, Olga replied that she was just back from London, where she had visited Adrian Stokes in his "amusing, 'modern' flat . . . divided up by curtains," and added that when she went to meet Don Arturo Brown at the Ritz, "he treated me to a tête-à-tête, not a party as expected."

To even the score, in his last letter of the year a petulant Ezra urged her to "make it new" when planning her repertoire: "He is very fond of her . . . [yet] she take it straight that he was awake a good deal of last night, getting disgusteder and disgusteder, and ready to throw up the whole damn concertization . . . nauseating to think of doing the old zuppa inglese, same trype you get six times a week at Aeolian [Hall]. . . . The natural contrast for Stravinsky is Bach . . . fergit she is bored / by looking up a Haydn /

AND a viola wiff vioLINN / piece for when comes Mr. Surly [Tibor Serly]."
He softened the rebuke with "Buon anno / an' yes'm, he wants her back."

Olga was still at Hook Heath with the Richardses in January 1935,
"twenty minutes from the nearest village shop (where nothing to be had),
two-and-a-half miles from Woking. It costs 5 shillings to go to London,
and [I am] chased with [the] hurry of missing the train back and keeping
dinner waiting," she wrote Ezra. Some ten thousand desertions were
reported in the Tyrol: "expect mostly lies, still she wishes He would write
Leoncina and tactfully ascertain whether all quiet there, if not could just
keep her at Sant'Ambrogio, or put her to the Ursulines [nuns' school]."

Pound, who was then using Rome Radio as a platform to expound his
economic theories, was highly critical of President Franklin D. Roosevelt's New Deal. "Wot's Frankie going to say tomorrow?" he wondered,
referring to the President's popular "fireside chats," then enjoying a wide
audience in the United States. He quoted Alice Roosevelt (of the rival
Oyster Bay branch of the family, as opposed to FDR's, of Hyde Park),
who "sez he iz 'nine parts Eleanor & one part mush.'" Olga, who listened
to the President's address distorted by short wave, adopted Ezra's views:
"His voice sounded awful . . . like the voice of a dead man hypnotized to
speak."

On April 6, 1935, a week before her fortieth birthday, Olga received sad
news from her stepmother, Katherine: "Your dear father has left us. . . .
The end was sudden, though his strength was declining since the first of
the year. . . . Father Sammon brought him Holy Communion and anointed
him, and immediately after, he began to sink away." The funeral was held
at St. Columba's Church, with burial in the family plot in Grove 10 of
Calvary Cemetery. "He had wanted so much to see you and Teddy again,
and always talked of going to see your little house in Venice. You were
very dear to your father's heart, Olga, and his lifelong separation from his
children was a cross hard to bear." Of her many regrets, the one that
bothered Olga most was that Edgar Rudge died without knowing he had a
granddaughter.

After her father's death, Olga again turned to her mother's old friend,

Katherine Dalliba-John, who consoled her with a generous gift: "I am sending you this little help, because I can leave you so little money after my death." When she returned to Florence for another concert in May, Ezra joined her and wrote another puff piece for *Il Mare:* "On the 7th of this month our musicians played in the salon of the well-known music patroness, Mrs. Dalliba-John in Florence, a salon frequented by Pizzetti, Mainardi, and others in the musical world. . . . [The poet] Eugenio Montale and other Florentine celebrities were also present." After he left, Olga said that "the earth seems to have stopped moving, but she supposes it really ain't."

From Rapallo, Ezra wrote that Gerhart Münch "has been nearly off his head with worry about his god damn country [Germany] . . . the problem of being interned in event of war." Pound was inviting other international artists to Rapallo: pianists Luigi Franchetti and Renata Borgatti, the Hungarian Quartet, and violinist and composer Tibor Serly.

In July, Olga joined Ezra and James Laughlin in a long-postponed motor trip to the town of Wörgl in Austria, one of two places where Silvio Gesell's stamp scrip—Pound's panacea for monetary reform—was accepted. Ezra would recall (in Canto 74)

> a nice little town in the Tyrol in a wide flat-lying valley
> near Innsbruck . . .
> > [where the] mayor of Wörgl
> > who had a milk route
> > > and whose wife sold shirts and short breeches
> > and on whose book-shelf was the Life of Henry Ford
> > and also a copy of the Divina Commedia.

They visited Mary at Gais and continued on to the Salzburg music festival in Laughlin's Ford, "one of the best trips I ever made," said Laughlin. When Ezra heard Toscanini conduct Beethoven's *Fidelio* at the Festspielhaus, Laughlin wrote in his memoir, "after about fifteen minutes, [he] reared up in his seat and expostulated quite loudly: 'What can you expect? The man had syphilis.' We trooped out and Toscanini didn't miss a beat."

Back in Venice in August, Olga noted, "everyone seems very cross and bothered, waiting for the guns to go off. They seem more annoyed at having to adunato [muster] than in having a war." One of her friends had bought a black shirt, symbolic of the Fascist Party. Pound was in Rome, where he heard "the Boss" (Mussolini) address the populace: "I mean he wuz on the balcony. . . . The troops have entered Abyssinia, which may be in the paper when you get this." He was, once again, in a "fury, trying to xxxpress his rages with a pen. . . . We murkns BORN awfully young."

Olga was with the Richardses in Hook Heath for another Christmas. She asked Frau Marcher to put aside some books for Mary, suggested Ezra might send their daughter sweets. Realizing the importance of having official documents for Mary in case of war, Olga proposed getting a certificate at the consulate in Paris stating that she was the sister of Arthur Rudge, and thus Mary's aunt and legal guardian!

News of the furor directed at Prime Minister Stanley Baldwin and Foreign Secretary Samuel Hoare over the negotiation of the Hoare-Laval agreement, which would give much of Abyssinia to Italy, was relayed to Olga by an eyewitness. She reported to Pound on December 20: "These Brits are incredible. . . . Hoare in tears, everyone furious. . . . She [Olga] furious on account of that prig . . . [Anthony] Eden getting the job."

"Baldwin has got a vote of confidence," was Ezra's commentary. "England now against dragging war into Europe . . . coal strike next / and the MONETARY issue the POINT."

"More celebrations on New Year's Day [1936] and the birthdays of the children—all cuts into time," Olga complained. "One little boy is quite charming, but *nothing seems to compare to Leoncina.*" In later years, she confided in her notebook, "Pride is one of the seven deadly sins, but there is no sin in a mother's natural pride in her children, which is founded on the cardinal virtues of love and hope."

Another winter concert season was beginning in Rapallo. Gerhart Münch was joined by an impressive group of musicians: Gabriele Bianchi from the Festival Musicale di Venezia, Yves Tinayre from Paris, and Tibor Serly from Leopold Stokowski's Philadelphia Orchestra. The programs, put together with Olga's collaboration, included chamber music by Telemann, a Bach cantata, Stravinsky's *Petrushka*, Bartók's Quartets, Mozart's

Sinfonie Concertante, and sonatas of William Young. Münch's brilliant rendition of Bach's *Goldberg Variations* concluded the first program.

It was becoming more difficult to entice an audience to Rapallo. After Mussolini rejected British Foreign Secretary Anthony Eden's concessions and invaded Abyssinia, the League of Nations Council declared Italy the aggressor and imposed sanctions. While Mussolini's actions tended to divorce the regime from the sympathies of the international community as well as many Italian citizens, the Pound circle continued to ignore the far-reaching consequences of this belligerent act.

With the impending threat of world war, the Amici del Tigullio took refuge in aesthetic concerns. "The Rapallo group resolved itself into a study circle," Pound announced, "with the immediate intention of hearing as many of the 310 concerti of Vivaldi as were available in printed edition, and executable by one or two violinists and a piano"—an example of how out of touch they were with the great political events that were taking place in Europe, the rise of Nazism in Germany and Fascism in Italy and Spain.

Ramooh wrote to Pound: "I am so glad we all feel the same about the Italian war. God spoke to Mussolini to take help to those barbarians. England has cut her own throat," she said, echoing the sentiments of certain long-time expatriates in Italy. Olga herself fell within Pound's influence. "Thank God the King [George V] is buried at last," she wrote. "Lord knows what those Brits are concocting under cover of the King's funeral."

In late January Olga was feeling revived and had started working again. Her photo appeared in the *Delphian* magazine above an article about the Vivaldi research. After an English Sunday afternoon at Hook Heath, "full of fuss and food," she was "so cold she is friz right through . . . and finding other people's family life exasperating—yeow!" Listening to Eliot's *Murder in the Cathedral* on BBC, she hoped Ezra had heard "Mr. Possum's" play, which in Olga's view was "magnificent, all except [the] end, which seems to tail off weakly."

For his part, Ezra—inspired by correspondence with Katue Kitasono, editor of *VOU*—for the first and only time considered a temporary change of domestic scene. "At least there iz one place she cd / go as hiz sekkertary, and that is Japan . . . no reason he shdn't have that damn purrfessorship fer a year, it was offered to ole Uncle William [W. B. Yeats]. No job & no glory, but if one went to tidy up [the] rest of the [Ernest] Fenollosa [collection] . . . there would be a excuse . . . she make a mental note."

"She all *for* going to Japan," was Olga's answer, no doubt aware that it was an impossible dream. Ezra never mentioned the subject again.

The Halcott Glovers invited Olga to join them in Cambridge. After learning of her relationship with Pound, Etta had written from their temporary quarters in Kampala, Uganda: "We often speak of you, my dear, and are refreshed that out of this increasingly depressing world of petty-minded nitwits there's one, at any rate, who has had the courage and generosity to face life and wrest from it all that seemed most worth having, *whatever the cost.*" They offered a house with staff at the university while Hal was working on a novel, and Olga eagerly accepted their invitation. "It will give me a chance to look up the Vivaldi mss. in the Fitz-william [Library]," she wrote Pound.

Among the rare treasures Olga discovered at Cambridge were the original manuscript of Vivaldi's Concerto no. 7 in A Major for Violin (with the name Fitzwilliam and date 1706 inscribed on the title page), and a large-scale masterpiece, *Juditha Triumphans,* about the biblical heroine Judith who beheads the Assyrian general Holofornes. "A sacred military oratorio" with Latin text originally written for the pupils of the Pietà Seminary in Venice, *Juditha* would have its modern premiere, the first performance in more than two hundred years, at the Accademia Chigiana.

9

The Red Priest of Venice

1936–1939

Long before the *Four Seasons* became part of the standard repertoire, Olga was drawn to the long-forgotten early-eighteenth-century composer Antonio Vivaldi, not only because he composed so prolifically for her instrument but because of his colorful personality. Red was Olga's color, and in midlife she tinted her dark auburn curls with henna to mimic the so-called Red Priest of Venice.

Count Chigi addressed her as "Miss Rudge-Vivaldi" and adopted a teasing tone in his letters when he wrote: "O prophetic apostle and devotee of that Antonio . . . as undeniably a great artist as he is a womanizer, a seducer of minors and an impenitent satyr! . . . I hope you will not be offended by the ways in which I speak of your 'beloved,' but the truth does not harm anyone, rather adds highlights to the image of our heroes, even when it shows them with their flaws."

Ordained a priest in 1703, Vivaldi became a teacher of music at La Pietà, a convent school for orphaned girls, and, in Ezra's words, "ran an opera company . . . traveling from Mantua to Vienna in company with a barber's daughter whom he taught to sing with great success, and with assistant nymphs." On Vivaldi's womanizing: "The idea of celibacy is a perversion of [the] idea of priest as initiator / droits du seigneur . . . the idea that clergy ought not to be tied up to one female may be sound in theory / but the Occident has gone daft on monogamy, and any other practice is too complicated for [the] present age."

En route to Paris in 1935, Olga stopped over to see the Foà family's collection of Vivaldi manuscripts at the National Library in Turin. After she had searched the card indexes without success, she was sent by the librarian to Professor Gentile next door at the university, where she introduced herself as a colleague of Gabriele Bianchi at the Accademia. Gentile instructed the librarian to hand over volumes 4 and 5, and Olga was among the first to see this vast collection. But she was in Turin for only one day, with no time to begin serious work in the archives.

Encouraged by Pound, she returned the next year and attempted to begin a thematic catalog. But when she asked for the same volumes, the direttore refused, saying that the government had a contract with Casa Ricordi, the prestigious house in Milan that published the works of many important composers.

"Ricordi has printed three or four concerti in ten years," Ezra advised her. "It will take 260 years at the present rate . . . to publish all of them. . . . Do they expect to prevent the performance of Viv[aldi]'s unpublished work for 260 years more?" He suspected the direttore was "trying to steal yr / catalog . . . I will raise hell in Rome if there is any dirty work."

Despite many obstacles, Olga unearthed 131 unpublished concerti at the library and set about copying them. "This area better for her than Venice, more like Paris," she wrote Ezra. "She is feeling rather stuffed with work, like the worm who didn't starve because the apple was too big."

"My own private opinion is that this collection is the remains of what Vivaldi himself sold to the Pietà when he made arrangements to leave Venice in 1740," she wrote Ezra. "A possible trail is made by the visit of Frederick Christian, Elector of Saxony, to Venice in 1740, when a concert was given for him at the Pietà. . . . [Vivaldi wrote] no operas after 'Rosmira' in 1738 . . . complained he wasn't appreciated in Venice as he should be, so I think V. goes off with or to the Sansonia people. One of the finest mss. in Torino is marked for 'orchestre de Dresden.' . . . I found bound volumes of his scores and asked, why bother to bind his working manuscripts? I realized they were gifts for the Emperor of Austria. He wanted to leave Italy and find a rich patron abroad."

Ezra had planned to join Olga in Turin, but again Dorothy was confined to the hospital in Genoa for a hemorrhoid operation, and "he cdn't figure a way to do it wif decorum an elegance, wot she has so impressed on him." He asked Olga to critique the Adams Cantos about the New England family that nurtured two presidents, John and John Quincy. "A 'specially beautiful bunch," she wrote, "beginning 'Revolution,' said Mr. Adams." Sometime in December she joined Ezra in Rapallo, and "his pa and ma gave her turkey and chocolates."

In February, she was back at the Chigi palazzo, installed in the green brocade suite with canopied bed often reserved for the Queen of Belgium. Count Chigi gallantly moved to a suite near the roof because—he told Olga—he wanted an unobstructed view of a former lady love's distant palazzo. Olga's relationship with the Count was one of mutual respect and friendship, and a chaste one. When very young, the Count had married an American—Bertha, the daughter of baritone Giuseppe Kaschmann. The marriage was annulled after a few years, and since that time the Count had admired many women but never settled his affections on another. He took pleasure in promoting young romances and arranged a wedding in his private chapel for two of the Accademia's most promising students, Giuliana Bordini and Riccardo Brengola, with the archbishop performing the ceremony and himself giving the bride away.

At the time of Olga's arrival, the Marchesa Fabiola Lenzoni, a middle-aged, aquiline and angular woman whose late husband had been one of the Count's closest friends, was the ceremonial matriarch presiding over the household. She was particularly fond of her fox terriers and had named each one for the notes of the musical scale—Ut, Re, Mi, Fa, Sol, La, and so on—of the eleventh-century theoretician Guido d'Arezzo. ("Ut" fed at the table from the Marchesa's own plate.)

While Olga was in Siena, she had rented the Venice house to her exotic friend the Marchesa Luisa Casati, who was temporarily down on her luck. ("The last time I saw her at Capri, at the Duchesse de Clermont-Tonnier's, she was still gorgeous, with white ostrich plumes—a bit Mistinguettish—and an enormous silver key," Olga recorded.) Dorothea Watts, who was looking after the calle Querini property, reported to Olga that La Casati arrived with "two ignoti, a pekinese and a black cat . . . with her famous leopard skin wrapped around her and carrying a candelabra (unlighted) in each hand. The *fondamenta* was lined with people calling out in Venetian, 'da dove viene questa vecchia strega?' [Where did this old witch come from?]."

When Olga returned to Rapallo in April, Pound was negotiating with Tibor Serly to lure the Hungarian Quartet for the concerts. The artist Stella Bowen, recently separated from Ford Madox Ford, visited her at Casa 60; later she wrote that Olga had "almost no material possessions, but her well-proportioned rooms furnished with big rectangles of sunshine had a monastic air . . . highly conducive to the making of music . . . with that incredible view of the sea!" Upstairs, Olga's room, was the heart of the house: a broad shelf for music and violin, a narrow bookcase, and chairs carpentered by Pound, the only spot of color an orange damask couch. In Mary's room, a few pieces known as "the Yeats' furniture" were added when Uncle William and his wife left Rapallo.

After a long silence, Olga heard from Ezra that another old friend, George Antheil, then head of the music department of David Selznick International in Hollywood, was composing scores for the Cecil B. DeMille western *The Plainsman* and Leo McCarey's shattering film about old age, *Make Way for Tomorrow*—a long way from being Pound's musical revolutionary. He announced the arrival of a son, Peter Richard, born to Böski, and apologized for not having followed through with the proposed concerts of 1932 and 1934: "[I] am particularly sorry to make Olga suffer for my innate stupidity."

Olga returned to the Accademia to oversee the opening of the summer session: sending a wire to the "Alta Patrona" Princesse le Piemonte, luring the Count onto the platform to introduce the speaker, and lining up the *docenti* on red and gilt chairs on the platform with him. And the Count did speak, "referring to Visconti di Madroni and his aristocratical traditions," she wrote, "and the Prefect came, and the Segretario TNF in a white suit."

In September 1937, Olga enrolled Mary, then twelve years old, in the Istituto della Signora Montalve at La Quiete, a convent school near Florence. To Ezra, Olga confessed: "She regrets a misspent youth and not knowing more, and that miserable Leoncina [is] growing up just as cocky and ignorant!" Ezra agreed to pay his daughter's fees, and Olga referred him to the Reverend Mother. "She can tell his darter that the way to Git Out is to learn English and frog [French]," was Pound's advice. "Having swatted to get her into the best scuola in Italia molto caro / she orter appreciate it and get edderkated."

Ezra was still corresponding with Münch, who was exploring the Vivaldi collection at the Sachsiche Landesbibliothek in Dresden. In Ezra's view, putting the Dresden Vivaldi catalog on microfilm, along with the manuscripts held by Turin and the other libraries, was the least expensive and most efficient way of providing students copies of the collections. When the Turin Library refused to collaborate with the others, Ezra took the matter directly to Italian Minister of Culture Bottai, who "phoned Torino instanter, to dig out Vivaldi" (Canto 92).

Olga was in Venice on October 29 for an "Omaggio ad Antonio Vivaldi" with David Nixon and Giorgio Levi, a program from the Estroharmonica performed for the first time since Vivaldi himself conducted. "Nixon [is] trying hard to play well—beautiful tone, no technique, no solfège, and no bluff—the same state she [Olga] wuz in 15 years ago, but don't know if he has her toughness." Nixon was "agitating to start a Vivaldi Society," with proposed headquarters in Paris, and asked Olga to be honorary secretary.

Mary's first trimester report, forwarded from La Quiete by the directrice, Signora Montalve, revealed that she was getting "edderkated": highest marks in English, religion, music, and *condotta* (conduct); above average marks in French, history, geography, mathematics, physical education, design, and German; below average in Italian and Latin.

She spent her first Christmas holiday with Olga at the Hotel Elefante. "It's cold work, doing the heavy chaperone in the snow, Olga wrote, "but very good air, getting on with the copying [of the Vivaldi scores] . . . enjoying meals and breakfast in bed . . . wishes Him here and *liking it* (which is unlikely)."

She was composing an article about the Vivaldi research for *Il Mare*, the Rapallo newspaper, and Ezra advised "NOT to waste yr. time on unessentials—you ain't cutting a cameo for the Naples museum." Another article about the Dresden collection published by an Italian periodical at Lake Como, *Il Broletto*, "set up a whole concert in small photos, half-tone."

When Mary was taken ill with what the Reverend Mother diagnosed as a light case of flu, Olga rushed to her bedside. "It looks more like a stomach upset," she reassured Ezra, "no cause for worry. . . . Hiz cheeild iz better, and talking—[I am] much impressed—all about Gabriele d'Annunzio."

In Florence, she noticed preparations for Hitler's visit: "All the ugly, modern houses on the piazza to be covered with . . . arazzi [tapestries] . . . the Via Cavour, by a tunnel of flowers, so nothing will be seen of the houses. . . . The Sienese [are] het up over being told they wuz to parade [in] Firenze," she added. "The carroccio is part of the procession and symbolic of one taken at [the Battle of] Monteaperti. . . . the Count proposing to take half [of] Siena to keep his spirits up."

Another short holiday in March in the South of France. At Biot, she acquired several items from Lindy Shaw-Paige's cast-off wardrobe, including a complete skiing costume with boots. "The atmosphere [is] too Brit for comfort," she observed, with much talk about King Edward VIII's intention to marry the American divorcée Wallis Warfield Simpson. At Etta Glover's house in Le Lavandou, she met Ezra's old friend Richard Aldington, "[who] has written another awful novel . . . a sop to suburbia."

Ezra mentioned that H.D. (once married to Aldington), was "all steamed up with kind feelings toward you . . . wanting to know why she hasn't been *told* [about the birth of Mary]."

"She has nothing against H. D. . . . it's H. D. and *Bryher* I won't stand at any price," Olga retorted (having fallen out with Hilda after she abandoned Aldington to cohabit with Winifred Ellerman).

The crisis between Great Britain and Germany, always in the news, was a cause for alarm: "If she doesn't hear something sensible she will bust! They think [Anthony] Eden is a saint and martyr! The locals have read the *Daily Express* and worried about 'where the Italian government [is] going to find the money to pay for all this' and say it hasn't paid its debts to England."

On March 24, 1938, the newly formed Vivaldi Society gave its first concert in the stately ballroom of Ca'Dolfin, one of the most beautiful eighteenth-century palaces of Venice. Ruth Sterling Frost covered the event for the Paris *Tribune:* "[To] Miss Olga Rudge, the American violinist . . . a pioneer in these researches, much credit is due," she wrote. A second concert was to be held in April in the great salon of Frost's palazzo, Contarini degli Scrigni; a third would take place in the Pietà on the Riva degli Schiavoni, Vivaldi's own church.

In July, Olga was ensconced in the Palazzo Capoquadri on the via San Martino in Siena, her permanent lodging for many summers. She sent Leoncina a selection of books for her thirteenth birthday: *The Happy Prince, Uncle Tom's Cabin* (in Italian translation), and a Baroness Orczy thriller. Ezra—who had forgotten the date, July 9—received a letter from Leoncina "reprovin' me fer not having celebrated her anniversary."

Mary was studying solfège, Signora Montalve noted, and "when the child is ready to study either violin or piano, she will be prepared. . . . We have been well pleased with Mary's general behavior and her progress in her studies."

She had enjoyed the volume of Robert Browning poems Ezra sent, and her first solfège lesson had gone very well. She was trying to master a third language, English, with limited success: "I am with mama now, and are very happi. On next Sunday I will go to Venice . . . I am very desiderous to see you . . . I am very glad that all the tennis [courts] in Venice are open, so we can play a little."

The Center for Vivaldi Studies opened in August 1938 during Sienese Music Week, under the aegis of the Italian Academy with the support of the Ministry of National Education and Popular Culture. Olga was writing the introduction to the *Quaderno dell'Accademia* edited by Luciani, a collection of notes and documents illustrating the life and compositions of the Venetian composer.

Talk of war was unavoidable. One of Olga's colleagues was getting his old uniforms out, though the Count bet a thousand lire there would not be another war. The French consul was calling up the French pupils. Lonny Mayer, one of the Jewish students, was among those who had to leave: "She did not whine, showed up well [at the concert], so I invited her out to dinner with the tribe—fiancé Mr. Pink, mother, sister, cognato . . . [all are]

going to trek back to Switzerland, apparent that their money is nowhere irremovable."

Pound blamed the situation on the munitions makers and international bankers. After the first Czechoslovak crisis in September 1939, he wrote: "If they fight to make Skoda [the Czech weapons manufacturer] safe for the city of London investment, it will damn well blow 'em to blazes."

Olga returned to Signora Scarpa's on September 19; the calle Querini house was still rented out. In Venice "everyone [was] gibbering about war," she wrote Ezra. Their strong-minded daughter had "arrived alone at 252 . . . lugged heavy valises here herself!"

"Rothschild [the British financier] started buying 45 minutes before [Neville] Chamberlain told the House of Communes he wuz going to see Mr. Hitler," Ezra reported from England. While Dorothy was recuperating from the operation, his mother-in-law, Olivia Shakespear (the woman Pound had called "the most charming woman in London" in his youth), died at age seventy-four, and Ezra was sent to dispose of her accumulation of furniture and family memorabilia: "don't think it humanly possible to clear this place in less than una quindicina [a fortnight]," he wrote.

Olga, who had been readying the Venice house for Ezra's fall visit, was not informed about this sudden change of plans. "She don't like it," she replied. "In thirteen years the L'cna has had the benefit of His company for three weeks all told. The best years of her [Olga's] life have been spent in solitary confinement out of consideration for His family . . . it is the *limit* to expect her to be sacrificed now to their *furniture*."

She asked Ezra to call on her brother Teddy: "There is some annual dinner he comes to London for, the 'Artist's Rifles,' so he might be in town." Ezra met Teddy Rudge and his son, and they "managed a few calm words in bloody din of bloody grill room, with everybody howling to be heard over knives and orch[estra] . . . her li'l bro[ther] Ted is a marvel."

And, for the first time since the child's birth, Pound met Omar—then twelve years old. After his grandmother's death, Omar was left in the custody of a guardian during vacations from boarding school.

In Venice, Olga was "burst[ing] with rage at having let herself be shoved into such a humiliating position." She marked her next letter

"Long delayed explosion!" in red ink when she reviewed it in later years, but she did not destroy it:

> She gathers He getting tired of town life and not displeased at getting back to His old slippers . . . She admits she would hardly do Him onore anymore as a maîtresse to 'take out' . . . [but] He never even sees that it is damn unfair . . . that He should always have her front door key and come and go as He likes and she never has His . . . *they started even in Paris.* Mah!—little by little all that has been changed—and *not* from any fault of hers. She has never done anything to hurt His family . . . or worry His parents, *still* He doesn't trust her, and now I have got to explain this to the Leoncina—without making a tragedy of it!

Ezra reassured her that "he ain't lookin' fer novelties & bazars, and he iz comin' bak as soon as possible 'cause he purrfers St. Ambrogio with her in it to London or elsewhere without her." He had seen the world premiere of W. H. Auden and Christopher Isherwood's play, *The Ascent of F-6,* and was meeting "the Possum" (Eliot) in the vestry of St. Stephen's Church.

Olga was quick to apologize. "She take back anything narsty she might have said. . . . Does the Possum really live in the vestry, or is it a joke?" She was mourning the demise of Eliot's *Criterion* magazine, and Ezra mocked her: "the joy of my life, the Citharistria / the scraper of cat gut and reviver of Vivaldi / the egregious Olga, scandalized at my levity thus reproves me: 'I *liked The Criterion,* it was *respectable* / *none* of your other magazines are respectable / You have no feeling for the sorrows of yr / friend Possum.' "

She had been to Florence with Mary, who bought copies of Botticelli's *Primavera* at the Uffizi Gallery for her father and *The Birth of Venus* for their neighbor in Venice, Dolly Watts. Moidile was invited by a friend for an ice cream soda, "which she drinks patriotically as being American." When they saw the Hollywood film *A Yank at Oxford,* Mary expressed a desire to go to college. "*Please do not* disillusion her about it yet," Olga cautioned the child's father. She took Mary to have her photo taken and to apply for a passport, and they got back to Venice just as the sirens announced an air raid drill.

10

Overture to War

1939–1940

In the spring of 1939, Ezra returned to the United States for the first time in twenty-eight years. He had corresponded with senators and congressmen, expounding his economic theories in an attempt to convince them of the errors of the Roosevelt Administration. The time had come to go to Washington to straighten things out. He boarded the S.S. *Rex* in Genoa on April 13, Jefferson's birthday—"and *hers*," Olga wrote; "she hates being out of everything—yeow!"

"Glad you have come over in the nick of time, for eye-opening," wrote the Princesse de Polignac, who had preceded him on the *Queen Mary* and was ensconced in the Plaza Hotel. On his arrival, the *Herald Tribune* called Pound "a prophet who taught his generation to throw off what he called the 'smoke screen erected by half-knowing and half-thinking critics'." A *Sun* editorial heralded "that bearded wanderer upon the literary waste lands of our sorry world," whose "chief concern, literature, is now a minor theme in the Poundish symphony . . . immediately the talk turns to economics, propaganda, and what he calls 'left-wing Fascists' in Italy."

After elaborating his theories in New York, Ezra took the train to Washington, "the only inhabitable American city I know of." He stayed in

Georgetown with the Misses Ida and Adah Lee Mapel, old family friends he had not seen since they visited Paris in 1919. His first postcard to Olga was from Thomas Jefferson's honeymoon lodge at Monticello. He had viewed some of the Vivaldi scores in the Library of Congress, after lunching with "the boss" and the heads of the music and Chinese divisions. He was also invited to the Japanese Embassy, and he viewed the films of Noh plays at the National Archives. His old friend from the University of Pennsylvania, the poet William Carlos Williams, then a medical doctor in New Jersey, came down for lunch. "Uncle Jorje" (George) Tinkham, a Republican congressman from Boston whose economic policies Pound touted, fed him diamond-back terrapin, Maryland style. Ezra wrote Homer: "seen more senators—Bridges, Lodge, Dies, etc.—[had] a kind word from [Senator William] Borah in [the] corridor." To Olga: "A joke on me & FDR . . . Washington *Post* said that 'the only person in Washington Ez wants to meet is MRS. Roosevelt.'"

In Massachusetts, he visited the Adams houses in Cambridge, saw the philosopher Alfred North Whitehead and the poet Archibald MacLeish, dined with Harvard University's president, and heard Olga's friend Nadia Boulanger present a music school faculty concert featuring Vivaldi's *Four Seasons*. He then spent "2½ hours in an airless room bellowing his cantos into a microphone fer record wiff 2 kettle drums at his disposal." James Laughlin drove him to the Loomis (Pound's grandmother's) homestead, and afterward to the Laughlin estate in Connecticut, "a quiet-type country house . . . miles of rolling white birch."

He denied plans to repatriate: "He wants to come home . . . been here long enuff . . . [but] tarrying fer Hamilton [College] celebrashun."

Olga complained to Ezra that she might lose him "to some college cutie—or that Mrs. [E. E.] Cummings or someone similar put something decorative in His way." The role of "the other woman" was a difficult one: "She suffering from 'back-street-itis' . . . having met His wife and bin asked if I knew when He wuz coming back. . . . He might have found time to send her at least a few letters having a beginning, a middle and end."

When he cabled gladiolas to appease her, Olga copied Ezra's characteristic jargon: "She wuz walking down the salita and met a man with a 'normous bunch of flowers for her—& wuz she pleazed, & wuz *He* nice. . . . She will now go on being good."

On June 12, 1939, at the 127th commencement of Hamilton College, his alma mater, Pound was awarded the degree of honorary doctor of letters with distinguished company: Elihu Root, Jr. (doctor of laws), the Reverend Malcolm Endicott Peabody (doctor of divinity), and H. V. Kaltenborn (doctor of humane letters).

"Waal, he iz been degreed & is a D. Litt.!! About bust the commencement by heckling a s.o.b. that was spouting twaddle," he wrote Olga. (Kaltenborn, a veteran political journalist and commentator, had launched into a speech that was anti-Fascist, and by implication critical of Pound.)

Some two months after Ezra's departure, he was due to arrive in Genoa on the *Conte di Savoia*. Olga had left for the Accademia before he arrived, and Ezra did not like it: "He come bak to see her, dambit an she ain't here."

While in the United States, he had consulted an attorney to explore the possibility of legally adopting Mary to legitimize her status and secure a U.S. passport for her, in case they had to leave Italy suddenly. When Olga heard the news, for the first time in their fifteen-year relationship she "put her cards on the table" and stated her position in strong language that could not be misunderstood: "He has put her off every time she tries to get Him to consider [the] subject of [the] present triangle," she wrote. There was no reason to maintain a "marital front" out of respect for Dorothy's parents, since both were gone. "He has told her He did not believe in marriage . . . certainly no church would consider a marriage entered into as He told her His was, as sacred or binding." On the brink of war with its possible dislocations, it might be a good time to reconsider legitimizing her own—as well as her child's—status. But she strongly opposed "an adoption that would make it [her child] over to you and implicitly to D., while I would lose every right."

Another perceived humiliation occurred when Maestro Casella asked Olga to do typing and secretarial work at the Accademia in addition to her administrative duties. Her hurt and disappointment were obvious in the next letter: "I have no intention of being the devoted mother, drudging in the background so that my daughter may have advantages." When Ezra went to Siena, he found the door to the Palazzo Capoquadri apartment double-locked. "You are the LIMIT," he wrote hastily on a note he pinned to the door. But as always they reconciled and were guests of Count Chigi at the Palio.

Olga wrote to Ezra after he returned to Rapallo: "everyone seems to think the Boss [Mussolini] met with Adolf [Hitler] and going to turn 'round and help frogs [French] . . . have those dam Germans sunk a ship with 1,000 non-coms—or is it talk?"

"Mebbe still some chance of Eng[land] & Italy keepin' out of the shindy," Ezra replied. He enclosed a clipping from a Roman newspaper about Olga's friend Dorothea Watts of Newport, Rhode Island, who had been ordered to leave Bolzano province in the Tyrol—a restricted zone near Mary's foster parents—within forty-eight hours, in one of Mussolini's "political and military measures against anti-fascism and the espionage activities of Western nations."

On September 3, 1939, the long-anticipated war was declared by the Allies, England and France, and Germany. Along with news of his victories on the tennis courts, Ezra wrote: "Hitler apparently intends fer the moment to set pretty on his Siegfried line . . . [Hermann] Goering's speech vurry good . . . English fleet not here yet. . . . The only thing Eng[land] hasn't done is to putt [Anthony] Eden into [the] cabinet."

"All the Brits running 'round in gas masks and Him piling up tennis scores?" Olga commented. "Whoever will be editing His epistles in the year 2000 will be surprised." She sent for the Leoncina to come to Rapallo and introduced her, for the first time, to Father Desmond Chute: "The news [was] unexpected and a shock . . . [but] he did not ask questions . . . highly civilized."

Olga's greatest accomplishment of 1939 was to write the entry on Vivaldi in Grove's *Dictionary of Music and Musicians.* "The individual authors . . . are in themselves a guarantee for the value of their contributions," the editor noted, "involving much time and laborious research."

Vivaldi Week at the Accademia—September 16 through 21—took place in spite of the hostilities. Maestro Casella had revised twelve of Vivaldi's concertos, motets, and arias, along with the Organ Concerto in A and the Concerto in A Minor for four clavichords transcribed by Bach: "For this occasion," Casella wrote, "there was no question of presenting transcriptions, but of reconstructing the original . . . where intermediary scores were missing (second violins and violas), an attempt has been made to use the Venetian style." The concert version of the opera *L'Olimpiade* was performed for the first time since Vivaldi's death in 1741.

The Rapallo concerts continued in 1940, with a diminished audience: "Every activity, everbuddy settin' waitin' for one or other cat to jump." In June, Marshal Pétain, head of the French collaborationist government, signed an armistice with Germany, and on June 14 Hitler's army marched down the Champs Elysées through the Arc de Triomphe.

Olga noted that Ezra's letter of July 12 was the first opened by censors. His almost daily correspondence was written in Italian, as if he feared the censors might misunderstand English and confiscate them. He often commented on the news: "Eddie [King Edward VIII, after his abdication Duke of Windsor] appointed Governor of the Bahamas." George Antheil's brother, who was just beginning a promising career with the U.S. Department of State, was killed in an air crash in Finland.

Olga was concerned about Mary, who wanted to return to her foster parents in the Tyrol for the summer. "It may be all right, her going back to the soil, only . . . she will only be getting her head swelled by being most important frog in a small puddle. . . . I do not like small puddles, and when I get into them, my reaction is to dive completely under and pretend I'm not there."

She heard that Dorothy Pound and some friends were planning to travel to Siena in September for the Accademia concert week: "If His legitime calklating to join her cronies here for Scarlatti, this one will *not* be pleased."

Ezra had hoped to arrive in time for the Palio, but Olga wrote that there would be no Palio till the end of hostilities. Like many others, the Sienese imagined the war would end by September, when they would stage a "Victory" Palio. "If she wants to worrit about something," Ezra replied pessimistically, "at least base her troubles on the idea that cousin Adolf

[Hitler] will be in London by September 15th, after which 'spose the war will die down a bit."

Olga moved into a smaller apartment at 22, via Roma. "She has discovered the orchestrale get 40 lire a day, which is a lot more than she gets . . . being a perfeck sec[retary], but would rather tornare & essere une violiniste [be a violinist], if not a perfeck lady."

Ezra was going to the ministry of culture in Rome to explore the possibility of using Rome Radio as a platform for his economic theories, to earn some money to support his two families: "Waaal, mebbe papa bring home the bacon / not official, but sum under consideration dieci mille [lire]."

Everything was uncertain. After visiting Mary in Florence, Olga was expecting La Quiete to close before the next term: "Leoncina all right, thin, but hard as nails and shaping nicely." When she inquired at the U.S. consulate if any action had been taken on Mary's passport application, the consular officer put her off with vague excuses—he had not heard from Washington—and asked if Olga had been ordered to leave Rapallo; foreigners were already being evacuated from the coastal towns.

She returned to Siena, with "a concert every night . . . this place more like a monkey house!" Maestro Vannini had gone off to rescue his family from Viareggio (it was rumored that the English fleet would soon be out).

Ezra still planned to go to Siena for the final concerts. "What wardrobe she thinks he requires? . . . velvet getting a bit quaint, and nobody wears evening stuff 'cause it is wartime . . . white shirt and black tie *quite* enough with any dark suit. . . . I don't feel my presence needs any sartorial emphasis."

"She 'spose He doesn't need his velvet, but He will need to look towny, a lot of the Nibs or Nobs have accepted." They were to celebrate a special event in music—the first performance, after more than two centuries, of Vivaldi's oratorio, *Juditha Triumphans*. This epic masterwork, which had been lost to the world, was saved by Olga's diligence and curiosity when she discovered the score at Cambridge University's Fitzwilliam Library. After a brief overture for drums, horns, and string orchestra, the mighty chorus of soldiers in battle sings out:

The sword, carnage, vengeance, rage,
fear and want precede us.
In the hurly-burly of the fight
may the fortunes of war deal
a thousand wounds
a thousand deaths.

One can only imagine the conflicting emotions they—Olga, Ezra, and Mary—felt as their adopted homeland, Italy, was at war with England and France.

Ezra reported on the performance in one of his chatty broadcasts over Rome Radio: "Two years ago, the Chigi organization had the sense to devote the whole of the Sienese fest to Vivaldi. . . . [*Juditha Triumphans* is] a musical whoop in two parts, to celebrate the retaking of Corfu from the Turks in 1715, very timely and suitable as a bicentenary funeral wreath on redhead Vivaldi . . . better than the *Olimpiade* . . . Vivaldi knew more about using the human voice than Johnnie [Johann Sebastian] Bach ever discovered . . . he makes ole pop Handel look like a cold poached egg that somebody dropped on the pavement. . . . I would by god rather hear Guarnieri conductin' Vivaldi than Toscanini conductin' Beethoven in Salzburg."

Mary returned to Bruneck, and Olga complained that the child's letters had "slumped into [the] conventional Gais mentality. She is a perfect chameleon, natural at her age, but I think rather hard that she should always be exposed to other influences, considering the trouble I took to get her decent parents."

In Sant'Ambrogio, times were hard and lire scarce. Ezra wrote to Katue Kitasono in Tokyo that he had "cashed his last postal money order for 156 lire (about six dollars). . . . As I can't cash American cheques . . . and as nothing (now) comes from English publications, this thin line of supplies from the J[apan] T[imes] would be useful."

Reading the correspondence of this period, one might wonder why Olga and the Pounds delayed returning to America on the eve of the second major European conflict of their lifetimes. The embassy in Rome advised all U.S. citizens to leave Italy in May 1940 and sent several ships to evacuate them. At the onset of war, Pound's book royalties from Laughlin and Dorothy's inherited income from England were cut off, and Homer's pension checks from Philadelphia stopped. Passage from Genoa to New York was then three hundred dollars per person—a considerable amount of money at that time. Although the U.S. Embassy was offering financial assistance to all citizens who asked for it, Olga and the Pounds made no immediate attempt to leave.

In mid-October, Ezra explored the possibility of booking passage for five on one of the Pan Am clippers from Lisbon, but "niente sino al 14 novembre." Olga's major consideration was Mary: "I refused to go because I did not want to leave her, and the American consulate refused to renew her passport," she confided in her notebook many years later. She was still procrastinating in mid-October: "She . . . don't want to go such an expensive way unless necessary. . . . doesn't He think . . . it would be better to wait till spring? He will arrive after the party, as far as elections, and have to spend a winter in the cold. . . . It doesn't feel like a war here."

Ezra: "He don't want 'em to be on two sides of a blinkin' ocean fer indefinite."

At the last crucial moment—November 11, 1941—Homer Pound, then eighty-three, fell, broke a hip, and was confined to the Rapallo clinic. Rail transport through occupied French territory to neutral Lisbon to board a clipper would have been unthinkable for Homer, and Ezra would not consider leaving his parents behind.

On November 14, he telegraphed Olga: "Non vado in America—tornerò a Rapallo." A letter followed: "Thank gawd thazz over. . . . the clippah don't take nobody more till Decembah-middle, cause it's behind with the mail. . . . he ain't been so glad about anything for a long while . . . wow!. . . . She get her fiddle goin' [and] tell him how soon she ready to let anyone but him hear it."

I I

The Subject Is—Wartime

1941–1945

The war began in earnest. Ezra was in Rome expounding his economic and political theories on the *American Hour* for Rome Radio, for which he was paid 350 lire (then approximately twelve dollars) a broadcast. On January 23 he wrote to Olga: "made 2 discs yesterday . . . 9 discursi in a fortnight. . . . No goddam light / no goddam stamps / no tabac open . . . can't see—*God* damn hotel with no light! . . . typing in the dark / typing in the twilight / she decipher if she can."

He composed a poem for Katue Kitasono, his Tokyo correspondent:

Stage, a room on the hill among the olive trees,
the violinist playing the air of Mozart's 16th violin sonata
Then a finch or some bird that escapes my ornithology tried to
counterpoint (all though in key)
I suppose the subject is: War time.

The Rapallo concerts had ceased. "The foreign subscribers are gone . . . no Gerhart Münch, no pianist / no public."

In March, April, and May, Pound continued his *discursi*. After broadcasts, he visited friends in Rome: Gian Carlo Menotti, whose honored guest he would be at the Spoleto Festival after the war, and George Santayana, then writing his memoirs, "a bit older, not very lively." For more spirited company, he "exchanged yarns" with the Irish ambassador, Mac White.

Italians were noticing shortages. Olga wrote to Ezra about an unexpected windfall of meat: "A bistecca broke a leg and had to be killed . . . Sunday [it] was sold to the population in [the] little chapel above the church on [the] way to Monte Allegro. Talk about sacrificial rites! The butcher did the job in the chapel, and we waited our turns outside, while Mass was going on in the church." She was preserving orange marmalade and waiting for news of Ezra's return from Rome. Mary was writing the most difficult chapter of her novel, "having finished reading *The Bostonians* [by Henry James], now fallin' back on Jane Austen's *Emma*."

Natalie Barney and Romaine Brooks were installed in the Villa Sant' Agnese near Florence to wait out the war. Barney had listened to Pound over Rome Radio: "glad you are sticking to it . . . and was the violin surrounding your speech Olga's?" she wrote Ezra. (The recording of Vivaldi she heard in the background was not Olga.)

Olga returned to the Accademia in June and installed herself in a small flat near the market at 8 (vicolo) San Salvatore. Ezra wrote that he had made "three [broadcasts] in a row Fri / Sat / Mon . . . am developing prima-donnitis . . . as Gertie [Gertrude Stein] said, 'I am an *explainer*.'"

Olga had to apply for permission to return to Sant'Ambrogio: travel papers were required during wartime. Mary, now sixteen, was translating the Greek classics (at Ezra's suggestion). She wrote to her mother from Gais: "I am all right . . . [but] growing out of my clothes. . . . I hope very much that we may soon be settled all together." Ezra was at that time "considering a flat in Rome for us [that is, Olga and Mary] after the war. . . . Roma wd / be more amusin' fer the kid than Sant'Ambrogio."

The Japanese attack on the naval base at Pearl Harbor thrust the United States into the war with Japan, and soon with Germany and Italy. Pound's radio broadcasts ceased as he retired to Rapallo, in his words, "to seek wisdom from the ancients." When he joined Olga and Mary in Sant'Am-

Olga and Ezra on the Grand Canal in Venice, 1962: "What Thou Lovest Well . . ."
(Horst Tappe)

Olga in Youngstown, Ohio, 1896: "An April baby in a lace-trimmed, puffed-sleeve dress." (Courtesy of the Beinecke Rare Book and Manuscript Library, Yale University)

John Edgar Rudge, Olga's father: "Youngstown's most eligible bachelor." (Beinecke, Yale)

Julia O'Connell Rudge, Olga's mother, and her children (left to right): Arthur ("Babs"), Olga, and Edgar ("Teddy"), with Jimmie, the black bear cub. (Beinecke, Yale)

Olga at St. Anthony's Convent School, Sherborne, Dorset (Olga is third from right in the second row): "I am a universal favorite, but I am not vain about it." (Beinecke, Yale)

Olga in Paris in the 1920s, when she met Ezra: "An Irish adrenal personality."
(Beinecke, Yale)

Renata Borgatti, Olga's accompanist: "A Valkyrie writhing to be free." (Beinecke, Yale)

Natalie Clifford Barney ("Miss B."): "The wild girl from Cincinnati" *entre deux âges*. (Carl Van Vechten, courtesy of the Van Vechten Trust)

George Antheil: "The bad boy of music." (Carl Van Vechten, courtesy of the Van Vechten Trust)

Ezra, on a walking tour in 1923 (Olga was the photographer): "He took me to Ventadour . . . how elegant a gentleman . . . walking 25 kilometers a day with a rucksack."
(Beinecke, Yale)

The Hieratic Head of Ezra
Pound, by Henri Gaudier-
Brzeszka: "It won't look like
you." (Beinecke, Yale)

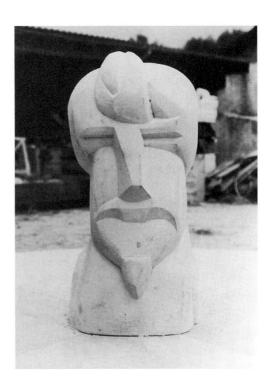

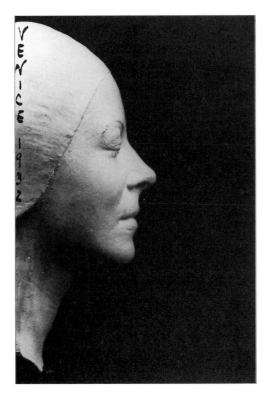

Olga's profile, by the Venetian
mask-maker Bonsuan (1932).
(Beinecke, Yale)

Olga with her daughter, Mary: "It was I who wanted the child." (Beinecke, Yale)

Premier Benito Mussolini, "Il Duce," in 1933, playing with a "leoncina." He inscribed the photo to Olga. (Beinecke, Yale)

Olga, the *segretarissima* of the Accademia Chigiana, Siena, Italy, in the 1950s.
(Courtesy of the Accademia Chigiana and the Beinecke Library, Yale)

Count Guido Chigi Saracini: "An El Greco grandee, courtly and aloof." (Courtesy of Count Chigi and the Beinecke Library, Yale)

Olga with Pablo Casals and his wife, Martita, who were among the many VIPs at the Accademia Chigiana in the 1960s. (Courtesy of the Accademia Chigiana and the Beinecke Library, Yale)

"Miss Rudge-Vivaldi" unveiling the bust of Don Antonio sculpted by Vico Consorti, a gift for Count Chigi on his eightieth birthday from the teachers at the Accademia. (Courtesy of Simonetta Lippi and the Accademia Chigiana, Siena)

Olga and Ezra's grandchildren, Walter and Patrizia de Rachewiltz, at Schloss
Brunnenburg. (Beinecke, Yale)

The last years: "Miss Rudge was the sea in which he floated." (Beinecke, Yale)

Ezra's grave at San Michele, the cemetery isle, where Olga took her place by his side in 1996: "A place of unlopped trees, of birds . . . 'not of one bird but of many.'" (Beinecke, Yale)

brogio for Christmas, he was still "trying to figure things out, to make up my mind about some things."

On January 26, 1942, Ezra's photo appeared in *Time* magazine above an article about his life in Rapallo, where he had "retired to continue his study of Chinese philosophy." "Because I stopped speaking on December 9th . . . I am not [compared to Lord] 'Haw-Haw'," he said, referring to William Joyce, the Brooklyn-born Nazi propagandist who was then broadcasting from Germany and was later executed by the British for treason.

Three days after the *Time* article appeared, he went back to Rome and picked up the broadcasts. The necessity to earn enough lire to support three households must have entered into his decision. But he insisted on a new introduction to the *discursi:*

> Rome Radio, acting in accordance with Fascist policy of intellectual freedom and free expression of opinion . . . [and] following the tradition of hospitality, has offered Dr. Ezra Pound the use of the microphone twice a week. *It is understood that he will not be asked to say anything incompatible whatsoever that goes against his conscience, or anything incompatible with his duties as a citizen of the United States of America.* [emphasis added]

Olga kept busy with the minutiae of daily life at Sant'Ambrogio: "sitting on the floor, making wicks out of cotton wool for the [olive] oil lamps" (candles had almost disappeared when the war began). "Fifty kilos of tomatoes drying on the roof. . . . She seems occupied all the time, even got around to a spot of practicing."

In late February Homer Pound, who had suffered in the Rapallo clinic for many months, died quietly in his sleep. Ezra had been very close to the Old Man, as he called his father. Mary wrote in her autobiography that her father came to her and said, "Il tuo nonno e morto. . . . he just threw himself on the couch and wanted to be left in peace and listen to music. Then he went to Rome again." The *American Hour* began transmission throughout the Axis countries.

Olga sent Mary to her foster family in Gais again during the summer harvest season. The Accademia was not open to students, but the Count invited her to continue with her administrative duties. He enclosed a concert program and a clipping about a thirteenth-century feud between the Tolomeis and the Salambenis, of interest to Olga because the Palazzo Capoquadri belonged to the Salambeni clan.

In carefully phrased Italian, Olga replied that she would not be returning to the Accademia that summer: "I have not been very well . . . I miss that lovely light Sienese air." Of the concert: "I do not believe that such important unpublished works have been performed anywhere, either in Italy or abroad, and . . . that other great Antonio [Guarneri] assures absolute perfection of execution." She continued to keep in touch with the Count throughout the summer and to listen to the Accademia concerts on the radio, including an all-Vivaldi program in August. Sebastiano Luciani was trying to get permission from the government to inspect the Vivaldi manuscripts in Turin; he hoped that Olga and Mortari, another member of the Comitato Coordinatori, would accompany him. Maestro Casella was already there in his studio.

Life in the coastal towns was difficult during wartime, food scarce. Mary returned to Casa 60 in the fall, but there was little of interest for an active teenager: "They ain't even a cinema to take the child to," according to Olga. When Ezra gave Mary a thousand lire as a Christmas gift, she asked to go to Rome with him.

Mail came irregularly to Sant'Ambrogio, often in batches, "dunno if for convenience of the old postino, or what," Olga pondered. In January 1943, she received notice that her house at 252, calle Querini in Venice had been sequestered. A Captain Piglini was occupying it.

A Mr. Bruers from the Royal Academy of Italy and a Milanese publisher had contracted to print an edition of Vivaldi's works, "wholly at the expense of the Royal Academy," the Count wrote, though Luciani and the Accademia would have full editorial control. He credited Olga for the Vivaldi revival and continued to tease her about her "priest, the little pig, not to say outright *swine*, despite all the love that he inspired in you."

In Sant'Ambrogio, Olga was happy to see the cherry tree in bloom after a difficult winter, and she opened the window wide to enjoy the sight. She was going through an orgy of housecleaning for Ezra's return. Mary was trying her hand at translating *The Cantos* into Italian and visiting Father Desmond twice a week for lessons in French and Latin.

In April, Mary went to Rome for the long-awaited visit with her father. "Her daughter is gettin' romanized," Ezra wrote. "I dunno as she will be wantin' to get back. . . . I parked [the] Sprig on the Menottis . . . looked very well in black at a dinner yesterday evening." Olivia Rossetti Agresti, a niece of Dante Gabriel Rossetti and an admirer of Il Duce, invited "the Sprig" to lunch; Princess Troubetzkoi, a Virginian by birth, a novelist and playwright who was broadcasting with Ezra on the *American Hour,* "fixed up something . . . for domenica" (a Sunday picnic that would have far-reaching consequences in Mary's life). Mary remembered that Allied bombers were then dropping propaganda leaflets over Rome demanding that the Fascist government surrender. She asked her mother if she could stay on indefinitely, but Olga warned that she must return by May 20 to have the *carta annonaria* stamped.

On June 22, Olga wrote: "There ain't no zucchini, and they ain't got no sugar to boil cherries [for homemade jam]. . . . [The] child continues diligent, thought of keeping her here till after her birthday, but p'raps better to send her off [to the Tyrol] soon as He gets back (an alarm last night)." Rumors still were circulating that residents of the seacoast would be sent inland.

Olga began to record in a ruled school notebook her life with Mary that wartime summer, their daily struggle to obtain food:

(June 25) Just before lunch, "Fish!" being called by the dwarfy good-natured woman from Zoagli covered with fish scales . . . sardelle, only 20 lire (12 last year). Lunch: fish cooked in oil with parsley & garlic, lettuce salad and quagliata [cottage cheese]. Merenda [tea]: first figs of the season. Supper: half cup of milk, remains of macaroni & beans, cold fish, bread & quagliata. Gave cat 1 / 2 fish head (rest treasured for tomorrow).

(June 27) End of month, not much in larder. . . . The little man comes 'round selling tape, pins, a companion piece to the fish woman—dwarfish, round shaved head, coat covers his hands, comes to [the] knees. [He] talks . . . counting points on his fingers. Subjects: love and religion . . . [if he] had a dozen corn stalks, he would eat one grain a day as "communion"—the sun rose every day & Christ rose every day on the altar, & the body of Jesus in the communion was the corn.

(June 29) [The] third of the "figurines" comes to my door: little old woman—gentle manners & a blessing hand . . . old-fashioned full-gathered skirt, needs earrings & a basket of fruit & strings of garlic to be a figure from a Presepio. The only male beggar—a stray dog—asks for the moon, i.e., a pezzetto di pane' . . . give him a lire & feel poverty-stricken at having no larder.

(July 3) EP arrives unexpected, bringing treat in honor of M[ary]'s birthday, a tin of marvelous paté de foie . . . *real* tea.

(July 7) Beans, with bit of speck [bacon] & oil. Figs (skin good to eat!) Pinolo [pine nuts] & pear skins & cores.

(July 8) [Mary's] birthday cake, castagna flour with candied cherries.

(July 16) Coffee from orange peel. [Max] Beerbohm's servant sent & showed how to make.

(July 24) Lin Yu Tang, the Chinese philosopher, said: "A well-filled stomach is indeed a great thing: all else is luxury of life." [Pound added the Chinese ideogram for the happy state of going to bed "warm, well-filled, dark and sweet."]

(July 25) More potatoes in a few weeks than in whole previous year . . . rabbit and chicken reappearing, and biscuits. Black market eggs, 7 lire each. Drought accounts for disappearance of salads and green vegetables.

Olga's diary ended abruptly. On July 19, 1943, a strong force of American bombers attacked the railway yards and the airport at Rome, and the damage was considerable. On July 25, Il Duce was arrested. Victor Emmanuel III, still titular King of Italy, asked Marshal Pietro Badoglio to take over as prime minister. The next day, July 26, Rome Radio carried one of Pound's broadcasts.

Ezra first heard the news of his indictment for treason—along with seven other broadcasters—over the BBC. He went to the American embassy in Rome, staffed by the Swiss during wartime, hoping to discover the official charges against him. The embassy had had no contact with Washington, so he learned nothing there. He returned to Rapallo to think things over.

On August 4, Pound wrote to U.S. Attorney General Francis Biddle, explaining his reasons for the broadcasts: "I have not spoken with regard to *this* war, but in protest against a system which creates one war after another. . . . I have not spoken to the troops, and have not suggested that the troops should mutiny or revolt . . . the American people should be better informed by men who are not tied to a special interest. . . . A war between the U.S. and Italy is monstrous and should not have occurred. And a peace without justice is no peace, but merely a prelude to future wars." His letter naively enclosed "an application for the renewal of the passport which you took from me when I called at your office." In Pisa, he would recall a line from that letter:

free speech without free radio speech is as zero . . . (Canto 74)

there are no righteous wars . . .
total right on either side of a battle line (Canto 82).

Ezra remained in Rapallo for the rest of August, waiting to see what would happen if the Badoglio government negotiated peace with the Allies. On September 6 he went to Rome again to resume the broadcasts.

On September 8, 1943, Italy capitulated to the Allied Forces. On the morning of September 10, while U.S. troops were preparing to occupy Rome, Pound checked out of the Albergo Italia and called on Olga's friend

Nora Naldi and her husband. They tried to convince him to stay with them, that the war would soon be over, but he refused, saying he was going to the Tyrol to see Mary. Nora offered him a rare black-market egg, some bread, and a cup of tea, then another hard-boiled egg and more bread for his backpack. Pound—at fifty-eight years old—set off on foot for his first long walking trip since Ussel and Ventador in the 1920s. He traveled the fifty miles from Rome to Rieti, spending "one night under the stars, one on a bench in Rieti" (Canto 84), before boarding a train going north with "a herd of the dismantled Italian army." He hopped another train at Bologna that took him as far as Verona, where he had to decide whether to go north to Bruneck or to the coast and Rapallo. In that area the trains were under efficient German control, so he decided to continue on to Mary in Gais.

On a clear September day, a traveler covered with dust and carrying a rucksack approached the door to the farmhouse. The Marchers presumed he was a beggar, and the frau was about to turn him away when she recognized his voice.

"Gruss Gott," "Der Herr!" "Tatile ist gekommen!" (Canto 78). A short time later, Mary returned to the farmhouse on her bicycle and fell into Babbo's embrace. She sent a telegram to her mother assuring her that her father had arrived safely, and Olga dutifully went down the hill to share the good news with Dorothy.

By the end of September a puppet Fascist government—the Repubblica Sociale Italiana—was operating from Salò in northern Italy. Ezra stopped there on his way back from Gais to be interviewed by the new minister of popular culture, Fernando Mezzasoma, hoping to broadcast again from Milan, the new center of radio propaganda. Many years later Pound wrote of this incident that it had been "great folly to have destroyed the batch of letters re / that," and only oral reports of that crucial time remain.

As the September season at the Accademia began, Count Chigi sent news to his "Carissima Segretarissima Olga": "At the end of this twelfth academic year, there are plenty of problems to deal with." A performance of Giovanni Pergolesi's *Il Maestro di Musica,* the second act of *La Traviata,* and Pietro Mascagni's *Zanetto* had taken place on the afternoon of the second. The voice teacher was being held prisoner in Sicily along with all of her family, but Signora Alfani Tellini replaced her and accomplished miracles. The Settimana Musicale Senese had been postponed until the next year, but more than one hundred students had already registered. "I hope that the next one may take place in an aura of *peace*," the Count wrote, "free of the nightmare of this most infamous slaughter."

"These terrible days go by with frightening slowness, and one loses one's sense of time," Olga replied. "The Poet is well, but I am very worried about him. . . . the 'liberators' coming to Europe to spread Mr. Roosevelt's Four Freedoms, the first of which is freedom of speech, will not forgive the Poet for having made use of his 'first freedom.' His position is vulnerable and could become dangerous."

On October 30, Ezra was back in Rapallo celebrating his birthday with "the Old Lady" (his mother, Isabel Pound), who miraculously produced turkey and sweet potatoes. At year's end, Olga noted that there were brioches at the cafés for the first time, with a few being sold openly at the bakery. Salt was still rationed but available on the black market for preserving pork ("Beerbohm's cook makes her own from sea water").

Ezra came for a Christmas lunch of ravioli. Food was becoming an obsession. Olga referred to the "dry writers" in literature (including Henry James), the "lack of food and drink in same." She preferred George Meredith's "constant reference to food and wine and J[ane] Austen's refreshing recurrences of mealtimes . . . Fanny, in *Mansfield Park*, mourning over 'the remaining cold pork bones and mustard on William's plate'." At a restaurant in December, while Ezra was away, she had chicken for the first time since the United States entered the war, and also macaroni and cheese, "as much as nearly a month's ration would be (38 lire, including wine)." On the day after Christmas, "the bakery under the clock was raided, a cartload given to the poor . . . got biscuits there the day before."

In his Christmas letter, Count Chigi sent news that the publisher Ticci was putting out volume 5 of the Accademia's *Quaderni*, including Mario Rinaldi's lecture "The Birth of Vivaldi." He assured Olga that her position was being held open for her, adding, "I have had no news of you, and I only hope that you are well."

In 1944, the Allied bombing of Rapallo, Genoa, and other coastal towns began in earnest. The Rapallo railroad bridge was destroyed, and communications between Rapallo and the rest of the world were interrupted. At the Capella dei Monti, a woman and the priest hearing her in the confessional were killed. Father Desmond Chute, the Anglican priest, had been deported as an enemy alien to work in a war hospital at Bobbio.

News came at last of the death of Winaretta Singer, the Princesse de Polignac, who had furthered Olga's early career and continued to offer financial support through the years. The Princesse was mourned by many in literary as well as musical circles; in Maurice Baring's words, it was "a great loss . . . the wittiest woman in Europe."

Olga wrote to Count Chigi: "It doesn't seem possible that this cauchemar [nightmare] we are living can go on much longer. . . . it was a great satisfaction to know that you continue your efforts in homage to Vivaldi. . . . [Mary] is not here now . . . it became necessary to let her take a job . . . a secretarial position, and [she] works very hard. . . . It has been eight months since I saw her . . . eighteen is a bit young to have to be on one's own." She passed along news from their mutual friend Emma Ivancich that her house in Capri had been seized and occupied.

The Count was pleased that Olga had received the *Quaderni* with the Vivaldi articles, and that Pound had also noticed them. "My Vivaldi mania is due wholly to you, my dear and most valuable secretary and inimitable collaborator," the Count wrote. "We continue to be spared by the 'heroic' enemy airmen [that is, the Allied forces], but in the countryside around us a number of things have been destroyed, among them the beautiful and historic Basilica dell'Osservanza, with its famous della Robbias." ("[T]he Osservanza is broken, and the best de la Robbia busted to flinders," Ezra would recall in Canto 80.)

"How it hurts to learn about the Basilica dell'Osservanza!" Olga replied. "I will pray for your city. . . . Here, too, there are always alerts, and in Zoagli, many people killed." Her reaction was typical of many on both sides during the war who noted only the bombing in their own neighborhoods, ignoring the devastation wrought in London and other European cities, with even greater loss of lives.

The Count was receiving many applications with fees paid, in spite of "the complete absence of means of transportation to Siena . . . and the general chaos." He was going ahead with plans to open the Accademia—the provincial governor had approved—and he hoped that Olga would return as soon as possible.

There followed a long hiatus in their correspondence. Olga's situation changed dramatically when the Germans constructed concrete walls to defend the beaches in Rapallo and issued an order for all inhabitants of seafront apartments to evacuate. In May 1944, Ezra and Dorothy were forced to move, with their household furnishings, from 12, via Marsala within twenty-four hours. They might have gone to Villa Raggio with Isabel Pound on the other side of Rapallo, "but it would have meant EP being very cramped, and another hill to climb," Olga remembered. "It would have been a kindness to EP's mother, who was alone, if DP had gone there—at least for weekends—but she [Dorothy] did not like her [mother-in-law]." To save Ezra's strength on the long walk to Sant'Ambrogio (and, Olga admitted, to keep him near), she invited the couple to move in with her.

Ezra's immediate concern was how to dispose of twenty years' accumulation of papers and books. Olga recalled that Pound himself carried the many little poetry magazines, reviews, and so forth—materials that were of too great interest (and eventual value) to throw away—to the new municipal building, the Casa del Fascio. The Casa del Fascio had a large room intended as a library, with empty shelves. "He took me there," she later wrote, and "I got the impression that he did this so I might be officially . . . recognized as a friend of his. We passed through a large room where a seduta [meeting] of local Fascists seemed to be taking place. I never had a dopolavoro card, useful for rebates on cinema tickets, etc., still less any Fascist tessera [membership card]. . . . The Rapallo concerts gave a rebate on tickets, but few, if any of the local Fascist officials ever came."

The rest of Ezra's papers were to be carted up the hill to Casa 60. But where to find containers to carry them? No porters were available to lift the heavy household effects up the steep hill, no men, no horses or mules, and no road for cars at that time. The Sant'Ambrogio flat was still as empty as Stella Bowen remembered it—six large rooms, with two comfortable Ezra-made arm chairs, a few small tables, books, and files. There was no telephone, no electricity, and only a tin hip-bath with rain water drawn from a cistern by bucket, shared by three other families, a cow, and several goats.

Not to have "all their eggs in one basket," the Pounds hurriedly divided most of their belongings between the Giuseppe Bacigalupos, who had room to spare, and Isabel Pound's apartment at the Villa Raggio. Baccin, the old peasant, helped carry the rest of the household things from the via Marsala to Casa 60. Olga left a note for Ezra: "Baccin will be at the steps of the salita Cerisola at quarter-to-ten domani lunedi. He can wait there as he has the wall to rest load on."

Mary was in Gais again for the summer, so Dorothy moved into Mary's room, the one with the best furniture—a bed, night-table, and enamel washstand that came from the Yeats's flat in the Villa della Americhe—and the only rug from the via Marsala. As Olga described that first evening: "I had made [the room] as comfortable as possible, spent the day helping to carry the Via Marsala [possessions] up hill. To help tide over the awkwardness—the three of us forced to converse at the end of a tiring day, I thought EP & D. would like me to show that I was minding my own business—I went to my room and played the Mozart Concerto in A major, as well as I have ever done. The next morning, E. told me that D. remarked, '*I* couldn't have done that.' (D. said nothing to me, good or bad or indifferent . . . pointedly spoke to me as she might have to a housekeeper.) I never played—or was asked to play—again. It was the last time EP had music at Sant'Ambrogio. After the first night, DP and EP sat listening in the dark to the BBC broadcasts." Dorothy referred to that time in only one letter to James Laughlin: "We spent a year up at Olga's house."

"We were all civilized people," Olga stated publicly of the ménage à trois, "with only the usual minor domestic irritations." On the surface, it appeared to many that the two ladies and one gentleman coexisted in harmony. They were all practiced in keeping "a somewhat Henry Jamesian attitude toward personal feelings," Mary observed. Olga did the shopping (she spoke better Italian), and contributed her meager income from teaching English at the technical school in Rapallo.

British writer Richard Aldington had earlier said of Dorothy: "The impression she gave was not of a woman [who was] . . . hurt and offended by infidelity. . . . Why should she object because her husband found the only trained musician in the world who would take his ridiculous caperings seriously?" Another friend who observed the couple remarked that Olga helped to use up Ezra's excess energy.

Later, after the triangular living arrangement had abruptly ended, Olga recorded her true feelings: "One solid year, Dorothy made use of me to the fullest, shared my house [while] I worked like a slave—cooking, cleaning, finding food—which I only undertook owing to her incapacity, so that E. should not suffer. I cannot understand the incredible meanness of the way she was behaving . . . in terror lest I have some advantage over her, considering our respective positions: she, with the war years' income saved up, a family legal advisor to fall back on and right to appeal to any of E's friends for help, a child provided for with no trouble on her part. I, with no rights of any kind—income completely knocked out by war—high and dry in a country I never would have lived in by choice except to be near E., having to improvise a living, with Mary."

Mary later recalled those months in her autobiography: "Whatever the civilized appearances, the polite behavior and façade in front of the citizens of Rapallo, hatred and tension permeated the house. . . . Never have I seen Mamile [Olga] cry so unrestrainedly as when she read Canto 81: the cry 'AOI!' is an outburst more personal than any other in *The Cantos,* and expressed the stress of almost two years when [Pound] was pent up with two women who loved him, whom he loved, and who coldly hated each other. . . . I had a glimpse of the madness and the vision: Zeus-Hera-Dione, the two different consorts of one god, one a sky goddess and one an earth goddess . . . many shades of emotion remain hidden, embedded in *The Cantos* as mythology."

On June 4, the Allies' armored and motorized infantry roared through Rome and crossed the Tiber River; the Eighty-eighth Division was the first to enter the Piazza Venezia, in the heart of the capital. Two battered German armies were fleeing to the north as five hundred heavy bombers joined lighter aircraft in smashing rail and road routes to northern Italy. The Eighth Army captured a number of strategic towns.

On June 5 at six o'clock, Pope Pius XII appeared on the balcony of St. Peter's to offer a prayer of thanksgiving to the Blessed Virgin and Saints Peter and Paul, guardians of Rome, and to give his blessing to the tens of thousands packed into St. Peter's Square. The Pope tactfully thanked both belligerents—the Allies and Germany—for having left Rome intact. Victor Emmanuel announced that he would step aside, as he had promised he would do after the liberation of Rome, and handed over all royal prerogatives to his thirty-nine-year-old son, Crown Prince Umberto, in a decree countersigned by Premier Badoglio.

In the United States, President Roosevelt hailed the capture of Rome, the first of the three major Axis capitals to fall, as "one up and two to go," and warned that "victory still lies some distance ahead . . . it will be tough and it will be costly." On the morning of June 6, the great Allied invasion of France under General Dwight Eisenhower was taking place on the beaches of Normandy.

12

The Road to Hell

1945

In the spring of 1945, the Rapallese were beginning to hear rumors—the Americans are coming! On April 25, the Italian partisans rose up against the Germans, and orders went out from the High Command not to resist.

On Friday, April 27, Olga—as was her custom every weekday morning —went down to Rapallo to meet her students at the Technical School, but there would be no classes that day. The students were being let out to celebrate the liberation. When someone told her the U.S. Army Command was headquartered at the Hotel Europa on the waterfront, she went there to show her passport and to speak to the officer in charge. But the officers were too busy to deal with expatriate Americans, so she climbed back up the hill.

The next morning, April 28, Ezra decided to go himself to explain to someone in authority his reasons for the Rome Radio broadcasts—"not in a spirit of surrender," he later explained to Mary. But the U.S. Army had moved on, and the officers that had occupied the Hotel Europa were on their way to Genoa, recently evacuated by the Germans. Ezra climbed back up the hill, and the two women with one man shared another strained, silent evening.

On April 30 Olga, understanding the seriousness of their situation, wrote an agitated letter to Mary in Gais, "in haste to give you a few addresses in case anything should happen to me." She listed the family and friends of most importance to her: Uncle Teddy Rudge, Mabel and Ethel Duncan ("our dearest friends, Mabel knew your *great*-grandmother Paige"), Don Arturo Brown, Adrian Stokes, Mrs. Cecily (Richards) Walters, Auntie Lou, Mrs. Ernest Harold Baynes ("if she is still alive"), Stella Bowen, Dorothea Watts Landsburg, James Laughlin, Reverend Desmond Chute, Lindy Shaw-Paige, Etta and Halcott Glover, T. S. Eliot ("to give you advice about your writing").

"Some furniture I left in Paris to be sold by Mme. Chauvin, 33 rue Dragon . . . [the] most important papers in my little dispatch case. . . . Your passport is No. 675 (April 19, 1941) [issued in] Firenze: see about getting a new one as soon as possible. . . . You know the jewelry I have . . . the large seal ring with Babbo's head, three gold bracelets, and a glass medallion with your hair and tiny gold coin." Among other keepsakes, "the d'Annunzio bird, my silver seal, my violin, my Japanese gown (with brocade sash), in the tin trunk in Venice—*most important!*"

Olga's "last words" to her only child: "Take care of yourself, and try to forget the war and be happy . . . read EP's works and study them well. . . . You have always been a joy and consolation to me. I believe happy times will come soon for you."

On Wednesday, May 3, it was Dorothy's turn to go down the hill to pay her weekly duty call on Isabel Pound. Olga, having heard that the Americans were back in Rapallo to stay, went down to see what she could find out. She waited for more than an hour at the office of Major Robinson, who, she was told, was the officer in charge. But the major was busy with local authorities and refused to see her. Olga wearily climbed back up the *salita*. At the entrance to Casa 60, she was surprised to discover the door locked. "Caro!" she called. No answer. Ezra was gone!

Just before noon, Pound had been working at the typewriter, with the Legge translation of Confucius open in front of him. As he recalled later, first he heard footsteps, then the butts of Tommy-guns beating on the door. The door was kicked open. Two Italian partisans he did not recognize, in shabby uniforms, entered the room. He knew instinctively that these were rough men, ready to shoot if he made the wrong move, but he did not know there was a ransom on his head. Later, he remembered "a bitch from below, Merlo's sister-in-law, with a look in her eye [that] meant she was after whatever rewards . . . she was prepared for the partigani."

"Seguici, traditore!" Ezra slipped the Confucius into his pocket and picked up the Chinese dictionary. He didn't know where they were taking him or for how long, so he wanted to take some work with him. The partisans gave him only enough time to lock the door and toss the key to Anita Pellegrini, the peasant woman who lived on the ground floor. Anita watched as he stooped to pick up one eucalyptus pip from the *salita* that goes up from Rapallo (Canto 80) and make a gesture with a hand at his neck to mimic a noose before they led him away.

When Olga returned and discovered Ezra gone, she hurried to the downstairs floor with the olive-press where Anita, through her tears, told her about the partisans' raid: "They have taken il poeta to Zoagli!" Olga did not delay to ask more questions, or to change from the light spring suit she was wearing, but hurried to the village on the other side of the hill, a half hour's walk.

The coastal bombardment had left Zoagli deserted by its inhabitants. "I was glad to see English troops quartered at Sem Benilli's castello, a local landmark," she recalled. "Gee, it was good to see those ugly British mugs again!" She discovered Ezra in the makeshift partisan headquarters, calmly studying the ideograms of Confucius in the book he had brought along in his back pocket. He was guarded by a posse of armed men and one civilian who, she assumed, was the new *sindaco*, or mayor, of Zoagli. She was surprised when the *sindaco* addressed her in the second-person singular "thou" form—*chi sei?*—"a most unusual familiarity." (In Mussolini's time, the old-fashioned *lei* was considered servile; after the war *voi* was banned as Fascist.) The *sindaco* had been questioning a Fascist prisoner. When he focused on Pound, Ezra asked to be taken to the American Command in nearby Chiavari to explain his position.

Olga was determined to go, too. "It was then one o'clock. I asked permission to go back to the British headquarters at Sem Benilli's to beg for something to eat." As Ezra later recalled the incident to Mary: "In the midst of the flurry, your sainted progenetrix [appeared] with DEElicious ham sandwiches. And if anyone says beer cans cannot be opened with a bayonet, they lie."

At four o'clock a car was requisitioned to take Olga and Ezra to Chiavari. The driver could not find U.S. Army headquarters, so he dropped them off at the partisan prison. The officer in charge recognized Ezra as *il poeta, amico d'Italia,* and refused to take him in without a written order. Pound still believed that as soon as the American authorities heard his side of the story, charges against him would be dropped. He asked to be taken to the U.S. Command to state his case, and Olga stuck with him. From Chiavari, they went by army jeep to Lavagna, where the occupying G.I.s were lounging about, fraternizing with Italian civilians who appeared happy to see them. The walls were covered with blood; in Olga's words, "They [the partisans] had been paying off old scores."

At U.S. Army headquarters, they found someone who had heard of Ezra Pound, the poet—the officer in charge, Colonel Webber—but the colonel didn't know what to do with him. He asked if they were hungry, and the K-ration box lunches tasted "very good indeed" after wartime shortages. Then he ordered them taken to the Counter Intelligence Center (CIC), a modern office building in the center of Genoa.

Earlier, in Zoagli, Olga had overheard two partisans discussing Casa 60, and she guessed they might have broken into her house. She asked Colonel Webber if he would send orders to the *sindaco* to protect her property. Olga was surprised at the new political pecking order: when the colonel gave the order to his Italian subordinate, the boy responded with a Communist salute.

It was getting dark at about seven o'clock when they arrived in Genoa. A young officer escorted them into a large hall with two *carabinieri* guarding the door and ordered them to sit down and wait. The straight-backed office chairs grew harder as the hours went by, Olga remembered. "In the distance, in another room, I could hear people crying, God knows what they were doing to them. It got to be nine, ten, eleven o'clock. We were left there *all night,* just sitting on those hard office chairs."

The next day, they remained in the same hall without food or drink and without speaking to anyone until, at 4:30 in the afternoon, two soldiers escorted Ezra into another office for questioning. He didn't return until seven. More K-rations for dinner. Then they were moved to an adjoining room, where Olga passed an uneasy night on a sofa, Ezra on two easy chairs pushed together.

She would recall those four days in a letter to James Laughlin as "among *the happiest of my life,* when I shared His cell (a waiting room in a business office) and emergency rations . . . incommunicado in the same room with Ezra."

The next morning, the *carabinieri* guard returned to heat water in tins for hot bouillon and coffee ("the first we had had in years"), and Ezra asked to send telegrams—to Dorothy, to Olga's brother Teddy, to their daughter Mary. He was taken away for another two and a half hours of questioning by Major Frank L. Amprim, who was later to figure prominently in the Ezra Pound case.

Ezra felt that he could talk freely with Amprim; at least there was a chance to explain his views to someone who understood what he was talking about. He was unaware that Amprim was not an army officer but an undercover FBI agent from the U.S. Department of Justice, sent to Rome to deal with war crimes.

Olga was feeling ill and asked to see an American doctor, but her request was ignored. At four o'clock, still weak, she was led in to be questioned by Major Amprim. When she told him she wasn't well, he released her after only a few questions. He had a friendly and patient manner, and took careful notes.

Olga and Ezra were left alone to talk privately between sessions. "It was your mother who saved me from stupidities . . . she was blessed with more sense of reality than I," Pound later wrote Mary. "It was her intelligence in making me see that I should not babble and joke about being 'the American Lord Haw-Haw'."

On the morning of May 6, while Ezra was undergoing another three hours of interrogation with Amprim, Olga asked for an Italian newspaper. She discovered in *Tribuna del Popolo* that Pound had been condemned as a traitor *in contumacia* (by default) by the U.S. government. When Ezra was led back to the waiting room, she told him the news. Naively, both were astounded that his broadcasts on Rome Radio, which he felt he had undertaken in good faith to enlighten listeners about the folly of U.S.

engagement in the war and the misguided economic policies of the Roosevelt Administration, were considered treasonous.

At two o'clock on May 7, Amprim called Ezra for yet more questioning. Afterward, he offered to drive Olga to Sant'Ambrogio. At Casa 60, he rifled hastily through Pound's papers and took some of the files with him. "The Major told me I must be prepared to testify in case there was a trial," Olga remembered. He offered to carry a few of Ezra's books back to Genoa, and restocked Olga's larder with rare items she had not seen since the beginning of the war: coffee, milk, and sugar.

After Amprim's departure, Olga went downstairs to question Anita, who told her that the partisans had returned to Casa 60 on the afternoon of May 3 after Pound had been taken away. When they attempted to get into Olga's apartment with ladders, Anita held them off until Dorothy Pound returned from Rapallo. They forced Dorothy to open the door. She was surprised that the partisans carried away only one old scrapbook of newspaper clippings, Pound's articles on political and economic topics from the Fascist journal *Meridiano di Roma*. Dorothy's diary entry for May 3 was brief: "They took *him* away today." Two days later, tired of waiting, she packed a small suitcase and walked down the *salita* to stay with Isabel Pound at Villa Raggio.

At Casa 60, Olga began putting Ezra's papers in order, hoping to find something useful for his defense. When Major Amprim returned a week later, his manner was still relaxed and friendly; he asked if he might stay for lunch. He was apologetic when Olga said she had only bread and coffee with milk from the army commissary. He returned Ezra's files, but took the old Model 90 Remington typewriter with the damaged *t* that Ezra had been working on. He reminded Olga that no one—not even the next of kin—could see or communicate with Pound until further notice.

The investigation was continuing. Olga waited for several anxious weeks with no communication from Ezra. Finally, on the morning of May 24, when she telephoned the CIC to inquire, the officer in charge told her that Pound had left under armed guard that same morning— destination unknown! Two days later she received a typewritten note dated May 24, postmarked Genoa: "Ziao . . . Talk is that I may go to

Rome oggi. Naturally hope to be able to pass via Sant'Ambrogio and get your news."

Ezra believed he was on the first leg of the journey to Washington via Rome when he was handcuffed to a black prisoner ("a murderer!" as Olga learned later) and loaded into a jeep by the military police. The caravan passed through Rapallo, but he was not allowed to stop or to leave messages.

The commanding officer, Lieutenant Colonel John L. Steele, was away from the camp in Pisa when they brought Pound in, and the officer in charge did not recognize the new prisoner or know why he was there. Cabled instructions from Washington called for "utmost security measures," with an added warning to "prevent escape or suicide." Strict orders were followed. Pound was issued an army fatigue uniform and told to remove his belt and shoelaces. A guard shoved him roughly into a corner cell with strong steel mesh used to make temporary runways for aircraft. Ezra said later that it reminded him of the gorilla cage in the Roman zoo. "They thought I was dangerous, a wild man . . . they were scared of me," he boasted to young acolytes at Saint Elizabeth's Hospital. "Soldiers used to come up to the cage and look at me. Some brought me food. Old Ez was a prize exhibit."

Army rations were shoved through the bars once a day; a can in the corner of the cage, seldom emptied, served as a latrine. When night came, and with it rain, one of the guards gave Ezra several blankets, but these offered little comfort on the damp concrete floor. Powerful overhead floodlights glared all night; it was impossible to sleep. The searing Italian sun bore down all day. He would later write in Canto 83:

No man who has passed a month in the death cells
        believes in cages for beasts.

After several weeks of good behavior, Pound was allowed a pup tent inside the cage to protect him from sun and rain. The sixty-year-old prisoner exercised daily, playing imaginary tennis and boxing to keep fit, but he began to feel dizzy and claustrophobic. The camp psychiatrist was called in. "Due to his age and loss of personality resilience, prolonged exposure in the present environment may precipitate a mental break-down," was his report. Pound was moved to the medical compound and given a standard-issue army tent. July came and went, but there were still no orders to return the prisoner to the United States.

Olga remained at Casa 60, not knowing where Ezra was—in Italy or America—trying desperately to get news of him. In the cage at Pisa, Pound was thinking of her when he wrote:

> O white-chested martin, God damn it
> 　　　　as no one else will carry a message,
> 　　say to La Cara: amo. (Canto 76)

Olga asked Ezra's young friend John Drummond, then a lance corporal in the British Army stationed at Allied Commission Headquarters in Rome, to make inquiries. When Drummond hunted down Major Amprim, he was somewhat reassured: "He [Amprim] appreciates EP's sincerity, integrity, and genius, but [will allow] no communication between Pound and his loved ones," he reported. Amprim was not permitted to tell where the prisoner was being held. Shortly after Olga received the May 24 note from Ezra, Dorothy, as next of kin, received her first letter. Remembering their wartime hardships, he had added a postscript: "Please see that Olga has enough money." It must have been difficult for Dorothy, but she took the initiative in writing: "I am enclosing one of the thousand lire notes that I found in his room soon after he was taken away. This, as you may remember, was *his* money, not mine. We never had a joint account at the Chiavari Bank. Mine [in London] is blocked."

Throughout that long summer, the two women exchanged polite notes at the Café Yolanda, a central meeting place in Rapallo. When Olga went to Genoa to send messages to Ezra from both of them, Dorothy protested. "That trip to Genoa was not a joy ride," Olga reminded Dorothy, angered by her pettiness; "I went 20 hours without food. . . . It is of vital impor-tance to safeguard E's reputation in every way . . . that cannot be done by bickering among ourselves or showing anything but a united front to strangers."

Their correspondence resumed a more cordial note on June 14 when Olga sent peace offerings, and Dorothy thanked her for "the home-baked loaf and the book you sent." She enclosed another lire note for Olga, "as I am expecting some money from England before too long."

Olga wired her daughter, still with her foster family in the Tyrol, explaining the seriousness of Ezra's situation. Mary said she was "very upset by your telegram. . . . The war is over, but I have never been in such an agitated state of mind as these last months." The U.S. Army had moved into the area, "some nice Hawayan boys, [who] have really charming manners, and some have fine Japanese aristocratic features. It must be lovely in Maway [Maui], they tell me." She was hoping to hitch a ride with them to Merano, and hence take the train Rapallo. "Everybody is scared of the Italians," she added, "and hope other Americans or English soldiers will come soon."

In July, Olga sent another welcome gift of food to Villa Raggio. Dorothy was glad to hear that "Mary is safe . . . the Old Lady [Isabel Pound] has asked several times for news of the child." She had reclaimed the via Marsala apartment from the occupying U.S. Army but decided to give it up. She would keep a room there for household goods, and she asked Olga to pack and send down Ezra's large brown suitcase with personal items. The books, still in packing cases, were left in his room at Casa 60.

In late August, Dorothy received official notification that Ezra was being held at the Detention Training Center at Pisa, where he had been all the while—one hour from Rapallo. Only she, as next of kin, was permitted to visit. On September 28, after "an awful journey," she was allowed to see Ezra for only one hour. His tent had a view of the mountains, she wrote Olga, and the camp doctor appeared "intelligent." "He [Ezra] looks wonderfully well in khaki, with plenty of woolens underneath, and army boots . . . food good, weight normal. . . . He is working on Confucius and has done some more Cantos . . . allowed to *receive* correspondence, subject to censorship, but only permitted to write to *me*."

Olga complained to John Drummond: "I just had a letter from D. [with] a detailed account of his woolen underwear, but no mention of important matters, such as whether he will conduct his own defense." On October 9, she wrote Ezra: "It's hard writing into the blue, never knowing whether you get it and having no answer. If I could only do something for you . . . but things go contrary for the moment . . . the depressing influence of Saturn 'til next March! I expect He will be out waving his wild tail again before long, *outside* the barbed wire of the DTC and *inside* the domestic reticolate [barbed wire]. The child [Mary] exhorted me to be a 'good loser' . . . reminded me of Violet Hunt's story of how you consoled her when [Ford Madox] Ford left her: 'You will soon be old, and then you won't care.' "

She added news of their mutual friends in Paris, lost during the war years: Jean Cocteau, Louis Aragon, Paul Valéry (all dead). Jacoboleff, whom she had met at Capri with Lindy Shaw-Paige in the 1920s with his *amante* Nadine Witowski, had joined Pétain's Vichy government during the Occupation. The Princesse de Polignac (dead, too), had left the Canal Grande Palace to her nephew, the Prince of Monaco. She was beginning to view Pound's enforced confinement as a mixed blessing: "I felt it the best thing they could have done for the *Cantos*, to shut you up for awhile. She is glad he has begun to sing again."

Ezra's situation improved when Lieutenant Colonel Steele, a Harvard graduate and former professor of economics at Boston University, returned from home leave to his post as commanding officer of the camp in Pisa. He was aware of Pound's reputation as a poet and had studied his theories of economic reform. He was also acquainted with Pound's friend in Rome, the poet-philosopher George Santayana. Under Steele's benign influence, Ezra was allowed to write on the old office Remington in the medical unit, punching away with his index finger, accompanying himself with a high-pitched humming sound. With no library but a well-stocked mind, he completed his finest work, the *Pisan Cantos*. Supplies were often short, and Pound used whatever scraps of paper he could find; parts of Canto 74 were composed on sheets of toilet paper. It was his custom to send the new Cantos to Dorothy, who forwarded them along to Mary (who had joined her mother in Sant'Ambrogio) to type clear copies. "EP has been singing in his cage, all right," Olga said, when a third large brown envelope arrived at the Café Yolanda on October 15.

Several days later, Olga went with Mary to the Yolanda to meet John Drummond. A very young G.I. entered the cafe, "whether by design or chance." He had dark hair and wore glasses and looked a bit shy. Drummond called him over to make the introductions. "So this was Omar!" Mary exclaimed. It was the first time Olga and Mary had met Dorothy's son, then in the U.S. Army of Occupation and on leave in Rapallo with his mother.

Drummond suggested that Mary, as Pound's minor child, should apply to visit Ezra at the detention center. Permission was granted for thirty minutes, once a month, but did not include her mother. Olga went anyway. In 1945, army jeeps traveled along the ancient via Aurelia where oxen had once been the principal beasts of burden, creating an almost continuous cloud of dust. Near the village of Metato, just north of Pisa, the U.S. Army had improvised the Detention Training Center for the Mediterranean Theater of Operations. The camp was surrounded by a half mile of barbed-wire fence held in place by concrete gibbets, with guard towers spaced at intervals. In this grim setting, Olga and Mary found Ezra.

"I'm very glad I followed your advice to the letter and asked only permission for Mary, result being that I was allowed in, too—as a *favor*, I have no *right!* Instead of the regulation half-hour, we had two-and-a-half," she wrote John Drummond.

She described their visit to James Laughlin: "Mary and I saw EP on October 17th. He is being well-treated and is in better health than before. He had got very thin on a war diet . . . now he has put on weight and is very calm and cheerful . . . looks younger than his age." Mary, more realistically, described Babbo in his cell as "grizzled and red-eyed," in a U.S. Army—issue shirt and trousers, unlaced shoes without socks, but with "his old twinkle and a bear hug."

Olga had not been back to the calle Querini since the war's end, and a serendipitous offer of transportation enabled her to go to Venice. "I wouldn't have undertaken such a trip . . . except suddenly a soldier friend arrived with a jeep and a few days leave, which gave us a chance to lay eyes again on the 'divine mud puddle' (as you call it)," she wrote Count Chigi. "My little house [was] emptied of the most important part of its contents . . . [but] things are beginning to go better for us now. I have finally received some money my brother sent six months ago."

Though Olga appeared cheerful, there was a dark current running through her correspondence. She had heard on the BBC that William Joyce, "Lord Haw-Haw," the British propagandist for the Nazis, had been condemned to death; his appeal had been heard on October 12. Joyce, who had been born in Brooklyn of an Irish Roman Catholic father and English Protestant mother, considered himself a true patriot, the messiah of a powerful new ideology that would restore an effete England to an idealized and heroic state. His broadcasts from Germany during the war fascinated—and infuriated—the British public. There were many parallels with Pound, who always considered himself a patriot trying to educate and enlighten misguided Americans who supported Franklin Delano Roosevelt's New Deal.

Olga wrote to her old friend Blanche Somers-Cocks, who had recently returned to Venice from Asolo, where she had been sitting out the war, that "E's position is very different . . . he never accepted orders as to what he should say. . . . I can't understand the length of time taken in deciding on E's trial. Yet I am told that time is working in his favor. One gets so little news. It seems ridiculous planning, when we might be pitchforked over to the States at any moment."

Ezra was pitchforked over to the States far sooner than she imagined. One quiet evening, on November 16, 1945, Pound was reading in the medical unit when two officers entered and told him to get together his gear—in only one hour, he would be flying back to Washington. He was escorted from the camp in the custody of two MPs, and not permitted to send messages to either Dorothy or Mary.

On November 23, the day before Mary's next scheduled visit, she and Olga walked down to Rapallo to make arrangements for transportation to Pisa. Olga wrote Ezra how she had learned of his departure for the States: "By chance, I had gone into the little sweet shop near the Castello, and the woman showed me the paper. . . . it was a great blow, not seeing you before you left. I can't imagine you in such a place . . . you are still *here* on the salita with me." It would be thirteen years before Olga and Ezra walked the *salita* together again.

In December 1945, Pound's temporary address was Cell Block 1, Cell 216, District of Columbia jail, from which he wrote to Mary, "vers de Noël": "Dearest child: Tell your mother I bless the day I first saw her, and

thank her for all the happiness she has brought me, a gleam of hope . . .
[but] *first must you go the road to hell* . . ."

James Laughlin described to Olga the situation as he viewed it on
January 4, 1946: "Poor E's predicament is a perfect symbol of what is
wrong with our 'civilization.' EP is now in St. Elizabeth's Hospital, and
there is little danger of his being brought to trial. The four doctors who
examined him—three appointed by the court, and one retained by us—all
agreed that he was seriously ill and unable to prepare his defense. . . . I feel
certain that after things cool down a bit the charge [of treason] will be
dropped, and later he will be let out. . . . The news of his illness will be
shocking to you, but I feel that it is providential. Had he been brought to
trial now, there is not a chance in the world . . . but they would have hung
him. . . . The mob is blood-hungry for victims and . . . there is nothing that
the little band of powerless intellectuals can do about it. . . . Fifty years
from now 'history' may well have stepped in and straightened the record a
bit, but that won't help the man who gets hung in the heat of the moment."

13

What Thou Lovest Well Remains

1946–1949

Like so many others, Olga was putting the pieces of her life back together after the war. Count Chigi urged her to return to the Accademia. La Scala in Milan was staging a new production of Vivaldi's *Juditha Triumphans* with conductor Antonio Guarneri (who had sent the academy five thousand lire for rights, to be added to their scholarship fund). "We will take up our work again . . . renewed and revitalized."

Mary, who had been in Sant'Ambrogio since Ezra's capture, returned to her foster family. She wrote to her father at St. Elizabeth's: "I am now convinced that it is best for me to become a good farmer. That will not interfere with my literary interest . . . I am not able to make mother understand this . . . she insists on my getting 'culture' before I become a farmer." On the first page of the journal she left behind, she had inscribed a quotation from Shylock's daughter's lines in *The Merchant of Venice:* "Farewell; and if my fortune be not crost / I have a father / you a daughter, lost." Olga recalled some thirty years later that it was "the *only* thing she left me before returning to Gais . . . if she intended to *hurt*, she succeeded."

The political situation in the Tyrol was still tense; the Austrian movement to take back the territory annexed by the Italians in World War I accelerated. Easter week saw a renewal of the old rites of spring, mostly pagan. Twelve villages assembled in Gais, with bearers of the cross dressed in Tyrolean costume. "Work in the fields is dropping little by little," Mary wrote. She had been to market to buy sheep with Herr Marcher, and "in the evening I enjoy the Tragic Muse." The "daughter lost" sent her mother gifts of butter, speck (bacon), a pair of socks, and wool for mending.

Olga shared her life in Sant'Ambrogio with Ezra. Her days, she wrote, "all seem much the same. In [the] morning, correspondenza; afternoon, downhill for three lessons . . . at noon, a sandwich tostato from the delicatessen (pastry better than pre-war) . . . translated a love letter into English for the cameriera of the lavandaia, then back to Rapallo to a devoted pupil, served *real coffee* . . . making enough to keep fed. . . . for 200 [lire] a day, one should be able to have meat, eggs and fish . . . [but] most of my pupils [pay] at old prices, and I don't know how to ask them to pay more."

Olga again focused her attention on Mary, who announced her intention to marry a young man she had met at Princess Troubetzkoi's picnic while visiting Ezra in Rome, Boris Baratti. He was the half-Russian, half-Italian scion of a family with "rickety titles," in Mary's words, and at the time of their courtship, penniless. He was, in Olga's view, a most unsuitable suitor.

There were heated discussions, and in April, Mary seemed to capitulate. To Olga, she wrote: "If you have some advice to offer me, I'll be grateful for it. I am feeling more sensible now. . . . When I first kissed Boris, I knew nothing about his title. I knew only that he was more clever than anyone else I had met—except Babbo, of course, he has no par." She confided that "Frau Marcher is not pleased at the idea of marriage because we are too young."

While Boris was visiting Gais, the young lovers discovered a castle near Mary's birthplace and began to dream of making it their home. Mary described the situation to her mother: "I took B. there and told him it was a pity such a nice old place should fall in the hands of a rich butcher in Bruneck who wants to make a hotel out of it. . . . He said it would be much better if *we* could have the castle . . . he would try to convince his father, a businessman mixing in politics (a monarchist). . . . His mother [is] a Russian princess who met B's father in Capri (she 20, he 25). At that time, B.'s father [was] very rich. They married, [had] three children—B.'s the eldest. The parents [are] not on very good terms . . . [his mother] is a very good painter, but a bit mad, keeping extravagant company, saying, 'My greatest mistake was to marry and to have children—I was born to be an avventuriera.' . . . His father [is] a more sentimental type. B. is on his father's side . . . has his own studio in Rome to avoid family scenes."

When Boris told his father he was going to see Ezra Pound's daughter, his father asked, "Why Mary *Rudge?*" Boris had heard about Mary's background from Princess Troubetzkoi, who told his father that Mary had used that name for convenience during the war. When Mary met Boris's mother in Capri, the mother said, "Scommetto che mi ha fatto nonna [I bet he has made me a grandmother]!" Mary confessed to Olga, "B. has not exactly been a 'good boy' up to now, but that does not worry me, because he has been frank about it."

In September, she visited Boris's father in Rome, and Olga went with her to look into the "state of affairs." She described Boris's studio to Ezra as "the room a young man in 1880 would have thought the latest thing— incredibly bad oil paintings, a female nude, a few old swords and daggers, worm-eaten panels of 'primitives.' " Boris's background, in her view, was equally unimpressive: "Friends of the Count's high up in monarchist and Vatican circles looked up [the] family. They are not known . . . no money. The father, and the son to a certain extent is beginning to take after him, is a very voluble talker, full of the most extravagant ideas, impossible to realize."

Ezra reminded her of his experiences as a young man about town in London: "minor follies, provincial taste, poses, etc . . . cd/ be mere juvenilia, but . . . if he is a liar, basta finito, & let M. find it out in time. . . . If you want to distract the child, you might take her to England—classic procedure—remove the young fem[ale] with an 'unexpected' invite to Spondon." On the other hand, "if the y[oung] m[an] is healthy & can support her that's a start—after two wars, males are scarce."

Olga confided in Count Chigi, who cautioned: "I will be so bold as to counsel you to use a lot of tact with your Mary . . . in the young the more love is thwarted the stronger it grows! Like those plants which, the more one prunes their small branches, the more their roots spread and take hold. . . . Pretend to go along with M's desire to get married, only asking her to wait a bit longer . . . buying time is the only possible weapon." If this tactic failed, he offered the Chigi chapel for the wedding with himself as *padrino*.

Mary agreed that "the wedding would be very beautiful in the chapel, very intimate." But as soon as Olga left Rome, the young couple decided not to wait for a fancy wedding in Siena. "Boris and I walked up to the Campidoglio, sighed with relief on seeing our marriage banns posted, and laughed over the ridiculous fuss and clamor." Between publication of the banns and the wedding, they planned to go to Gais for another look at the *castello*. The Marchers were preparing to kill a sheep for the celebration, and were disappointed when the young couple failed to appear. Olga next heard (from John Drummond in Rome) that the marriage vows of her only child and Boris had been exchanged October 17 and duly registered in the sacristy of the Church of San Saturnino.

Olga poured out her heartbreak to Ezra. "When I saw them in Rome, I was very much against a religious marriage," she wrote, for her lifelong belief in signs of the zodiac had warned her against it. "This whole affair started under cattive stelle . . . a bad Saturn, when Cancer women come under [the] influence of unworthy men." She cited the wedding registration at San Saturnino, and 17, a bad number for that date.

Ezra answered on his new stationery with the letterhead "J'aime, donc je suis" (borrowing from Descartes' "Je pense, donc je suis"): "Waal, she has done all she cd/ to impede Sprig & thazzat. . . . in my present [position], don't see that [I] cd. have done more than emit a few cautions. 1. git health certificate—you need 'im 'ealthy—fer kids. 2. Some brains, soz not to be bored to death. 3. a gent, fer various raisins. . . . I also said nuts re/ titles being eyed, that ain't the point anyhow."

The Count invited Olga to return to the Accademia as director of the new Vivaldi Library, and her life in Siena resumed its hectic pace. The Center for Vivaldi Studies opened on November 4, 1946, and the *Bollettino* praised "the Center's intelligent and hard-working Secretary [who] has earned wide acclaim for these studies . . . [and] the first Thematic Catalogue of Unpublished Vivaldi Concerts." Yet she felt that her exhausting labors often were unappreciated by the Comitato Coordinatori, the triumvirate of Luciani, Casella, and Mortari.

She had not given up the battle to go to the States, but the Count advised patience, "especially if the Poet counsels you against it. You would risk leaving needlessly, and once there, being of no help, even a source of added worry for him."

Olga persisted. "I can't understand you making *no* reference to my coming," she wrote Ezra. "If you don't want me, for God's sake, say so."

His answer left no doubt: "Yes, he wd/ be pleez to see her ANYWHERE OUTSIDE this continent. But SHE damn well NOT set foot in this country . . . has she ever heard of the last Depression. . . . When a man is down a wellhole, you don't help by jumpin' in on top of him."

Olga resigned herself to enjoying the diversions of Tuscany. En route to an attractive old *tenuta* near Cotormignano that had once been visited by King Victor Emmanuel, she was driven through "the most beautiful Sienese country, side roads bordered with quercia, yellow and red," and "the bridge Tolomei crossed when being sent to the Maremma, a very high one arched over the Rosia."

The next day, she stopped at Francesca Frost's Castel del Diavolo in Florence, "tower and sala, very old—had been used by contadini as a stalla—on a hill in an orto of olives." The villa had been reconstructed before the war by a German-American painter, and Francesca's room, with a raised platform bed, was "suitable to act a Shakespeare play in." It was a twenty-minute walk from the center, "can't bother to wait for transportation, the bridges all broken [by wartime bombs], trams are more trouble than comfort." Some of the street names in Florence had been changed since the war, she wrote, even the Piazza Vittorio Umberto. "The Florentines are blue about the condizione di pace, they hate the English! It is beginning to unite them."

She motored in style with the Marchesa Fabiola to the Count's "annual feed for the seventeen Contrade, each rappresentante of [a] Contrada found mille lire under his serviette. . . . His Nibs [Count Chigi] is 67, talks about belle gambe a lot, and goes to sleep in his chair after dinner, snoring loudly—very disconcerting from someone . . . so very stiff and proper."

She had accompanied the Count to a screening of Walt Disney's *Fantasia*, "an amusing Mickey Mouse to music of *Apprenti Sorcier*, conducted by Stokowski, incredibly *cabotin*" (Olga's almost untranslatable French word for deliberately affected, or "ham" acting). The Count was a great aficionado of American films—in his youth, of Ziegfeld Follies girls—and liked to consider himself au courant in all things American. He would avidly thumb through copies of the *Saturday Evening Post*, then the most popular American magazine, though Olga suspected he could not read a word of English.

Olga took leave from the Accademia for a few days in the new year of 1947 to see to her calle Querini house and to call on old friends in Venice. Blanche Somers-Cocks, recently returned to the Palazzo Bonlini, gave a vivid account of the wartime vicissitudes of the British colony in Asolo. Olga learned that her house had been rented to Dottore Francisco Giacomelli for 250 lire a month; then Guido Talloni, an artist who once painted Pound's portrait, was put into the house by the Fascist authorities. She wrote to the officer in charge of war reparations, Major G. K. Cavanaugh: "I take it that Dr. Giacomelli's agreement to sublet my house to Sig. Talloni till December 15, 1945, cannot be considered binding?" She had left valuable books, household linen, china, et cetera in a locked cupboard, and asked if an inventory had been taken: "If my house has been dismantled to allow someone to store their own furniture in it, I see no reason why I should be expected to accept their valuation of the house *un*furnished."

Back in Siena, she passed along news of the political situation: "The new regime is going to split into 12 dipartimenti. . . . Siena and Grosseto is the Lega dell'Ombrone, and Siena [is] agitated lest it comes under Firenze. Professor Vannini is a very ardent supporter of a Sienese republic, with the Count as first President. A great deal of joking re. same: the Count being monarchist, Vannini anarchist, and me, republican (1st, as American; 2nd, as Irish; 3rd for Vivaldi and repubblica Veneziana)."

Ezra suggested that the Accademia might consider producing his second opera, *Cavalcanti,* based on the *Sonnets and Ballate* of the thirteenth-century Tuscan poet Guido Cavalcanti, whose works Pound had translated and published in 1912 (including the familiar stanza, "Donna mi prega"). When composing the new score, he heeded Olga's advice: it would not be as difficult to perform as *Le Testament,* with simple 4/4 rhythm and bel canto flow. But "economia is the order of the day," Olga reminded him, and since her present job was what one might call a sinecure, "it was not for her to scare the amministrazione by suggesting further expenses."

She described the picturesque scene in winter: "snowing again in Via di Città . . . the girls and young men caught without hats look very bal poudre. . . . chat at meal times (quite Shakespearian) between His Nibs and the butler, Sabatino—considered an oracle on the weather by reason of his corns! The Count likes to mimic his way of talking, like a dog with a sore throat barking in Sienese. . . . The Marchesa spends three hours a day on crossword puzzles, three hours at cinema, and three hours solid gossip on family affairs of Sienese and Florentine aristocracy—a little goes a long way!"

She had not been with Ezra for almost two years and was relieved when a long-awaited letter from the U.S. vice-consul in Florence advised that her passport could be renewed upon presentation of evidence that she had made definite travel plans. But again Pound voiced strong disapproval: "the idea of anybody being ass enough to cross the ocean . . . puts up his blood pressure . . . anybody, who starts for this country under one millun $$ is ipso facto *nuts.*"

Olga was beginning to look back with nostalgia on the Paris years in light of her present position. "She does not doubt what He says about difficulty of life in the States, but has she been treated to such comfort during 15 years at Sant'Ambrogio? He not think it was easy for her, coming from rue Chamfort. . . . I would like to send you a letter of Egerton's (I found in the wreck in Venice). It would show you the kind of thing I *had* and did not respect—karma! I suppose one doesn't get such [a love] twice in a life. . . . I am butting my head against a wall. And He probably getting consolation elsewhere." With rare insight into Pound's personality, she added: "If I am hurt or unhappy . . . your reaction is anger at me . . . you simply don't see—it's as unconsciously done as if you had pinched my finger in a door you had locked."

In Olga's view, Pound's mother would be an asset in the United States when his case went to trial, but she had not been able to find a sponsor. Father Chute had paid 2,025 lire for Isabel's passport to be renewed and made arrangements for her to leave on the June 29 sailing of the S.S. *Vulcania* for New York. But after writing to a number of friends in the Philadelphia area, including the Heacock sisters, to find a temporary residence, Olga found no one who would take her in, and the Presbyterian Home was beyond her modest means. In the end, Isabel "did not feel secure" with the travel arrangements, and having heard from Dorothy that she would be allowed only three fifteen-minute visits a week at St. Elizabeth's, she decided to remain in Rapallo.

Mary was preparing for the arrival of her first baby, Olga's first grandchild, at the Fonte di San Martino Casa di Cura in Merano. She was feeling well, taking long walks to Schloss Tirol. "The nuns tell me the full moon has a strong influence, perhaps [the baby will arrive] in two days."

The child was born at one o'clock on April 8, five days before Olga's birthday. "While I lay waiting, the first bud of the magnolia tree under my balcony burst open," Mary wrote. "I had the moon through the window, a good alleviation of the pains. . . . Babbo has written a boy must obviously be called Walter in honor of Walther van de Vogelweide—today is also [the day of] St. Walter—and Siegfried, for my special predilection for the Nibelungen hero and for Boris's capostipite [founder of the de Rachewiltz family, from which Boris was descended]. . . . The baby has blue eyes and blond hair like Babbo's, a nose like Boris's, and the general opinion is that he looks like me."

Later, after she returned to the schloss: "I am in a continuous state of bliss. . . . Our baby has already grown out of his first-size jackets . . . his bluish color has changed to a bright pink, [he] keeps his eyes open and assumes [a] quaint expression which somehow reminds me of Babbo. . . . The nun in charge is of Gais, she knew me as a little girl."

Olga was back in Rapallo in June, corresponding with the Count: "I found a difficult situation here with old Mrs. Pound . . . however, her broken arm is already mended—87 years old!" Isabel could not stay on at the clinic because they needed her room for more serious cases, and she could not stay at home alone, so the only solution was to take her to Mary, a two-day journey by car. Olga complained to Ezra that the car and chauffeur, the hotel, extra tips for service, and lunch at Bozen "cost as much or more [than] auto-pullman." She wondered "how the Old Lady recounted the trip? . . . His Lady Ma seems to have got surprising strength back to wield a pen."

Isabel's letter to her son focused on the mountain scenery, not the hardship of the journey: "I regret you do not know the wonderful beauty of the road, under the rocky shore of Lago di Garda," she wrote in careful Spencerian hand. Though her mind was still bright, her body had suffered: "One leg refused to function, even with the help of two [walking] sticks. . . . I am too shaky to write, so I shall leave correspondence to Mary, [but] she has too many demands on her time."

Back in Siena for the summer session, Olga observed the Tuscan countryside with an artist's eyes: "Sunday, His Nibs took us out to Viscona, a fattoria [farm] on top of a hill looking over one-half the world—a lunar landscape, now the grain has been cut—the Fontana, a rain-water pond in a crater, blue from the sky . . . on same, 42 white oca swimming and two pair of white bue down to drink in stone troughs . . . a horse and foal, brought out to be shown, a nice cat on the rafters, several hungry-looking cane da caccia tied, and puppies loose, turkeys galore and chickens—the famblies won't keep them in common, but dye them various [colors] and let [them] out loose to eat on threshing-room floor—result, a real palio."

Still unable to travel to Washington, Olga's first act of 1948 was to prepare for publication, at her own expense, a carefully edited selection of Pound's wartime radio broadcasts, to be titled *If This Be Treason* . . . She sent the manuscript to Julien Cornell, Pound's lawyer, for his critique and advice. "I chose talks which I could reprint *entire*. I have not even corrected spelling mistakes. . . . Other[s] . . . it would not be advisable to reprint entire, not because they contain anything treasonable—far from it—but because they might be considered *libelous* . . . [but] anyone unprejudiced reading the booklet would gather . . . that E. was not an 'adulator' of Fascist leaders, had kept his independence."

Cornell advised against distributing the booklet, though he found nothing treasonable in it. After visiting Pound at St. Elizabeth's, he wrote to James Laughlin (who forwarded the letter to Olga): "I had not seen Ezra for about a year, and was impressed with the further deterioration of his mind. His delusions have become more clearly defined. . . . Dr. Over-holser says that he is willing to testify that E. will never get any better, also that he does not require hospitalization."

Laughlin also refused to support *If This Be Treason . . .* "You don't grasp the facts of the situation," he wrote Olga. "It does not matter what E. said over the air. If he had only said Jesus was a good man, it would still be treason if he had been paid to do it by an enemy government, with whom we were at war. That is the whole nub." Eliot, whom Olga consid-ered Ezra's true friend, also registered his dissent: a limited *selection* from the documents would have no legal value for Pound's defense.

Laughlin undertook to help Olga financially: "Ezra has expressed the wish, and D[orothy] has approved, that all his royalties from the books I publish should be paid to you until further notice. I hope you won't make a fuss about taking this money." He had visited Pound, who "said for me to explain that there was much he could not put in his letters to you because they are read. He has enemies on the hospital staff who communicate with the enemies outside—or so he thinks." Dorothy Pound, he reported, had aged a little, "is terribly intense, and completely centered on Ezra. I got the impression that she does exactly what he says, not the other way around."

"The absolute refusal to face facts is a strong family trait," Olga agreed. "Both his mother and Mary show it to a marked degree and D[orothy], I should imagine, has acquired it. . . . I won't make a fuss about taking [this] money, and thank him kindly for the thought, but nothing has happened to change her feeling about using his money at *this* distance." (She did not object to Laughlin's keeping it for her in case of emergency.)

"The reason she would like to come to the U.S.," she wrote Ezra, "was the same that made her leave a comfortable flat and friends in Paris for bare rooms and solitary meals at Sant'Ambrogio . . . but no-one understands her likes and dislikes."

Ronald Duncan, one of the first of the young writers to attend the "Ezuversity," understood. "I have always suspected Cornell and Laughlin of typical Yankee facetiousness," he wrote Olga. "*It is essential that you go to America, and drive through Laughlin's and Dorothy's attitude of acceptance.* There are a vast number of people in the States . . . and I include Dorothy, who relish the situation of having their own pet genius all tied up in the cage. . . . Ezra has only two real friends, that is Eliot and yourself." Duncan explained his position, and Eliot's, to Laughlin: "We both came to the conclusion that Olga was the best thing for Ezra—but what can we do about it? . . . Eliot is the one person of authority who can, as it were, both advise Olga and pull strings for Ezra."

For his part, Ezra's advice was "do as little as posble/ she wdn't if I were out, i.e. she play the fiddle when she wants, but not scratch fer corn. Siena [is] too useful to lose, but not to get buried under."

Back in Siena, Count Chigi was having his portrait painted "in a truly magnificent uniform of the Knights of Malta—red vest, blue-black coat with large white 'X' on shoulder." Olga was again subject to "black melancholy, gets nothing done . . . will try to get a month or so at Rapallo, but the climate and loneliness there is depressing." Mary had been translating sections of Pound's Cantos into Italian, and, in Olga's view, "the child did some good ones, but whether or not she's capable of anything *now* is doubtful."

In early February, Olga had received an urgent *espresso* from Mary: "nonna gravissima." Her grandmother, Isabel Pound, had been ill for three weeks, requiring a nurse at night, and Mary, with no servant to help, had been caring for her in the daytime. Olga telegraphed twenty thousand lire "to save the Old Lady from wanting anything necessary," then took the next train to Bruneck.

On February 14 she wrote Ezra: "glad I went up and did what I could." The "proud Presbyterian peacock" (as Ezra called his mother) had been suitably laid to rest. "Before the Old Lady became unconscious, she asked, 'When will I stop having to be a person?' and said that Homer had come for her."

"If it's any consolation to Him, and it is to me, [she] was fitly arrayed . . . très grande dame [in] a pale pink satin jacket, a lace scarf round her head, then wrapped in a large red Paisley shawl, very Chinese in color, with pine branches laid over her. Mary, Peter [Rudge], and I lifted her into the coffin and screwed down the lid. Then all the boys and the old grave digger carried it to the foot of the steps, and it was dragged down the hill on a sled to the grave, just near the little chapel on same hill as [the] schloss, only lower. I had your cane—the old grave digger took it from my hand to measure against [the] coffin, as he feared he had made [the] grave too small—it was giusto. He started to shovel in earth. But Peter (a year younger than the others, and not so 'clever') said, 'if none of the rest of you are going to say a prayer for her, I will, though I don't know any but Our Father.' So the last tribute paid [the] Old Lady was not in Italian . . . blood is thicker than water."

Back in Rapallo, Reverend Chute was holding a requiem mass for Isabel in the chapel. "You've been a brick," he congratulated Olga. "Without you, [the burial] . . . might so easily have been sordid [but] was turned into beauty . . . not only the sled, but everything she would have liked. E[zra] will approve."

After examining his mother's checkbook and papers at the castle, Olga wrote Ezra: "There is no money *left* . . . Boris has spent thousands on archivio expenses looking up the Baratti family. . . . Mary seems hypnotized with B. He seems to hold the purse."

She wrote Father Chute about her suspicions, questioning the pretentious "crowns and coronets" on Boris's stationery, and enclosing a genealogy signed by "Principe L. Boris Baratti de Rachewiltz, Conte di Lucca, Fossano, Bestagno, and St. Agnes, Signore di Carvere." (Boris claimed he was entitled to use Conte di Fossano until he was twenty-one; after, as *primogenito*, he had the right to Principe de Rachewiltz.)

Father Chute replied that he had seen the couple, and in his view they appeared happy and in love, devoted to their child. "I feel sure Mary has been straight, only inexperienced," he reassured Olga. "She's taken my preachments well." He agreed that "heraldry is an expensive hobby," and suggested that Count Chigi might research the family in the Almanach de Gotha. But "*you*, Olga, are the one [Boris] most wants to impress."

Mary was considering returning to England with her cousin Peter, who had spent the past year in the Tyrol working at the schloss. "I told her not to do anything on the wrong side of the law, i.e., leaving home with Walter without her husband's consent," Olga wrote to Pound. "If she and Boris ever wanted to part she would lose her rights to keep Walter."

Olga vented her bitterness in a letter to Ezra discovered in the archive, evidently reconsidered and never posted: "You were right in not wanting a child. I was wrong. I have been wrong from the start, and no way to clean up the mess. . . . You put j'aime, donc je suis on your note paper. I don't know who you love now. If you loved me, you would have wanted me to come, even to see you five minutes in a corridor. . . . No-one would believe . . . how you humiliated me when I wanted a child, and how I had to choose between it and you. You never noticed it until it was old enough to amuse you. Yes, I know Confucius says you can't reason when feeling resentment. But I feel it. You are now trying to train the young. You showed no such tenderness to me when I was young. Now I am old, and of no use to you."

In spite of her bitterness, Olga was singleminded in her determination to go to St. Elizabeth's. She wrote to Samuel A. Silk, then assistant superintendent, "requesting certain information in re. the patient, Ezra Pound." The reply gives an idea of the poet's adaptation to life in the hospital: "It is Mr. Pound's mental quirk not to face any facts which are not in conformity with his preconceived beliefs . . . he is very cleverly able to distort reality to suit his own purpose. . . . When his ward was taken onto the grounds, he insisted on keeping apart, refusing to sit on the benches reserved for the group. . . . During the early part of his stay, he would lie upon a blanket spread for this purpose . . . but for the past several months, he has had a very satisfactory collapsible aluminum chair, in which he sits on the lawn to take the sun. . . . [He] constantly complains of great fatigue and weakness . . . less evidenced when he is working on his manuscripts in his room alone."

Julien Cornell stated his view of Olga's position in a letter to Laughlin, which Laughlin then forwarded to her: "I am afraid this situation is completely beyond my poor powers as a mere lawyer. I think there is a good prospect that Ezra could be sprung . . . [but] unfortunately for Olga, Dorothy has the whip hand . . . not only the legitimate wife, but also the legal representative of her insane husband, and she has the funds to take care of him, which Olga lacks. . . . I am afraid Olga will have to give him up. Even if she could get to the States, Dorothy might make it difficult for her to see Ezra. The final decision in such matters would be made by Dr. Overholser, who is a sympathetic and tolerant person, but I would not predict his attitude in such a triangular situation."

"I do *not* intend to give E. up," Olga wrote Laughlin, "not because I have delusions of any happy ending as far as I am concerned . . . but because I have a feeling of responsibility." She considered Dorothy incapable of making the necessary decisions that Ezra was in no condition to make himself.

Olga resumed correspondence with Ezra on May 22, passing along the news that Boris had been to London to take Mary back. She accused Ezra of "complete hardhearted ignoring of my feelings," but closed the letter, "with love (if there is such a thing except for note-paper headings)." At this juncture, Pound relented and agreed to her coming, though no definite date was set. "Summer is best, at least [a] chance to sit on the lawn . . . but do it right (with introductions, etc.) . . . from that playboy gal, Francesca [Frost]."

In early July, Olga wrote from Sant'Ambrogio: "She is xxxceedingly triste here alone. . . . He read those [Chinese] odes—the percentage of desolate females is high in them, and no-one telling them it wuz their fault, instead of their misfortune. . . . She has bin practicing a little, and enjoying it." She had played Bach, Pergolesi, and Corelli with Reverend Chute, who always stood by with tea and sympathy. "As for leading the orchestra . . . she no longer has the strength or the illusions. This year, she will be in the second violins [at the Accademia] . . . how much fun will be got by them [students] out of [the] elderly sec[retary] appearing in that capacity!"

Aldous Huxley had been in Siena, "very sympathetic, said he knew you years ago in London with Tom Eliot." Bernard Berenson came twice to lunch; he was trying to raise funds for repairs to San Marco in Venice, "asking $20,000 through the efforts of Mesdames Bliss, Beale, and Bacon, sassiety matrons in Washington . . . got $16,000, but says nothing done for 'Aht' xcept in [the] name of Saint Snobbery."

She described in terse staccato a postwar vignette of the political situation in Siena, where the Communist Party had reigned since the fall of

Fascism. "At a meeting in front of the Monte dei Paschi [Bank], someone threw a bomb, four guardia wounded. . . . The contadini came into Siena, unarmed—their women were waiting for them and handed out bastoni . . . [then] a general strike, everything hermetically shut, Communist posters against the 'Governo degli assassini,' government posters asking population to assist at this morning's funeral." Olga went with the Count to the Duomo, near the headquarters of the Fedel Terra, a peasant Communist association. "The procession had hardly got past the turn which leads to the Via di Città when more spari, people started to run. . . . The Sindaco, a Communist, came to the funeral in his official capacity . . . someone shouted, 'fuori il Sindaco,' which was taken up by the crowd, and shots fired from the Fedel Terra balcony . . . armoured cars came out of the prefettura courtyard, immensely applauded . . . [and] the coffins [were] brought back."

The Accademia opened the fifteenth with half the teachers missing, making it "very hard to concentrate on anything." Peter Russell, one of Ezra's disciples and founder of the Pound Society in London, came to Siena. He had met the poet Eugenio Montale, later a Nobel Prize winner, at a café favored by the Florentine literati, and Montale had launched into a long tale about Pound's red-haired mistress, "well calculated to shock a young Englishman before the days of permissiveness." Russell was inspired to visit Olga. To her eyes, he was "a nice young man—been all 'round Italy following his Cantos, Mantova, Venice, Rimini, etc., I think a 'serious character' " (a term of approval Pound used in Canto 114). Thus began Olga's correspondence with "his enthusiastic Russell," which continued for many years.

"My own problems are becoming less important to me," she wrote Ezra, "[but] the life of a segretaria is a dog's life. One's head continually filled with other people's concerns. . . . Had my violin cleaned, looked over by the lutero here, but I have no time or strength or place to play . . . so much going on, she doesn't know if she is on her head or heels."

At St. Elizabeth's, Ezra remembered "the flurry in Siena, and the 999 things for her to do, and he ain't complainin' about anything save her wasted energies. . . . He prefers her not to waste energy on hack work any peon can do."

She had recovered her sense of humor when she described a new arrival from Bombay who appeared at Count Chigi's board: "The Indienne is . . . out to get H.N. [His Nibs], considers the black head in the Saracini arms symbolic that a black woman will return into the family. . . . She read the Count's hand, gives him six years more . . . says she can renew his youth . . . leaves the drawing room to 'retire' before the others, [and] H.N. will duly conduct *her* with ceremony a quarter-hour later to the Swan Room. So far, the Indienne reports a kiss on the forehead. The problem . . . troubling His Nibs is how to keep the Indienne here without 'keeping' her."

In Olga's view, the Count's obsession with "the Indienne," one of the students at the Accademia, came from his "desire to escape from the lagnanze [complaints] of the now dreary Marchesa, and an element of sadism which delights in tormenting, having something inferior and humble always there to pick on . . . a remarkable man, in spite of all."

Sir Steuart Wilson, then head of programs at the BBC, and his wife, a cellist, were among the distinguished guests at the week-long series of concerts in 1949: "a great relief to meet people who speak one's own language—I don't mean the English language—but who can get one's point of view." The conductor for sacred music was Guido Cantelli, a talented twenty-eight-year-old who later, in 1956, died in a plane crash.

On September 29: "Finito la Settimana! . . . His Nibs does not have the courage to keep the Indienne 'per sempre,' so she is leaving, having charmed everyone. . . . [She] came into the little office where I was writing late at night in a beautiful orange sari and little censer chasing evil spirits with incense!"

An excursion to San Gimignano with the Chigiana Quintette playing in the Sala Dante was a great success, but the Count did not travel with them. He held a strong dislike for San Gimignano that stemmed from when he had been sent there as a youth by his family to separate him from a young sweetheart. To eradicate the memory, he had sold the Torre facing the piazza that he inherited from the Chigi-Saracini clan, and never went back.

Olga found that the hill town had been invaded by Twentieth Century–Fox filming *Prince of Foxes,* a costume-adventure movie notable as one of the first postwar productions made on location in Europe. The piazza was full of their decorations, "festa with floats that must have come from the

Viareggio carnival, some enormous plaster figures on horseback, Walt Disney faces and grotesque plaster heads projecting from the windows of the towers . . . all the population dressed as Italian peasants, the cloister of the Duomo used as a wardrobe department." She asked Ezra to imagine an Italian historical film with Hollywood trimmings and English voices, and "that unspeakable Orson Welles" in the leading role.

In October, Olga arrived in Rapallo after circling around the peninsula for fifteen hours due to a washout. A thunderstorm had blown in during the night, "the like she [has] never seen—continuous flashes." The next morning, she went down to circulate a petition to be signed by the citizens of Rapallo—"clergy, doctors, bank cashiers, shop keepers"—attesting that Pound had never at any time been a member of the Fascist Party. One of Ezra's many friends led her to the barber shop where they accosted customers sitting around in their lather and coerced them to sign on the corner of a dressing table. "Nobody ever thought of Him as a Fascist, but as an American citizen who sympathized with certain things in the [Fascist] regime," she wrote later to Peter Russell.

Olga was starting a translation of Enrico Pea's *Il Romanzo di Moscardino*, but she felt "she let Mr. Pea down badly . . . he was worrying, and Jaz [Laughlin] . . . waiting to publish, [but] she can't work at things like that with her head stuffed with other people's affairs."

In October, Mary and her family moved into their permanent home, Schloss Brunnenburg. A former watchtower for Schloss Tirol (which gave its name to the district), Brunnenburg perches high above the valley of the Adige, a half day's drive from the Brenner Pass. The main tower is Roman, the outside walls eleventh century. In the nineteenth century, an eccentric German added the crenelated turrets that reminded Olga of illustrations in her beloved *Grimm's Fairy Tales*. The schloss had almost fallen into ruin when Mary and Boris moved into one top room of the tower. "[Mary] apparently feels she has done well for herself in life," she wrote Ezra. In the postwar Tyrol, she noted, "they've got Swiss cigarettes hidden under the cows. . . . You can buy Swiss watches cheaper than in Switzerland."

She received news from Count Chigi that the Marchesa Fabìola Lenzoni had died suddenly. "I suppose I shall have to go back to Siena, so as not to lose [my] job and offend Chigi too deeply."

In late fall, at the Castello Alpiano, the Count held court in the *fattoria* dining room for "choice specimens" of the Italian aristocracy. "Marchese Teoduli looks the spitting image of [King] Victor Emmanuel (their arrière grandmère's were sisters)." A magnificent lunch was served, guinea hens roasted on a spit with *salvia* tucked under their wings, dolce with *ʒabaione*, bananas (reappearing for the first time since the war).

In Washington, Ezra was "still laffin'" over the election" of Harry S. Truman. He suggested that Olga invite the President's daughter, Margaret, then making a career as a soprano on the concert stage, to come to Siena as a *Borsa d'Studi Honoraria,* which would increase the prestige of the Accademia in America. Ezra's great friend T. S. Eliot had just been awarded the Nobel Prize, an honor Ezra had coveted in the 1930s but forfeited forever by engaging in the wartime broadcasts.

A letter from Laughlin again advised Olga to delay her visit to Washington: "Ezra for the moment does not want legal steps taken to get him out [of St. Elizabeth's], which might lead to a trial and unfavorable newspaper publicity . . . but he remains absolutely devoted to you."

At year's end, Olga was resigned to her position, with a more realistic understanding of Ezra's character: "She minds being locked *out—mah,* she can't change Him, and she supposes she will have to change herself. She may turn into something He will like better—but then perhaps she might like Him less?"

In his first letter of the year 1949, Ezra mentioned four holidays set aside for the inaugural and parade of President Truman, in spite of "slush, slop, sleet and snow." He congratulated Olga on her very accurate translation of Enrico Pea's *Moscardino,* said she was becoming "a literary chicken as well as musicologist." He hoped she was well paid for her efforts, though he suspected it was "little or nawt?"

Eliot, the loyal friend who had dedicated *The Waste Land* to Pound, "il miglior fabbro," visited St. Elizabeth's in early 1949. "[He] says we may have to wait several years before it is worthwhile trying some new step [for his release]," Olga passed along the news to Peter Russell. "I don't think public opinion is going to get very 'het up' over E. [at St. Elizabeth's]. . . . It's just another place for people to 'go,' makes them smug and pleased with themselves."

She was in Rome to meet Ronald Duncan, another ally, the week of February 16, when Pound was awarded the Bollingen Prize for Poetry and became the center of heated controversy. In 1943, during Archibald MacLeish's tenure as Librarian of Congress, an annual prize for poetry had been proposed by Allen Tate, then consultant in poetry at the Library. The idea was approved under Luther Evans, who succeeded MacLeish, and he thought at once of the Bollingen Foundation, established in 1945 by philanthropist Paul Mellon and his wife, Mary Conover, as a source of funds for the award. The Mellons offered a grant of ten thousand dollars, one thousand of which was to be awarded each year for the best book of verse published during the preceding year, and a body of Fellows in American Letters was named to make the selection. On March 4, 1948, the creation of the Bollingen Prize was announced to the public. A year later, in November 1949 at a meeting of the Fellows at the Cosmos Club, Tate revealed the unanimous choice for the first award, Pound's *Pisan Cantos,* published by New Directions in 1948.

Evans warned that "the reaction would be emotional rather than intellectual." And it was—launched by two long articles in *Saturday Review* by Robert Hillyer. When the *New York Times* of February 20 picked up the story—"Pound, in Mental Clinic, Wins Prize for Poetry Penned in Prison Cell"—Ezra was attacked as pro-Fascist and anti-Semitic in a series of debates in publications of the era. This continued unabated until August 19, when a joint committee of the U.S. House and Senate ruled that the Library of Congress should abstain from giving the award, and administration of the prestigious Bollingen Prize was transferred to the Yale University Library.

Olga was happy to be out of the fray and back in Sant'Ambrogio. She installed the first stove in the cottage in early 1949, and lit the fire in the evening for tea. Other modern conveniences were coming to the hillside villages, and the newly installed electric lights were more to her liking than the gloom of the Palazzo Chigi. "But will he come back *here?* And will he want to *stay* if he does? Or will she find there is someone else? And the little crumb of time she been spending her whole life waiting for, to be divided in still more briciole [tiny pieces]."

Several of Ezra's young disciples were planning pilgrimages to Sant' Ambrogio, and Olga warned Peter Russell before his visit: "Be prepared for a simple life—no thousand dollar vino, no plumbing . . . it's off any carriage road, so bring country boots, old ones, [the] salita is tough on shoes."

Mary Barnard, another young poet who corresponded with Pound and visited him at St. Elizabeth's, had written to Olga: "I saw him in October, he was looking very well . . . allowed to go outside in Dorothy's custody. . . . We had no talk that was unchaperoned . . . I wanted an opportunity to say things about the difficulties of your situation without meddling too much, [but] no chance."

When a package arrived from Eliot for Olga's birthday on April 13—at the time of the eclipse of the moon—she shared the gift with Ezra's young friends in Sant'Ambrogio. "Mary Barnard took 'Mr. Eliot's Spam' as she might have taken the Sacrament, Peter Russell went for the bacon, [D. D.] Paige lapped up the milk," she wrote Eliot. Yet she questioned the sincerity of some of Pound's newly won disciples.

She was bothered most by the presence of D. D. Paige, who had arrived with his wife in 1946, installed himself in the Pounds' former flat on the via Marsala, and started to work on an edition of Pound's letters. Paige, a University of Pennsylvania graduate then teaching at Wellesley College, had visited St. Elizabeth's and gained Ezra's confidence. Olga disliked Paige's intrusion on her privacy. It was Dorothy, she alleged, who had allowed Paige into the via Marsala studio, with access to personal correspondence left in open boxes "without even a string around them. . . . I did not set foot in the via Marsala apartment after 1943 [or] allow Paige access to my flat in Sant'Ambrogio."

In Olga's view, the young Englishman John Drummond was a better friend and more reliable editor. Drummond, then living in Rome, had first come to Rapallo before the war to study with Pound, and he sided with Olga. Pound's bibliographer Donald Gallup, an objective witness who met Paige by chance at the Accademia Chigiana, said he had purchased the carbon copies Pound had made of his letters, which Paige edited for the

Beinecke Library "at Pound's request, to give Paige a little money to operate on." But Paige's transgressions continued to be a sore point between Olga and Ezra.

She wrote Eliot a perceptive critique after the publication of *The Letters of Ezra Pound:* "I am still not convinced about the omissions. Are not 'omissions' just what always show up most glaringly? Won't people . . . think the book one-sided and imagine what has been left out worse than the truth . . . an attempt at whitewash? If some of Ezra's *outrageous* letters were included (many of them date long before his mis-called Fascist period), people . . . would see that E's radio speeches continued a line of talk definitely his *own* over a long period of years, in no sense 'Fascist propaganda.' "

That autumn Mary announced that another grandchild was on the way, expected in late February or early March 1950. "I like a simple and quiet home," she wrote her mother, "and hope I'll be able to go through life without a separation or divorce. . . . I hope Walter and the rest will do all the things . . . I should have done, and that they'll inherit not only [their] grandfather's tendencies, but also his genius. I could wish for nothing better in the way of a child and husband and home."

Boris had obtained two decrees from the Corte d'Apello—the first to legalize the Order of Canossa and Corona di Ferro and title of Principe de Rachewiltz in October 1948, the second to secure diplomatic rights and immunity in August 1949. Ezra approved of the change of surname from Baratti to the titled "de Rachewiltz." In his view, it was "a show of spirit, and last line of defense against rising tide of imbecility, demi-Xtens [Christians], etc." But Olga never could reconcile herself to Boris's pretensions.

At the end of October, she had almost given up the battle to visit St. Elizabeth's. In bitter frustration, she posted this letter: "She doesn't want to let His birthday pass without a word, [but] if He wants to see her, He can arrange to do so. Only the greatest possible sincerity can affect any change." (There was no closing message of endearment.)

Once again, Ezra firmly vetoed her plans: "ARRANGE indeed—az if tickets were free—DEEP sympathy . . . she now Herkules & the Trachinae."

The depressing year ended with the death of Sem Benilli, one of the most important citizens of the little town, "lying in the portineria of his ex-castello." Olga's pessimistic mood was obvious when she quoted this verse from Canto 81: " 'What thou lovest well remains'—does it? Yes, if he means the sun, moon and stars, Mozart sonatas, even solo parti del violin, but one loved them at ten years old, and it seems a big price to go through . . . just to find one has really nothing more than what one started out with."

14

A Visitor to St. Elizabeth's

1950—1955

The Fifties began with new life, and Olga passed along the good news: "Born—Washington's birthday, a granddaughter, Patrizia Barbara de Rachewiltz." The answer from St. Elizabeth's: "*Banzai!* Warn't sure if Mlle. X arrov on 22nd, but thought so—hadn't calculated the Birthington Washday."

Ezra sent other news from Washington: Mrs. Eleanor Roosevelt, the President's widow, was to have her own television show, James Laughlin was in Aspen skiing, Holy Year rates reported in the press at the luxury hotels in Rome, the Hassler and the Excelsior, were a minimal six dollars per day. The ambiance at St. Elizabeth's was often bizarre: "Just received, in a confidential whisper from the Colonel, that 'Hitler' is right here on this ward, going by the name of Jones."

Olga was still lobbying for Ezra's release. She had met Ernest Hemingway in Paris with Ezra in the 1920s, and she recalled this meeting when appealing to "Hem" and other literary friends for help. She received in reply a "peevish letter from Mr. Hemingway":

Dear Miss Rudge:

I will try to be as short, and . . . as blunt as you were . . . You ask what I actually have done for Ezra. I obtained monitorings of Ezra's broadcasts during the war—Ezra was my true friend, and I wanted to see what sort of an ass he was making of himself, so that I might come to his aid when it was necessary. His broadcasts, which contained occasional pieces of excellent sense and brilliance, were really awful, and I saw that there would be a difficult problem whenever the war was over and he was a prisoner.

At the time . . . I was in Germany fighting, my oldest boy Jack was wounded and a prisoner, and I knew nothing of Ezra's fate. When his attorneys wrote me . . . I made a statement . . . that he was of unsound mind when he made his broadcasts after the U.S. entered the war. . . . If Ezra is released at this moment, as of sound mind, to be tried, he would receive a sentence of from ten to fifteen years. . . . He made the rather serious mistake of being a traitor to his country, and temporarily he must lie in the bed he made.

If I were a King or a President or even a divisional commander, I would pardon Ezra instantly, kick him in the ass, ask him to have a drink and tell him to use his head if he has one. But I am only his friend, and can only use my head in his behalf. I hope this answers your questions as bluntly as they were put. To be even more blunt, I have always loved Dorothy, and still do.

Hemingway's letter contributed to Olga's depression; she could not concentrate, was "in a state nervosa." Its closing statement must have wounded her deeply, but she did not admit it when she wrote to Ezra: "Sounds like a hangover—[but] full of expressions of affection for Him."

Mary sent photos of Patrizia's christening. The child's hair, dark at birth, now had a reddish cast like Olga's and Ezra's. "Fotos rec'd. of tribal unity," Ezra wrote; "'tenny rate, yu got a *family*."

Olga joined the family at Brunnenburg for Easter and the April birthdays: "Moidile looking very well and slimming rapidly . . . very efficient with Patrizia Barbara—only baby wot come across wot don't smell!" Mary prepared a *festa* for her mother, complete with the "first birthday cake I've had since before the flood." Olga was happier about their situation: "Them children are living in Paradiso all right . . . Walter [is] a very charming child, great sensitivity to the sound of words." The alpine path was too steep for the little ones to climb, and she was planning to buy a donkey to carry the children from Brunnenburg to Merano. A donkey cost less than a double baby carriage, she considered, and the Count had offered to order the animal from Sardinia through his *fattore*.

Life at the ancient castle was not always an earthly Paradiso. In early June, the dining room ceiling collapsed, breaking furniture and china and smashing a clock, requiring repairs costing more than half a million lire. Uncle Teddy appeared in their time of need, to Mary's eyes, a benevolent genie: "The most sensible man I've ever met. I would say a Saint, if that wouldn't sound funny."

Back in Siena, Olga found the same intrigues and uncertainties, the population doubled, the streets a hell with camions, cars, and vespas, the concerts spoiled by traffic noise. One pleasant diversion from the "zoo" was a performance of Verdi's *Don Carlo* in Florence with Count Chigi.

Referring to the Chigi family motto, *Micat in Vertice* (Shining at the Summit), Ezra queried "if Chigi knows his Mycat, or vortex, is out of Svetorius Caesar's soul risen to heaven—so [the] star allus on top over his statue?"

In July 1951, Olga returned to Paris, her first visit to the "Center of the Universe" since the war; she had been "fearing disappointment at coming back after all these years, but it is . . . more beautiful!" As Suzanne Baumgartner's guest on the rue de La Fontaine in the Sixteenth Arrondissement, she was just around the corner from the rue Chamfort where the concierge, to her surprise, recognized her: "nothing changed, except *me!*"

She was to represent the Accademia Musicale Chigiana at the Third International Congress of Music Librarians (July 22–25) sponsored by UNESCO. A cocktail party hosted by the publisher of a music review, and a visit backstage of the *foyer de danse* of the Paris Opera with congress members, were highlights.

Julien Cornell, Pound's lawyer, was also in Paris, which gave Olga an opportunity to meet with him. A graduate of Swarthmore College and Yale Law School, Cornell was a Quaker, an idealist, and a pacifist, to

Olga's eyes "a curious specimen, but nice—also *hopeful*." Cornell believed in a world federal government to maintain peace, and from the outset he treated Pound's defense as another civil liberties case.

Olga called on many old friends. Nadia Boulanger invited her to an end-of-term fête for her pupils (mostly American). Mabel de Courcy Duncan, recovering from an operation, was "lying, half-sitting, Etruscan-tomb fashion, very thin, cheerful, memory a bit uncertain. . . . Ethel, with ear plugs [hearing aids] now hears, and manages everything." Natalie Barney was still holding court in the rue Jacob salon, "dusted, but not renovated, [and] asked me to lunch, both times alone, [was] able to talk."

The *librairie* in the old neighborhood had expanded to three shops; Olga had first known its owner, Mademoiselle L'Avocat, as a girl of fifteen selling in a tiny bookstore. She was saddened to see the grand salon of the Pomairols on the rue Saint Dominique unfurnished and ruined by dividing walls, "no valets in livery—only one aged employee, who knew nothing about the Pomairols."

The Salle Pleyel, the venue where she had performed in her youth and Pound had presented the concert version of *Le Testament de Villon*, had been remodeled and completely changed, "not *French*, a rag-bag—no Parisians!" She tried to get in touch with Jean Cocteau, sans success, and went to the Opéra, thinking he might be at the rehearsal of his ballet *Phèdre*, then being performed in honor of Nijinsky. But there was no chance of attending the ballet, as the house was sold out. She considered a concert by the renowned violinist Joseph Szigeti "un disastro."

There was a luncheon reunion with that suave man about town Arturo Brown "incredibly the same—only better." The admiration was mutual. Don Arturo complimented her grey hair as very becoming. She pampered herself after so many lean years: "bought meself a hat, a blouse, a pair of dark-blue transparent gloves, elbow length." Everywhere, she was reminded of Ezra: "Now He pull up His sox, and reflect on the possibility of getting here."

After Paris, Olga went on to London. She stopped at Faber & Faber, Pound's English publisher, for tea with Eliot, "very frail, but kind about offering help re. my passport . . . thought it bad for me to be cooped up in Italy." He offered a check for a hundred pounds to pay her expenses, which Olga refused. After a leisurely dinner at the Hotel Connaught, Eliot gallantly saw her home in a taxi. She later attended a matinee of Eliot's successful play *The Cocktail Party,* and admonished Ezra to "encourage His friend, the Possum, who *does* love Him, she *feels* it."

There was a pleasant weekend with Ronald Duncan at his country home, Welcombe, "most beautiful and unspoiled, not even a petrol station, soft air, drizzle of fine rain on one's face." She liked Duncan's wife, Rosemary, and considered the children well brought up. But Duncan's play, *Stratton,* in Olga's view was "a flop!—all these young men trying to do too much and too quickly."

She was staying with Peter Russell in exchange for having put him up at Sant'Ambrogio; he was "a very clever young man, where he will land [is] another matter . . . like [Richard] Aldington (pre-war), as a *Times* critic?"

Next was a family reunion with Teddy and his family at Spondon. Peter, who had been living with Mary in Brunnenburg and working on the farm until a tractor accident injured his knee, was en route home to recuperate when Olga met him at Paddington Station. John, her other nephew, had been sent down from Malvern School "in disaccordance with [the] authorities." Olga complained to Ezra about her talented brother's wasted life, but he wisely reminded her: "A country doctor [is] as useful as just more d—- easel pixchoors—don't see why not as sazfakery a life to the liver."

On the way back to Italy, Olga stopped over in Paris for a night and a day to see the Duncan sisters again, but she was too late: Mabel "died last month shortly after I saw her and was buried at Dinard—Ethel has now *become* Mabel."

Back at the Accademia, she sent the *Bollettino* to press during the heat wave of August, "completely demoralized . . . she never reads a book, hears no music, just talks to people she will never see again." Though she often considered her efforts in vain, she had helped to put the Accademia "on the map." An illustrated article in *Terra di Siena,* a quarterly magazine of Italian tourism, touted its efficient *segretaria* as "la vestale del Centro Vivaldiano." *Time* devoted two columns to the Accademia and Count Chigi, "the last of the truly civilized." Due to Olga's efforts, his eight-hundred-year-old Palazzo housed one of Europe's finest music libraries.

Some 250 young people from thirty countries were in residence that summer; the 70 most talented would study under violinist-composer Georges Enesco, guitarist Andres Segovia, and conductor Paul van Kampen in intensive two-month courses. Olga was putting together a concert of American music, with the Quintette playing the Aaron Copland *Sextet* with clarinet.

Clotilde and Alexandre Sakharoff were teaching a course in dance. Olga remembered attending their performance in Paris with her mother and Teddy, when Teddy was on leave during World War I. "They made the mistake of giving a performance in the Chiesa—poor Alexandre was too old, *ridiculous*."

She outlined for Ezra the crises and trivia of a "Specimen Day" at the Accademia:

9:30 Newell Jenkins, American direttore d'orchestra, re. American concert . . .

10:00 Mr. Wathan—to color-photo various pictures in coll[ection] . . . discovers the Cleopatra, the Vestal Virgin, & the Holy Fambly . . .

10:30 Female from Sweden, with guitar case, ready for Segovia— turn her on to Swiss flautist for musique d'ensemble.

3:30 Photog. arrives, picture taken in "lion" dress, for Him.

4:30 Flautist . . . to play Mozart 4th & C.P.E. Bach quartette . . . best all 'round musician here.

6:00 Count arrives, disgruntled, telegram from Segovia [who] can't come till 1st week Sept.

6:30 Argue with Vannini about putting pressure on R.A.I. [Rome Radio] to broadcast "Intermezzi," *not* the Cimarosa opera . . . try to salvage American program . . .

8:00 We will dine . . . have to change dress and doll up. Sister
Gertrude, American nun, turned up . . . telephoning and
interruptions, one walks kilometri in the Palazzo, but the heat has
broken.

The Direttore dell'Archivio, whom she called "Little" Cecchioni,
amazed her. He was "the neatest and cautious-ist of old bachelors," but he
came in after dinner "incredibly tight." She had never seen anyone drink
to excess in the Palazzo. He talked like an encyclopedia for two hours,
"boiled down to 'the end of civilization in ten years' — doesn't want to wait
to see it, he'd rather be dead," Olga commented, and then added, "*her own
sentiments.*"

In September the violinist and composer Enesco was in residence for a
two-week course, bringing his wife, the Princesse Cantacuzene. "I had
heard of the extreme poverty of their lives in Paris," Olga noted. "His
choice of Siena was due to his being happy to see her again in palatial
surroundings." Enesco had had a heart attack in London two weeks before
the session began and was unable to manage the steps and the long walk to
the violin classroom upstairs. So a room was fitted up for him in a passage-
way on the lower floor; with an electric fan at full blast behind him, he was
able to keep going. His class was crowded with composers and young
orchestral conductors — Antoine de Bavier and the Queen of Belgium
were among those who never missed a lesson — and young Yehudi Menuhin played Bach concertos with him.

The concert of Musica Contemporanea Americana ("wangled after
months of angling") was a great success, and opening night of the Teatro
dei Rinnovati on September 16 recalled evenings with Ezra: "It hasn't
been spoiled by ghiribizzi [Canto 80]," she wrote, "but how can she enjoy
it without Him?"

In November, Olga joined Mary and the family at Brunnenburg: "The
view from the back windows . . . very Chinese . . . where rocks [have]
broken off, a steep ravine with trees, chestnuts, the most beautiful yellow.
Yesterday it rained, they came up out of the mist with Schloss Tirol
perched on top, more beautiful than a sunny day. . . . His daughter a bit on
[the] thin side, but looks better for it. . . . We cut off Walter's topknot in

attempt to give him a real 'Buster Brown' or 'Enfants d'Édouard' cut, pleasing to his ma and grandma, but not to him. . . . I intend getting him a black velvet Russian blouse to wear with his lace collar."

The kitchen, "where we have meals, now it's cold," was a pleasant room with a large basket of red apples from Walter's orchard on top of the white-wood kitchen dresser. A still larger wicker basket held Patrizia, "sitting up and taking notice of boy-blue brother, the kind of picture wot would make some poor painter's fortune as a cover for *Home* magazine — so American!"

To Olga's eyes, Mary was "much more sensible than I ever was, in many ways, older, but she has had wot she wanted with a minimum of waiting, whereas I have been rotted with waiting, and now it [is] too late. She can cut a loss, and I go on sorrowing."

Ezra asked Olga to send a photograph of herself, but she refused: "Why should He want photos of her as she is now? He has left it too long. She doesn't think she would have the courage to see Him now if He *were* here." "Xmas is upon us again," she continued; "not feeling festive, but will make [the] effort for the young."

Early in 1951, Mary left the castle with her cousin Peter when he returned to England. She was beginning to share some of her mother's disillusionment with her marriage. "Nothing has turned up in the way of letting flats . . . no point in my going back, not knowing where the next money [is] coming from. . . . If I have enough patience, Boris will get on to something regular in time . . . he wants me back," she wrote her mother. She had been visiting Oxford, Bath, and Exeter: in Ezra's words, "motoring all over England looking fer [a] farm fer young Peter." "I think she is (quite unconsciously) making a refuge for herself and infants — and could do worse," Olga wrote.

She was at the Palazzo Bonlini with Blanche Somers-Cocks in late February, in Venice to assess the war damages to the calle Querini house. She spent all one day at the consulate and with lawyers, got to the Piazza San Marco in the evening, "just a bit of mist and people hurrying, not a soul she knew — like limbo might be."

In early March, she went to Rome for a long interview with a legal adviser to Americans seeking reparations and submitted a damage claim to the U.S. vice-consul, listing the valuables in the Venice house when Captain Piglini was tenant (May 1940–January 1945):

Antique brocade robe & obi (200,000 lire)
300 books, including 10-volume *Complete Works of William Shakespeare*.
First edition of *The Wasteland*, by T.S. Eliot.
First edition of *Apes of God*, by Wyndham Lewis.
2 volume Ovid, Bodini ed. (300,000 lire).
Antique Persian carpet (150,000 lire).
Tami Koumé oil painting (200,000 lire).

Pound's Ovid, bound in boards (mentioned in Canto 76), had disappeared when the *sequestratario* emptied the shelves and put her books in a damp basement. These were the only material possessions left to Olga at fifty-six—but she had priceless memories.

Boris was in Rome researching a book comparing Confucianism with the religion of ancient Egypt. "We always get on well," Olga wrote, "but after lunch, I nearly fell asleep . . . a gift of gab—a bit much." In spite of her doubts about him, Olga turned over the damage claim to her son-in-law, who, as an Italian citizen, stood a better chance of getting a fair price. She was shocked to discover, when the claim was settled, that instead of the two million lire she had expected, "Boris, without consulting me, had accepted 100,000."

Unlike Olga, Fifi Drummond, a Roman senator's daughter, was impressed by Boris. In her view, he was of the same tradition as her *avvocato* father; she worried about her British husband's long silences. With Fifi, Olga had attended the Teatro Eliseo production of Arthur Miller's *Death of a Salesman* (*Morte di un Commesso Viaggiatore* in Italian), which had been "calculated to destroy any illusions in re. life in the States."

Olga picked up correspondence with her stepmother in Youngstown. Katherine Rudge was "surprised and pleased" to hear from her: "I tried to reach you through the Red Cross during the war, with no results," she wrote. Katherine wisely advised against her coming to Ohio to live. She could not offer hospitality in Youngstown, where she had made a home with relatives, and after Olga's long absence, "it is better to remain among your friends than to come to a few tired old people who are dropping out of things. . . . You will not find anyone here much interested—fifty years is a long time."

Olga was at the Palazzo Chigi to celebrate the Count's seventy-first birthday: "For a man who has so many 'friends,' surprisingly few remembered." The Marchesa came back from Florence, bringing a new tie and some large pears, and Olga contributed a plate of mascarponi cheese, "not often seen in Siena, he likes—but [not] at [the] end of [the] long stuffy lunch with bad champagne—ils ne savent pas vivre!" She viewed his position perceptively: "an old man . . . with the pack closing in, waiting for the spoils."

On the way back to Rapallo, Olga met Gabriela Mistral, the Chilean poet and Nobel Prize winner then living in a villa at San Michele by the sea. "Female Gabe a remarkable specimen," she wrote Ezra, "full of good will and sound sense, a sense of humor—anti-Fascist, so much so that she had a guardiano tailing her." A friend had called her a "jolie juive" years ago, but Donna Gabriela said she was 'not jolie nor juive'. When she was a little girl, her grandmother used to read the Bible aloud, and it affected her writing. She also spoke fondly of the Chilean poet Pablo Neruda, who at that time was a political refugee in France.

Olga was happy to be back at Casa 60 for the summer, to smell the honeysuckle on the *salita*. "He wouldn't recognize the Rapallo shop fronts, all modernized," she told Ezra. "The Café Yolanda [is] going in for ices, and Dante (the waiter) in a white coat." Reverend Chute invited her to play the violin with an English friend, Cecilia Kynaston, on viola: "We did Mozart and Corelli, Purcell trios, and the Bartók two-violin duets [Tibor] Serly gave me, which [I] have never had [a] chance to try."

She was back at the Accademia in September for the Settimana Musicale, dedicated to Verdi, beginning with the choral excerpts of *Nabucco* and *Falstaff*. She asked Ronald Duncan to come, and to bring Pound's score of *Le Testament de Villon*, which she was planning to take to Washington. Caresse Crosby also came to Siena. Caresse had first visited Ezra at Howard Hall in 1945 and remained a steadfast friend through the years at St. Elizabeth's. On their most recent encounter, she had found Ezra surrounded with "not very interesting young men," and felt that his old friends "were getting rather shoved out of things." This strengthened Olga's determination to go to Washington.

After the annual music festival, Olga returned to Venice to set in motion the necessary repairs on the calle Querini house. At a November concert at La Fenice, "so many Chigianist names on the program that she had to go, in spite of a deluge of rain," she wrote to the Count. "Ettore Gracis was directing, and the duo Corini-Lorenzi were soloists; the cellist di Kunert, and little Vianello (percussion). I find it very moving to see 'your' young musicians getting such a welcome." A documentary about the Accademia was then showing at the Olimpia Cinema, but she had been too busy fighting it out with the *acqua alta,* which was receding at last, leaving the *zattere* covered with crabs.

She sent condolences to the Count on the death of His Highness Prince Sigismundo Chigi, a Grand Master of the Order of Malta, a Chigi cousin. After making an unaccustomed journey to Rome for the memorial service at the Villa Malta on the Aventine Hill and accompanying the body to the Verano Cemetery, the Count was lauded with speeches and an honorary parchment at the Choral Society's annual banquet. On Saint Cecilia's Day (November 22), there was a benefit concert for the flood victims, and he reminded Olga that "crabs are very good to eat, if prepared properly!"

Throughout that winter, Olga complained of her despair and loneliness, being shut out of St. Elizabeth's and hence out of Ezra's life. She continued to make plans for traveling to America, renewing her passport at the U.S. consulate in Florence. But she added: "I wish I had the courage to eat it—like Garry Davis!" (referring to the World War II fighter pilot who had destroyed his U.S. passport and encamped on the steps of the Trocadero, at the time the meeting place of the United Nations in Paris, in protest against the war—*all* wars.)

Eliot and Laughlin opposed her visit. In their view, Pound's reputation would be compromised by having "the other woman" in Washington, knowing that his wife Dorothy had lived in an apartment near St. Elizabeth's since 1946. They feared that the "yellow press" might pick up on Olga's arrival and spark unwanted publicity.

Olga went ahead with her official request to visit patient 58102 in

Chestnut Ward, which was granted by Dr. Samuel Silk, acting superintendent. She booked third-class passage on the S.S. *Italia* out of Genoa,
posting her first letter to Ezra from Gibraltar: "She ain't occupying the
bridal suite . . . nine hundred immigrants got on at Naples, buona gente,
three in a cabin for four . . . [but] found [the] shower room functions, got a
top berth, [and] am doing well." Her circumstances improved when she
went to the purser's office to collect mail. Noticing correspondence from
the Accademia, the purser explained that he was also a lover of good
music—his aunt had a Steinway, and the Trio di Trieste practiced on it. He
handed over a pass to first class with his blessing for the rest of the trip.

There was also a letter from Pound. "O.K., you bin put on as custodian,
and can take me out to grass from 1–4 p.m. Will be at window at 1, if you
don't see me, yowl!" Ezra had asked Olga to bring her violin "to play the
Jannequin for 5 or 6," but Olga refused: "He never realized that it [is] as
great a strain for her to play for 5 or 6 as for 500 or 600. She is *not* going to
play the violin until she can make a proper comeback, and that is *that*."

It was not the season for Ezra's nostalgic eucalyptus pips or favorite
apricots, but she was bringing two small suitcases containing copies of the
Cavalcanti opera, a few *oro* (gold coins), clippings, the Accademia *Quaderni*, the Villon score ("will do the copying myself in Washington"), and,
for sentimental reasons, his gift of a flask of perfume in a tiny red heart.

Olga did not linger to visit friends in New York; instead she immediately caught the Pennsylvania Railroad to Washington. She received a
warm welcome at Caresse Crosby's red brick row house on Q Street in
Georgetown. Crosby, who had been Pound's publisher in Paris in the
1920s, had moved to Washington during World War II to open a contemporary art gallery as a venue for war-exiled artists. She was then publishing *Portfolio*, an innovative literary magazine for promising young writers, and lobbying for Women Against War.

Olga timed her visit to St. Elizabeth's for her fifty-seventh birthday,
April 13. The hospital occupies a group of venerable red brick buildings in
southeast Washington across the Anacostia River, and from the grounds
high on a hill an unsurpassed view of the nation's capital stretches as far as
the eye can see. The wife of a former superintendent whose hobby was
horticulture supervised the landscaping, soliciting donations of rare trees

and plants from governments around the world. In fine weather, nonviolent inmates were permitted to wander on the well-maintained grounds, and some, like Ezra, exercised on the tennis courts. The main building, dating back to the 1860s, originally housed Civil War wounded, mostly amputees, but in more recent history it had become an institution for serious cases of mental illness.

Pound was first an inmate of Howard Hall, a dreary building for the criminally insane, but soon was transferred to Center Building, which in Ezra's time housed elderly patients suffering from senile dementia. The superintendent, Winifred Overholser, assigned him a room near his office at the end of the second floor hall, where he could keep an eye on the poet.

Olga was permitted three visits of three hours each. While Ezra joined her on the lawn in the afternoon, Dorothy was discreetly absent. No written record remains of their first reunion after seven long years, but Olga recalled in a taped interview: "You feel that you've got a few minutes to—[a long pause]—it was not the kind of thing that he would have discussed by letter, nor would I, except indirectly."

Back in New York, Gibner King, a friend from Ohio, took her to the Old Vanderbilt Hotel: "all them past glories filled with *such* people!" Another evening, a teacher at the Julliard School invited her to join the musicians before a concert. She booked passage on the S.S. *Vulcania*, due to arrive in Cannes May 17 (with stops in Halifax and Genoa). In her first letter to Ezra from aboard the ship, she wrote: "He forgive her for argyfying, it's only [that] she doesn't want Him to miss a chance. He gave her a beautiful trip. Gratz! . . . He go on being wonderful. He *is* wonderful."

The "argyfying" was a result of Olga's determination to seek Pound's release from the hospital, and his equally strong desire to maintain the status quo. Olga objected strongly to John Kasper, one of the young followers at St. Elizabeth's, who had first corresponded with Pound as an admirer of his poetry. A recent graduate of Columbia University, Kasper was working toward a doctorate in English and philosophy. He would later cause Pound's supporters embarrassment when he was revealed as an anti-Semite and a racist who was outspoken in his support of the Ku Klux Klan.

Olga wrote again aboard the *Vulcania:* "This one, who expected after having at last seen Him to want nothing more than to lie down and die, has accomplished the viaggio di ritorno in a most serene state of mind, re-signed to going on in this vale of tears. . . . As far as *she* [is] concerned, sitting on His lawn is paradise . . . watching His trees and His birds with Him has been the only time she felt really relaxed and contented all these years."

While Olga was away, Mary had "muddled up matters in re. her pass-port," having gotten a sworn statement from England that Lieutenant Arthur Rudge had been killed in 1918 and therefore could not have pro-duced her in 1925, "without consulting me, or worrying what conse-quences it might have . . . result, [she] got a passport [in] San Marino, [as the] daughter of EP and OR . . . will have to produce proof, which there ain't, and can't be."

Back at the Accademia in June, Olga was "writing on an ornamental concrete bench near an artificial lago covered with slime, and water spi-ders, no swans, at Castel Berardenga [Count Chigi's country estate], where *He* once came for an Accademia picnic." She wished for an Italian Proust to describe the scene, the long table with the Count at the top, set in front of the small chapel containing the family tombs.

In September, Olga's stepmother, Katherine Rudge, was buried next to her husband in the family plot at Calvary Cemetery. Olga always appreci-ated the fact that Katherine worked in her old age ("she did this volun-tarily"), so that she and Teddy could keep their inheritance. "The only reason to sell the Youngstown property is so the proceeds could be used to get Him out," she wrote Ezra. The guilt caused by not telling her father about Mary's birth still weighed heavily on Olga's conscience; in her view, the conflict with Mary was an ironic payback for her actions.

Saint Cecilia's Day was observed with Mass in the Chigi chapel, the courtyard spread with laurel leaves and hung with *contrade* banners. The Count's friends (the few who remembered) sent flowers to be placed on the statue of the saint, and various nuns and *beghinas* assisted and kissed the plaster foot of the saint, which pleased the Count: "He seems to think he is building up a legend."

Mary, who had not seen her father for seven and a half years, planned to go the United States in the spring, and Olga worried about the effect the hospital—seeing Ezra in such a place—would have on their daughter.

Reluctant to have Mary spend the first days alone in a hotel, she wrote again to Caresse Crosby, who had put her up in Georgetown: "You were such an angel to me. Could you help us again this time?" She offered in exchange a month at Mary's castle or her house in Venice.

Mary sailed on the S.S. *Independence* from Genoa in March. She arrived at Crosby's house on the twelfth, and Caresse delivered her by taxi to St. Elizabeth's. "Spent [the] whole afternoon with Babbo. . . . he is wonderful, except for the waist line, just like Rapallo. He talked all the time for my 'education,' like ten years ago," Mary reassured her mother. "After my second day, Dorothy was usually present; after the first week his regular visitors returned." Mary described the young people Ezra collected as "third rate . . . sloppy and ignorant, a new species of human beings in appearance and behavior . . . what a waste of his fine mind!"

One exception was William McNaughton, the son of *Time*'s Capitol Hill correspondent, author of a best-selling biography of Harry Truman. After a dispute with his father, Bill was working as a taxi driver in 1948 when he went to St. Elizabeth's for his "admissions interview" to the Ezuversity. He visited Ezra every Tuesday afternoon and Sundays, and later he was an attentive friend of Olga's when he was stationed near Venice on the battleship U.S.S. *Nimitz* with the Mediterranean fleet.

Mary met other interesting visitors at St. Elizabeth's: novelist Katherine Anne Porter, Huntington Cairns of the National Gallery of Art (with Pound's collaboration, translating the *Odes* of Confucius), and Kenneth Clark, the English art historian.

Omar came every day, and agreed with Dorothy that they should not attempt to hurry Pound's release from St. Elizabeth's—a "do-nothing" stance that infuriated Olga. Mary wrote her mother: "I am trying to make as many contacts as possible, [but] it is not easy, with Babbo's attitude. . . . At social occasions, as long as I was the charming young princess with a fairytale castle in Italy, everything was fine . . . but as soon as I met anyone I thought could help Babbo, [it was] an unpardonable breach of etiquette."

Mary attended the book signing of Caresse's memoir, *The Passionate Years*, at the Crosby Gallery on April 1, and Pietro Lazzari, a then unknown gallery artist, painted her portrait. Later, Professor Craig La

Driere invited her to read the Italian translation of Pound's first Canto at the Catholic University.

While Mary was away, Olga had the two grandchildren at Sant'Ambrogio, plus a third child Mary said she had rescued from a Roman orphanage, two-year-old Graziella. "This place is a Paradiso terrestre, with those three kids running 'round—children [are] necessary to complete the picture." Ezra urged her to devote more time to the violin. "Yes, she should be playing, [but] when does she ever get time for herself?" she answered. Mary's children "had come to that period in life when a grandmother was useful," she explained to Ezra. "Mary told me she was 'always afraid of me.' Mary's brats [are] not afraid of me, though I keep them in order, show no favoritism."

Blanche Somers-Cocks stopped by for a week's visit on her way to Menton, and at eighty-one was a perfect guest, a "great help with the children—sews, mends, plays with them." She remembered Somers-Cocks "sitting up in bed, happily reading Yeats, living on yoghurt, rusks, fruit, writing letters, darning the children's socks, making herself useful— though *deaf, really* deaf, since a young woman."

When Mary arrived back unexpectedly, instead of bright, burnished kids waiting for mama's arrival she found Patrizia sulking from some scrap with "Cri-Cri" (the family's nickname for Walter). "I am all for formal politeness, which makes life possible," Olga stated, one of her unbending principles.

The young people invited her to the castle for Christmas and "hoped till the last minute" she would come, but Olga preferred the solitude of Sant'Ambrogio. "Have kept out of any Rapallian entanglements. . . . Anita [Pellegrini] is going to bring me a plate of their Xmas dinner, i.e., lasagna." She was enjoying the simple life, "the luxury and joy of this place after the Palazzo Chigi . . . to look out of the window first thing in the morning, to rejoice in the sight of five healthy cabbages growing below, to climb that salita in the dark, and sit on a bench with stars to look at."

James Laughlin, in Europe on a skiing holiday, visited Olga at the Accademia in the new year. He adopted Pound's style when writing to "the Venerable" at St. Elizabeth's: "I was in Siena, and found The Lady in good form, tho' much concerned and agitated over your predyk-cement. She had us to lunch at the Palazzo, with the Old Boy [Count Chigi], who is . . . behaving like a very spoiled young lady from Philadelfia . . . he is a gonna shut down the hackademya fer spite if the Gov't. whacks off his patrimonio, which is rough on The Lady. . . . we had better get mobilized and find her a genteel and not overly-arduous position of a litcherary or musical nature. . . . Lozza snow here, powerful cold, dunno how these [Italians] stand life in their palazzi." He had also visited "old [Bernard] Berenson," and commented: "he keeps *his* hot, with profits from swappin' with the Lord Duveen . . . [a] spry old joker at age of 89 . . . [with a] sharp tongue!"

Olga continued to urge Eliot and Ezra's other literary friends to lobby for his release. When the question of a presidential pardon was raised, the U.S. Department of Justice advised that Pound could not be pardoned until he had been found guilty; he could not be found guilty until he had been put on trial; and he could not be put on trial until he had been declared sane.

Another important obstacle to Pound's release was Dorothy, his legal guardian. She could not afford the high fees of a private facility and felt that Ezra was doing well where he was. She did not admit, perhaps even to herself, that she wanted to keep Ezra where no other woman could reach him. As Mary Barnard remembered Dorothy at St. Elizabeth's: "She is very tense over Olga. You would have thought that in the last twenty years one of those women would have thrown him over for good, or that one or both of them would have resigned to the situation, but no. After Dorothy withdrew, I got a briefing [from EP] on what to say and what not to say to Olga . . . being mainly 'patience and fortitude'."

These roadblocks were increasingly frustrating to Olga, who was trying, once again, to get to the United States. She invited Clare Boothe Luce, the American ambassador in Rome, to visit the Accademia, hoping to win her support, and peppered Pound's friends and colleagues with a steady barrage of correspondence.

Early in 1955, Olga was still waiting to see if a friend could wangle free passage to the States. She was at Brunnenburg on Whitsunday, when Patrizia Barbara Cinzia Flavia de Rachewiltz received her First Communion: "a day of great clarity and contrasts, blue mountain ridges laced with snow, little girls in long, full white lace and loose curly hair on the green meadow under flowering cherry trees." Her granddaughter wore the dress Julia O'Connell had designed for Olga's First Communion, and Olga took pride in family continuity.

She continued to make plans, pleased that Eliot would be in Washington on or about the sixteenth. Blanche Somers-Cocks had attended a meeting of Peter Russell's Amici di Pound in Rome and agreed with Olga that "a real rumpus is needed . . . the years pass, and he becomes forgotten by those who hold him prisoner."

When Olga arrived in Washington in early June, Caresse Crosby had been called to Paris following the death of her son, Billy Peabody, so she booked a room at the Women's Equal Rights Club on Constitution Avenue with women of many different backgrounds. "I had not lived in the States since 1904," she recalled, "and thought it a chance to learn about *them*. Instead, they started telling me all about Italy, from what they read in the newspapers."

D. G. Bridson, who observed Ezra during the time of Olga's visit, wrote that "the beard [was] no longer [an] aggressive dark auburn, [but] white with an almost Confucian cut. He was also far less erect, less alert and agile." "Grandpa" was the persona Pound adopted in the presence of young scholars who visited him: Hugh Kenner, a student of Marshall McLuhan at the University of Toronto, future author of the groundbreaking work *The Pound Era;* Guy Davenport, avant-garde writer and professor at the University of Kentucky; David Gordon, an expert in Chinese art and history, then at the University of Maine in Orono; and Dellum Simpson, author of a work about Basil Bunting. The poet Charles Olson, later of the Black Mountain School in North Carolina, then living in Washington, was the acolyte of whom Pound wrote: "Olson saved my life." Hangers-on who did not know Pound or his reputation as a poet came because "Gramps" was a colorful character who saved snacks from his lunch to feed the squirrels (and the young people).

A number of young women came, among them Sheri Martinelli, a painter in her thirties who had a studio in Georgetown. A visitor described Martinelli: "golden hair falling down around her thin shoulders . . .

dressed in blue jeans and a checkered blouse, [she] suggested a frayed and faded survivor of the early bobby-sox days." She found her way to the hospital with "Steff," the sister of Stanislaus Yankowski, a Polish scholar helping Pound with translations. Sheri was born Shirley O'Brennan to a large Irish Catholic family, and her father drank to excess, rather like James Joyce's. She had gone to New York in her late teens, worked as a model, and married a painter, Ezio Martinelli. They moved in the hippest circles in Manhattan until she drifted into drink and drugs. After the marriage ended, she came to Washington. She said that she had waited all her life to meet a "holy man," and Ezra Pound fit that image.

For a time, the admiration was mutual. A magazine article reported that "Mr. Pound considers Miss Martinelli's paintings better than anything done 'since 1527.'" Sheri became a member of Pound's inner circle, and since the hospital required Ezra to be accompanied by a family member outside the ward she often substituted for Dorothy as his "adopted" daughter. Sheri hinted that Ezra had considered legal adoption. In later interviews, Martinelli insisted that she and Pound were lovers, which is unlikely, because visitors were not permitted in the ward after 4:30 in the afternoon, and there was no privacy on the hall at any hour.

For many months, she visited Ezra almost daily, observing the scene with an artist's eye: Dorothy's "luminous beauty, with almost celestial Botticelli perfection, a winter rosebud with tiny touches of pink, . . . soft hair falling with a golden aura about her face." Silence surrounded Dorothy, she remembered, but the refined English lady would surprise everyone by saying things quite out of character: "imbecile, idiot!" She also quoted Dorothy as saying she liked having Ezra in St. Elizabeth's: "At least I know where he's sleeping tonight."

And then there was "the other lady." Sheri was witness to Olga's 1955 visit. She was sitting at the right hand of Pound one afternoon when Dorothy failed to appear. Then Olga came, "a royal presence, with marble-like, sculptured features, her back stiff and erect, professional-looking, a *trained* person." Her hair was carefully "marcelled" in waves, and she was wearing a lovely lavender and white summer dress, with matching lavender parasol to protect fragile skin against summer sun.

No one knew who Olga was, but Pound looked up with a "bad little boy" grin, an expression that said, according to Martinelli, "anything can happen now . . . when you looked into EP's eyes, you could see he was only four years old." Olga "stared like a lioness" when she saw the attractive young woman sitting close to Pound. "In a magnificent fury, she [Olga] lifted the folded parasol over my head. I could see she was reading my face, and when she looked into my eyes she saw—'iggurance.' She waved the parasol over me, but never did bring it down."

Olga did not record this encounter at St. Elizabeth's, but she failed to live up to her promise to "keep off the grass." There was an "argymint"— so devastating that Olga, for the first and last time in their relationship, broke off all correspondence with her lover. The only comment she jotted in her notebook more than twenty years later was: "If Dorothy had not told me a lie in answer to a direct question *before* I saw EP, I would have been prepared and not gone over the deep edge."

A letter from Mary to her mother offers some clues to Olga's state of mind after the visit: "I can't see how you can separate yourself from Babbo," she wrote. "I understand he has hurt you very much, but he still needs you more than ever. . . . D[orothy] is certainly not acting like a lady . . . all the falsehoods and subterfuges, etc . . . [a] situation [that] has gone on for thirty years, I do not see how he could alter [it]." She assessed her mother's position: "Your best weapon is that you are much calmer and look younger and better than you have in all these years. . . . Don't be too hard on Babbo. All of us should give him as least trouble as possible, after all he has gone through."

Pound's "painter of Paradise" attracted undesired publicity when the *Washington Post* reported Martinelli's arrest on a drug-related charge. Archibald MacLeish rebuked Ezra for mixing with such people. Ezra's retort: "Sheri acquitted, jury out five minutes."

There is no record of Olga's visit to her father's grave or to relatives in Ohio in 1955. She stopped in the Philadelphia suburbs to see Esther and Priscilla Heacock, the sisters who headed the "dame school" Ezra attended as a child, cousins of her late Uncle Harold Baynes, the naturalist. Baynes's ninety-three-year-old widow (her mother's sister, Louise O'Connell) had lived with the Heacocks before they gave up housekeeping. A published writer herself and member of the Author's Union, this lively old woman was then staying in Jenkintown with Miss Clare Warren, who had been a friend of the senior Pounds before they moved to Italy.

Olga's long correspondence with Louise Baynes had ceased entirely during the war. Since Olga always considered herself close to Uncle Harold and Aunt Lou and remembered fondly childhood visits to New Hampshire, the estrangement is puzzling. A clue may be found in a 1936 letter from Louise, then living on Bailey's Island, Maine, to Olga's brother Teddy: "I wonder what I have done to offend Olga," she wrote, "certainly nothing intentional." She expressed surprise that Olga was doing "secretarial work," and added that "she [Olga] must have had association with a great many people with interests similar to her own; it seems strange that so attractive a girl should remain unmarried." For anyone as fiercely proud of her independence as Olga, this must have rankled; moreover, as the mother of Pound's child, she considered herself married in the eyes of God. On this visit, she was saddened to see her aunt failing, and misunderstandings were forgiven or forgotten. Olga sailed from the port of New York, not to return until 1969 when she came back triumphantly with Ezra.

15

A Piece of Ginger

1956–1962

W hile Olga's personal life suffered and her talent diminished, she still held a respected position at the Accademia Chigiana. For the twenty-fifth anniversary celebration in May 1956, Arthur Rubinstein came to perform the works of Chopin. The summer session enrolled a number of promising young people. Zubin Mehta, a former student, came from India for an all-Tchaikovsky evening. Daniel Barenboim conducted Beethoven in August, and the versatile Claudio Abbado led a program of Wagner, another of Bach. Count Chigi disdained contemporary composers (and shut the door to the *salottino* to block out the sound), but he did not allow his prejudices to influence his staff when Olga invited violinist Yvonne Astruc to perform works by Aram Khachaturian and Igor Stravinsky.

She remained in Siena over Christmas to see the lights go on again at the Teatro dei Rinnovati for a program of Basque music and dance, and tried, unsuccessfully, to put Ezra out of her mind. For the first time since their "argyment" at St. Elizabeth's, she sent a New Year's message: "Bear no grudge, to the Rudge!" Ezra did not reply.

The Accademia year began with the Kammerchor Philharmonia di Vienna. Soprano Elizabeth Schwarzkopf arrived in March, violinists

David Oistrakh and Joseph Szigeti in May, the Ballet from the Palais du Chaillot in June. With the passing years, the small regional academy had won international renown. As Count Chigi had anticipated, the world's great musicians came to him. Olga arranged their schedules and accommodations, catering to the whims of temperamental performers and maestros. There was little time for reflection; her hectic schedule was interrupted by brief respites in Rapallo and visits to Brunnenburg.

At St. Elizabeth's, a young Texan, Marcella Spann, had joined the Pound circle. Her reserved demeanor was in marked contrast to the exuberant Martinelli; her hair caught neatly in a chignon indicated a "serious character." She had come to Washington, after college and a job in New York, to teach at a junior college not far from the hospital. Pound was impressed by the shy young woman, a student of contemporary American poetry, and assigned her to compile an anthology, *From Confucius to Cummings.*

Meanwhile, Pound's friends in the literary world were agitating for his release. As early as January 1957, Archibald MacLeish, T. S. Eliot, and Robert Frost co-signed a letter to Attorney General Herbert Brownell requesting a review of the Pound case. After a long delay, Deputy Attorney General William P. Rogers (who was soon to replace Brownell) answered, inviting Frost and his colleagues to come to Washington.

But before further action could be taken, a controversy erupted in February that seriously compromised Pound's position. The *New York Herald Tribune* launched a four-part series of articles under the headline "Segregationist Kasper Is Ezra Pound Disciple," linking Pound to John Kasper and the Ku Klux Klan.

It was not until the following October, when the adverse publicity quieted down, that Frost felt the time was ripe to go again to Washington. Attorney General Rogers received him but remained noncommittal. MacLeish felt that the petitions to the Attorney General were getting nowhere, so he wrote to Secretary of State Christian Herter, suggesting that the poet's continued incarceration was damaging American prestige in Europe. At the same time, Frost was carrying on negotiations with the White House. "He did a lot for me, I must never forget," Frost was quoted as saying.

Public opinion was beginning to turn around. An editorial in Henry Luce's *Life* stated that whatever Pound had done in wartime Italy he had suffered enough, and that his case should be reconsidered. The publisher's wife, Clare Boothe Luce, former ambassador to Italy, was said to have been moved by the respect and esteem in which Pound was held by the Italian people. T. S. Eliot was responsible for keeping the cause alive in England. Ernest Hemingway joined the chorus: "Ezra Pound is a great poet, and whatever he did, he has been greatly punished. I believe he should be freed to go and write poems in Italy, where he is loved and understood."

In the spring of 1958, Frost paid a third call on Rogers, and this time the Attorney General listened patiently, and assured the poet that the U.S. government would no longer oppose Pound's release. But first, an attorney would have to prepare the necessary paperwork. Thurman Arnold of the Washington law firm of Arnold, Fortas & Porter was engaged. Dorothy Pound, her son Omar (now a teacher in Boston), and a miscellaneous group of Ezra's disciples were on the benches at the hearing before Judge Bolitha J. Laws on April 18. Sworn statements were read from many celebrated writers: Marianne Moore, Carl Sandburg, W. H. Auden, Robert Fitzgerald, Hemingway, and MacLeish. Dr. Winifred Overholser testified that Pound's "further confinement can serve no therapeutic purpose. Ezra Pound is not a dangerous person, and his release would not endanger the safety of other persons . . . or interests of the United States."

Mary, at Brunnenburg, listening to Italian radio, heard the good news and relayed it to her mother. Olga was disappointed that Ezra would leave the hospital, not as a free man, but in the custody of his wife acting as "Committee for Ezra Pound," released to her "with bond, under such terms and conditions as will be appropriate to the public good." He chose to remain in Chestnut Ward for three weeks after his release to sort books and papers until the "Committee" could make arrangements for their return to Italy. When Dorothy booked passage on the S.S. *Cristoforo Colombo* sailing July 1, Marcella Spann went with them as secretary.

Before returning to Italy, Pound visited his childhood home in Wyncote, Pennsylvania, then owned by Mrs. Herman L. Gatter and her son Carl, and visited his former teachers, Priscilla and Esther Heacock. From

Wyncote, the party traveled to Rutherford, New Jersey, for a brief reunion with William Carlos Williams and his wife, Flossie.

Omar was in New York to see them off aboard the Italian luxury liner, acting as buffer against reporters. The three adults shared one small cabin, No. 128, tucked away at the end of a corridor in first class. When Ezra disembarked in Genoa, he was photographed wearing an open-necked sport shirt, slacks, and his "first new hat in thirteen years," a sombrero. More photographers, more reporters. Pound "hailed his adopted nation with a fascist salute," the press reported, although many interpreted the gesture more benignly as holding his hand over his eyes like a visor to guard against the glare of the Italian sun. When asked the simple question of when he had been released from St. Elizabeth's, he replied with a grand metaphor: "I never was. When I left the hospital I was still in America, and all America is an insane asylum."

The party traveled on to Verona, where they stayed overnight, until Mary came to take them to Brunnenburg. In Mary's words, "For how many years I had prayed for just this meeting . . . Babbo coming down the path! We were all swept off our feet and too happy." Her birthday on July 9 was the occasion for a village celebration with dancing and fireworks, a great welcoming party to which the villagers brought flowers and music and torches and drums. At night, when the others retired to their rooms, "Babbo would sit in the dining room and talk to me for hours," she said, "as though it were now his turn 'to fill in the gap,' of the years at St. Liz."

Olga was not there to welcome the man she loved. One can imagine her feeling of isolation and pain, as that other woman—Ezra's legal wife—usurped what she considered her rightful place at the castle with Ezra and their daughter.

In January 1958, Olga heard from her brother Teddy, living out his life not far from the Rudge family ancestors in Spondon. He was anticipating retirement from practice as a country doctor with a pension of six hundred pounds a year and would sell his place to be near his son John, then a prosperous dairy farmer, soon to be joined by the other son, Peter.

Teddy's letter was followed by distressing news from the Heacock sisters in Wyncote: "Cousin Louise's mental condition has become a problem," Esther wrote. "She thinks she is persecuted, [that] someone is spying on her and will kill her!" In more rational moments, the ninety-three-year-old had expressed a desire to go to Italy to live with her niece. Olga was still pondering how to shoulder this additional burden when the sisters wrote that Louise had been moved to Friends' Hospital in Philadelphia. The last close member of Olga's mother's family, Louise Birt Baynes, succumbed on February 25, 1958. At her request, her body was cremated, and the ashes were scattered over Mount Chocorua with her husband's.

A specific bequest of two hundred dollars was left to her niece, Olga, in Aunt Lou's will; an equal amount to Edgar M. Rudge and sons, Peter and John, to the Heacock sisters, and several close friends; the residue of her estate of some fifteen thousand dollars was to be divided equally among the above, after donations deducted for several bird clubs.

When she received the news in Sant'Ambrogio, Olga wrote to Esther Heacock, as executor: "Auntie Lou's legacy . . . comes at a moment when . . . my Youngstown tenant is falling back on his payments, [it] all goes to the bank to pay off the mortgage." The sisters had sent several books written by Uncle Harold, the naturalist. "Mary's twelve-year-old will enjoy having these," Olga wrote; "many I had seen years ago [and] now can appreciate much more. It is such fine writing, and the point-of-view is so sound, so unsentimental. So much trash . . . is being given to the young."

Just before Christmas, Ezra told James Laughlin (who distributed his book royalties), that he had been persuaded to make recordings at St. Elizabeth's only on the condition that the first hundred dollars per month would go to Spann. "If I konk out, I don't want Marcella stranded in Europe."

Olga heard from an unidentified gossip that Marcella had replaced her as Ezra's lover. When she expressed this latest fear to Laughlin, he replied: "The Rapallo rumour about the Texan is sans basis. Neither I nor Bob [Robert MacGregor], who saw her there, discerned anything of the kind." As further reassurance, he added, "$1,000 for the Venice house loan awaits when you need it."

In the beginning, life at Brunnenburg was idyllic. In Mary's words, "The family had been trained for a demigod, and as such he came . . . with

his wife Dorothy and his secretary Marcella, Committee and bodyguard.
. . . He [was] in great need of shelter and tenderness, so that he might write
Paradise. . . . So beautiful were the days that all later suffering is forgotten,
'and for one beautiful day, there was peace' " (Canto 117).

In February, Ezra picked up correspondence with Olga for the first time
since the encounter at St. Elizabeth's. "Thanks for the silence," he said.
"Mary has a gordorful heredity from both sides. . . . I don't know what you
two blew up about. *Possibly similarity* . . . plus Isabel [Pound]. . . . If I ever
get out of this morass, I will let you know." A week later, he expressed his
own despair and malaise: "feeling like [the poet Juan Ramon] Jiménez for
these months (he spent a year expecting to die each day) . . . attitude has
kept me groping like a fish."

"Don't know if a mother is much use to a girl who has always wanted a
father—perhaps some of the Old Lady's [Isabel's] nervous strain [was]
caused by absence of a male parent in her youth," Olga replied, not
recognizing how close she had come to analyzing her own situation. "I
have heard very seldom from Mary since your arrival. She has not crit-
icized her father to me, even to the extent of saying 'how like his mother'
he is."

She reminded Ezra that his books and other belongings must be removed from Casa 60 because the owners were considering selling the
house. Through the years Ezra was at St. Elizabeth's she had considered
herself caretaker of his property and stayed in Sant'Ambrogio to see that
the valuable memorabilia were preserved. There was no reason for her to
be there now; she wanted to get on with her own life.

"I told Mary that I wanted everything taken at one time, for *my* convenience and peace and quiet, [it] is not intended as a declaration of war. I
have enjoyed the Gaudier [Brzeska bust] and the books, have no interest in
the furniture. My permission to enter the house is given to *you* and to *no-
one* else" (implying that Dorothy and Marcella were not welcome). "I am
glad you are feeling better . . . am all right myself, trying to follow [the]
precepts you had posted on the wall of Rapallo to encourage the population: 'così vivere che i tuoi figli e i loro discendenti ti ringraziano' [Live in
such a way that your children and their descendants will be grateful to
you], and 'L'arciere che manca il centro del bersaglio cerca la causa

dell'errore dentro se stesso' [When the archer misses the bull's eye, the cause of the error is within himself]."

The old *contadino* Baccin, who had cared for Olga and Pound since they first came to Sant'Ambrogio, died in June. Olga sent flowers to Anita and the family Pellegrini "da parte di EP." "Such things mean a lot to these people who . . . stood up for you, with no thought of any advantage."

In many ways, it was a sad time. From California came news from Böski Antheil that "Smitty," who wrote his first two violin sonatas for her on the rue Chamfort, had died suddenly. And from England, news of the death of Kathleen's father, the patriarch of the Richards family, devoted friends of her youth. Kathleen thanked Olga for her letter of condolence and asked for news of the Accademia and the music world they shared: "I envy you having attended [Alfred] Cortôt's Chopin classes. . . . [There are] far too many musicologists these days . . . music is too much subjected to scientific research, instead of being played and enjoyed for its own sake."

Olga missed out on another major event in the life of the man she loved when Mary flew to Berlin with Eva Hesse, the friend from Munich who had translated Pound's work into German. They went there to see his version of *The Women of Trachis* performed in that language. After completing his work on the Confucian *Odes* at St. Elizabeth's, Pound had begun a translation of Sophocles' *Trachiniae*, an idea that came to him from reading the Noh plays translated by Ernest Fenollosa, and wanting to see what would happen to a Greek play given the same medium. There was a strong autobiographical element in the plot, Herakles transferring his love from his wife Deianira to Iole, one of the captured women of Trachis. The long-standing tradition of Noh plays in Germany dated back to 1906, and the theater—the largest in Berlin—was packed.

Eva reported to Olga in Sant'Ambrogio: "The Noh elements came over well, and the audience streamed home in excited discussion. . . . At the end of the year, you'll have netted somewhat over a million lire, a nice Hemingway-like sum." She did not know that Mary, not Olga, would benefit from this bonanza in royalties.

Olga returned to Siena in June for the summer session of the Accademia. Proofreading the illustrated brochure to be sent out to prospective students, she noted that the enrollment fee had increased to over ten thousand lire, but inexpensive lodgings were still available at the Casa degli Studenti on the via del Porrione. She wrote again to Ezra, in the chatty tone she used to report her activities: "Vanni [Scheiwiller, Pound's publisher in Milan] sent in *Mauberly*, with M. Jean's *Incoronazione*—all your ole monstres sacrés. . . . What I ain't learned about monstres sacrés! Cortôt and Casals—83 and 84! The antics of the octogenarians show considerable joie de vivre, so cheer up, you haven't got there yet." She noted that Bernard Berenson had died at ninety-three, "owing to culpable negligence in not taking the Duck-egg's [Duchess's] advice in going to her dentist, hence a poisoned jaw."

Pound's life at Brunnenburg was no longer idyllic. After the first euphoria dissipated, he felt confined in the mountain retreat; it was hard to keep warm after winter set in. There were difficulties with Marcella Spann, almost the same age as his daughter. "I grew jealous and I grew angry," Mary admitted. The Pounds, accompanied by Marcella, fled to Rapallo and settled into rooms at the Albergo Grande Italia.

Olga wrote again to Ezra in October: "Where has He got this idea that He is responsible for other people's happiness? You used to rub into me that if I suffered, it was on account of my own imperfections, not to blame it on someone else. . . . As I remember my catechism (Roman Catholic), despair is one of the three worst sins, i.e., sins against the Holy Ghost, the other two being presumption and sodomy (which last [is] not your trouble). . . . It seems quite Confucian, the middle way, between presumption and despair."

Pound's answer: "DEEspair / the Possum says it in *After Strange Gods* / didn't seem to be my trouble, 'cause I had PREsumption, pride, vanity, baldanza [arrogance], & got used to bein' the life of the party, or thinkin' I was, *and* having worn out everyone's indulgence, I ain't blaming anybody else for the defects of my kerr-akter."

Early in 1960, Olga let the Venice house for one year (with an option to renew) to Lester Littlefield, a highly cultivated Dartmouth graduate with roots in Ogunquit, Maine, then living in Paris. An admirer of Pound, he had visited St. Elizabeth's in 1956 and continued to correspond with him.

"Is it possible EP remembers me?" he wrote to Olga. "I remember climbing a circular iron staircase at St. E's to his doorway, and being warmly greeted by EP, arms outstretched and head thrown back, like some lord in the upper reaches of the Inferno." (In *The Cantos* Pound wrote, "and Lester brought the *Odes* to St. Elizabeth's.") Littlefield found "handsome little 252 . . . in apple-pie order—the sun pours in each day from the Cipriani courtyard."

As Olga anticipated, Casa 60—the cottage she had occupied for so many years in Sant'Ambrogio—was sold, but she soon found a place up the hill let by Signore Cesare Beltrami. She described it to Esther Heacock as "a tiny cottage, equally un-getattable, but with a lovely view." A thank-you note from her grandson for the gift of the *New Hampshire Bird Bulletin* was enclosed, with a photograph of a blackbird "that remained a widow because of a cat that went on top of this tree!" Walter was already planning to apply for a scholarship to an American university.

In early January 1961, another letter from Ezra at Brunnenburg: "Perfectly monstrous Christmas here, under perverted circ[umstance]s / if he gets into Purgatory, he'll be lucky." Mary described the December morning when "I found the Christmas tree lying on the floor. A bad omen . . . if love be not in the house, there is nothing." Soon after, Olga received a postcard with scenes of bookstalls along the Seine and the nostalgic message, "The Christmas that might have been."

Later in the same month, another poignant letter: "Why couldn't I have come to you? . . . Crazier when I got out of bughouse than when in. *Inside* was where he belonged for *comfort*, no responsibility, able to be lord of creation with no fuss / . . . O some way to roll back [the] curtain and get to good years that he ruin'd. . . . May be still time . . . how much time he will be given, now he looks like a Tyrolese devil mask?"

Disillusioned with life en famille, Ezra again fled Brunnenburg, this time to the Rome apartment of Ugo Dadone, a retired military attaché and friend of Boris's. The poet Donald Hall, who interviewed Pound for the *Paris Review*, described Ezra as he found him there: "His eyes were watery, red, weak. As he spoke, he separated the words into little bunches: 'You have driven—all the way—from England—to find a man—who is only fragments,' then his face would sag and he would collapse onto a sofa into silence; then he would jump up in five minutes and begin the cycle again, his speech newly vigorous and exact."

On May 10, 1961, Dadone summoned Mary to Rome. He could no longer care for her father, he said; the doctors thought his heart was failing. Mary found Ezra very weak, and entered him in the clinic J. Pini, recommended by Dadone.

Olga visited him there May 14. To her eyes, J. Pini was "as near the atmosphere of St. Elizabeth's as could have been found." Ezra's room on the ground floor opened onto a garden, but the gate was always kept locked. Ezra was confined to his bed, could not be encouraged to eat, or to drink water. After a long silence, he said, "There's an *eye* watching me." Olga feared he had indeed lost contact with reality, but the same afternoon she *saw* the eye of one of the attendants, looking through a crack in half-open shutters!

She kept a careful log of visits to the clinic, and wrote Ronald Duncan: "Thanks to the [John] Drummonds, I was able to get to Rome weekends—the last two weeks, every day, twice a day." Her devotion remained unflagging, even at sixty-six years old, while holding a demanding position at the Accademia and having to endure a physically exhausting five-hour train ride from Siena to Rome. This pattern continued until June 15, when Ezra showed no progress and Olga—with Mary's consent—decided to move him back to Brunnenburg.

Mary came down in a hired car. "He [Ezra] curled up on the back seat like a foetus," Olga wrote of their return. They stopped over in Florence for lunch, though Ezra ate nothing, and reached Merano late that evening. Ezra was too weak to ascend the mountain, and the two women deposited him in the Sanatorium Martinsbrunn, the Casa di Cura on the Fonte San Martino.

Her commitment to the Accademia prevented Olga from spending the rest of the summer at Martinsbrunn, but she continued to correspond with Ezra. Early August was an especially busy time. The British ambassador had been to Siena, as had Adlai Stevenson, the former presidential candidate, who was staying with his sister at her villa in Florence. Olga was responsible for arranging lodging, meals, concert tickets, and other entertainment for the illustrious guests. With her erect posture and the discipline of a trained violinist, she remained charming, well dressed, and efficient, seldom showing the strain and heartbreak over Ezra.

On August 14 Pound suffered a relapse, and Olga was summoned to Martinsbrunn. He was being fed intravenously, and she confided to Ronald Duncan: "I thought the end had come, but came back here [Siena] the 17th as planned, so as not to show him I thought so. . . . [I] telephoned Mary that evening—he had taken a turn for the better, the doctor said it was miraculous!" Walter had brought a jar of Chinese ginger from London, which in her view was "most unsuitable." But not to disappoint the child she said, "perhaps a little bit, when he felt better." The next day, "E. demanded a piece of ginger, after which he asked for a ham sandwich—he had had nothing but [IV] injections for two weeks! . . . [he] is gradually picking up."

He was sitting up when Olga arrived in October. "He *can* get well . . . *is much better* than when I saw him in Rome," Olga wrote Duncan, "mind clear, not in the terrible state of anxiety and self-reproach." But when Duncan, the only nonfamily member permitted to enter the closely guarded sanctuary, arrived at Martinsbrunn, Ezra was still lying in profound silence during much of the visit.

Several months later, Olga wrote, "he was commencing to walk 'round the room without a stick, fairly serene and content." The doctor was waiting to consult with a famous specialist from Innsbruck before risking a prostate operation.

Duncan urged Olga to encourage Pound to make a will, but she hesitated: "Even if I would risk a misunderstanding with E. (and I won't), a will would have no legal value now that he has a 'guardian.'" In her view, the will that Ezra had already executed, before the war, "may or may not have legal value. . . . It . . . names M. 'literary executor' when she reaches the age of 18, until then, her mother (OR) guardian. . . . Don't you think she [Mary] has proven herself a capable young woman who has always worked for E's best interest?"

"Two things stand out in my mind after seeing you the other day in Merano," Duncan wrote Ezra. "(1) Your sense of remorse hasn't got a leg to stand on. Please stop worrying about trivial details. (2) Mary's loyalty.

You are lucky to have somebody who loves you as much as this and has your work so much at heart . . . make certain that it is Mary who has the power to say 'yes' or 'no' about your work."

Olga was back at the Accademia for an evening concert with the Oistrakhs, *père et fils*, playing Bach and Vivaldi: "An expensive orchestra directed by [the] celebrated lion-tamer, Sergiu Celibidache, *murdered* a Vivaldi concerto—got hopelessly lost!" The Count had just returned from a wet day in the country on the anniversary of his uncle's death ("accidentally shot while out shooting, made His Nibs his heir sixty years ago"). She had been asked to unveil a bust of Vivaldi at the inauguration ceremony in the Parco di Villa at Castelnuovo Berardenga, the Count's country retreat, a handsome three-story eighteenth-century building in a woodland setting with the towers of Siena visible some twelve miles in the distance. She was also engaged in the editing and writing of the scholarly introduction to the Vivaldi letters for the *Journal of the American Musicological Society*, while trying desperately, through correspondence, to give Ezra the will to live. When there were no replies to her letters, she sent a new pen and encouraged Ezra to "spend a little time doodling . . . it will come back by degrees."

"Please go on," she wrote. "Does He know that Natalie's [Barney's] friends are thinking of a tribute for her *85th* birthday? I suppose it wouldn't be proper for me to say, 'I thank you, Natalie, for Him!' (I mean, introducing Him, 20 rue Jacob?)"

In November, Lester Littlefield asked to extend the lease of the Venice house through 1963, but Olga refused. She was keeping the house for Ezra to come back to. She reported an item of interest in the press: "President Kennedy doing something to please. . . . His friend Mrs. [Alice Roosevelt] Longworth [who had visited Pound at St. Elizabeth's] invited to meet [Pablo] Casals [at the White House] after fifty years."

Back at the Accademia in December, Olga was learning to play the *flauto dolce* (recorder), "a heavenly sound, or can be, and not physically tiring." Antoine de Bavier had turned up for lunch on his way to Rome, and she was preparing Bach's *St. Matthew Passion* for the Tempio Malatestiano on December 25. "Still waiting for news," she wrote. *"What is she waiting all her life for* (now agli sgoccioli [reaching the last drop])? She would like to see Him . . ."

Olga returned to Martinsbrunn for Valentine's Day. She was in Bologna, waiting in the station café on her way back to Siena, when she wrote Duncan: "E . . . had a bad spell ten days ago (it's that beastly changing catheter business), now back to where he was before, i.e., eating, showing interest in newspapers . . . surprised Mary by being dressed and *ready to go out* a few days ago . . . walked as far as the gate and back with no fatigue. He worried me by [sending] a telegram, 'Keep hoping.' I was expecting bad news . . . instead, he was admitting that there *was* hope . . . a great step." Soon after, Olga received a letter from Ezra asking if there was a possibility of Anita Pellegrini putting him up at Sant'Ambrogio. He recalled with nostalgia how he had tried to walk up the hill alone when last in Rapallo, but when he got to the landmark eucalyptus, he discovered the old donkey path was being surfaced with cement and temporarily impassable. "You deserve ten years for us to go over the pleasant things, from rue Chamfort onward," he wrote, remembering "the walk along the Seine for N[atalie Barney]'s party (I kept the rue Chamfort key for years after) . . . the Piazza and the cloistre, the Capoquadri, and Roma, that uncomfortable room near the Corso, and the case for the brick balustrade to the stair, Calle Querini, she always finding things for him, and he snarly, she forgiving the snarl—her way with Anita and the people at Sant'Ambrogio, her kindness to people, him blind, with inferiority complex." (He echoed these sentiments in Canto 113: "in every woman, somewhere in the snarl is a tenderness.")

In March, Olga heard the Vivaldi *Gloria*—with chorus, orchestra, and *soli* from Florence—performed at the Teatro dei Rinnovati for the first time "since [Alfredo] Casella conducted same in Chiesa di San Francesco in 1939 . . . the 'Agnus Dei' as beautiful as [the] one in Bach B minor Mass." No news from the Alto Adige: "Hope all is serene and that He will tell them females what *He* wants. Please reassure everyone (including Himself), I am *not starving* and don't need *financial aid*. If He comes to Sant' Ambrogio, He only need think about His own expenses, which should be less than Martinsbrunn."

"I would be ready to receive *Him* in ten days or two weeks," she wrote on March 2. "Since one can't *count* on the weather . . . He and Mary could spend the first night or two at Villa Chiara, see the urologist, and face the bit of a walk to Casita 131 rested. . . . Yeats' ex-bed and bedtable had a lick of paint and other contrivings . . . so if He feeling up to the simple life, glad to see Him when He likes." She reminded Ezra that Dottoressa Elfreide Bacigalupo's old father "used a catheter for the last twenty years of his life, and got around all right."

On April 7 she wrote a letter to Duncan "in haste—am painting, cleaning, contriving . . . EP is expected here, just before or after Easter. . . . *please*—don't tell *anyone else* about this, I mean EP's coming. The situation is extremely delicate, so for the moment consider this *top secret*."

Olga was determined "to set the record straight" in her notebook entry of April 25, 1962: "EP motors from Tirolo with Mary to stay with OR. . . . I was not trying to entice Him from Brunnenburg, but when He was well enough to move, He came back to me at Sant'Ambrogio—and stayed. I gave up my job and took over."

Mary's autobiography recorded the events leading up to their reunion: "[It was] a long illness . . . but he recovered. And by the time the magnolia I had first seen in bloom when my son was born was in full bloom once more, he came out and walked in the garden. It was decided that as soon as he was strong enough to travel, I would take him back to Sant'Ambrogio for a visit. And ever since, he and Mamile have been taking care of each other."

16

The Last Ten Years

1962–1972

After his reunion with Olga, Ezra was moved to the Villa Chiara, the Casa di Cura of Dr. Giuseppe Bacigalupo, whose mother, Elfreide, had been Pound's doctor before the war. A clear case of prostatitis had been "shamefully neglected." Olga never forgave the doctors at St. Elizabeth's for having dismissed the patient without a complete physical checkup. Yet a urologist from Genoa and Dr. Bacigalupo were both of the opinion that an operation was unnecessary at the time.

The doctor had shown Olga how to manage without a nurse. A local woman came in the mornings for two hours, a *contadina* they had known for more than thirty years, whom she could trust. "I made a fire on the hearth, and E. read Cantos out loud until bedtime, making notes and corrections . . . most touchingly considerate, no trouble at all."

She kept a daily log, like a trained nurse, of Pound's meals and medications:

7:15 breakfast: orange juice, few spoonsful porridge.

1:30 lunch: riso in bianco, cold chicken, gruyère cheese, banana cream w[ith] apricot.

4:00 tea: pane integrale, peanut butter, biscuit, tea.

8:00 supper: pastina in brodo, soft-boiled egg, 3 cooked apricots. (Medicines: 10g. miroton, 20g. sympatol, 1 ducolax, lucidril.)

Ezra disdained the regimen, and he jotted this random comment in Olga's notebook: "My bestial idiocy at Dadone's [is] past any measure. . . . If he had (three years ago) . . . given me a proper large glass of castor oil, and lemon 'on the rocks,' i.e., plenty of ice, followed by real coffee, all these doc bills & catetere [catheters] could have been avoided. B[acigalupo] approves the model to replace leaky inner tube . . . swears he can remake normal men."

Olga sent a note to Dorothy Pound at the Albergo Italia, enclosing a map with instructions to reach Casa 131 if she wanted to visit her husband: "Take a taxi to the 'Eucalyptus' . . . where the via Primavera joins the salita . . . you then will have to walk about 7 to 10 minutes (cars cannot station there). . . . [The salita] joins the Via Aurelia above the Casa di Sole." The junction of the road where the eucalyptus and cedar appear to grow from one root—called "l'eucalipto" by the locals and taxi men— Pound mentions in Canto 76:

> from il triedro to the Castellaro
>   the olives grey over grey holding walls.

When Ezra's bladder infection reappeared at the end of May, the blood count was very high, and the doctors recommended an emergency procedure to prevent uremic poisoning. Dorothy, as legal guardian, was required to sign the forms. Olga noted that she "paid purely formal visits, one-half hour June 15th, at my request, [to] give the surgeon permission to operate."

The procedure took place June 19, under local anesthetic. "He has been doing well, yesterday was up for [the] first time," Olga wrote Duncan, "takes an interest in books and newspapers. . . . All this has shown that . . . his fits of depression and not wanting to eat were not mental, or cussedness, [but] due to poison in the blood. . . . I shall not go to Siena this summer. . . . Mary can come down for a week or so every now and then and take over if necessary. . . . I intend to see this thing through. Dr. Bacigalupo . . . has known E. over 35 years and understands his kinks, doesn't get put off by his manner . . . is *very fond of E*."

When Ezra was released from the Villa Chiara on June 30, he returned with Olga to Sant'Ambrogio, and Dorothy Pound left Rapallo with Omar the same day. Dorothy wrote, after arriving at Brunnenburg, that she was glad the operation was successful, but "I hope now they will leave the poor man alone." She enclosed a check "for Ezra's keep," and added, "please reimburse yourself for warm undershirt and any other expenses. We generally allow 60,000 lire a month for food." She continued to send monthly checks, but kept the purse strings firmly in hand: "No money is supposed to be his 'own' nowadays."

Mary and the children came to Sant'Ambrogio while Olga returned to Siena July 22 for the nineteenth Settimana Musicale Senese. She wanted to be there for the second performance of Vivaldi's *Juditha Triumphans* (about which she wrote a scholarly abstract for the Accademia *Bollettino*).

Lester Littlefield was still "guardian" of 252, calle Querini; Marianne Moore and two Bryn Mawr classmates traveling in Italy and Greece had visited him at Olga's house that summer. Olga retained the right to use it two months of the year, and on September 25—as soon as Ezra could travel by train—she took him back to the Hidden Nest.

He was strong enough to attend a dinner on the thirtieth to celebrate his election to the Academy of American Poets hosted by the Society of Venetian Writers. While Olga remained quietly in the background, Ezra was becoming an international celebrity. An interview with photographs appeared in *Time* (translated from *Epoca*) in April 1963.

They returned to Sant'Ambrogio for Ezra's second prostate operation at the Villa Chiara. "Dorothy was responsible for the second operation—as Committee, she had to decide," Olga noted bitterly; "the one chosen left him impotent." But she was fair enough to acknowledge that the alternative operation might have killed him.

Ezra had recovered sufficiently to travel to Siena for the final concerts of the season at the Accademia. Olga was warmly received by the Count and former colleagues, but she appeared to feel no regret at giving up her prestigious position to care for Pound. She heard that, in her absence, Pablo Casals and his wife, Martita, felt they "were not treated with enough red carpet, and left in a huff."

The couple returned to Sant'Ambrogio at the end of August. Mary, in the States again, had gone to Boston to visit Robert Frost and to thank him for helping to secure her father's release. She was just in time, for Frost died a week later. She also went to Brooklyn to see Marianne Moore in her apartment there—"packages, books everywhere, the best knives too tarnished to use"—but to Mary's eyes, Moore was "perfection, handsome, temperate and considerate, humorous and talented."

In early September, Olga and Ezra returned to Venice via Rimini. Ezra requested to see for one last time the church of San Francesco with the tomb of Sigismundo Malatesta, a monument to the fifteenth-century ruler and his mistress Isotta, central figures in Cantos 8 through 11.

On his birthday, October 30, the Cini Foundation celebrated with a publication party for the Italian translation of the Confucian *Odes* and, according to Olga, "a large crowd were enthusiastic." Later, Olga recorded that Ezra had tremendous applause when appearing on the platform at "a poetry-prize do" in Padua. Constant travel, which Ezra seemed to enjoy, failed to lift his deepening depression. "There were more causes than I realized, i.e., not physical," Olga acknowledged.

Horst Tappe, the photographer who had wangled an invitation to the calle Querini to record Ezra's life, recommended La Prairie clinic in Clarens, Switzerland, specializing in the treatment of nervous disorders. Lester Littlefield agreed that Dr. Niehaus's treatment "gave Pope Pius some six or more years of life." When Olga delivered Ezra to the clinic on November 18, they shaved off his beard: "I found E. red-faced like a monkey's behind—but when the redness disappeared, [he was] still handsome, showing a likeness to Homer," she remembered. "He was disintoxicated, and never had catatonic symptoms again." Dorothy Pound paid the bill but complained to Olga: "Did you know when you took Ezra to Montreux the prices which reign in Swiss cliniques? You should have given me warning." Olga was determined to restore Ezra's health and equilibrium, whatever the cost.

The couple remained in Venice through the winter. Mary Jane Phillips-Matz, who lived in the second house down the alley from No. 252 in the 1960s, and after 1969 just across the canal from Olga's house, remembered the "trim, gray-haired woman who . . . fed stray cats and . . . began to cosset our three toddling daughters (and the son born in 1966), serving afternoon tea and cookies, and when they were older, the elderly man who lived with her taught them to play chess." The two women shared an interest in music, and both were from Ohio. "From her I learned how to serve ample meals on tiny trays that inevitably ended with poached pears or soft desserts with colorful names, 'Spotted Dog' or 'Resurrection Pudding.' The smell of burnt logs hung in the living room, as did the scent of pungent eucalyptus."

Phillips-Matz remembered Olga as energetic, intelligent, high-spirited, a mine of common sense, who punctuated every sentence with "Capito?" "She taught me to layer newspapers under sweaters and coats to keep warm, to wrap a light blanket like a kilt for extra protection during afternoon naps. I helped to mop up water from the canal that crept into the hall during an acqua alta. Her closets and mine were filled with clothes that had seen ten or even twenty seasons. She taught me a great deal about what she called, 'making do,' how to make a bed on steamer trunks. Loans flowed from her house to mine . . . repaid promptly on both sides. After great loss, we grieved together. After lunches at Montin's or Cici's, we exchanged memories of childhood visits to Mt. Chocorua." Poignantly, she recalled "the day she played for the last time and put her violin away, without a trace of self-pity or regret."

In February 1964, four months before the seventh Festival of Two Worlds, Gian Carlo Menotti came to Venice to arrange the Italian premiere of the *Last Savage*. Mary Jane's friendship with Menotti dated back to the 1950s. A decade later, she was director of public relations, general manager, and fund-raiser for the Festival. Charles Matz, who was then Mary Jane's husband, offered to introduce Menotti to Pound. "Did you know," Matz asked, "that Pound once wrote an opera?"

"You mean the libretto?"

"No, the music. . . . He used the poetry of François Villon, *The Testament*."

Matz took Menotti to the Hidden Nest, and as the vespers rang at Santa Maria della Salute the composer and the poet talked about music—Pound, a poet who for a time turned composer, and Menotti, a composer who often turned to poetry and drama. Olga played the tape of the BBC broadcast of *Le Testament*, and Menotti asked for permission to perform the opera in Spoleto in the summer of 1965.

Olga and Ezra had just settled in for another winter when Pound's venerated friend T. S. Eliot died. Pound was the last survivor of the generation of poets and writers ranging from Yeats to Hemingway, and the death of Eliot left him "very sad and deeply stricken."

On sudden impulse, and after consulting Eliot's widow, Olga purchased air tickets to attend the January 4, 1965, memorial service in Westminster Abbey. Sir Alec Guinness read from the *Quartets*, and other old friends delivered eulogies. After the ceremony, the couple returned to the Eliots' flat to spend several hours alone with his widow, Valerie. After, Ezra wanted to see his Wyndham Lewis portrait at the Tate Gallery.

They were in the taxi on the way to Heathrow when Olga noticed ads for Aer Lingus, and spontaneously suggested a detour to Ireland, the home of her maternal grandparents. In Dublin, they visited Georgie Yeats, widow of "Uncle William," and viewed the paintings of Jack Yeats, the poet's father. The only literary people Ezra asked to see were Patrick Kavanagh and Austin Clarke.

Back in Venice, Pound was invited to read from the Confucian *Odes* at a Dante Commemorazione at the Cini Foundation on the island of San Giorgio Maggiore, sharing the stage with Nobel Prize winner Eugenio Montale. Caresse Crosby had invited the couple to attend a poets' seminar at the Castello di Roccasinibalda, but Olga declined; Ezra was saving himself for the Spoleto performance of his opera in July, though she hoped their friend Gianfranco Ivancich "would bring us to you for a day before returning to Rapallo." She described herself as "cook and bottle washer, sec[retary], counter-irritant and soporific, all in one bottle, and sometimes I feel as if the bottle had been given a good shaking before taking."

Olga's account of "Ezra Pound in Spoleto," drafted in her notebook, gives a behind-the-scenes glimpse of the 1965 performance of *Le Testament de Villon* and the poetry week preceding it at the Festival of Two Worlds: "By genius, I mean 'an inevitable swiftness and rightness in a given field, the trouvaille, the direct simplicity in seizing the effective means' [a quotation borrowed from *Guide to Kulchur*]. Pound found all these attributes in Gian Carlo Menotti when they met to discuss . . . *Le Testament de Villon.*"

The production was staged as a ballet choreographed by John Butler, with Carmen de Lavallade and other dancers, the stage bare but for a gibbet. The conductor, Herbert Handt, sang a role.

Thomas Schippers conducted a new production of *Otello,* and to Olga's eyes, his wife Nonie Phipps was the undisputed "queen" of the Festival, sharing a box with their Venice neighbor Wally Toscanini, daughter of the conductor Arturo. Also on the program were Pierre Louÿs's *Chansons de Bilitis,* set to the music of Claude Debussy (again, choreographed by Butler after a concept of Vera Zorina), and *Abram and Isaac* (from the Chester Miracle Play), staged by Rhoda Levine with music by Benjamin Britten.

"First, poets of different nationalities and divergent ideological viewpoints," Olga recalled, "who . . . read their own works on stage at the Caio Melisso Theatre" (a dramatic setting built for chamber operas on the medieval cathedral piazza). Desmond O'Grady was master of ceremonies. Charles Olson, Pier Paolo Pasolini, Lawrence Ferlinghetti, and Allen Tate were there; Pablo Neruda (who "looked like a prosperous businessman"), Stephen Spender ("in a striped sweat shirt"), and Yevgeny Yevtushenko. Ezra, in a light linen suit and canvas shoes, seated in Menotti's box, read with the aid of a microphone—not his own poems, but Marianne Moore's translations of La Fontaine, Robert Lowell's "imitations" from Dante, and his own translations of the Confucian *Odes* and Montanari's *Saturno.*

Pound, then almost eighty, appeared "thin, slight and weak," his soft voice cracking as he "reached up to the hatrack of memory." He received a standing ovation. "Everything about Spoleto was fine for Ezra," Olga noted, "the air, the people. Life in the Palazzo del Duomo was exceedingly pleasant. He did not find Menotti's stairs too steep to climb, and the local bread was much to his taste. The 12 o'clock concerts in the theater across the way were a daily joy to the man who had written: 'The magic of music is its effect on volition, a sudden clearing of the mind of rubbish and the re-establishment of a sense of proportion'." After, there were unexpected meetings with old friends in the piazza: Benedetta Marinetti, Yvonne Casella, Caresse Crosby, Buckminster Fuller, John Drummond, Desmond O'Grady, Isamu Noguchi (who spoke of Brancusi and Gaudier). "In late afternoon, sitting at the window, he [Ezra] might listen to rehearsals outside the Duomo, the swallows he loved making themselves heard above the orchestra. How better could 'an old man rest'? He rambled 'round the city at all hours, stopping for ice cream, or speculating on the Arena as a possible setting for *Women of Trachis* (if Menotti would write the music he wanted for it). He returned to Spoleto each time with joy."

After Spoleto, Caresse Crosby sent Robert Mann to meet the couple at the Rome station and to have Ezra carried on a *chaise à porteur* to the eagle-shaped fortress of Roccasinibalda, her World Peace Center and Italian Yaddo Colony. The castello, designed by Michelangelo's contemporary Baldassarre Peruzzi, is carved out of sheer solid rock in the Abruzzi mountains of Rieti province. At the back, there is a hanging garden with towering cypresses and a swimming pool where, at sunset, Caresse's guests used to gather for cocktails. The Great Hall in the north wing was a succession of large, empty spaces with coffered ceilings and huge open fireplaces. The sparsely furnished bedrooms, Olga remembered, had paneless windows that opened onto the Turano valley below, and were uninhabitable for five or six months of the year; the swooping and darting of bats interrupted her sleep. Since Roccasinibalda rises above the clouds, she felt as if she were on a floating island.

The castle was cold and damp that summer, and Ezra could never find a room warm enough to suit him, though he spent long sunny hours in the courtyard, Caresse recalled. The "rambunctious, combative" youth of the Twenties, who had arrived in Paris bronzed and *negligé* to dance a "voo-doo prance" with her at the Boule Blanche, had become "a tired old man with listless eyes and a shock of white hair." There were days when he didn't say a word, just whispered "yes" or "no" to direct questions, and his mood swings were dramatic, "by turns, alert and energetic, despondent and apathetic." Frances Steloff, owner of the Gotham Book Mart, a gathering place of the literati since the 1920s, was also in residence that summer and remembered that when photographers came, Olga refused to pose with Ezra "for reasons of propriety."

Caresse's memoir, "What in the World?" about her life as a peace activist and co-founder with Buckminster Fuller of Citizens of the World, was soon to be published by *L'Herne*. She had visited Ezra at St. Elizabeth's in February 1946, and was asked by psychiatrists to give her opinion in his sanity hearing: Was Pound completely out of his mind, or as she had known him in the 1930s? "I said truthfully, 'as I had known him.' I loved and admired him then, as I always have, *never* thought him a traitor."

Back in Venice, the calle Querini nest was not as "hidden" as it had been in the 1930s: "We have had a German TV crew on our heads, hands and feet! . . . the director, a clumsy brute, doing a documentary for EP's birthday." Academics, journalists, and biographers came, along with the merely curious who found Olga's number in the telephone directory. "They ring my bell and announce they are writing books that will tell 'both sides.' *Both* sides?" she queried. "What do they think we are? Ezra Pound is no pancake."

Olga kept Ezra on the move as an antidote to depression. The couple celebrated his eightieth birthday in Paris. At Samuel Beckett's play *Fin de Partie*, Ezra whispered to Olga as the protagonists spoke the dialogue from trash bins, "C'est moi dans la poubelle." They did not stay after the performance to speak to the Nobel Prize–winning author, but Beckett— not wishing to subject the old poet to a long climb up to his apartment— came himself to pay a call on Pound and stayed for more than an hour.

After nearly sixty years Natalie Barney was still holding court in her salon. A German documentary film crew recorded their visit to the rue Jacob, accompanying them around the garden and up the steps to the Temple à l'Amitié.

Barney's birthday gift to Ezra was a long-awaited trip to Delphi. The poet George Seferis, the 1963 Nobelist, who had translated Pound's poems into Greek, took them home to meet his beautiful wife. Ezra "saw no-one but Greek friends," Olga recalled. Zizissimo Lorenzatos arranged a picnic on the beach near Soúnio (with chilled pomegranate juice that Ezra remembered for its *color*). They had the place to themselves in November after the tourists had gone. With another Greek friend, they attended an outdoor exhibition of modern sculpture, including a Gaudier-Brzeska dog that "did not fill EP with enthusiasm." The highlight of the trip was the "sacred fount" at Delphi that Ezra had visited only in his imagination when writing *The Cantos:*

> Castalia is the name of that fount in the hill's fold,
> > the sea below . . .
> Grove hath its altar
> > under elms, in that temple . . . (Canto 90)

After Ezra joined Olga in 1962, she had begun to throw the coins for the *I Ching* readings daily for both of them. In 1966, she started to record her findings in a series of blue school notebooks ("to put some order into my affairs"): "These hexagrams have always been made, usually in the morning, first thing after breakfast . . . commencing with mine, read aloud to Ezra, then his," she noted. (Pound mentioned the *I Ching* in Canto 102—"50 more years on the Changes"—inspired by Confucius's saying, "If many years were added to me, I would give it to the study of the Book of Changes.") On the flyleaf of the first notebook, he scrawled: "Olga = Courage."

The earliest notebooks contained only the hexagrams, but soon Olga began to record Pound's health, diet, response to visitors, and dreams, interspersed with her own thoughts and reminiscences of childhood, family, and friends. The notebooks also included "notings down" that Olga happened upon when thumbing through *The Cantos, Guide to Kulchur,* and other (often undocumented) sources, for example: "Curiosity, that's my advice to the young—have some curiosity," and "A good deal of literature seems to spring from hate, but something vital emerges from the fragments, which is not hate" (translated from the Italian). The so-called *I Ching* Notebooks provide a valuable record of the last ten years of the poet's life and are closely interwoven into the text of this biography.

Ezra began suffering from severe depression again and was admitted to the Fazio Clinica delle Malattie Nervose e Mentali of the University of Genoa on March 11, and he remained there until April 16. Professor

Cornelio Fazio, who examined Pound, wrote this report: "The patient was . . . almost completely silent, uttering only a few words when questioned, impaired physically, often refused food. . . . Sometimes, prompted by external situations (travels, environmental modification), Mr. Pound exhibited fairly normal activity and interest. . . . Ideas of self-accusation and hypochondriacal delusions were always present. . . . These ideas and the general inhibition could probably account for the refusal of food. . . . It seemed as if the personality of the patient had always been on the autistic side . . . so that a psychotic-like situation came out permitting, and perhaps encouraging, poetic activity."

Pound had been under the care of a young specialist, Romolo Rossi, who prescribed Tofranil, a powerful drug that left him in what Olga described as a "catatonic state." She telephoned Dr. Bacigalupo, who moved him out of the clinic.

In Olga's view, travel was a better way to restore Ezra's equilibrium. They went to Ravenna at the end of May to hear Antoine de Bavier conduct Bach's *St. Matthew Passion* in the Church of Sant'Apollinaire. Ezra was invited again to Poetry Week in Spoleto in July, and read "most beautifully." They heard a fine performance of the Verdi *Requiem* in the square before the cathedral conducted by Zubin Mehta, and Olga recalled that she had first met Mehta when he was a promising new student at the Accademia.

Later that summer, news came from Siena that Count Guido Chigi Saracini, her mentor and benefactor since the founding of the Accademia in 1932, who had furthered the careers of Mehta and many other young musical stars, was dead. At the time Olga was too preoccupied with Ezra's care to attend the memorial service. Without revealing the depth of the mixed emotions she felt about the "zoo" and its master, she wrote to close friends: "He is greatly missed. The Accademia is not the same without him."

That November, a tidal wave brought the highest water in Venetian memory; they were trapped in the house for forty-eight hours. The water soon reached the cheekbones of Gaudier-Brzeska's Hieratic Head, and before it stopped rising it reached table height and stayed there all the next day. "But the most striking thing was the *dead silence*."

In another determined effort to restore Ezra's health, Olga checked into the Hotel Blankreuzhaus in Basel, Switzerland, in January for a consultation with Dr. Poldinger of the Psychiatrische Universitätsklinik. Dr. Poldinger prescribed antidepressant drugs and reassured her that there would be an increase of the mood-lifting effect in the spring. They traveled on to Zurich, and visited the Joyces' graves. "The other graves had little Christmas trees and wreaths with candles, as is the custom there," Olga remembered, "but Joyce's name (with Nora's) was nearly illegible, on a stone hidden in the grass." The following day, Ezra sat patiently for a portrait sketch by Oskar Kokoschka at his studio in Villeneuve.

When Dorothy Pound heard they were considering an invitation to speak at the Folger Library in Washington, she wrote: "For mercy's sake, don't take EP into the USA." In a later letter, she described Olga's position as "rather like leading 'round a performing bear!"

An unexpected visitor from America arrived in the summer of 1967, the poet laureate of the Beat generation, Allen Ginsberg. Olga described the encounter in Spoleto: "We went . . . to Mozart's *Don Giovanni* with Thomas Schippers conducting and the Henry Moore sets. During the first interval, AG chose to present himself to EP (sitting in a stall near the gangway), stopping the flow of people behind him. . . . We had arranged to meet friends in the theater bar . . . when a group of poets (including AG) arrived to pay their respects to EP—accompanied, naturellement, by TV. They kept muttering mantras and tagged on when EP tried to get out of the crush and go up to congratulate Schippers backstage."

Ginsberg next turned up in Sant'Ambrogio. He sat under a tree in a wooden chair and sang Hare Krishna to Ezra, then went inside for the promised lunch. Ezra refused to say anything the whole afternoon until Ginsberg commented that Paul Morand had "jazzed up" the French language. Olga asked, "What was that book by Morand you liked so much?" (which Pound had translated into English). Ezra answered "*Ouvert la Nuit* [Open All Night]," and went on eating his spaghetti. "It was like being with Prospero. There was no weight in the silence," Ginsberg said. Later, Olga received this note: "Thank you for your sweetness to me, while I stayed so long. I love Mr. Pound, and did not know how to leave. I hope he finds peace."

The same month, Olga corresponded with the British critic Cyril Connolly, whom she had never met, protesting remarks in his article about Louis Zukovsky. Connolly had written that he could not forgive Pound for condoning the actions of the Nazis at Belsen and other concentration camps. Olga defended Ezra. During the war, she said, they were cut off completely, with no news, only one radio, and when Ezra was in the Pisan camp, he had not heard about the atrocities or, she insisted, he would have written about them in *The Cantos*. Many of his good friends were Jews— she mentioned Luigi Franchetti (a grandson of a Rothschild), Giorgio Levi, Lonnie Mayer—and some had appeared at the Rapallo concerts. This was the beginning of a long correspondence—and friendship—with Connolly.

After years of waiting, Olga at last had her prize. One observer noted that "Miss Rudge was clearly the sea in which he [Pound] floated. She cleaned, she shopped, she stoked the old stove." And she appeared to enjoy every day with Ezra. "Why is it, in old age, dancing seems better? We had a gramophone, dancing with Him to Vivaldi [was] His idea!" After many lonely Christmases past, she now could enjoy the holidays with her lover. They saw the New Year in with "His new couch, Vivaldi, rain on the roof, dinner on a tray, later chocolates and grog—hot!"

Their daily lives followed a familiar pattern: Ezra did yoga exercises before breakfast, "spontaneously." Lunch at the Pensioni Montin or Cici, visits with friends, walks along the Zattere, a light supper at home (Olga strictly monitored Pound's diet). In the evening, Ezra often read selections from *The Cantos*.

Along with notations about Ezra's diet and daily activities (and eye-glasses purchased), Olga noted their current reading—a preface to C. G. Jung's work, important to Pound because of Jung's interest in the *I Ching*. In answer to Olga's query if it made sense, Ezra replied: "The things one calls chance being a result of more laws than one knows."

They celebrated Olga's April birthday with Else Bernheim and Joan Fitzgerald at Fitzgerald's studio viewing the just completed bust of Ezra; he was pleased with it. Many old friends—and often curious strangers— found their way to the calle Querini. Mrs. Philip Barry, the playwright's widow and Grace Kelly's aunt, was sent to them by Caresse Crosby. The poet Paul Blackburn, who translated Provençal poets following in Pound's tradition, brought a beautiful Andalusian goblet and pine cone. Ezra said it reminded him of an Aztec idol he saw at St. Elizabeth's, a symbol of male-female copulation. Böski Marcus Antheil turned up—after more than thirty years! Julien Cornell, Pound's lawyer, arrived from Washington with his wife, and Dorothea Watts Landsburg returned to her former home on the calle Querini.

Correspondence came from an unexpected source in Ohio. Richard Hammond, who had last visited Olga in Paris in 1928, informed her that an urban renewal program was in progress in Youngstown; the building of a new post office had increased the value of her father's Boardman property. Rentals were building up in her account, and Olga realized it might be wise to hold on to the lots. But she asked Hammond to explore the possibility of a sale: "I do not foresee leaving anyone any property."

In July the couple traveled to Spoleto to see Menotti's 1968 production of *The Saint of Bleecker Street*, which Olga pronounced "Magnificent!" There were concerts every evening, Thomas Schippers conducting Mozart and Vivaldi, another opportunity for Olga to have lunch with Simonetta Lippi, Schippers's assistant. Lippi's father had been a musician, and Simonetta shared with Olga a love of music. An enduring friendship developed, and after Lippi followed Schippers to his post as conductor of the Cincinnati Symphony Orchestra, she credited Olga with teaching her all she knew about managing a conductor's busy schedule.

Menotti sent them home to Sant'Ambrogio in his chauffeur-driven car, and two days later Ezra was strong enough to walk to Monte Allegro, where they discovered their names in the old hotel registry for the year 1924.

During this era, Olga began to record Ezra's dreams in her notebook. In an early one, he saw Olga dancing in a window: "Me?" "Yes." "Was I dancing nicely?" "Yes." "What kind of dancing?" "Oh, that Ceylonese bending."

In another, Eustace Mullins of Staunton, Virginia, one of Pound's acolytes at St. Elizabeth's, starred in an unlikely Freudian drama. Ezra and the poet Hilda Doolittle, his young sweetheart, were staying with the Mullins family when Ezra learned that Mullins had raped H.D.

"I said if there was any produce, he would have to support it. He might have said 'please,' I said. It wouldn't have been difficult for you to use persuasion."

Olga: "Were you annoyed? Was she [H.D.] recognizable?"

Ezra: "Yes, I was annoyed. Both recognizable."

On September 5, Olga booked the 9:12 P.M. sleeper to Paris, where they were invited to stay in M. L. Bardevant's studio flat. After a nostalgic lunch at La Coupôle, they visited Natalie Barney on the rue Jacob. The courtyard surrounding the Temple à l'Amitié was in shambles and the house appeared "derelict," but Barney herself was "better than two years ago—she asked about my violin." They went on to the Brancusi studio and the Gaudier-Brzeska room at the Musée d'Art Moderne, and enjoyed a superb lunch with James Laughlin and his wife, Ann, at the five-star Tour Eiffel restaurant.

Olga booked a sleeper the same night to arrive in Venice the next morning. Ezra's only complaint was an ache in his shoulder (he would never admit pain, so Olga had to deduce it from his actions). He was also suffering from diarrhea, impossible to hide and doubly difficult for Olga, who was unable to wash the soiled clothes while traveling. She noted other physical infirmities of advanced age: he was developing a cataract, and "for the past year, EP [has been] slightly deaf, so that conversation, when many are participating, tires him and he retires into himself with fits of needless anxiety, but never enough to keep him from doing anything which pleases him—going out to meals, theater, travel, with no special fatigue, no aches or rheumatism." He endured his bête noire, a tub bath, "without tears."

At the year's end, they were settled in again at the Hidden Nest. Ezra read aloud from Yeats one evening, Olga read the tarot cards the next. They discussed "oddments" in the news and viewed photographs of the *Apollo 8* spacecraft (Olga was astonished that nothing but the crust of the earth was showing). The couple spent Christmas Eve reminiscing over old photographs discovered in a suitcase.

On the first page of the 1969 notebook, Ezra wrote this tribute to the woman he loved: "For the gift of life, sensibility and courage—those two were the opening bars of the Jannequin (Olga's)—never admit defeat!"

Desmond O'Grady, the poet who had been at the dock in Genoa to meet Pound in 1958, came to stay with them in Sant'Ambrogio. He read from the works of Patrick Kavanagh one peaceful evening, and on others, Ezra and O'Grady concentrated on the chessboard. But days later, while reading *The Cantos*, Ezra erupted angrily, following a pattern of erratic behavior that Olga was at a loss to explain.

Mary came to visit. She and Ezra took long walks to the Castellaro, and there was the appearance of a close family. But on the third day, while Mary was helping to prepare lunch, she shattered a perfume bottle Olga's brother Arthur had given her some sixty years before on Hill Road in St. John's Wood. It was an accident, but to Olga's eyes it was symbolic of the basic discord between the two women.

The season persisted windy and cold, colder, coldest. Casa 131 was a contadino's cottage, and the only warmth came from the open fireplace with pine cones to burn. Ezra's cough persisted, and Olga attempted to cure it with the housewife's old-fashioned remedy, chicken broth and rice. Her thoughts often returned to Hook Heath and the supportive environment of the Richards family many years before.

She wrote to Kathleen, hinting at the loss she secretly felt in giving up music to be Ezra's companion: "Remember the Hill violin? You? Your father? You were always such a united family, it becomes difficult to remember which—a kindness to me, among many . . . a Hill copy of a Strad, 'The Messiah.' . . . I did practice all during the war, and was playing better, too. [But] I have not had time for fifteen years now to practice, and you know what a violin needs. You ought to have it . . . where would you like it to go? If I am able to get to England when it gets warmer, [I] will bring it."

In April, the couple returned to Venice. Ezra was suffering from stomach cramps and similar complaints of advanced age, but was able to enjoy a performance of Verdi's *Don Carlo* at La Fenice. On April 13, he jotted in the notebook: "It's her birthday. He brings nothing but good wishes and bad deeds." Count Vittorio Cini, head of the foundation that bears his name, and his wife, Kiki, honored Olga on her natal day with a dinner party for nineteen. When Valerie Eliot arrived in Venice for the celebration, the Count "charmingly explained that he put Valerie on his right instead of me, because she was a 'straniera.' I feel myself Italian."

As a hostess gift, Valerie brought a pair of shoes, to Olga's eyes the act of a warm and caring person. "May I say how much I admire the way you take care of Ezra . . . so sweet and patient with everybody, no matter how tiresome they are," Valerie wrote after returning to London. Back in "EP's Kensington," she was reminded that "we had our wedding breakfast at 10 Kensington Church Walk where Father Wright, who married us, lived."

On the fifteenth, the couple celebrated again—at Harry's Bar, then luncheon at Torcello. When Olga asked Ezra what historic character he would have chosen to dine with, his answer was "Chaucer."

On May 11, Olga awakened Ezra early to catch the train to Rome. Another hour to the Citadella, where he was to sit on the platform for the awarding of the Premio Letterario. Ezra was silent, but the poet Olma read from Mary's translation of *The Cantos,* a "very moving" event.

Their busy schedule continued until June 4, when they left their Venice garden at 1:45 P.M., arrived at JFK Airport at 8:30 the same evening, and went directly to the Hotel Schuyler on Forty-fifth Street, a hotel Olga had used in the past, apparently unaware that the neighborhood had gone downhill in the fourteen years since her last visit. James Laughlin was surprised to hear they were staying there; he did not even know they were coming to the States.

Ezra had been invited by Mrs. Hugh Bullock, then president of the Academy of American Poets, to attend the academy's thirty-fifth anniversary in the board room of the New York Public Library and the presentation of a fellowship award to Richard Eberhart. Valerie Eliot was at the library editing a new edition of *The Waste Land,* which included Pound's extensive annotations, and joined Marianne Moore, Robert Lowell, Margaret Cohen, Lewis Freedman, Norman Holmes Pearson of Yale, and Ezra, who "would arise in a most courtly fashion to shake hands when any admirer came up to speak to him."

The following day, the couple drove with grandson Walter de Rachewiltz, then studying at Rutgers University in New Jersey, to Norfolk, Connecticut to stay with James and Ann Laughlin at Meadow House. Laughlin was to receive an honorary doctor of letters degree from Pound's alma mater, Hamilton College, on Sunday June 8. Olga, Walter, and the Laughlins drove to Clinton, New York, for the commencement. As Laughlin described the event:

> Because they thought the academic procession might be too long . . . they gave him a special entrance from the side . . . very dramatic. There was a silence, and the audience began to get restive, then Ezra entered, led by the master of ceremonies . . . with his stave, and when the president introduced him with a graceful little speech, saying that he had had his own Doctor of Letters there thirty years before, there was a tremendous standing ovation from the students. Ezra looked beautiful in his academic robes, and sat on the platform beside me.

They drove back to Manhattan on Monday and settled in at the Laughlins' Bank Street apartment in the Village. Ezra was up every morning at seven o'clock, taking a hot bath and shampooing his hair without complaint. "Each day, Olga worked out some little project for him," Laughlin remembered. "When they were not invited out, I would have little dinner parties for them at the Dorgene Restaurant opposite the White Horse Tavern in the Village. Ezra barely spoke, but he followed conversations." At another dinner party honoring Marian (Mrs. E. E.) Cummings, Robert Lowell read from her husband's works, and Lowell and the others went back to Bank Street after. Valerie Eliot and Djuna Barnes came on Djuna's birthday, bringing champagne. Ezra was "stimulated and brilliant," Olga recalled; "[he] takes the ladies downstairs (in slippers)." They also called on Marianne Moore, incapacitated and in a wheelchair, at her charming but cluttered Brooklyn apartment.

Walter drove his grandparents to Germantown to visit Priscilla and Esther Heacock, the Quaker sisters whose family, Ezra recalled, had owned a floral business on Fernwood Avenue when he attended the Chelten Hills Dames' School. The sisters were long-standing friends of Olga's Aunt Lou and Uncle Harold Baynes, the naturalist; Esther herself had become an accomplished photographer of birds. Surprised to see that Olga had taken Dorothy's place, they conceded that "she has evidently cared for him for so many years."

The next morning, Olga flew to her birthplace, Youngstown, Ohio, to inspect the property left in her father's estate. A parking lot occupied the site of the Rudge family home on Bryson Street. After discussing the situation with Richard Hammond and an officer at the bank, she created a trust, with Hammond, an old family friend, as trustee. She was delighted to meet her two young cousins (one, a nun in a teaching order). She hurried back to New York the same evening. Walter and his grandfather had been in all day; Ezra refused to eat, fearing that Olga would never come back. But the next morning he was up early to go with Walter to the Hans Arp exhibit at the Guggenheim Museum. On the last evening, Mary Hemingway, Ernest's widow, treated them to dinner at four-star Voisin.

Back in Venice, the house was being repainted, so Olga escaped with Ezra to Rome for the Fourth of July celebration. She recorded another significant dream.

Ezra: "It was on the 4th of July that I hurt myself climbing over a picket fence. I scraped the skin in the crotch—didn't hurt my balls."

Olga: "How old were you?"

Ezra: "Oh, eight or nine."

Olga: "I thought it was your father . . . ?"

Ezra: "Yes, I don't know how old he was, a small boy, swinging on a swing and the rope broke. That's when he got that cut, you could put your hand into his side that far, lost one testicle—never could do athletics."

Olga: "Was he always telling you to take care?"

Ezra: "No!"

Olga: "Your mother?"

Ezra: "She never mentioned the subject at all."

A few days later they were in Spoleto. They found "all serene" at the Menotti palazzo. As in seasons past, the Festival of Two Worlds was a time of reunion with old friends: Simonetta Lippi, Buckminster Fuller and his wife Ann, Sally Fitzgerald and Stephen Spender's daughter, Isamu Noguchi and Willem de Kooning. Anthony Hecht wrote, and read, a poem dedicated to Ezra. When Ezra was invited to choose one of his own poems to read, he was so depressed Olga feared he could not go on with it. She got him onto the stage, where he sat quietly with six others—and at last, read. Listening from the box, Olga pronounced it "Magnificent!" They met the Spenders and others in the piazza after, and Noguchi and Menotti discussed staging Ezra's *Women of Trachis* the next season.

They were in Rapallo for another memorable happening on July 20, 1969, when an American spacecraft landed human beings on the moon for the first time. As they watched the *Apollo 11* drama on television at the Café Dante (formerly the Yolanda), Olga asked, "Should the astronauts have left the American flag on the moon—or that of the United Nations?"

Ezra: "The American."

Olga: "Which do you consider of greater importance, the discovery of America, or the landing on the moon?"

Ezra (without hesitation): "Landing on the moon."

They were back in Venice in October, when critic Cyril Connolly, a dandy of the early 1920s—then very plump with a bald spot, "looking like a Roman poet in exile"—arrived. In Canto 76, recalling his early years in Venice, Pound had written:

> by the soap-smooth stone posts where San Vio
> meets with il Canal Grande
> between Salviati and the house that was of Don Carlos . . .

Remembering, Connolly wrote a colorful account of Ezra's eighty-fourth birthday party:

> The soapstone posts are still there on the corner of the Canal San
> Vio . . . 'the house that was of Don Carlos' is the Palazzo Guggen-
> heim. Our host, Count Cini, was an old friend, an outstanding octo-
> genarian whose fortune is devoted to his foundation on the island of
> San Giorgio. . . . The Count was a gourmet. . . . We had place cards
> and menus and rows of gold-engraved glass goblets. I shall never
> forget the white truffles in cheese sauce. . . . We ate persimmons and
> local muscats and white figs, while the Count's beautiful Roman
> wife cut up an apple for Mr. Pound. After luncheon, the guests
> gathered 'round while the Count toasted the Maestro in Marc de
> Bourgogne. . . . His birthday party [was] a mixture of Americans

and Italians, painters, sculptors, writers. Peter Russell, now living in
Venice, read a poem in his honour; we drank champagne, and a
cake arrived with eighty-four small candles. The patriarch gave two
great puffs like the Cyclop's bellow, and blew out all the candles.

On Christmas Day 1969, a walk on the Zattere. Olga and Ezra were
having lunch outside at the Pensione Cici, watching the passing scene. In
late afternoon, the three Matzes came to the calle Querini, and Mary Jane
read Chaucer in front of the fire. "When I got to 'Merciles Beaute,'" she
said, "Ezra told me to read more slowly. Once he corrected my Columbia
University Chaucerian English, and my voice was trembling as I read the
line, 'Your eyen two wol sleye me sodenly / I may the beaute of hem nat
sustaynel.' I did not dare to look into his eyes." After the visitors left and
the house was quiet, they picked up their chess game in front of the fire.

The twenty-sixth was another fine day for lunch outside at Cici, and
Walter came as they were finishing, bringing a gift of maple sugar for
Ezra. Walter was in good form, but Ezra was "somnolent." He would not
get up the next morning, so Olga took lunch up to his room on a tray and
was able to talk with Walter without interruptions.

At year's end, they were alone again. Olga put on records of Bach and
Yves Tinayre singing the Villon opera, and they toasted with Hennessey's
Fond de Verre.

Early in 1970, both suffered from depression, due in part to the severe
winter and prolonged bouts with influenza. Olga corresponded with Dr.
David Shaw of the department of neuropsychiatry, West Park Hospital,
Epsom, Surrey. "I would be delighted to see him [Pound] when he is in the
UK," Shaw replied. "However, long-standing depression in the 8th decade is notoriously resistant to treatment . . . [with] other problems of
metabolic changes of aging. I do not think his hopes should be raised too
high." To Olga: "I was interested to hear of your annual bout of hiberna-
tion (cyclothymia). . . . You could try anti-depressants. Some people have
been helped by Lithium."

Other correspondence came from an unexpected source: Omar Pound
at Cambridge. He was planning to visit them in Venice. "I never cease to

be amazed (and grateful) for the astonishing way you care for EP. Terribly exhausting, and no time off. Bless you for it!" he wrote.

Olga's efforts were not unappreciated. On her seventy-fifth birthday April 13, Ezra wrote this paean of praise, "To Olga":

> If there was a trace of beauty in anything, she saw it.
> For fine and just perception and a level gaze,
> For courage in face of evil,
> For courage in time of adversity.
> If anyone ever deserved the spring with all its beauty, she did.
> What her memory brought her was always some trace of fineness
>   of perception.

Dorothy Pound wrote to the couple in Venice in early spring: "Rapallo is now quite unpleasant. All winter there are floods of old people, and now—Easter and onwards—one caravan-load after another. The bay is already surrounded by bathing huts. I greatly hoped to see Ezra, it's more than a year." She added the distressing news that "Sunday p.m. somebody got into my room and opened the little dispatch case, extracting several rings (I do so regret my engagement ring from Ezra). . . . They left the English money and passport untouched . . . must be Mercury transit across the Sun!"

On July 21, 1970, a "Petition for Order to Make Monthly Payment to Patient's Companion" was filed by Caryl S. Terry, attorney for Dorothy Pound, "Committee for Ezra Pound," in the U.S. District Court for the District of Columbia.

> For a number of years, Miss Olga Rudge has acted as the patient's
> companion, fulfilling the functions of both housekeeper and
> nurse. . . . it would be advisable to provide Miss Rudge with some
> remuneration for her services, since it would be extremely
> expensive to hire persons to perform the services she presently
> performs. Therefore, the Committee requests that an order be
> entered authorizing her to make monthly payments to Miss Rudge

in the amount of $100 per month as compensation for her services to the patient.

However benign the intent, the petition placed Olga in a subservient position; the one hundred dollars per month was not sufficient compensation for the blow to her pride. She had long accepted the sacrifice of taking on the responsibility of Ezra, and had come to terms with "appearances." But it must have rankled to be Ezra's "housekeeper and nurse" in the eyes of the world.

Cyril Connolly was one correspondent who clearly recognized Olga, not as Pound's companion but more as a second wife. With a series of turbulent affairs and three marriages behind him, he was now three years older than his fifty-three-year-old father-in-law. His blond and pretty third wife, Deirdre, was expecting another baby. Would Ezra agree to be godfather by proxy? Cyril had dreamed that an old leather hatbox arrived from Venice, inside which he discovered a small child with a note from Ezra pinned to it: "I am sending you a wunderkind—his mental age is four!"

Connolly apologized for the publication of a recent article calling Robert Lowell "the greatest living American poet." He had meant living in *America,* he explained diplomatically. As a resident of Venice Pound was, in Connolly's view, "*the* greatest living American poet"—but "I only got to know his work well in the last few years."

Valerie Eliot invited the couple to come to London, but Olga regretted that they couldn't go. She reported their busy schedule of the previous year: "We hibernated in Venice—as good a place an any other in winter, [then] went to France . . . a choreographer friend had a spectacle during the Fêtes Jeanne d'Arc . . . three days in Paris, Orleans in May . . . to Rome [in] early June for two performances of Noh [plays], then to Spoleto, where Gian Carlo Menotti has lent his flat to E. for the Festival the last five years . . . as always, something or someone of interest."

Back in Sant'Ambrogio "heat, *muggy* heat." But the "coup de grace" to Olga was "the Noel Stock book [a new biography of Pound] *and* the favorable press it has received."

James Laughlin had written the author, an Australian professor then at the University of Toledo, in Ohio: "It seems to be crammed with information and facts . . . and reads well . . . looks like a triumph. I hope that all the family will be pleased, including Olga."

Olga was not pleased. "Ezra has not *seen* him since 1960 (*or* written him) except for a half-hour in Venice two (or three?) years ago. . . . [Stock] was a friend of DP's . . . (details in the book, EP says, could *only* have been given by her)."

Olga never forgave Stock, and from this experience she acquired a distaste for all biographers (in her daughter Mary's words, they appeared as "hogs after truffles"). She complained to Valerie Eliot that "all human sentiments are being crushed out of [me]."

Olga and Ezra were in Venice for the rest of that summer with many visitors, some welcome and some unwanted. "The filthiest of the hippies invading Europe . . . sit 'round here on dirty pavements, just like the pigeons. . . . I got rid of one hippie by the simple expedient of *turning the hose on him*." Canaletto paintings, she observed, "portrayed a clean Venice —nary a pigeon."

When Robert Lowell arrived, Olga "got in some other people," and Ugo Fasolo read his "Pigeon" poem, their grandson Walter followed with Ezra's translation. Then Lowell read from his recent collection, *For the Union Dead*. "Ezra sat on a hard chair from dinner till midnight, and no-one said 'perhaps we should not keep E. up too long,' or 'how wonderful he is able to do it.' "

During Pound's birthday week in October, Gianfranco Ivancich stopped by, bringing a recent issue of William Cookson's *Agenda* dedicated to Ezra, which pleased him. Mary arrived with granddaughter Patrizia on the twenty-ninth. The morning of his eighty-fifth birthday, Ezra announced that he had "dreamt of *leopards*" (possibly remembering the Roman zoo in the early days of their liaison). At Joan Fitzgerald's suggestion, Olga celebrated Mass with Mary and Patrizia at San Moise and took Communion. Count Cini rang up with *auguri* for Ezra, and came later, bringing a bottle of champagne. Other devoted friends stopped by: Lotte Frumi ("[with] a repertoire of Jewish jokes"); the "beautiful blond," Lisalotte Hochs; Fasolo, Fitzgerald, and Gianfranco Ivancich.

Mario Casamassima brought a copy of *Spots and Dots: Ezra Pound in Italy,* photos by Vittorigo Contino of Ezra in Venice, Siena, and Rapallo, recently published by Ivancich. Count Cini thumbed through it attentively, Olga recalled, and offered to promote the book. When the count left, a woman from Mondadori, the publisher, with a copy of Mary's translation of the *Antologia.* Laughlin remembered "a good letter from Mary describing the birthday celebration, which was fairly quiet, except that a lot of reporters turned up."

Pound's reputation as a leading Modernist poet was growing. Luigi de Maino, an editor from Milan, wanted to publish one of Ezra's early works, and came to interview him. When he asked which of the works they should publish, Ezra replied "*Sextus Propertius*—the best, of course." ("E. could make decisions without any suggestions from me or anyone," Olga noted.)

The next morning, a photograph of Olga with Ezra, Buckminster Fuller, and Guido Cadorin appeared in *Il Gazzettino.* For many years she had avoided such publicity, "for reasons of propriety," but at this point in life she had given up the pretense.

The year 1971 saw Mary's debut as a writer. *Discretions* (echoing the title of Pound's *Indiscretions*), published by Atlantic Monthly Press in the United States and Faber & Faber in England, revealed to the world for the first time Mary's childhood with foster parents in the Tyrol. Her descriptions of visits with her mother in Venice showed psychic pain: Olga, the strict disciplinarian who admitted "little talent for motherhood," inspired fear and longing in the little girl, not understanding and love. In Olga's view, she had been trying to instill in her daughter the same discipline and perfectionism drilled into her by Julia, qualities necessary to become a concert violinist. But to Mary growing up, discipline came across as disapproval, a feeling that she never measured up to Olga's high standards.

Olga was deeply wounded by Mary's revelations. "What good was she doing unleashing her spite and repercussions to her own and her children's damage?" Olga wondered. What she minded most was Mary's claim that she had not wanted the name of a "dead man"—that is, Arthur Rudge, the brother whose name Olga had listed on Mary's birth certificate to save her the embarrassment of an "unknown" father. Olga recalled that she had given Mary a blanket that had been Arthur's to take to La Quiete, and Mary mysteriously lost it.

Olga wrote to Peter du Santoy of Faber & Faber, pointing out the alleged "inaccuracies" in Mary's book. One particularly objectionable passage—"I shared Tate's [Herr Marcher's] bed"—Olga protested vehemently: "If OR and EP had known, *I* would have taken her away!" This was, in her view, pure fiction.

At the time of publication Mary was in Ghana assisting Professor Leonard Doob of Yale with anthropological research. For several years, Doob had lived in Merano while studying the region, and developed a close friendship with Mary and her family; Mary dedicated her book, "To Leonard." *Discretions* widened the breach between mother and daughter, and for many years Olga could neither forgive nor forget.

Her early collaboration with Ezra on *Le Testament de Villon* was at last being recognized. Robert Hughes, a young assistant conductor of the Oakland Symphony in California, was staging a new version based on the original orchestrated by George Antheil in the 1920s. With his companion, Margaret Fisher, he came to Venice to consult Olga about the production. He observed that when she arranged tea, "it was a *proper* tea, Victorian proper." And even at this advanced age, Olga displayed great energy, staying up late to talk about Ezra and his work for seven hours. But she drew a line in the conversation when talking about her private life, a line that she would not cross.

A young couple from New York, Christopher and Mary Mendenhall Cooley (whose father was on the board of the Metropolitan Museum of Art), came to stay at 252 while looking for a house of their own. They bought a place with a garden in Dorsoduro, remarking how lucky they were to find it. Cooley remembered Olga saying: "The hardest thing is to cope with *good* luck. We can all cope with *bad* luck—there's no choice—but few people are smart enough to cope with *good* luck."

In December 1971 Ezra was ill with a slight case of flu; she hoped to get him out again soon, but it was too cold and windy and there were high-water alarms. Yet they attended a solemn ceremony at San Giorgio to mark the death of another giant from the Paris years, Igor Stravinsky. Olga and Ezra listened from their places of honor near the altar rail while the mayor of Venice read Pound's poem "Night Litany," with its haunting refrain, "O Dieu, purifiez nos coeurs!"

The days—and hours—of Ezra's last year ticked by, meticulously recorded in Olga's notebook. A telegram from Brooklyn on February 7, 1972, informed them that Marianne Moore had died in her sleep. Olga arranged a memorial service at St. George's English Church in San Vio, and Father Victor Stanley conducted the Anglican rites at 5:30 the next evening. Ezra read, without faltering, Moore's poem "What Are Years?"

What is our innocence
what is our guilt?
All are naked, none is safe. And whence
is courage: the unanswered question . . .

In early April, Alberto Piscetto, a translator for the Russian Congress Dostoievski, arrived in Venice. Olga sat with Olga Branca of the Cini Foundation, Ezra with Alberto, around a horseshoe-shaped table with the *congressisti*. Olga described the Russian voices and stance as "pure *granite* —a prova di bomba [bombproof]!" Alberto, "a brilliant conversationalist who knew everybody," went back to the calle Querini with Viktor Sloski and greeted Ezra with a big bear hug.

Venice was still suffering from bone-chilling cold and the heat was off, so Olga made up the divan for Ezra downstairs near the fire. The next morning, *"Surprise!"* (twice underlined by Olga), "a delightful aubade!" Students from Minnesota State College, in Venice to sing at St. Mark's Cathedral, were serenading at daybreak. "E., as usual, shy, but got him to show himself at the window to say thank you. Then all came in and went upstairs to meet him, in groups." On Olga's seventy-seventh birthday, "E. celebrated by making morning coffee, which he carried up to me." Dinner that evening with translator Piscetto, the artist Guido Cadorin, and Professor Ghayyam Singh of Belfast, who had known Montale and F. R. Leavis. Olga pronounced all good company.

The days continued full to the brim, punctuated by special events. Photographer Henri Cartier-Bresson paid a farewell visit on the sixteenth. In May, a lecture by Sir Kenneth Clark, who greeted them cordially at the

Ateneo Veneto; in June, the Verdi *Requiem* at La Fenice conducted by Thomas Schippers. The house in Dorsoduro had a revolving door for Pound scholars. Leon Edel, biographer of Henry James, got high marks for "very good conversation," but added to her labors. As an example of the difficulty of caring for Ezra in his last years, she noted: "When interested, he [Ezra] forgets his preoccupation with the 'water works' . . . changed linen three times, with maximum hysterical comment to drive one mad! But if I stop, it means getting into the hands of paid help."

Olga was ruthless in discouraging unwanted visitors. D. D. Paige invited himself to Venice in June, bringing his second wife and young child of five. They would stay at the Pensione Seguso, and wanted to meet Pound again. Olga turned them away without a thought. Time was too short. On one of the rare cool days of summer, Olga read to Ezra from a book about Kierkegaard. "*Slow* reading does not seem to tire him. [I] forget how *slowly* he always read to himself." When Ezra felt up to it, they traveled to Lucca to visit Enrico Pea, the poet whose work Olga had translated, who resembled "a jovial Santa Claus."

Another controversy as divisive as the one over the Bollingen erupted in 1972 when the nominating committee of the Academy of Arts and Sciences in Boston awarded Pound the Emerson-Thoreau Medal, and the council of the Academy overruled it. According to James Laughlin, a close observer, "the pot continued to boil . . . in a way very favorable to Ezra, and there have been a great many letters to the editor in various newspapers, even editorials."

Dr. O. B. Hardison, director of the Folger Shakespeare Library in Washington, a member of the Academy, resigned in protest over the council's decision. He invited Ezra and Olga to Washington for a reading at the Library. They were in Friuli with the Ivanciches when the letter came, and failed to reply. Dorothy Pound (writing from Calford Green, Haverhill, Suffolk) heard the news and urged them not to go; the trip would be too hard on Ezra. "Omar has 'parked' me in a nursing home about twenty miles away," she wrote, "an extra person in the house was too much for Elizabeth. The personnel [are] very thoughtful; clients, about ten or twelve, *not* given to being pleasant . . . lovely grounds, one can walk on stone paths. I am hoping Omar and Co. will be back next weekend." All of her letters to Ezra closed with a term of endearment, "à toi."

Another vexation for Olga arose when she learned that Mary's *Discretions* was being published in translation in Italy. "A rather undiplomatic thing to do," Laughlin wrote Noel Stock; "it will simply increase Olga's hostility [to Mary], if the book is circulating . . . among her Italian friends."

In September, another event to remember: breakfast at Caroline de Robilant's palazzo to view Pope Paul and his cortège passing on the Grand Canal. They joined a small crowd near the Accademia before the Pope was "stuck up on a platform before St. Mark's," in Olga's words.

Olga's gift to Ezra on his last birthday was an antique bed with provenance of Isabella Stewart Gardner's family. Joan Fitzgerald came to help Olga assemble the parts. Some were missing, and Olga said it resembled "a comic strip, trying to puzzle the matter out." At last, "E. in bed—a miracle. He allowed me to sluice him in [the] tub, so all clean in a new clean bed."

Pound's dream: Vivaldi in Siena. Piscetto's *prete* had gotten someone in the Vatican to celebrate Vivaldi. "I was looking for you," Ezra said, "after we got there, I had forgotten the hotel." "Did you find it?" "No, I just woke up."

When Ezra felt strong enough for luncheon at Pensione Cici, he cut a distinguished figure: ivory-handled cane, newly laundered lavender shirt with wide collar, monocolored yellow tie. As they walked along the Zattere—a not unusual happening—a young German poet followed and introduced himself. At the Cici, Ezra hung his hat outside the *pensione* dining room according to custom, his scarf on a brass hook, and carried the cane inside, then took his place with Olga among the "regulars."

The next morning, new injections activated the bladder, and Ezra was a difficult patient: "wet off and on all day . . . a constant drip." Olga never complained, but took a *tranquillina* at the moment of washing and dressing Ezra. Ezra objected to the "cackle" of Diana, the nurse who gave the injections. The situation reached crisis proportions on the eleventh, when he flooded. Ezra was "better, but very bad-tempered" over the weekend.

On the sixteenth, the "usual free fight to get him under the shower and dressed—how long can my strength last?"

The twentieth dawned cold and grey, and Ezra was in bed all day. Their neighbor Mary Jane Phillips-Matz came in the evening, and Olga noted that Ezra got in some good conversation about the Hirshhorn Museum in Washington and the National Cathedral (a member of Mary Jane's family had designed the stained-glass windows). The "Nobel Prize [has] been and gone," Olga wrote—"not that E. ever spoke of it, but people did." His grandson Walter said of Pound at the end of his life, "He was like Oedipus at Colonnus—beyond grief."

Telegrams of good wishes for Ezra's birthday were arriving. The notebook entry for October 29 read: "Very foggy, also rain. [Ezra took] a glass of boiling water at 5, drops of Guttolax at 9 a.m. Cup of black coffee. No fever. Later, passata di legume, cups of apple water, apple puree. Fever [in the] afternoon (37.2 1/2 C). E. wet all day. 10g. Guttolax last thing."

On October 30, Ezra's last birthday, Olga jotted: "7 a.m., no results from Guttolax, a demi-tasse cafe. Broth with pastine at teatime." The artist Guido Cadorin, still groggy from a recent heart operation to install a pacemaker, came with a little pupil; Lisalotte and Manfredo, Joan Fitzgerald, the Bernard Hickeys, the Chris Cooleys, Rosso Mazzinghi, Lotte Frumi soon after. Peter Russell brought a poem. Ambrosini sent flowers and sweets. Lester Littlefield, a bag of goodies from Fauchon's.

There was plenty of champagne, Olga remembered. Ezra was lying on the bed in apricot pajamas under an apricot blanket. Olga was firm about not allowing more than two at a time to go up. She took the supper tray to Ezra at 8:30, when the Ivanciches went to Cici's to get sandwiches for the guests. (A waiter came back with a complete birthday dinner.) Ezra, unassisted, blew out all eighty-seven candles on the cake. After getting Peter Russell and Chris Cooley to leave at quarter to ten, Olga was still cleaning up at 12:30, too tired to sleep.

On October 31, she threw the I Ching as always, first thing in the morning. "HSIEH = Deliverance" was the prophetic message of the hexagram. Ezra felt considerable discomfort in his stomach, but no great pain. The congestion continued all day until late that night, when Olga became alarmed and called the ambulance boat to take Ezra to the municipal hospital, S.S. Giovanni e Paolo. Stoic as always, Ezra refused a stretcher, came downstairs with his hand on the wooden rail that had been put there in the 1960s, "when EP came back to stay—it was the *last* thing in the house His hand touched." He walked along the calle Querini to the Fonda-menta Ca'Bala and climbed into the gondola unassisted.

As Olga related the events of their last hours together:

> The next morning, Joan Fitzgerald came to the hospital . . . she insisted on my resting, held his hand for the intravenous. He said, "Take your hand away!" I, of course, never rested, nor did I leave the room from the time we got to the hospital. The doctors . . . were kind, attentive and conscientious. . . . [I] had no impression of his being in pain (he was always uncomplaining of physical pain). After that, more intravenous, then a tube in [the] nose . . . which evidently gave him relief, so much so that he dropped asleep, tired out, but peacefully breathing, and we were alone. . . . There were no last messages, no 'death-bed repentance.' I did not know, though sitting with his hand in mine, *when* he had gone until the nurse came in, turned up [the] middle light.
>
> Caro! When death came it was beautiful, and you went, smiling. I held your hand and was glad.

17

Olga Triumphant

1972–1996

T he hospital room was needed. Ezra's body was taken to the bare *camera ardente*, which was opened up for him and then sealed until eight o'clock the next morning. Olga was not allowed to stay the night. News of his death went out over radio and television immediately, and soon the international news services picked it up. Olga was the only eyewitness to record the scene in the *camera ardente* and at Pound's memorial service.

> Ezra Pound lay under a tattered but beautiful ancient brocade, old gold and green, scattered with real roses. His granddaughter Patrizia whispered, "Nonno, under his Botticellian cloak." By the bed . . . candles in silver sconces brought from the Palazzo Ivancich that had burned there at Christmas gatherings . . . on opposite sides, two Venetian artists drawing last sketches. The warmth and informality of "the Venetian way" cancelled out any thought of "the American way" of death. Snatches of conversation: ". . . and when Prince Oltrepassino died—a great piece of patterned brocade—kids running in from the street—a cat sat there licking himself, then stepped over the prince."

Senator Vittorio Cini, founder of the Cini Foundation, was the first to offer condolences. Olga asked his permission to have the funeral service in the Church of San Giorgio Maggiore, one of the most beautiful churches in Italy; "its position on the island of the Foundation ensured order." Senator Cini sent his private secretary to the abbot of the Monastery of San Giorgio, the Reverend P. Egidio Zaramella, who promised to conduct the service himself the next day, and to ask the pastor of the Anglican Church, the Reverend Victor Stanley, to assist. Official pallbearers were chosen from a list of Pound's most distinguished friends: Professor Vittorio Branca of Padua, a Dante scholar with the Cini Foundation; Ugo Fasolo, president of the association of writers of the Veneto; Professor Giuseppe Santomaso of the Venetian Academy of Fine Arts; Dottore Gianfranco Ivancich.

Ezra's body was taken from the *camera ardente* to the Benedictine monastery until the next morning, when the coffin was placed in the central nave of San Giorgio outside the altar rails.

Anita and the Pellegrini family, after driving all night from Sant'Ambrogio with the two sons and grandchildren, were discovered sitting on the steps of San Giorgio Maggiore at six o'clock. Grandson Walter and his father, Boris de Rachewiltz, had been in the United States but arrived in Venice in time for the service.

Father Zaramella read the brief Roman Catholic burial rites in Italian, and Reverend Stanley blessed the coffin in English. The Gregorian plain chant of the Benedictine friars and music by Monteverdi wafted softly in the background.

More than 120 friends signed the commemorative book: Silvana and Vanni Scheiwiller and Luigi de Maino from Milan; Sir Ashley Clarke; Wally Toscanini, the Countess Castelbarco; Christina Thoresby; the artist Guido Cadorin; Charles Matz; Francesco Messina; Emmanuela Straram Mangiarotti; Simonetta Lippi and her sister, Contessa Angela Piccolomini, from Rome; Franco Montanari; professors Bernard Hickey and Alto Sergio Perosa; Aldo Camerino, a Venetian writer, and his wife Gina Vivante; Lotte Frumi; Janice de Luigi Lifton and Lester Littlefield; Desmond O'Grady; Rolando Monti; Giorgio and Liselotte Manera; Rosso Mazzenghi and family from Genoa; Professor Donald Queler of the Italian national television station, and his wife; Christopher and Mary Cooley; Signor Puccelli from Rapallo; Dottoressa Zaira Amman Semenza.

Gianfranco Ivancich had gone early in the morning on November 2 to choose a burial site for Pound in the evangelical section of the cemetery of San Michele dell'Isola, in the north lagoon close by the graves of two other cultural giants of the century, Igor Stravinsky and Serge Diaghilev.

"Ezra Pound wished to be buried in Idaho," Olga noted, "in view of the Sawtooth Range. He had made known in writing to his Committee in 1967, [but] legally he was not free to manage his affairs. 'Venice or Rapallo, wherever I happen to be, she knows my wishes'—he left the arrangements to *me*."

A black, gilt-edged gondola, gondoliers dressed in white, a coffin covered with a blanket of wreaths from Venice and Sant'Ambrogio—there were no flowers in the church—left the mooring of San Giorgio. Olga whispered a line from *The Cantos:* "For the gondolas cost too much that year," recalling Ezra's early days in Venice.

From a room on the Riva degli Schiavoni, overlooking "the far-shining lagoon," Henry James described "the faint shimmering airy watery pink; the bright sea light seems to flush with it, and the pale whitish green of [the] lagoon and canal to drink it up." Olga saw San Michele as "a place of unlopped trees, of birds: *'not of one bird, but of many . . .'* " She recalled that young Ezra, newly arrived in Venice, had been inspired by a painting—*Processione a San Michele*—to write a poem, "For Italico Brass," dedicated to its artist.

> From boat to boat, the bridge makes long its strand
> And from death's isle, they on returning way
> As shadows blotted out against far cloud
> Hasten for folly or with sloth delay.
> When thou knowest all that these hues strove to say
> Then shalt thou know the pain that eats my heart
> Some see but color and commanding sway
> Of shore line, bridge line, or how are composed
> The white of sheep clouds in the wolf of storm

That lurks behind the hills, shall snap wind's leash
And hurl tumultuous on the peace before
But I see more.

One wonders if Pound, who professed to "see more" at the death isle in 1907, had foreseen his own final resting place some sixty-five years later?

Father Victor Stanley accompanied the family and some twenty close friends to San Michele to perform the last rites. After the others left, Joan Fitzgerald and Desmond O'Grady stayed behind with Olga, Mary, and Patrizia. O'Grady threw a fistful of clay on the grave, and "we departed, leaving Ezra for the last time. I have never felt so lonely in my life."

Olga had sent a telegram to Omar Pound at Cambridge: "After three days illness, Ezra died in his sleep—please break news to Dorothy." It arrived too late. According to James Laughlin, when Omar flew to Venice with Peter du Santoy of Faber & Faber, Olga had gone ahead with the funeral, "despite Omar's having telephoned asking her to delay it . . . rather harsh, but I guess the poor thing is quite distracted." Olga was accused by English friends of having hastened the funeral so that Omar would not be present, but she insisted that she had made desperate efforts to stop it. "EP's . . . son [was] known in Venice during the last ten years by his absence. . . . he came once and was treated with courtesy," she said. She had always felt sorry for the boy.

On November 4, when Omar and du Santoy finally arrived from England, Olga returned with them to the gravesite. They "spent an evening with the entire de Rachewiltz family," Laughlin remembered, but "all discussion about family matters was . . . at cross purposes. I hope they can find a way to work out their difficulties without getting into the hands of lawyers."

Dorothy Pound maintained the stiff upper lip typical of a British matron under the most difficult circumstances. "I regret that the funeral itself had to be so hurried, as several queries have come as to when—where," she wrote Olga. "I have never been to the Cemetery Island, and am glad it seems such a pleasant spot. . . . my fervent thanks to yourself for looking after Ezra so carefully." She signed with her full married name, Mrs. Dorothy Pound, a subtle reminder no doubt understood by Olga.

She vented her anger about the way she was treated by the press to her former neighbor Mary Jane Phillips-Matz (Olga had been mentioned as Pound's "housekeeper" in the obituaries). Phillips-Matz, later the biographer of Verdi, was one of the first to acknowledge Olga's importance to the life and work of Pound: "How deeply felt is your contribution to what we all know—or 'see' as [Jorge] Casteneda means 'to see' against 'to look'—how much energy was yours, how many ideas, how much strength. Only the perspective of history will give the world a sign . . . but when I think of your gifts, your culture, your intuitions . . . few people have any comprehension."

The mourning that began on All Saint's Day continued throughout the years. Olga's life resumed its customary rhythm, but the entries in the notebook reflect the emptiness, "the gradual dropping off the bandwagon, which after a brief period, disappeared and was replaced by the garbage van . . . the enfin seule motif in its original meaning came back to mind."

A daughter-in-law of the artist Italico Brass came to the calle Querini to bring photographs of her husband as a child with his father, Italico, long dead; a self-portrait by Brass with a background of a procession on the bridge, another of the boy Ezra with Aunt Frank and a friend (his nurse?) on their first visit to Venice. Olga preserved the photos for their granddaughter, Patrizia.

She returned to Rapallo on November 21 and was surprised to see Father Chute's chapel at the Duomo still lighted with candles from the Mass that had been held in Ezra's memory the week before. Anita had kept a little light burning for him at Sant'Ambrogio. Olga started to work immediately sorting books and containers of memorabilia: "Did not see anyone all day after lunch, work[ed] late, dead tired—*His silence!*"

Back in Venice on December 4, she again used work to dull the pain. She was considering how to divide the first floor, to shut off Ezra's bed and armchair corner. While her practical nature took charge, quotations from *The Cantos* expressed her deepest feelings: "not love, but that love flows from it ex animo, and cannot ergo delight in itself, but only in the love flowing from it." (Canto 91).

On December 5 she went to the *municipio* to have the death certificate stamped: time of death, *ore* 20:00 (8 P.M.), from data given by the Ospedale Civile. The clerk wrote *celibe* on the form, apologetic, but there was nothing about wife or children on the passport. (The clerk had mistaken Dorothy Shakespear Pound, the next of kin, for a sister.) "He would have, *must* have, laughed in heaven!"

Mrs. Hugh Bullock acknowledged Olga as the poet's true heir when she sent condolences from the Academy of American Poets, expressing "deep sympathy . . . and appreciation for her devoted friend, Mr. Ezra Pound, elected as a Fellow of the Academy in 1963 by a majority vote. . . . The quality of his work and the counseling that he generously gave to his peers make him a giant in the history of literature." That was Olga's reward for the years she loyally stood by Ezra.

Biographers were still her bêtes noires. The latest, David Heymann, claimed (falsely) to have been to the house in Venice and to have met the couple. He was close to the mark when he described Olga in her seventies as "petite and whitehaired, with finely-honed features; she struck me as resilient and matter-of-fact. Olga carried the brunt of the conversation [while] Pound watched us with piercing eyes." Though his comments had the ring of truth, Heymann had never visited the Hidden Nest and, according to Olga, borrowed the material from *Spots and Dots* and an interview on Italian television with Pier Paolo Pasolini.

She continued to throw the I Ching coins for hexagrams for herself and for Ezra every morning: "There is no reason why I should bother with these things . . . just to *remember* and have the illusion . . . that He is still here, and if He should be here at the same time every morning, to know that I am here, too, and *waiting*."

The first Christmas since his death was a time of remembrance. She could find no wreaths except those made with artificial flowers, so she concocted one out of newspaper rolled and covered with green plastic branches held in place with gold string, and tufts of gold flowers. When she telephoned Liselotte to tell of her despair over the wreath, her friend offered pine branches, a little gilded box of sprigs, and nine red candles. Accompanied by friends who had been at the gravesite in November, she took the launch to San Michele, tidied the grass, changed the brown candles on Mary's wreath from the Tyrol to red, added carnations and the gilt bunch. The young Mangiarottis and Ivanciches were summoned to light candles and told to make a sign of the cross and to say a prayer for Ezra.

Early in the new year Olga suffered another loss. Her Venice tenant, Lester Littlefield, collapsed of heart failure in the Milan station on his way back to Paris and was rushed to Fatebene Fratelli hospital. Olga did not want Lester to suffer alone, so she took the train to Milan, arriving around midnight, too late to go to the hospital. The next morning she was told that Littlefield had been moved to the city morgue. She "found dear Lester looking calm and dignified, all the noble qualities in his face dominant, he [being] one among ten or more sheeted figures," then went to the funeral home to make the arrangements and to notify Lester's cousin in Ogunquit, Maine.

A posthumous *espresso* from Lester dated January 27 was waiting when she arrived home in Venice. She had been planning to fly to London in February for the memorial for Pound at the Mermaid Theater with Stephen Spender, W. H. Auden, and Cyril Connolly. Littlefield had written that he would like to go with her, but he had already booked a reservation on the train to Paris for the next day, January 28: "I am 60 today, feel 120 physically, and a foolish and trusting 18 in spirit."

Olga sent news of Littlefield's death to Connolly. "Lester was a thoughtful and generous friend," she wrote. He had spent the last two years near her and Ezra, had offered financial help: his gift of a thousand dollars would enable her to make trips to America and London. "Ezra wrote that I was 'the loneliest of them all,' and I am."

A vexing controversy erupted between Olga and the Gardner family of Boston, whose antique bed Olga had purchased in good faith as Ezra's last birthday gift. "Joan [Fitzgerald] lent it to you in an emergency last October," Elizabeth Gardner wrote. "This bed, one of a pair made with matching upholstered headboards, was my mother's, *never for sale*. I cannot believe you intend to keep someone else's property." Gardner was still claiming the bed—and Olga stubbornly refusing to return it—in October 1975, three years after their first correspondence. In the end, Gardner agreed to buy another bed if Olga would return the purchase price, "so that we may put an end to this episode . . . particularly distasteful because of your gossip, which reaches me from all quarters."

Olga sent Gardner a check, but her friendship with Fitzgerald was damaged beyond repair. To a later observer, the entire affair may seem pointless, but to Olga's eyes it damaged her reputation among the close-knit circle of Anglo-American expatriates in Venice. Christina Thoresby, the organist at the English church and one of Peggy Guggenheim's oldest friends, was mentioned by some as the source of the gossip about the bed.

Living in the heart of Venice with its gossip and intrigue was claustrophobic for Olga, who agreed with Rose Lauritzen, a Belfast-born resident, that Venice was "like a gossipy Irish village." Rose and her husband, Peter, the American art critic whose pointed beard looked like the sheriff of Nottingham's, were accepted members of establishment Venice, forgetful of their colorful past. The bohemian group in Venice then revolved around Geoffrey Humphries, whose studio on the Giudecca was famous for tuna-fish-and-rice parties. There was always tension between that unconventional coterie and recognized members of the establishment whose leaders, Sir Ashley and Lady Clark, were the most revered couple, with the gravitas and charm one expects of a former ambassador to Rome and his wife. The Clarks lived then on the *piano nobile* of the Palazzo Bonlini, former home of Blanche Somers-Cocks, where Lady Clarke had created one of the finest "English" gardens in Venice.

Two new friends entered Olga's life at this time: Philip and Jane Rylands. Philip had met his Ohio-born wife in Cambridge while he was reading history of art, enjoying the cachet of being the nephew of George (Dadey) Rylands of King's College. The couple had driven to Venice in 1972 in a Volkswagen camper to find permanent digs in the prestigious Palazzo Ca'Torta. Philip soon became involved with Sir Ashley's restoration and fund raising for Venice in Peril, while Joan contributed a "Letter from Venice" to the Rome-based *Daily American*.

In the summer of 1973, a Family Agreement concerning Pound's estate was signed by all parties, creating a trust into which royalties and other earnings of the estate would be deposited. There would be three trustees, Mary, Omar, and Dorothy's attorney (who was also administrator of the estate). Since Mary and Omar lived abroad, they would be represented in the United States by delegates—Professor Leonard Doob of Yale and Walter Pilkington, the librarian at Hamilton College, respectively. "From these earnings a very decent pension is to be paid to Olga," James Laughlin noted.

Olga drafted a letter to Laughlin about the agreement: "The Trustees have far too much power and far too little knowledge of EP. None . . . knew Ezra before the war. [They are] trying to squash a man born in 1885 into the . . . hats Eva H[esse] and Hugh K[enner] are wearing in 1973."

She had to turn down an invitation from Laughlin to visit him in Norfolk. "[I] won't take on any trips until some money rolls in," she answered. "Have spent over $2000 for [a] copy of [the] Gaudier head for the grave, as EP instructed." She had asked Isamu Noguchi to design a base for Gaudier's Hieratic Head, and Gianfranco Ivancich went with him to the Henraux marble yard in Pietrasanta to give instructions to the stone cutter.

In late summer, Donald Gallup, curator of American literature at the Beinecke Rare Book and Manuscript Library, visited Brunnenburg and encouraged Mary to sell Pound's papers to Yale University. On October 30, Ezra's birthday, Yale announced the establishment of a Center for the Study of Ezra Pound and His Contemporaries, with Mary named curator of the archive. Members of the committee for the center were Gallup, Frederick W. Hilles (professor emeritus of English literature), Louis Martz (then director of the Beinecke), and Norman Holmes Pearson. In Laughlin's words, the archive "is hedged about with a considerable number of rather stiff restrictions . . . no personal or family letters can be looked at by anyone until ten years after Dorothy's death."

Scholars would gain access to the collection sooner than anticipated. One year and one month after Ezra died, Dorothy—his wife of more than fifty years (thirteen faithfully spent near St. Elizabeth's)—died in her sleep, on December 8, 1973. One can only speculate about Olga's true feelings when the rival she had disdained for so many decades, and in the end accommodated herself to, was gone.

In the same month, the Donnell Center of the New York Public Library on West Fifty-third Street was observing the poet's death with "A Quiet Requiem for Ezra Pound," taped interviews by many whose work he had influenced, including James Joyce, who wrote: "It is twenty years since he first began on my behalf. . . . There are few living poets who could say . . . my work would be exactly the same if Mr. Pound had never lived."

"The highlights [of the late '70s] are mostly of things 'not done,'" Olga wrote in her notebook. "I shall be eighty next April . . . I confess to feeling very shocked to find lives used for the ending. . . . Venice is a spider's web that I am anxious to get out of." But she remained close to Ezra at San Michele. Ezra's umbrella cane was "a help in walking and standing" on pilgrimages to the gravesite. One morning she planted "Chinese-looking" pink-and-white dahlias. "Caro, does my fussing disturb you?"

Through the miracle of modern aviation, Olga—who first traveled by horse and buggy—left Venice for Milan at eleven in the morning on November 11, 1973, and landed at JFK Airport at 10:30 the same night. The next day, she took a taxi to Grant's Tomb to see the neighborhood where she had lived as a child with Julia and her two brothers, "no people, but the leaves to scuffle through, the sun and gold-leaved trees. [I] feel an air of old times, calm, quiet."

She went on to New Haven the fifteenth to have lunch with Mary and Donald Gallup of the Beinecke Library, and discovered in the archives photocopies of Pound's delightful letters to *his* first love, Mary Moore of Trenton. "What a joke, Caro!" she noted. "Me, enjoying His love letters to another woman!"

She was with Mary at the Beinecke when Archibald MacLeish came for a conference; she "would have liked a quiet talk with him, but do not think Mary really wanted that." There was still difficulty in keeping off argumentative subjects with her daughter.

Olga next visited grandson Walter at Eliot House in Cambridge and enjoyed what she later described as the "highlight of [my] visit to the States . . . 1939 recordings of Ezra—magnificent!" On the train back to New York, she took with her a volume of the avant-garde poetry of Charles Olson, whose work was influenced by *The Cantos,* and who had visited Pound at St. Elizabeth's. The collection provoked a violent reaction, she said: she "literally vomited . . . in a plastic bag containing said book! Have never done such a thing in public before."

Mary Jane Phillips-Matz, who was then living in Manhattan, went with

Olga to the Museum of Modern Art, where they viewed the works of the futurists and cubists, in "EP's friends' corner"—Francis Picabia, Fernand Léger, Jacob Epstein—and Gaudier's *Birds Erect*. The Brancusi on a raised, carved platform made her think that the Gaudier Hieratic Head "would look wonderful similar."

On the plane back to London, her neighbors the Arrigo Ciprianis (of Harry's Bar) were seated behind her and helpful in making the transfer in Milan and home to Dorsoduro by taxi. Early the next morning she went to San Michele to be alone with Ezra, "a beautiful sun and faint mist . . . no birds, the leaves on Ezra's tree, all fallen."

Well into her nineties, Olga was an omnivorous reader with an inquiring mind: "Must remember Greek letters . . . Milton's daughter learned enough to read to her father," she observed. "All this Italian verbosity is bad . . . read *French* to learn *to write in English*."

Rereading Yeats, she discovered that Lady Gregory's son Geoffrey was killed in Italy in 1917 in an air battle, like her brother Arthur. She recalled Yeats quoting Lady Gregory's praise of "writers pursued by ill luck, left maimed or bedridden by the War—the injustice of what seems to her the blind nobility of pity." Olga added her own wisdom: "Yeats puts his finger on the right word: *pity,* a characteristic always of EP, from feeding the stranded actress at Wabash, to feeding La Martinelli on the lawn at St. E's with left-overs. *But he did not pity me, because I do not like pity?*"

At year's end she recorded a quotation from Confucius: "Things that accord in tone vibrate together . . . things that have affinity in their inmost natures seek one another." After another cold winter, the Easter service at San Giorgio (on Olga's birthday, April 13th) brought back poignant memories.

Family ties were increasingly important as she grew older. On May 20, Teddy—the only surviving member of Olga's birth family—who had driven from England via Germany and Bolzano, arrived, "true to form, on the dot of a quarter to one. . . . talked poor Teddy to death . . . he is a good and remarkable egg!"

She took a sentimental journey in August, stopping first in Verona to revisit Vittoriale, Gabriele d'Annunzio's villa, where she discovered, "in a suitable but unlighted place," Romaine Brooks's fine portrait of the World

War I flying ace. Fifi Drummond joined her on the train to Gardone, and they continued on to Sirmione, the lakeside oasis of sumptuous gardens and olive groves at the end of a peninsula on Lake Garda—the inspiration of poets since the time of Catullus. Dante had stopped there, followed centuries later by Goethe and Byron. Ezra had discovered it on a walking tour with Dorothy and Olivia Shakespear in 1910, and returned in the 1920s with Olga.

When Fifi returned with her to Rapallo, they visited Father Chute's memorial chapel and lighted candles for Ezra and the Reverendo. Ezra's cat was waiting at the Casa, pleased to see the shutters open to his mewings—a cat, Olga said, that "could look me in the eye, straight and hard." She read accounts of an earthquake aftershock at Brunnenburg and noted "the remarkable coincidence of an earthquake in yesterday's I Ching— "when I throw the coins for hexagrams, I feel *my* hands going through *His* motions."

Mary visited, but—after broth with tortellini and one glass of red wine—"the argument (about what?) got out of hand, and at 9:30 she went off with her valise in a fit of rage." Olga gave her daughter the benefit of the doubt, viewing Mary's ill humor as the result of having "too much on her shoulders." But after returning to Brunnenburg, Mary wrote an angry letter accusing Olga of "lying about Graziella." For the first time, Olga learned that Mary's foster child, Graziella, was Boris's daughter. "EP never said, or wrote—to me at least—anything to show that *he* had been informed. We *both* would have thought the truth . . . a *good point* in Boris's favor. As it was, it looked as if the 'Knights of Canossa' wanted 'a good work among the poor' on their prospectus."

On January 14, 1974, the active octogenarian jetted off to London, and after a nostalgic visit to 10 Church Walk, Ezra's home in his youth, she had another heartfelt reunion with Teddy. They went to Westminster Cathedral, recalling Ted's years as a choir boy (when Olga first noticed Irish shamrocks on the stalls). Next, to the National Portrait Gallery for a screening of D. G. Bridson's documentary film about Pound, the last time Olga and Bridson would meet.

In March, Omar came to Venice to collect the sculptures by Gaudier-Brzeska lent by his mother for an Alliance Française exhibition. Olga gave

Omar lunch and a receipt for the Gaudiers. He left gifts of Earl Grey tea (which she liked), and photos of Ezra and Dorothy, circa 1935 (which she did *not* like).

At a lecture at the Ateneo Veneto attended by a room full of old women, she introduced herself as the oldest inhabitant of Venice on her April birthday. If not "the cruelest month," April was to be approached with caution: "*My* month—be careful of it!"

In Sant'Ambrogio on Easter morning, superstitious *contadini* urged her to go down to the sea and wash her face first thing, and when she came out, to take up a stone and throw it behind her. Easter bells at San Pantaleo serenaded her while she was taking breakfast with the birds. She was readying Ezra's room for a welcome visitor on June 12, Leonardo Clerici, a Pound scholar, who "seems to be studying with the mind of a grandson . . . told me that 'Ezra' means 'help' in Hebrew." Clerici accompanied Olga to the Rapallo cemetery to put flowers on Homer Pound's grave, and won high praise as a houseguest who was very patient, good company, and cooked supper.

Her brother Teddy's second son, John Rudge, arrived next with his wife Pearl. Olga noted a family resemblance between John and his aunt Olga—"[John is] as loquacious as I am."

In July, granddaughter Patrizia and her new husband, Pim de Vroom, visited after their wedding at Brunnenburg, which Olga had not attended; "if it had been a true family reunion," she wrote, "I would have." As one guest recalled the wedding: Pim's long-haired friends arrived from Holland in bluejeans, the international costume of the young of that era, a contrast to the well-dressed and coiffed Italians. Boris, the father of the bride, played a recording of Pound's translation of the marriage song from the Confucian *Odes*, and after the ceremony two white doves were released from their cages to go free. But the birds clung to the wall, terrified —not a good omen—and indeed the marriage, like so many others that begin with high hopes, did not last.

After seeing the couple in Venice, Olga considered Pim "a nice young man, well brought up, sensitive. . . . P[atrizia] seems thinner, which brings out the good lines of her face." She took them to San Michele to see Gaudier's Hieratic Head on the new Noguchi-designed base.

In her later years, Olga was becoming an icon. At a Cini Foundation reception, U.S. Ambassador Richard Gardner approached and introduced his wife. Christopher Winner interviewed her for *Newsweek,* but Olga still refused to talk about herself, only about Ezra and his poetry: "I never pretended to be an expert in things I didn't know about. . . . the most important thing in *The Cantos* is 'the quality of the affection.' "

She kept in touch with other poets from Ezra's world. Stephen Spender, at another Cini Foundation reception, announced that "Olga Rudge has just told me that Robert Lowell is dead." Olga had last seen Cal Lowell with Ezra in New York, and recalled his troubled life with bittersweet memories.

Distressing news from England on September 14: her beloved brother had been taken to West Suffolk Hospital; she suspected he was dying. He sounded very weak when she telephoned but asked—typical of Teddy— "How are *you?*" Olga urged her grandson to drive to Norfolk to call on his great-uncle, but Walter failed to do so. She harbored "heavy thoughts" about Walter: "the hearts of others—and my own—are a dark forest," she wrote in her notebook, paraphrasing Dante's *selva oscura;* then she remembered her daughter's visit, when Mary left in a rage—"not dark forests, but dark *jungles!*"

Elena, the housekeeper, was the first to come with the news that Count Vittorio Cini, who had arranged Ezra's funeral at San Giorgio, had died on September 18. "He was a fine 93," Olga reminisced; "it seems only yesterday that he turned up with two bottles of champagne, iced, for Ezra's 85th." She never dreamed of the dead, but felt their presence: "I have to stave off everyone who wants to invade their time and space." The next day dawned bright and sunny after days of downpour, "most beautiful and unexpected," for the Cini service at San Giorgio. She felt deeply another loss on October 9 of Father Victor Stanley, the priest who had read the Anglican rites at Ezra's memorial.

Olga had just finished reading Pericles, "the house copy marked by EP." She considered Bernard Berenson's *The Last Years* "perfect reading for 80-year-olds . . . both EP and BB had *wide views* of relationships and of life." William Cookson's edition of Pound's *Collected Prose* was found wanting; he referred to Olga's translation of Cocteau's *Mystère Laïc,* but failed to mention her extensive Vivaldi research or to include Ezra's music reviews in *New Age,* which she considered among his finest prose. "My real pleasure in life is to make notes that no-one will read," she wrote, not imagining that scholars in the future would sift carefully through every page of her notebooks.

A beautiful dawn on Ezra's October 30 birthday. She went to San Michele early, "in the morning sun." Rereading Canto 91,

> the body of light come forth
> from the body of fire

she was reminded of "the last beautiful dawns we saw together, through the big tree one could see from my bed with the white satin cover at 'La Collina.'" Throwing the I Ching coins, the morning ritual, turned up "skilled fire" (her sign, Aries): "She kept Him warm, at least that!"

Mary telephoned on the thirty-first: "she let me talk, we seem *nearer.* Nearer and nicer . . . let us go on from here."

Olga was following in the footsteps of her mother, Julia O'Connell, as a pillar of the Anglo-American community. The new rector of the Anglican Church, Reverend Robertson, accompanied her to San Michele in November; she was present for the Thanksgiving service with other members of establishment Venice—the Clarks, the Guinesses, the Lauritzens, and Peggy Guggenheim—as Canon MacDonald prayed for the newly elected President, Jimmy Carter.

Teddy, still weak but holding his own, called with Christmas greetings. Olga talked with Mary and the family at Brunnenburg and learned that Patrizia and Pim were expecting a baby, Olga's first great-grandchild: "I hope all goes well for Patrizia, that they will *all three* grow up to live in daylight and not in a false fairy story cum Disney 'castle,' i.e., none of that mawkish 'little Prince' and 'little Princess' stuff."

On New Year's Day, Olga wrote to Valerie Eliot: "Get slower and slower, seeing less people, *remember* more." A dream before waking: "Someone crouching by [my] bed, and holding [my] hand. EP? Mother? A curious . . . metamorphosis in my dreams, Mother becomes EP." Ezra had been the comforting, guiding presence in Olga's adult life that Julia was in her childhood. "Shall not homing man tread like a ghost where he cares most?" she wrote, inspired by the Confucian *Odes*.

Word reached Olga of the death from congestive cardiac failure of another correspondent and confidant, Cyril Connolly—in his seventies, younger than she. One of the last friends to visit Connolly in the hospital had read aloud, at the patient's request, Pound's poem "Tomb of Akr Caar."

Time reported the death of Tibor Serly, her accompanist in the 1930s at the Rapallo chamber concerts, and she was more than ever aware that she had outlived many performers of her own generation and some who were younger. "She should have tried harder to keep music," she reflected. "EP—no-one—understood my not being able to *play* unless I practiced, and found [a] place to do so . . . a very deficient musician, yes, but even He noted 'a delicate firmness.'"

At eighty-three, Olga was constantly in motion: to Munich for a screening of a film about Pound that included his first recordings on Telefunken (1967), and a meeting with their old friend Eva Hesse. In May in Venice, Liselotte Hochs displayed Olga's portrait in a *vernissage* that ended with a formal dinner in the garden, and Vittorio Branca introduced the D. G. Bridson film about Pound in another showing at the Cini Foundation. When Lia Sicci stopped by to enlist her help in the cause of "Women's Liberation," Olga listened but commented that though she was a liberated woman herself, she refused to join any organization.

Yet she contributed ten thousand lire for the Festa della Madonna della Salute on August 5 in appreciation of the Rapallese friendship and support on Ezra's behalf. She was "putting her house in order" in Sant'Ambrogio; for the first time considering installing a shower in the kitchen and Mary's room. (They were accustomed to bathe in an iron tub, or in the sea like the *contadini*.) In an orgy of cleaning and rearranging, using an old toothbrush to dust the book edges, she was reminded that Ezra used a toothbrush to dust down the black cat who waited for him at the top of the *salita:* "Hiz cats—Tiger Tim and his Black Lady—verrry thin, verrry ravenous. [He] climbs up a tree to look in, but can't jump, as his jumping-off branch 'bin cut . . . your cats, Mr. Pound, long-lived cats. 'Persistence,' he would say . . . am I turning into one of those horrible old women who devote themselves to cats?"

Early in January 1979, Olga was off to Milan for a lecture at the Teatro Eliseo by Dr. Thomas S. Szasz, professor of Psychiatry at the New York State University Hospital in Syracuse, with whom she had corresponded about Ezra's condition. "It was a great event in my life to have heard and seen you in action," she wrote Szasz. She suggested that 1985, the centenary of Ezra's birth, would be a fitting date for a "public retraction of any accusation of un-American activities," and contrasted public opinion in the United States to "the more civilized attitude of EP's friends in *Europe,* and of the *press* in Italy." The "explainers and exploiters" who followed Pound reminded her of "small children walking 'round in grandpa's shoes cut down to fit his size."

A poignant family reunion on August 1. Olga was summoned to England for the funeral of her last surviving brother, Edgar Marie (Teddy) Rudge—at eighty-three, a year younger than Olga. Ted's children, Peter and Elizabeth, picked her up at the station and drove to the family home, Four Winds, through "lovely country Mother would have loved."

"Peter [was] doing splendidly in a difficult situation," she wrote. "A Protestant Church and a Catholic priest, Father Sleight, who did Teddy justice. Peter read the Lesson very well." They walked to the grave, then back to Four Winds for lunch with at least forty of Teddy's friends, to show his paintings and old photos that her mother had, first at 12 Hill Road, then on the rue Chamfort. "Everyone was very kind to me, seemed struck with my resemblance to him [Teddy]. . . . Now that Teddy is gone, His Cantos are the only place I find a record of our *childhood*—Chocorua, the land of the Maple!"

Another memorial took place on August 27 at the English church, for Lord Louis Mountbatten, victim of an Irish terrorist bomb planted in his boat while sailing with grandchildren and young members of the royal family. William McNaughton was with Olga as she signed the guest register in her distinctive hand, OLGA O'CONNELL RUDGE. It was important to her to make a statement that she was of Irish descent: "There should be *one* Ireland—if the English show sense, they will get out in style."

The social life of Venice picked up in the fall. At Giorgio Manera's party, Olga wore a lion-print dress Ezra used to admire; she had sent a scrap of it to him at St. Elizabeth's, which he fastened to the bars of his window. The Rylandses invited her to Palazzo Ca'Torta to meet a "large and lolling Stephen Spender" (Olga's words), who wanted to talk about his son, then studying painting in Siena. She was "flapi" (her word for a confused and upset condition): "Too much talk! Too much food! Too much drink!" She was happier in the company of winged friends, especially in winter—"grated bread for the birds, so they could eat more easily."

Peggy Guggenheim died just before Christmas. In the *calle*, Olga happened upon the young Rylandses with Peggy's and Lawrence Vail's son, Sinbad, and Thomas Messer, director of the Guggenheim Museum in New York. Under the terms of Peggy's will, they let it be known, it was her wish to be cremated, the ashes to be buried in her beloved dogs' graveyard. Olga considered her own burial: "perhaps to be cremated in Venice, if it were possible to cremate EP's remains at the same time."

Nearing her eighty-fifth birthday, Olga kept to an active schedule, entertaining visitors from around the world, taking long walks in Venice, traveling continuously in Italy, England, France, the United States. The photographer Sarah Quill came and asked her to sit in the window with the strongest light. "A few years ago, I would have worried about the results," Olga said, "but now I don't care—a few wrinkles, more-or-less . . . I lost a tooth this morning!"

"The things that excite me *now* are reading, the book 'coming alive.'" In Canto 77, she discovered "Jactancy," and jotted the definition in the notebook: "'Jactitation' (law), of marriage, offence of claiming to be a person's wife or husband" ("they can't get OR on that"). Another *pensée:* "Osmosis of persons? (consoling thought). There is no marriage, or giving in marriage, in heaven? The thing is not to break the thread, the light—'the sun's silk, tensile,' (Canto 90)—the stars, the body of light. His writing is her clock, as [the] sun in these transcriptions, her greatest—her only—consolation."

Mary called from the Netherlands to announce the birth of another great-grandchild, Cyril Gautier, "a handsome blond boy, with long limbs, seems happy, Patrizia idem." Olga wanted Patrizia to name one of the children Ezra, but "she went out of her way in naming *two* sons to slight her grandfather."

In later years, her reputation for acid wit and abrasive comments was well earned—for those who did not know her well, she was a tiger, but to close friends a paper one. She was often gracious to total strangers with a genuine interest in Pound. The U.S. cultural attaché in Trieste, Sterling Steele, sought her out and asked her to dinner with a young Fulbright scholar. She invited both back to the calle Querini for a cup of her favorite Earl Grey tea. When Steele returned in March as U.S. consul, bringing his wife, June, Olga wondered if the "VIP treatment *at last* from the U.S. authorities was personal kindness, or a change in tactics toward EP?"

The patriarch of the Ciprianis, whose great-grandson had been named Ezra to honor their enduring friendship, died in April. As Olga followed the coffin to San Michele, she was painfully reminded again of her journey there with her Caro.

Celebrations of Pound's ninety-fifth birthday began in April 1980 on the seventy-fifth anniversary of his graduation from Hamilton College. Others followed in unlikely places: Saint Andrew's Presbyterian College in North Carolina, with guest speakers Mary Barnard, Sister Bernetta Quinn and her daughter Mary. *Paideuma*, a new journal of Pound scholarship edited by Professor Carroll F. Terrell, began publication at the University of Maine.

The highlight of 1980 was a trip to New York on the new supersonic Concorde. At this advanced age, nothing seemed to surprise her. In New York, she was given celebrity treatment, avoiding the long queue at the Museum of Modern Art's blockbuster show of Picasso's paintings. The next day, a "beautiful drive to New Haven" to Mary's digs at Saybrook College; Mary was then curator of the Ezra Pound Collection in the Beinecke Rare Book and Manuscript Library. Olga described to Isamu Noguchi the "ten glorious days" at Yale, looking out on his Rock Garden, "watching the shadows on your 'rocks'—what a place to work!"

Back in Venice, Philip Rylands had been named administrator of Peggy Guggenheim's art collection, and Olga was invited to the opening. Like her mother, she always sought interesting company: "*C'est toujours le beau monde qui gouverne* (Canto 77): the best society that reads the best books, possesses a certain ration of good manners, of sincerity, frankness— modulated by *silence*."

The Vivaldi research in the National Library in Turin was bearing fruit in the unusual popularity of the once almost forgotten Red Priest; his works were being performed at major venues throughout the world, the *Four Seasons* included in the standard repertory of classical music. At the Goldoni Theater in May, his mandolin concerti: "beautiful orchestral effects and very fine ensemble, all Italian." Again at La Fenice in September, the Manchester Chamber Trio performed the violin sonatas, a violin solo with cello and cymbals. At San Giorgio Maggiore in October, the acoustics were "splendid for pianissimo play, but loud playing re-bombate eat one another."

Lawrence Pitkethly came with a camera crew from the New York Center for Visual Arts to interview Olga for a documentary film, *Ezra Pound: An American Odyssey*. The Irish-born American Pitkethly won Olga's affection by telling stories of his uncle, a painter known for his portrait of an Irish harper. After the director left, she sent a postcard of Blarney Castle "to me darlin', the Irish harper, who can charm tough old women, even down the garden path," signed with the inimitable "Olga *O'Connell* Rudge."

Walter's wife Brigit was delivered of a son by Caesarian section on April 21 (missing Olga's birthday by only one week). "BANZAI! Will go and lay [the] news at San Michele instanter!" Olga journeyed to Brunnenburg at Pentecost for the baptism of Michael Ezra with water from "the Castalian Spring" at Delphi. At last she had a great-grandson named Ezra. The family had been working on the farm with students from St. Andrew's College at the castle for a summer seminar. Another film crew had been there and departed, and "for one beautiful day there was peace" (Canto 17).

A call from Fifi Drummond announced the death of Olga's friend and confidant Ronald Duncan on June 5, a great loss. She suggested to Mary a memorial mass in the courtyard at Brunnenburg (a "fallen away" Roman Catholic, in later years Olga often observed the rituals of the church). Sadly, news of Böski Antheil's death in California arrived a week later.

On the twentieth, she traveled to London for a private viewing of Gaudier's Hieratic Head at Anthony d'Offay's studio on New Bond Street: "remarkably clean, *white*, absolute—on a square base—nothing else in the room." The next day, nephew Peter motored in from Norfolk to join her as Sir Alan Bowness's luncheon guest at the Tate Gallery. Olga ordered trout: "I haven't had since He fished them in Friuli."

On the tenth anniversary of Ezra's death—All Saint's Day—Giorgio Manera went with her to the memorial at St. George's Church and after to San Michele. They joined the crowds of Venetians going to decorate the graves of their loved ones on the Day of the Dead when the ferries are free.

At Christmas, Olga again fulfilled her role as mother, grandmother and great-grandmother, at Brunnenburg. Walter met her in Bolzano and escorted her to the Schloss, where she was ensconced in the tower room with a magnificent view of the Alps. Her great-grandchild Michael Ezra was, to her eyes, "a fine baby, up to standard, amiable, and cousins, ditto." Walter awakened her in the morning with "a heavy tray, and THE freshest egg I've ever eaten since grandmother first learned to suck eggs in 1895!" After lunch, he walked her through the agricultural museum over the sheep sheds, and a "very ingenious arrangement" of rooms for the students from St. Andrew's College. A tempting swing, which "grandma" took a turn on, brought to mind Robert Louis Stevenson's *A Child's Garden of Verses:* "Oh, how I like to go up in a swing / Up in the sky so blue / Oh, I do think it the pleasantest thing / Ever a child could do." "I have a vague remembrance [of] the tune. Teddy, 'Babs' [Arthur] and I had a happy childhood. [I] am glad to see Demian, Cyril and Michael Ezra having one, too."

At supper, more visitors, and Brigit was "a very elegant padrona di casa." Olga changed into party clothes—a black dress worn with a red sweater, her gift to Ezra—for the Christmas tree with real candles and the traditional opening of presents. She had not forgotten the lost art of flirting, and found Graziella's husband "physically the best specimen . . . seen for a long time."

Robert Hughes, a young symphony conductor, called from California early in the new year to request Olga's presence in San Francisco March 24 at the dress rehearsal of *Le Testament de Villon*, followed by luncheon with the Italian consul. All travel expenses were to be paid in advance; a round-trip excursion air ticket required her to stay for a month. Olga did not hesitate but cabled a triumphant "Yes!" Hughes remarked later that Olga —after traveling for a day and a night—was still radiant and enthusiastic, her "translucent, perfect skin, and benevolent face, transcendent. She had not added a pound since her youth—the perfect figure of 'Aphrodite.' "

The re-creation of the 1926 concert version of *Le Testament de Villon* was performed by the Arch Ensemble for Experimental Music at the Herbst Theater March 28, with Hughes conducting. Thomas Buckner sang the Villon role; Jan Curtis, a mezzo-soprano, "Heaulmière" (Ezra had called it "the fireworks of the piece"); John MacAllister, a bass, was Bozo. Toyoji Tomita designed, constructed, and performed on the cornet-de-dessus, the five-foot-long medieval instrument that introduced the opera.

The slight, white-haired woman on the front row next to the Italian consul listened intently to the all-Pound program: Three Pieces for Solo Violin, which Ezra had composed for her, and the *Plainte pour le Mort du Roi Richard Coeur de Lion* by Gaucelm Faidit, arranged from late medieval music, pieces that Olga had performed as a slow movement interlude in her programs. *Fiddle Music,* the most performed and shortest of Pound's violin works (published in the *Transatlantic Review* in 1924) was played by Nathan Rubin, who also premiered *Al Poco Giorno,* a Pound work from Olga's manuscript collection. "Ezra assigned pitches to the exact rhythms of Dante's poem," she remembered.

On Easter Sunday, she joined Walter and Brigit in Cambridge. The easy informality of the young couple delighted her: "I *eat* and *sleep* (at night) as I have not done in *years.* . . . an enormous breakfast, brought by Walter, who arranges pillows, etc. as a matter of course—no fuss, Brigit equally easy-mannered." The apple of her eye, great-grandson Michael Ezra, was "on his toes, looking at new things."

Back in New York at the Gotham Book Mart, she renewed her friendship with owner Frances Steloff, another octogenarian and legendary figure in the literary world, whom she had met at Caresse Crosby's Castello di Roccasinibalda. Among Olga's purchases was Rebecca West's *The Meaning of Treason,* first published in 1947, an account of the post—World

War II trials, notably that of Lord Haw-Haw, the broadcaster of Nazi propaganda to Britain.

Mary Jane Phillips-Matz raced around the city in taxis with Olga to see the apartments where she and her mother had lived and accompanied her to the airport on April 13. "She was lugging . . . an old raincoat of Pound's, into which she had pinned several things of her own. . . . We drank fruit juice out of cans and nibbled on crackers . . . the best birthday party ever. She waved happily from the gate, and elegant as always, disappeared down the jetway."

Life in Venice continued at the same lively pace. When Joan Guiness came to tea, Olga offered a cup of Earl Grey, which delighted Guiness (she reportedly imported a supply of Jackson's from London): "I can't bear Italian tea—dead mouse floating in a cup, we call it." The second birthday of George Augustus James, the Rylandses' first-born son, was celebrated on June 18. Philip was taking on another worthwhile cause, organizing the first circulating library of English books in Venice. Only centuries were milestones in that ancient city—a concert at San Giorgio Maggiore marked the one thousandth anniversary of the Abbazia Benedittini with music by Gregorio Zuchino, a monk of the year 1600.

In late July, Gabriele and Luisa Stocchi drove her to Sant'Ambrogio. She awoke at dawn in Ezra's bed. Birdsong, which continued for almost an hour, and the bells of San Pantaleo inspired a quotation from Yeats in the notebook: "all happiness depends on the energy to assume the mask of some other self . . . all joyous or creative life is a rebirth as something not oneself, something which has no memory and is created in a moment and perpetually renewed."

She was closing her safe deposit box in Rapallo and listed its contents: two gold coins; a copy of Antheil's *Ballet Mécanique;* "Dawn Song," Pound's first published poem (in *Mumsey* magazine, 1905); Ezra's letters to his parents of the same era; an early edition of the *Little Review;* letters from Hemingway and Miró, a note from Maurice Vlaminck; letters to Olga from Stella Bowen and James Joyce—a few of the treasures accumulated in some eighty-eight years.

On the anniversary of Ezra's death, Bill MacNaughton accompanied

Olga to San Michele. On such autumn mornings the *fuoci fatui*, will-o-the-wisp gas fires from the decomposing bodies, bathed the graves in a misty light. McNaughton was surprised to find Olga still recording hexagrams of the *I Ching*, not only for herself, but for Ezra: "It is like examining one's conscience daily, part of my convent teaching," she said. "When I have cleared my mind with *The Cantos* and *Guide to Kulchur*, I feel as if He was coming closer, that the mist is rising, and that soon I may see Him plain, sitting there in His chair."

Jane Rylands was organizing a seminar at the Gritti Palace with three generations of Pound's "other family"—Olga, Mary, and Walter—for the University of Maryland's European Division. When Walter spoke, Olga noted his resemblance to her younger brother Arthur, "his sagoma [shape] and carriage in a new woolen suit, woven from sheep he had sheared himself!" He was "quick on the uptake—like myself." A Chinese dinner at the Rylandses' Ca'Torta ended with ginger, reminding Olga of "the ginger Walter bought his Nonno in 1960, which brought him back to life." Grandson-in-law Pim de Vroom won kudos for helping to put the slides in order for another showing of "The Last Ten Years"—scenes of Venice, London, Zurich, Spoleto, and Rapallo, ending with Natalie Barney's Temple à l'Amitié in Paris in 1968—of which critic Robert Vas Dias remarked: "Toward the end, the face becomes set in monumental haggardness, the figure . . . like a Giacometti."

On Christmas Eve, Olga arranged the figures of Ezra's *presepio* on the mantelpiece, jotted a passage from the Confucian *Odes:* "I am alone / look up to moon and sun / In my thoughts the long pain / the road is so long, host / shall he come again?"

She was astonished to discover in the February 4 *La Stampa* that Boris de Rachewiltz, her son-in-law, was implicated in the sale of arms to the Arabs. She immediately telephoned Mary, who "gave correct information re. Boris." The Rylandses had mentioned a sale of arms by G.I.s stationed in Italy, so she telephoned Jane to set the record straight: it was possible that Boris felt an obligation to help Arab friends who had helped him in his archeological research.

There was more unwelcome publicity when her son-in-law was

imprisoned in Belluno. Olga asked lawyer Giorgio Manera to represent Boris when his case went to trial, and offered funds put aside for her own funeral expenses for his defense.

The *convegno* to commemorate the centenary of Pound's birth, initiated by Vittore Branca and the Cini Foundation, was held at San Giorgio Maggiore May 30 through June 1. It was Branca, Olga recalled, who first introduced the Noh plays to Italy in 1950. Mary, Brigit, and Michael Ezra came down from Brunnenburg for the conference, and Walter, then visiting his father in Belluno, would arrive later. On the feast day of the Natività of Maria in July, Olga called Mary from Sant'Ambrogio and was told that Boris was "still in the same box." Later, Antonio Pantano, en route from Brunnenburg, stopped by with the news that according to a recent law passed by the Italian legislature, Boris would soon be released.

Back in Venice, Olga was an honored guest on many occasions: the inauguration of the Cini Museum and dinner with Sir Ashley and Lady Clark; a benefit concert at the Associazione Amici della Fenice (of which Giorgio Manera was president) for the awarding of a *premio* for young pianists. Manera's sudden premature death and memorial service at San Trevaso on October 25 was a great sorrow.

She was buying candles for the Madonna della Salute on November 19 when Archbishop Arndt approached and kissed her hand in the midst of the crowd. She asked his help with her current crusade, "détente with Protestants, Catholics, and Jews—a Daniel is needed to explain that EP did not dislike Jews."

For the rest of her life Olga defended Pound against charges of anti-Semitism. During the war, she maintained, they had no contact with the Nazi soldiers who occupied Rapallo, and since they received no news from the war front in Germany Pound could not have known—and condoned—the horrors of the Holocaust. Many of their friends were Jews, and she recalled that she and Ezra had attended the synagogue in Venice with Giorgio Levi when it was dangerous to do so.

Mary telephoned with plans for Christmas at Brunnenburg, but Walter had passed on her remark about the tower not being a suitable place for "old, rickety people on account of the rickety steps," and she suggested that Olga might prefer to spend the holiday in Venice. And she did.

Christmas Day with Archbishop Arndt and his wife, who always "make one feel welcome, though he doesn't remember names" (she was reminded of Homer Pound, who filed names away in his "forgettery").

The Lawrence Gays, her hosts in San Francisco, were the first to call on New Year's Day. Larry knew someone close to the Ministro della Giustizia in Rome, and wanted to help Boris. But first he needed more information about the accusation and date of arrest. Olga, who had not heard from Mary since Christmas, telephoned Brunnenburg to ask. For the first time, she heard the news: "*Boris is out!* He was there for Christmas!" She was angered at Mary's rudeness in not letting her know. The next day's post brought photos of the family around the Christmas tree with the three great-grandsons, and of Mary and Boris's thirty-first wedding anniversary, from which she had been excluded, rubbing salt in old wounds.

She was honored at another celebration of the centenary of Pound's birth, a *Pommeriggio per* Ezra Pound, on February 2. Valerie Eliot, Giuseppe Santomaso, and her daughter Mary were among the participants in the *convegno* held in the theater some thirty meters from the Piazza di Spagna. Olga presented her slide lecture, "The Last Ten Years," to another distinguished audience, including Indro Montanelli, director of *Il Giornale,* Milan's leading newspaper.

She was called upon to assemble Pound memorabilia and photos for another young broadcaster from Radiotelevisione Italiana, who came to interview Ezra's "companion" in the centenary year. At ninety, Olga was gaining recognition in her own right as a Venetian celebrity. Graham Thayer, executive producer of the BBC, arrived without warning. At her birthday reception at the Gritti Palace, she was surrounded by journalists "who would like to get a photograph or two on the terrace before the sun goes down."

A high point of the year—and of Olga's life—was a ceremony June 9 in the Campidoglio in Rome. "*I* am to be given an award, i.e., *me!*" she noted with astonishment. This modest woman from Ohio made her way from the Via del Teatro di Marcello up the wisteria-decked *cordonata* past the two majestic statues of Castor and Pollux to the piazza designed by Michelangelo for Charles V's triumphal entry. At the Palazzo Senatorio (Rome's Town Hall), she was awarded the prestigious Adelaide Ristori Prize for merit in the field of music. In the presentation speech, Nino Guillotti praised Olga's research and organization of the works of Vivaldi into a thematic catalogue, her thirty-two years as executive secretary of the Accademia Musicale Chigiana in Siena, and declared Olga Rudge "a national monument."

In June, Professor Carroll F. Terrell of the University of Maine invited her to attend the Ezra Pound Centennial Conference. David Moody of the University of York accompanied her to Orono: "She traveled on her own from Venice [to London]. I was asked to 'look after her' on the nine-hour journey from Heathrow to Bangor, Maine, but she needed no looking after. She was the coolest and most independent of travelers. . . . For the duration of the journey, she entertained and instructed me with her conversation . . . civilized talk, not chat, mostly about Pound. . . . [Olga Rudge] was an extraordinary woman in her own right."

In Maine, she was the honored guest of the community of Pound scholars and disciples—poets Patrick Kavanagh and Allen Ginsberg, James Laughlin of New Directions—and for the first time she saw Pound's translation of *The Women of Trachis*, performed by the Maine Masque theatrical group.

In Venice, Jane Rylands was drafting a proposal to establish an Ezra Pound Memorial Trust to preserve 252, calle Querini as a memorial to Pound, with Vittorio Branca of the Cini Foundation, Valerie Eliot, Gian Carlo Menotti, and Isamu Noguchi among the trustees, and an advisory board of family members. The preliminary draft dated September 1985 made clear that Olga, as the founder, intended for the foundation to benefit Ezra's and her descendants, "by putting the major assets . . . into the care of a charitable foundation . . . to relieve her heirs of the burdens of taxation and maintenance." The house would be a research institution six months of the year, and from November through March, available as a residence for the family.

Venice gossips viewed the trust as an attempt by the Rylandses to control Olga for their own personal gain. Joan Fitzgerald claimed to have seen a document in Olga's own handwriting stating that it was never her intention to transfer the house to a foundation for literary scholarship. Bill McNaughton, who visited Olga during this era, saw the tangle with the

Rylandses as an imbroglio involving "skullduggery, the gondolieri intelligence network, alarms and counter alarms, threats of a suit and countersuits, in other words, a very sordid business."

The Rylandses packed away papers and memorabilia intended for the library into several old trunks and removed them, presumably for storage in a safe place, to a warehouse of the *gondolieri* on the nearby Zattere. In Fitzgerald's view, the Rylandses had "stolen" at least one trunk filled with valuable papers, but she had no proof. At some point, Walter and Mary went to Venice and removed the trunks to Brunnenburg. Mary has said that people like the Rylandses *made* her mother's life in later years—but she gradually came to see that they were using her, as an icon.

For many years Olga had considered a memorial to Pound in his native United States; Ezra had expressed a wish to be buried in Hailey, Idaho, the place of his birth. In early October 1985, when opportunity knocked, this far from typical ninety-year-old was on her way there. She and Mary were to be honored guests at the centenary celebration (October 30, 1985) of Hailey's most famous—and controversial—native son.

One can only imagine how the residents of this small Western town viewed the woman touted as "Ezra Pound's mistress" (though she insisted, "I was never supported by Ezra"), who had once lived in a ménage à trois with Pound and his legal wife. She was wearing a modish traveling costume and perky hat, a hand-woven plaid shawl draped dramatically over her shoulders, and carrying a rubber-tipped umbrella "more for pointing than support."

Richard Ardinger, editor of Limberlost Press, held Olga's shawl while a cameraman positioned her for a television interview. The white frame house where Ezra had been born was behind her, and poets were reading their work in the front yard. On this beautiful fall afternoon, the sun was bright, the sky was clear blue, but the leaves were falling with a gusting wind. The interviewer was primed with a question: "What kind of man was Ezra Pound?" "He was a good man," Olga replied, steadying herself with the umbrella tip, "he was a *manly* man."

Later, Olga and Mary fielded questions about Ezra in Hailey's Liberty Theater. "Pound was *not* a Fascist," Olga insisted, holding a microphone in one hand, patting the table to stress the point with the other. "His name was Ezra . . . don't you think Jews would be comforted to hear a man by the name of Ezra on the radio?" Mary also defended her father: "Have you ever *read* the work of Mussolini? Or did you just hear what other people have said and written about him?"

Back in Venice a week after this exhausting journey, she wrote William Cookson in England that she had taken a collection of Ezra's photos to Zoagli for the new exhibition hall and returned the same day: " a little too much going on for this 90-year-old!"

In 1987, the Comune di Venezia placed a commemorative plaque on the house at 252, calle Querini—*Olga*'s house, the house her father had bought for her in 1929: "In un mai spento amore per Venezia EZRA POUND, Titano della poesia, questa casa abitò per mezzo secolo [In his never-extinguished love for Venice, Ezra Pound, titan of poetry, lived in this house for half a century]." Scholars and the curious continued to come from distant lands to sign the guest book. Rajiv Krishman from Kerala, India (via Christ's College, Cambridge); Gabrielle Barfoot from Belfast, and Desmond O'Grady of County Cork, Ireland; Professor Walton Litz, of Princeton University; Mary and Polly Andersen from Hailey, Idaho; Erica Jong, author of *La Serenissima;* Christine Stocking, a little-known artist from Milwaukee (who filled a page with a Dali-inspired sketch).

It was a time of reconciliation with Mary and the family. In her birthday gift to Olga, "A Little Book for Your Thoughts," Mary had written on the flyleaf: "Mary's thoughts these days are mostly 'What does my mother think, feel, dream?' " Walter sent photos of great-grandsons Michael Ezra and Nicholas Thaddeus (born in 1986) with him at Torre di Angles, the highest peak of the Tyrolean Alps at Val Venosta (Olga noted in the margin, "chips off the Old Block").

When Carroll Terrell came to Venice for a Pound symposium in 1988, he visited the gravesite at San Michele with Olga. She "pushed through all of us," he remembered, "tossed away her cane, and . . . tearing the grass away from the tombstone, said, 'I pay good money for them to maintain this . . . but I'll do it myself if I have to.' "

The daily jottings in the notebook were becoming more difficult with each passing year: "This page has taken me *one hour!*" (She checked the clock: two minutes past midnight.) "Mind racing, pulse irregular—appetite for food and 'desultory reading,' my mother used to reprove me for, good as ever." An incomplete draft of a letter (possibly never posted): "Old people are dreadful, always know more than you want to know and insist on telling it!"

Commenting on a recent broadcast about the Princesse de Polignac, another nonagenarian, Olga jotted: "a woman making the best use of her last years, exercising her mind, learning Greek, practical—glasses, pencils, notebooks on all floors—discriminating gourmet, calm, no fuss, kind but not sentimental." She might well have been describing herself. "In my youth, I was easy on the eyes," she wrote. "I get more compliments now, but they mean less—I know better." She was pleased by Father Desmond Chute's remark after years of separation during the war: "Olga, you are growing old gracefully."

Coda

It All Coheres

Life alone in the Venice house was becoming too difficult. Mary came to take Olga home. Schloss Brunnenburg rises out of the mountain mist like one of the turreted fairy-tale castles of the Brothers Grimm that Olga had read in childhood. Reaching the castle requires taking a bus or funicular to the village of Dorf Tyrol, or a half-hour's hike up a steep mountain road past chalets of the German-speaking natives who unofficially refuse to accept their Italian citizenship.

In 1991, the Fourteenth International Ezra Pound Conference convened at Brunnenburg, with four generations of Pound's "other family." Mary's suite adjoined the rooms Walter, his wife Brigit, and their children occupied in one wing; Olga was ensconced in the tower. The lifestyle of the titled de Rachewiltzes is unpretentious: Walter conducts tours of the agricultural museum; Brigit cooks for the family and the St. Andrew's College students during their semester abroad. As Ezra discovered, the castle is difficult to keep warm in winter; fireplaces and old-fashioned green porcelain stoves, remnants of the Austrian epoch, are beautiful to look at but give off very little warmth.

In the 1990s, Olga was still holding court, reclining on a daybed and pointing out to visitors the panoramic view of the Alps from her picture window: "Mother always insisted we live in beautiful places." A portrait of her brown-eyed Irish mother, Julia O'Connell, was proudly displayed on the opposite wall, alongside a genealogical chart of the first families of Ireland, a photo with Ezra on the mulepath to Sant'Ambrogio. *The Complete Works of William Shakespeare*, bought long ago from a London book dealer, rested on a nearby shelf.

"My memory isn't so good," Olga admitted—"I am almost one hundred years old!" But to the friends and the curious who made their way to the Sudtirol to view the "monstre sacré," she showed remnants of the witty, sharp-tongued, mildly flirtatious woman she was in her youth. With almost total recall, she related childhood escapades, intriguing stories of her years at the Accademia Chigiana in Siena and the stopover in Turin at the National Library that unearthed the Vivaldi archive. When the conversation turned to Ezra, she grew silent, though her eyes lighted up with words she could not express.

She was still lively and alert at the one hundredth birthday party, April 13, 1995, in the salon of the castle, celebrated with a concert of works by Vivaldi, the Red Priest, followed by a light supper. Great-grandson Michael Ezra helped to blow out the one hundred candles on the cake. Peter Rudge, Teddy's son, traveled from England to join family, friends, and Pound scholars from near and far to pay homage to this remarkable woman.

Olga lived for another year. Her daughter Mary recalled the events of the last day of her life, March 15, 1996. Michael Ezra fell and injured his leg while they were having lunch, and Brigit left the table to rush him to the doctor. When they returned, Mike was on crutches, so Nicky, the ten-year-old, helped his father move Olga to the big wicker chair for her afternoon nap. "She was very happy, she loved their attention," Mary said. At 3:30, when Mary went up to the tower to offer her tea, "she simply did not open her eyes, but sat in a very relaxed position—as though she had chosen her own day and hour."

"There was to be a vernissage in the apartment that's now an art gallery, so most of the friends who had come last year for her hundredth birthday came up in the evening to take leave of her. She looked so beautiful in her kimono [the red one that her primo amore, Egerton Grey, had brought from Japan]. The first night I put her on her bed with the windows open, so all the valley and the mountains were close to her. The next day we brought her to the courtyard chapel (St. Michael's), and she stayed there until Tuesday. Sunday, St. Patrick's [Day], the priest from the village came for the Rosary with the village people and local friends and the students. The grandchildren and great-grandchildren read passages from *The Cantos,* and Professor Singh wrote a beautiful poem. One of the students played 'I did it my way . . .' on the saxophone, and brought tears."

Tuesday morning, Mary went to Venice to arrange for another service at St. George's English Church, San Vio, in Mary's words, "very beautiful, with Vivaldi music." The friends who were with Olga for Ezra's memorial stood by, in death as in life—Lisalotte Hochs, Olga Branca of the Cini Foundation, Lady Frances Clarke, Sir Ashley's widow, and Joan Fitzgerald (who had forgiven her trespasses). "The sun shone brightly as we [went] down the Canal Grande and over to San Michele," Mary remembered. Olga was buried to the left of Ezra, taking her place by his side, where she wanted to be.

In an obituary note, David Moody wrote of "her constancy towards Pound through all his vicissitudes, her self-sustaining inner strength . . . the independence of spirit to match his genius."

But the final word must be Olga's: "I think of my dead. They are nicer than the living. A great deal to be said for dying—a sifter, the dross falls away. I am glad I believe in life everlasting, Amen—Caro!"

Notes

The primary sources of this biography are the Olga Rudge Papers, Yale Collection of American Literature (MSS54 YCAL), Beinecke Rare Book and Manuscript Library (herein cited as ORP/YCAL); family memorabilia in three old trunks that I was privileged to research at Brunnenburg during OR's lifetime, now held by the Beinecke Library (cited as 1996 addition, ORP/YCAL); the Ezra Pound Collection (MSS53 YCAL: Series 2, Family correspondence, also held by the Beinecke Library, herein cited as EPC/YCAL; and MSS52 YCAL, cited as the EPAnnex).

Series 1 (ORP1): The Rudge–Pound correspondence, interfiled and chronologically arranged in Boxes 1–32. (I have followed the original text, omitting the use of [*sic*] when punctuation and spelling are idiosyncratic.)

Series 2 (ORP2): General correspondence (Boxes 33–92) of OR and others is alphabetically arranged under correspondent's name (third-party correspondence in Boxes 91–92).

Series 3 (ORP3): Notebooks are divided into two sections: *I Ching* notebooks (Boxes 93–99), daily records of the years 1966–86 arranged chronologically, containing flashbacks to earlier events recollected by OR in later life; and Research notebooks (Boxes 99–101), transcripts of important correspondence and materials collected by OR "to set the record straight," arranged alphabetically by title or subject).

Series 4 (ORP4): Personal papers (Boxes 102–24), writings, memorabilia, and notes, OR's further attempts to document her life.

Series 5 (ORP5): Financial papers (Boxes 119–26), bills and receipts, leases, EP's funeral expenses, etc., arranged alphabetically by type of material.

Series 6 (ORP6): Printed material (Boxes 127–34); and Series 7 (ORP7), Newspaper clippings (Boxes 135–41), collected by OR and arranged alphabetically by subject and type of material.

Series 8 (ORP8): Music (Boxes 142–47), an important section documenting OR's musical career, scrapbooks, notices, and clippings of OR's early performance history, concert programs, Vivaldi research, the history of the Concerti Tigulliani, arranged alphabetically by subject and type of material.

Series 9 (ORP9): (Boxes 148–54), photographs of OR and EP, family members and friends, notables in the music world and other world figures; two early albums of Olga and friends at Capri (1921) and others in the mid-1920s and 1930s.

Series 10 (ORP10): (Box 155), Rudge family correspondence, childhood photos of OR and her parents; Julia O'Connell's scrapbook of her singing career.

At the head of each chapter's notes I have noted principal sources for that chapter. Quotations from these sources are not cited, assuming the reader will have no difficulty in tracing them in the principal source.

The following are abbreviations of proper names frequently cited in the notes:

OR	Olga Rudge
EP	Ezra Pound
JOR	Julia O'Connell Rudge
JER	John Edgar Rudge
AR	Arthur Rudge
EMR	Edgar Marie (Teddy) Rudge
ECG	Egerton Charles Grey
KRD	Kathleen Richards Dale
KDJ	Katherine Dalliba-John
GA	George Antheil
HP	Homer Pound
IP	Isabel Pound
DP	Dorothy Shakespear Pound
GCS	Guido Chigi Saracini
MdR	Mary de Rachewiltz
JL	James Laughlin
RD	Ronald Duncan
DC	Father Desmond Chute

I OLGA AND EZRA IN PARIS (1922–1923)
Principal source: OR–EP correspondence, ORP1 / YCAL.

p. 1 "They stayed to themselves": OR, taped interview with P. D. Scott, Berkeley, Calif., 12 Oct 1985.

p. 1 "civilized man"; "some correlation": Gourmont, *Natural Philosophy*, tr. Ezra Pound, 295.

p. 2 "Irish adrenal personality": Antheil, *Bad Boy*, 122.

p. 2 Oriental-motif jacket: ("I don't know that Ezra would have noticed me if I had not been wearing that jacket.") OR, taped interview with P. D. Scott, Berkeley, Calif., 12 Oct 1985.

p. 2 "wild girl from Cincinnati": Secrest, *Between Me and Life*, 320.

p. 2 "between a chapel and a bordello"; "folded up like damp handkerchiefs": Interview with Bettina Bergery, in ibid., 317.

p. 3 "Who is that?": OR interview, in *Ezra Pound: An American Odyssey* (film), ed. Lawrence Pitkethly, 1981.

p. 3 The poet's robustness; patriarchal attitude: Anderson, *My Thirty Years' War*, 243–44.

p. 3 "Cadmium? amber?": Ethel Moorhead in Norman, *Ezra Pound*, 276.

p. 4 "without finding a congenial mistress": EP to Picabia, in *391* magazine (1922).

p. 4 "The rent is MUCH cheaper": EP to John Quinn, summer 1921, EPC / YCAL.

p. 4 "as poor as Gertrude Stein's": Hemingway, *A Moveable Feast*, 107.

p. 4 Stein did not find Pound amusing: Stein, in Norman, *Ezra Pound*, 245.

p. 5 "a beautiful picture": Daniel Cory, "EP, a Memoir," *Encounter*, May 1968.

p. 5 Porcelain figure; basketwork of braids: EP, "Medallion," *Hugh Selwyn Mauberly*.

p. 5 Their next meeting: OR, Research notebooks, ORP3 / YCAL.

p. 5 Visitors who came: Interview with Robert Fitzgerald, in Norman, *Ezra Pound*, 310.

p. 6 "He sang it to me": OR, Research notebooks, ORP3 / YCAL.

p. 6 "Me scusi tanto": OR to EP (pneumatique), 21 June 1923.

p. 6 "that Mephistophelian red-bearded gent": Antheil, *Bad Boy*, 117.

p. 7 "as wildly strange": GA to EP, [nd] 1923, EPC / YCAL.

p. 7 "note how elegant": 1996 addition, ORP / YCAL.

p. 7 "I noticed when we commenced": Antheil, *Bad Boy*, 121.

p. 7 "a riot": "The Mailbag," *New York Herald* (Paris), 22 Dec 1923, ORP8 / YCAL.

p. 7 "My piano was wheeled out": Antheil, *Bad Boy*, 133.

p. 8 "a very pretty sonority"; Pound's pieces: Irving Schwerke, "Notes of the Music World," *Chicago Tribune* (Paris), 15 Dec 1923.

p. 8 "Can this really be . . . music?"; "heaven-sent . . . repose": Louis Schneider, "Futurist Music Heard in Paris," *Chicago Tribune* (Paris), 12 Dec 1923, ORP8/YCAL.

p. 8 "practice the Mozart": EP to OR (pneumatique), 1 Dec 1923.

p. 9 "Dolcezza mia": OR to EP, 23 Dec 1923.

2 JULIA AND HER DAUGHTER (1895–1909)
Principal sources: Julia O'Connell scrapbook, in Family papers, ORP10/YCAL; Mahoning Valley (Ohio) Historical Society publications; OR's unpublished autobiography, 1996 addition, ORP/YCAL; OR–JOR correspondence, ORP2/YCAL; *I Ching* notebooks, ORP3/YCAL.

p. 10 "I did not know": F. M. Ford, in MdR, *Discretions*, 154.

p. 10 Youngstown in 1895: *A Heritage to Share: The Bicentennial History of Youngstown and Mahoning County, Ohio*, 142.

p. 11 "that mad Irish girl": M. J. Phillips-Matz, "Muse Who Was Ezra's Eyes," *The Guardian* (Manchester), 6 Apr 1996.

p. 11 Aunt Frank had heard O'Connell: OR, *I Ching* notebooks, ORP3/YCAL.

p. 11 "took my mother to Boston": OR to Cyril Connolly, 15 June 1970, ORP2/YCAL.

p. 11 "My mother was . . . capable": OR, unpublished autobiography, 1996 addition, ORP/YCAL.

p. 12 The "grand concert" programs are in Julia O'Connell's scrapbook.

p. 12 "Miss O'Connell sang"; "beauty of the brunette type": Carrie Harrison, "Some of Our Women Abroad," [nd], ca. 1892, Julia O'Connell scrapbook.

p. 12 Marriage at St. Paul the Apostle Church: Thomas W. Sanderson, ed., *Twentieth Century History of Youngstown and Mahoning County, Ohio*, 634.

p. 13 Rudge family history: Rev. Thomas Rudge, *History of the County of Gloucester*, by the Rector of St. Michael's Church, [nd], cited by OR in Research notebook, ORP3/YCAL.

p. 13 The two brothers homesteaded: Joseph G. Butler, *Youngstown and the Mahoning Valley*, 3.

p. 13 "My home . . . was near Ross-on-Wye": George Rudge to OR, Family papers, ORP10/YCAL.

p. 14 George Rudge's death: Rev. E. M. O'Callahan, "Final Summons" (obituary), *Youngstown (Ohio) Vindicator*, 6 Dec 1906.

p. 14 "My parents did not quarrel": OR, *I Ching* notebooks, ORP3 / YCAL.

p. 14 Arthur's acts of derring-do: OR, *I Ching* notebooks.

p. 14 "like a cat dragging kittens": OR autobiography, 10.

p. 14 "Once married, [Julia] saw herself": OR autobiography, 11.

p. 15 Olga remembered sledding: OR, author interview, Brunnenburg, 1993.

p. 15 Among Olga's keepsakes: OR, Family papers, ORP10 / YCAL.

p. 15 "desultory reading": OR, *I Ching* notebooks.

p. 15 "All of my life": OR autobiography, 16.

p. 15 New York summers; Mount Chocorua: OR autobiography, 14.

p. 16 Uncle Harold: *Country Life,* obituary of Ernest Harold Baynes, Feb 1914.

p. 16 When Olga was nine: OR, *I Ching* notebooks.

p. 17 Saw a "sea-lion or porpoise": OR to JOR, [nd] 1904.

p. 17 "I know Madame": OR to JOR, [nd] 1904.

p. 17 "Votre fillette est . . . charmante": Mme. Pharaïlde to JOR, [nd] 1904, ORP2 / YCAL.

p. 17 "Only twelve days": OR to JOR, 12 Dec 1904.

p. 18 "Let me tell you": JOR to OR, 13 Jan 1906.

p. 18 "Could you send": OR to JOR, [nd] 1906.

p. 18 First Communion: OR, *I Ching* notebooks, June 1976.

p. 19 "Mrs. J. Edgar Rudge has entire charge": Announcement in *The Musical Courier* (New York) 1909, Julia O'Connell scrapbook.

p. 19 Julia in expatriate community: Julia O'Connell scrapbook.

p. 20 "Mrs. J. Edgar Rudge is residing in London": *History of Youngstown,* 364.

p. 20 "The money didn't come": OR autobiography, 13.

p. 20 "The first room": Ibid., 20.

p. 20 "I used to take my pup": OR to Patrizia deRachewiltz, [nd], ca. 1980, 1996 addition, ORP / YCAL.

p. 20 "In the musical circles": OR, *I Ching* notebooks.

p. 21 "the little old gentleman": OR autobiography, 14.

p. 21 Olga's mother's friends; "little shop on Duke Street": OR, *I Ching* notebooks.

p. 21 Ten-volume set of Shakespeare's plays: OR autobiography, 14.

p. 22 "a good Klotz": OR autobiography, 14.

p. 22 "[Olga Rudge] is of a serious nature": Music review, ORP8 / YCAL.

p. 22 "payer de sa personne": OR autobiography, 14.

p. 22 Katherine Dalliba-John: OR, *I Ching* notebooks.

p. 22 "moated grange"; "truly Dickensian old maid": OR, *I Ching* notebooks.

p. 23 "only one small hotel": OR, *I Ching* notebooks.

p. 23 "hopping about the Grand Plage": E. Glover to OR, 17 Feb 1936, ORP2 / YCAL.

3 HALCYON DAYS NO MORE (1910–1918)

Primary sources: Edgar Marie (Teddy) Rudge's diaries, Research notebooks (Box 101), ORP3 / YCAL; Arthur Rudge's World War I letters, Family papers (Box 155), ORP10 / YCAL; Music notices and reviews, ORP8 / YCAL; JOR, EMR, and AR correspondence, ORP10 / YCAL; ECG to OR, ORP2 / YCAL; *I Ching* notebooks, ORP3 / YCAL.

p. 24 "Mother always insisted": OR, author interview, Brunnenburg, Oct 1993.

p. 24 Lease of 2, rue Chamfort: Financial papers, ORP5 / YCAL.

p. 25 "floating memory": *I Ching* notebooks, 1980.

p. 25 "rue Chamfort's terrain": OR, author interview, 1993.

p. 25 "Our love was living proof": C. Stroumillo to OR, 12 July 1983, ORP2 / YCAL.

p. 26 Martinus Sieveking: OR, *I Ching* notebooks, 1984.

p. 26 "For the first time": Julia O'Connell, *Youngstown Telegram*, [nd] Mar 1916, ORP10 / YCAL.

p. 27 "Madame de Saucisson": OR, *I Ching* notebooks, 1976.

p. 27 Hôtel of the Marquis: OR, *I Ching* notebooks, 1983.

p. 27 "My mother would take me": OR, *I Ching* notebooks, 1983.

p. 28 "a flowing cantabile": *The Times* (London), 9 Nov 1914.

p. 28 "that very capable young violinist": *Musical Courier* (New York) Feb 1914, Music reviews (Box 146).

p. 29 The Duncans' widowed mother: OR, Biographical notes, ORP3 / YCAL.

p. 29 "an attractive man": Egerton Charles Grey, obituary, *Biochemical Journal* 23 (1929).

p. 29 "favored fairy forms": ECG to OR, 5 Nov 1914.

p. 29 "You never guessed": OR to KRD, 10 Sept 1974.

p. 29 "There is no letter": JOR to AR & EMR, [nd] Aug 1914.

p. 30 "Germany has declared war!": JOR to AR & EMR, [nd] Aug 1914.

p. 30 "no fruit at all": JOR to AR & EMR, 8 Aug 1914.

p. 30 "We could see them": OR, Research notebooks, ORP3 / YCAL.

p. 31 "There was a fever": Rupert Brooke, from Alan Moorhead's *Gallipoli*, quoted in Kirchberger, *The First World War*, 91.

p. 31 All notes from EMR's journals (1914–15) in re his service in military hospitals in Paris in World War I are in Box 101, ORP3 / YCAL.

p. 32 "She has acquired a warmth": *Jewish Chronicle* (London), 9 July 1915.

p. 32 "our brave men" *Dover and County Chronicle*, 10 July 1915.

p. 32 "Apart from the thrill": OR, Research notebooks (Box 100), ORP3 / YCAL.

p. 32 "My 'first love' explained": OR, Research notebooks (Box 100).

p. 33 "All British" concerts; "distinctly promising young artist": Music reviews (Box 146).

p. 35 "I have a little bedroom": EMR to AR, 12 Aug 1916.

p. 35 "[Miss Rudge] played with great distinction": Music reviews (Box 146).

p. 35 "an imaginative work": Music reviews (Box 146).

p. 36 "Miss Rudge . . . is emphatically a musician": *Morning Post* (London), 8 Nov 1916.

p. 36 "The first recital": JOR to EMR & AR, 10 Nov 1916.

p. 36 "His [Paray's] musical gifts": *Westminster Gazette*, 29 Nov 1916.

p. 36 "Hypothesis of the Subconscious Mind": ECG to OR, 9 Dec 1916.

p. 36 "Egerton's attitude toward 'love' ": OR, *I Ching* notebooks.

p. 37 "Something romantic, Mother!": OR, *I Ching* notebooks, 1979.

p. 37 "the streets are irregular": AR to JOR, 4 July 1914. (This letter and the following are from ORP10 / YCAL.)

p. 37 "I went round to see him": AR to JOR, [nd] 1914.

p. 37 "To master the air": *I Ching* notebooks, 1981.

p. 37 "The machine I shall fly": AR to JOR, 25 Sept 1917.

p. 38 "We had no holiday": AR to JOR, 28 Dec 1917.

p. 38 Arthur's squadron was posted to the Veneto: AR to JOR, 23 Mar 1918.

p. 38 "I did not tell Mother": OR, *I Ching* notebooks, 1982.

p. 39 "London Applauds Americans' Works": *Musical America*, 15 Apr 1918.

p. 39 Teddy in an exchange of prisoners: AR to JOR, [nd] July 1918.

p. 39 "This morning on patrol": AR to JOR, 20 July 1918.

p. 40 "Death, for me": AR, in memoir of Choura Stroumillo, enclosed in letter to OR, 12 July 1983.

p. 40 "[Arthur] was the hero": C. Stroumillo to OR, 12 July 1983.

4 LOST LOVES (1918–1922)
Principal sources: *I Ching* notebooks, ORP3 / YCAL; ECG–OR correspondence, ORP2 / YCAL.

p. 41 "Do not worry about me": JOC letter to OR, [nd] 1918 (Box 70) ORP2 / YCAL.

p. 42 Paris critics: Music notices and reviews, ORP8 / YCAL.

p. 42 "The performance [was] sheer good work": J. H. Glover to OR, 19 Nov 1919, ORP2 / YCAL.

p. 42 Violoniste de l'orchestre at Théâtre Caton: Music reviews, ORP8 / YCAL.

p. 42 *crepe cuore* ("Mother died of—not angina"): OR, *I Ching* notebooks, 1979.

p. 42 "the terrible sight—MOTHER!": OR, *I Ching* notebooks, 1979.

p. 43 "Ted and I were alone": OR, *I Ching* notebooks, 1979.

p. 43 "My mother left her desk"; a gift from Auntie Lou: OR, *I Ching* notebooks, 1983.

p. 43 "I do not believe": ECG to OR, 4 July 1920, ORP2 / YCAL.

p. 44 "Some months must still pass": ECG to OR, 3 Aug 1920, ORP2 / YCAL.

p. 44 "If I had let my mother": OR, *I Ching* notebooks, 1976.

p. 44 "She had enough": MacKenzie, *Extraordinary Women*, 113.

p. 45 "[She] was outwardly Greek": Ibid., 110–11.

p. 45 "innocent, proud, eccentric": Painter, in Diliberto, *Hadley*, 147.

p. 45 "[Cleo] had suffered": MacKenzie, *Extraordinary Women*, 113.

p. 45 "William Atheling" review: *New Age* 44, 25 Nov 1920.

p. 46 Villa Cimbrone: Maria Odone, "A View from the Bay," *Daily American* (Rome), 9 Mar 1965, in 1996 addition, ORP / YCAL. (OR's marginal note: "stayed there as guest of Lord G's sister.")

p. 46 Nepenthe, "gleaming": Secrest, *Between Me and Life*, 123.

p. 46 "The mountains and the sea": MacKenzie, in ibid., 300.

p. 46 "change the background": MacKenzie, foreword to *Extraordinary Women*.

p. 47 "a rich American widow": MacKenzie, *Extraordinary Women*, 124–25.

p. 47 "her daughter was very delicate": Ibid., 128.

p. 47 "had reached the delicious state": Ibid., 127.

p. 47 "legendary and self-invented": Secrest, *Between Me and Life*, 297.

p. 48 A pictorial record: Box 148, ORP9 / YCAL.

p. 48 "There is another possible element": EP to OR, 22 Jan 1929.

p. 48 "When he refers to her": OR to EP, 25 Jan 1930.

p. 49 "I [am] still suffering": ECG to OR, 21 Dec 1921.

p. 49 "I hope that my mother": OR, *I Ching* notebooks, 1976.

5 A MARRIAGE THAT DIDN'T HAPPEN (1923–1926)
Principal sources: OR–EP correspondence, ORP1 / YCAL; OR's notes on Mary's birth, Personal papers (Box 105), ORP4 / YCAL; Music reviews, ORP8 / YCAL.

p. 50 "so *frozen* on the phone": EP to OR, 23 Feb 1924.

p. 50 "Have had the miseries": EP to OR, 25 Feb 1924.

p. 51 "There was only one object": ECG to OR, 22 Dec 1923, ORP2 / YCAL.

p. 51 "There was no discussion": OR-EP "chronology," Research notebooks, ORP3 / YCAL.

p. 51 "Are you coming the 19th?": OR to EP, 15 Mar 1924.

p. 51 "she ended her life": EP to HP, 25 Mar 1924, EPC/YCAL 2 (Family correspondence).

p. 51 *L'Histoire du Soldat* "Well done": OR to EP, 24 Apr 1924.

p. 51 Difficulties en route to London: OR to EP, 24 Apr 1924.

p. 52 "Too late to instruct you": EP to OR, 9 May 1924.

p. 52 "an enterprising young violinist": *The Lady* (London), 15 May 1924.

p. 52 "there was humour and subtlety": *The Observer* (London), 15 May 1924.

p. 52 Pound "composes rather as he writes"; "there were endless repetitions": *The Lady* (London), 15 May 1924.

p. 52 "essentially commonplace": *Daily Telegraph* (London), 12 May 1924.

p. 52 "very successful": Olivia Shakespear to DP (enclosure in EP to OR), 11 May 1924.

p. 53 "I think her fascinating"; "stirred up old things": OR to EP, 11 May 1924.

p. 53 "We have the Salle Pleyel": EP to HP, 21 June 1924, EPC/YCAL.

p. 53 a "XV-century piece": EP to HP, 19 June 1924, EPC/YCAL.

p. 53 "Adrienne Monnier and I": Beach, *Shakespeare & Company*, 132.

p. 53 "gargantuan feast of cacophonies": Louis Schneider, "Music in Paris," *New York Herald* (Paris), 9 July 1924.

p. 53 "by far the most interesting": *Chicago Tribune* (Paris), 9 July 1924.

p. 54 "She doesn't honestly think": OR to EP, 20 Oct 1924.

p. 54 "I disagree": KRD to OR, 16 Oct 1924, ORP2/YCAL.

p. 54 "Xe una bbrrrava ragazza": EP to OR, 22 Oct 1924.

p. 55 "perhaps in the afternoon": EP to OR, 9 Nov 1924.

p. 55 "piantato un figlio": Personal papers, ORP4/YCAL.

p. 55 "Just telegraphed 'no' ": EP to OR, 29 Nov 1924.

p. 55 "It'll be *Rapallo*": EP to HP, 28 Jan 1925, EPC/YCAL.

p. 56 "OR, as early as 1923": OR, Personal papers, ORP4/CAL.

p. 56 "Yes, Ez is 'married' ": Tytell, *Solitary Volcano*, 179.

p. 56 The *New Freewoman:* EP to OR ("suggesting a *roman à clef, not* case report"), ORP5/YCAL.

p. 57 Etta Glover, "a broad-minded woman": EP to OR, 26 Feb 1925.

p. 57 "mi hai lasciato": OR to EP, 28 Feb 1925.

p. 57 "There was no concert": OR to EP, 4 Mar 1925.

p. 57 "lots of ugly old crocks": OR to EP, 11 Mar 1925.

p. 57 "Sirmione [is the] ideal place": OR to EP, 11 Mar 1925.

p. 57 The venerable Albergo; "her uncle's dead": OR to EP, 17 Mar 1925. (Ernest Harold Baynes died 20 Jan 1925.)

p. 58 "Usually full-grown birds": Ernest Harold Baynes, in *Wild Bird Guests* (New York: Dutton, 1915).

p. 58 Mussolini "is surely a nice man": OR to EP, 17 Mar 1925.

p. 58 "I think extremely well of Mussolini": EP to HP, [nd] 1926, *see* Paige, ed., *Letters of Ezra Pound*, 205.

p. 58 "plumb on [the] roof": EP to OR, 4 Mar 1925.

p. 58 "maybe she'd better have an 'alliance'": EP to OR, 13 Mar 1925.

p. 58 "This life of an escaping criminal": OR to EP, [nd] June 1925.

p. 59 "fish a basso": EP to OR, Paige Carbons (EPC/YCAL), 10 May 1925.

p. 59 Birthing customs: EP to OR, 9 June 1925.

p. 59 "the cappellano came": OR to EP, [nd] June 1925.

p. 59 "don't put them in petticoats": OR to EP, [nd] June 1925.

p. 59 "All you appear": EP to OR, 9 June 1925.

p. 59 "a dead man's name": OR, *I Ching* notebooks, 1978.

p. 59 "Am writing to Olga": GA to EP, [nd] 1925, EPAnnex/YCAL.

p. 59 "It wasn't the Caesarian": OR to EP, 18 July 1925.

p. 60 "I felt as if the boy had died": OR notes, Personal papers.

p. 60 "Wot! Feet first": EP to OR, 19 July 1925.

p. 60 "I did not want E. to see me": OR notes, Personal papers.

p. 60 "doctor says I can get up": OR to EP, 19 July 1925.

p. 60 "pericolissima operazione": EP to OR, 20 July 1925.

p. 61 "no-one has seen any connection"; OR notes, Personal papers.

p. 61 "'Fraid he hasn't been": EP to OR, 20 July 1925.

p. 61 "HERS and nobody else's": OR to EP, 20 July 1925.

p. 61 Ezra's choice, Polyxena: EP to OR, 20 July 1925.

p. 61 "About His coming": OR to EP, 20 July 1925.

p. 62 "Night before last"; "There is a contadina": OR to EP, 22 July 1925.

p. 62 "I would have stayed on": OR notes, Personal papers.

p. 62 "La mia leoncina": OR to EP, 22 Oct 1925.

p. 63 "IF she has any . . . ideas": EP to OR, 25 Sept 1925.

p. 63 "No sense of Olga's going": EP to GA, 14 Nov 1925, EPAnnex/YCAL.

p. 63 "Natalie was under the impression": EP to OR, 7 Dec 1925.

p. 63 "D[orothy] is in Cairo": EP to HP, 24 Dec 1925, EPC/YCAL.

p. 64 Mussolini in Rapallo; "EP . . . was not interested enough": OR, *I Ching* notebooks, 1976.

p. 64 "early to bed with *Napoleon*": OR to EP, 28 Feb 1926.

p. 64 "You should have come back": OR, *I Ching* notebooks.

p. 65 "D. has been half ill": EP to OR, 20 Mar 1926.

p. 65 "'Troppo incomodo' is probably": OR to EP, 29 Mar 1926.

p. 65 "She's such a high blue": EP to OR, 31 Mar 1926.

p. 65 "I've got a new violin sonata": GA to EP, [nd] 1926, EPAnnex/YCAL.

p. 65 "Ch'è il fine del mundo": EP to OR, 8 Apr 1926.

p. 66 Critic praised Olga's performance: *Chicago Tribune* (Paris), 18 May 1926.

p. 66 "An HER lookin' ": EP to OR, 28 Apr 1926.

p. 66 "George Antheil's Ballet"; "The carefully upholstered": *Chicago Tribune* (Paris), 20 June 1926.

p. 66 "The music was drowned out": Beach, *Shakespeare & Company*, 132–22.

p. 66 *Le Testament de Villon:* The original score, with EP's marginal notes, in Box 143, ORP8 / YCAL.

p. 67 "not quite a musician's music": Thomson, *Virgil Thomson*, 83.

p. 67 "Dare say it went fairly well": EP to Arturo Brown, 30 June 1926, EPC / YCAL.

p. 67 "Miss Rudge has developed": "Who's Who Abroad," *Chicago Tribune* (Paris), 15 June 1926.

p. 68 "Olga is the seventh gate": GA to EP, 13 Aug 1926, EPAnnex / YCAL.

p. 68 Hemingway accompanied Dorothy: Ernest Hemingway to DP, *Selected Letters*, ed. Carlos Baker, 742.

p. 68 "next generation (male)": EP to HP & IP, 11 Oct 1926, EPC / YCAL.

p. 68 "Fitzgerald's trans. of Omar": Paige, ed., *Letters of Ezra Pound*, 180.

p. 68 "I divine that you have": W. B. Yeats to Olivia Shakespear, 24 Sept 1926, in Norman, *Ezra Pound*, 283.

p. 68 "taps, tests, analyses": EP to HP, 18 Nov 1926, EPC / YCAL.

p. 68 "gee-lorious" curls: EP to OR, 19 Nov 1926.

p. 69 "doing some wild telegraphing": EP to HP, 22 Dec 1926, EPC / YCAL.

p. 69 "Over the chaos": MdR, *Discretions*, 14.

6 THE HIDDEN NEST (1927–1928)
Principal sources: OR–EP correspondence, ORP1 / YCAL; *I Ching* notebooks, ORP3 / YCAL; Music reviews, ORP8 / YCAL.

p. 70 "what sort of reception": "Music Notes," *Chicago Tribune* (Paris), 28 Jan 1927.

p. 70 "I learned from collateral evidence": EP to Huddleston, 1 Feb 1927, EPC / YCAL.

p. 70 "GOD, CHRIST": EP to OR, 31 Jan 1927.

p. 71 "the first . . . American-born musician"; "slabs of sound": *New York Herald* (Paris), 19 Feb 1927.

p. 71 "That Mr. Antheil's music": *New York Herald* (Paris), 8 Feb 1927.

p. 71 "Mussolini complimented Miss Rudge": *New York Herald* (Paris), 3 Mar 1927.

p. 71 Mussolini "played well for an amateur": OR interview, *Sunday Times* (London), Oct 1985.

p. 71 "unusual honor": *Youngstown Telegram,* Mar 1927.

p. 72 "Olga and I are now": GA to EP, [nd] winter 1927, EPAnnex/YCAL.

p. 72 "Berenson is a very great critic": EP to OR, 17 Mar 1927; description of I Tatti in this era, *see* Wineapple, *Sister/Brother,* 159–60. (OR visited I Tatti 5 Apr 1927.)

p. 73 "photograph was sent": *Town and Country,* 15 May 1927, ORP8/YCAL.

p. 73 "He does the Ravel": OR to EP, 24 July 1927.

p. 73 Olga's visit to Il Vittoriale: *I Ching* notebooks; *see also* OR to EP, 31 Jan 1934.

p. 74 "Have now seen it": EP to OR, 24 July 1927.

p. 74 "Waal, I 'spose": EP to OR, 17 Aug 1927.

p. 74 Reunion with Egerton Grey: *I Ching* notebooks, Feb 1976.

p. 75 "He rejoices that she should possess": EP to OR, 10 Sept 1927.

p. 75 "As to her PA": EP to OR, 12 Oct 1927.

p. 75 "Yes, he sh'd pay some attenshun": EP to OR, 1 Nov 1927.

p. 75 "I went in the sled": OR to EP, 19 Jan 1928.

p. 75 "I grew up like one of them": MdR, *Discretions,* 15.

p. 76 "We hung 'round": OR to EP, 10 Jan 1928.

p. 76 "They decided . . . a circus"; "The young man": OR to EP, 15 Mar 1928.

p. 76 "Elle est une princesse": EP to OR (enclosure), 16 Mar 1928.

p. 77 "like a concierge's loge": OR to EP, 2 Apr 1928.

p. 77 "I had the idea of musical toys": *I Ching* notebooks.

p. 77 "I think you will agree": ECG to OR, 12 Mar 1928.

p. 77 "All the air went dark": OR to EP, 25 Mar 1928.

p. 77 "She hopes it is not his intention": OR to EP, 16 Apr 1928.

p. 78 "not particularly happy": MdR, *Discretions,* 52.

p. 78 "I have touched up": GA to EP, 23 Apr 1928, EPAnnex/YCAL.

p. 78 "I went to Miss Kraus": GA to EP, 9 July 1928, EPAnnex/YCAL.

p. 78 "Will He take a passage": OR to EP, 16 Apr 1928.

p. 79 "in some place where": OR to EP, 26 June 1928.

p. 79 "A contadino came along": OR to EP, 9 July 1928.

p. 79 "We had been warned": OR to EP, 10 July 1928.

p. 79 "She hopes He stop writing": OR to EP, 17 July 1928.

p. 79 "*if* he remembers me"; "The permanent residents": OR to EP, 14 July 1928.

p. 80 "introduced himself and promised": OR to EP, 29 July 1928.

p. 80 "a new turn . . . with the knees": OR to EP, 17 July 1928.

p. 80 "The good doctor shows": OR to EP, 22 July 1928.

p. 80 "his ugly face": *I Ching* notebooks, 1980.

p. 80 "one of those pure frank English girls": OR to EP, 29 July 1928.

p. 80 "get all the sea salt": EP to OR, 23 July 1928.

p. 80 "The architetto . . . attaches himself": OR to EP, 8 Aug 1928.

p. 81 "He regrets his absence": EP to OR, 14 Aug 1928.

p. 81 "She hasn't got": OR to EP, 13 Aug 1928.

p. 81 "The unforgivable sin": OR to EP, 8 Aug 1928.

p. 81 "He was taken ill": M. deCourcy-Duncan to OR, 15 Aug 1928, ORP2 / YCAL.

p. 82 "He not expect her": OR to EP, 3 Sept 1928.

p. 82 "I was very sorry": JER to OR, 22 Sept 1928, ORP2 / YCAL.

p. 83 "It was the house": OR, Research notebooks, Box 100, ORP3 / YCAL.

p. 83 "Gretchen is very cockawhoop": EP to OR, 25 Oct 1928.

p. 83 "Here am I": Greene to OR, [nd] Oct 1928.

p. 83 "I could put a chattière": OR to EP, 8 Nov 1928.

p. 83 "He think next step": EP to OR, 10 Nov 1928.

p. 83 "He doesn't want cage": OR to EP, 14 Nov 1928.

p. 84 "To call it the smallest house": OR to EP, 1 Nov 1928.

p. 84 like "three matchboxes": Desmond O'Grady, *Agenda* (EP Special Issue), 1980.

p. 84 "am having downstairs done": OR to EP, from Pension Seguso, [nd] 1928.

p. 84 "My system of decor": EP to OR, 31 Dec 1928.

p. 84 "I think you'd be happier": EP to OR, 9 Dec 1928.

p. 85 "No, you God Dam fool": EP to OR, 12 Dec 1928.

p. 85 "She feels that He ought": OR to EP, [nd] Dec 1928.

7 THE BREAKING POINT (1929–1931)
  Principal sources: OR–EP correspondence, ORP1 / YCAL; Music reviews, ORP8 / YCAL; *I Ching* notebooks, ORP3 / YCAL.

p. 86 "I have tried very hard": OR to EP, 21 Jan 1929.

p. 86 "I do not think life": EP to OR, 22 Jan 1929.

p. 87 "Am I supposed to want"; "When he first knew her": OR to EP, 25 Jan 1929.

p. 87 "She fed up with hartists": EP to OR, 26 Jan 1929.

p. 87 Pound's narcissism: Cody, "Ezra Pound: The Paris Years," 18–19.

p. 87 "There is no greater joy": OR to EP, 8 Mar 1929.

p. 88 "The two Adrians": OR to EP, 8 Feb 1929.

p. 88 "*impresario* and *impressed*": OR to EP, 3 Mar 1929.

p. 88 "I have been told": GA to EP, 1 Feb 1929, EPAnnex / YCAL.

p. 88 "Our concert would draw": KRD to OR, 14 Feb 1929, ORP2 / YCAL.

p. 88 "Miss Olga Rudge": *The Guardian* (Manchester), 3 June 1929.

p. 88 "these two very fine artists": *Musical Opinion*, [nd] July 1929.

p. 88 "the Landosk": OR to EP, 30 Sept 1929.

p. 89 "The Blue Spill": draft (133 pp.) Box 115, ORP4/YCAL.

p. 89 "I've got to do *something*": OR to EP, 19 Nov 1929.

p. 90 "An' he IS damn well": EP to OR, 19 Nov 1929.

p. 90 "Orl rite, she arrange it": EP to OR, 21 Nov 1929.

p. 90 "He was very nice": OR to EP, 26 Nov 1929.

p. 90 "Dad duly and properly pleased": EP to OR, 26 Dec 1929.

p. 90 "lunch at the Hotel Rapallo": EP to OR, 28 Dec 1929.

p. 90 "mild curiosity": OR to EP, 29 Dec 1929.

p. 90 "It is curious how Yeats": OR, *I Ching* notebooks.

p. 91 "It is so damned hard": EP to OR, 21 Jan 1930.

p. 91 "She doesn't think": OR to EP, 25 Jan 1930.

p. 91 "He never said": EP to OR, 18 Jan 1930.

p. 92 "He has been seriously ill": EP to OR, 24 Jan 1930.

p. 92 "absolutely essential that she continue": OR to EP, [nd] Jan 1930.

p. 93 "I have perfect faith": Adrian Stokes to OR, 12 Aug 1929.

p. 93 Casa 60: Rolando Monti painted a gouache of the house, and "EP at St. Elizabeth's spoke of the 'yellow house' he hung in his tiny room, which delighted him" (OR, *I Ching* notebooks).

p. 93 "convoluting into bouquets": MdR, *Discretions*, 115.

p. 93 "It was *good* olive oil": OR taped interview, *Ezra Pound: American Odyssey*, 1981–82.

p. 94 "with as much success": Bowen, *Drawn from Life*, 145.

p. 94 "first dinner-coated meal": Yeats to Olivia Shakespear, 2 Mar 1929, ORP2/YCAL.

p. 94 "we had sun": Guggenheim, *Out of This Century*.

p. 94 "Those people didn't know": OR, *I Ching* notebooks, 1977.

p. 95 No sign of intimacy between them: Author interview, Giuseppi Bacigalupo, Rapallo, July 1993.

p. 95 "the dawn of a new era": Waverly Root, *New York Herald* (Paris), 25 May 1930.

p. 95 "full of new charm and rich rhythmic verve": *New York Herald* bureau (Berlin), [nd] May 1930.

p. 95 "badly handicapped": *New York Herald* (Paris), 9 May 1930.

p. 95 Mr. Carr, an English gentleman: OR to EP, 19 Aug 1930.

p. 96 "She hasn't had time": OR to EP, 22 Aug 1930.

p. 96 "My stay in Venice": Adrian Stokes to OR, 31 Aug 1931.

p. 96 Adrian "a beautiful young man": OR, *I Ching* notebooks.

p. 96 "She hasn't any place": OR to EP, [nd] Oct 1930.

p. 96 "I will not be able": JER to OR, 29 Sept 1930, ORP2 / YCAL.

p. 96 "Nothing decided about the flat": OR to EP, 5 Oct 1930.

p. 97 "I wish I could get enough": OR to EP, 3 Oct 1930.

p. 97 "the whole idea": OR to EP, 2 Nov 1930.

p. 97 Sale of grand piano, Renata Borgatti to OR, 7 Oct 1930, ORP2 / YCAL.

p. 97 "She plunk in on hi sassiety": EP to OR, 12 Sept 1930.

p. 97 "the state of murkn industry": EP to OR, 16 July 1931.

p. 97 "Mussolini is trying to make trouble": JER to OR, 22 July 1931.

p. 97 OR's 1930–31 (and other) passports: (Box 111), ORP4 / YCAL.

p. 97 "I asked her [Ramooh]": OR to EP, 23 July 1931.

p. 97 "She [Mary] enquires"; "I assure you the young man": OR to EP, 20 Aug 1931.

p. 98 "sua figlia professes": OR to EP, [nd] Aug 1931.

p. 98 "All right / DAM it": EP to OR, 22 Aug 1931.

p. 98 "majestic and beautiful like a queen": MdR, *Discretions,* 21–22.

p. 98 Mary's early visits to Venice: MdR, *Discretions,* 47 ff.

p. 100 "Mamile's resentful, disappointed eyes": MdR, *Discretions,* 66.

p. 100 "The differences between Mary and me": OR, *I Ching* notebooks.

p. 100 Details of their daily lives: OR's 1931 diary (Box 106), ORP4 / YCAL.

8 RARE AND UNFORGETTABLE LITTLE CONCERTS
(1931–1936)
Principal source: OR–EP correspondence, ORP1 / YCAL.

p. 103 Olga's world of music; Don Arturo: OR to EP, 11 Nov 1931.

p. 103 "something French": OR to EP, [nd] 1931.

p. 104 He had heard they weren't pleased: EP to OR, 14 Nov 1931.

p. 104 "excess nervousness": OR to EP, [nd] 1931.

p. 104 "the little Yehudi": OR to EP, 27 Nov 1931.

p. 104 "la matinée musicale": *Figaro* (Paris), 9 Dec 1931, ORP8 / YCAL.

p. 104 "Some said they liked it": OR to EP, 6 Dec 1931.

p. 104 "She's 'sposed to git": EP to OR, 24 Dec 1931.

p. 104 "with talk of the League": OR to EP, 24 Dec 1931.

p. 105 "the complication being": OR to EP, 31 Dec 1931.

p. 105 "wotter baht HIM lookin' "; "as fer eatin' ": EP to OR, 21 & 29 Jan 1931.

p. 105 "provided a hand-me-down": OR to EP, 25 Jan 1932.

p. 105 "*He* gets larger and larger": OR to EP, 17 Jan 1932.

p. 105 "You set the seal": E. Glover to OR, 31 Jan 1932, ORP2 / YCAL.

p. 106 "trying to get some": OR to EP, 2 Jan 1932.

p. 106 "where does the money": OR to EP, 27 Jan 1932.

p. 106 Marquise de Belboeuf ("Missy"): OR to EP, 3 Feb 1932.

p. 106 The artist Tami Koumé: OR to EP, 23 Feb 1932.

p. 106 "a tout-Paris house": OR to EP, 23 Feb 1932.

p. 106 "Parisian life": EP to OR, 14 Feb 1932.

p. 106 "Lord knows where": OR to EP, 27 Apr 1932.

p. 106 "The child cries": Johanna Marcher to OR and EP (Box 57); letters from Mary Rudge (the child) to OR in Boxes 64–66), ORP2 / YCAL.

p. 107 "It was enough to break": OR to EP, 18 May 1932.

p. 107 "Offer Olga tour": GA, enclosure in EP to OR, 1 May 1932.

p. 107 "I have noticed his good intentions": OR to EP, 7 May 1932.

p. 107 "But whether that wily bird": OR to EP, 22 May 1932.

p. 107 "Last night was a wonderful fête": Arturo Brown to OR, 5 June 1932, ORP2 / YCAL.

p. 107 "We go nowhere": KDJ to OR, 3 June 1932, ORP2 / YCAL.

p. 108 "Frid began to show interest": OR to EP, 5 Aug 1932.

p. 108 Settimana Musicale Sienese; "Siena on my map": ORP8 / YCAL.

p. 108 "She got any bright ideas?": EP to OR, 3 Apr 1933.

p. 108 "ciao, amore": OR to EP, 1 Jan 1933.

p. 108 "the excessive rent": OR to EP, 9 Jan 1933.

p. 108 "in disgrace, because we practiced": OR to EP, 8 Mar 1933.

p. 109 "very bucked up": OR to EP, 5 Nov 1932.

p. 109 "wuz pleased to see": EP to OR, 5 Apr 1933.

p. 109 "the UNSPEAKABLE Dale": EP to OR, 9 Apr 1933.

p. 109 "astonishingly fit": OR to EP, 24 Apr 1933.

p. 109 "worryin' when she gets a good hand": OR to EP, 29 Apr 1933.

p. 109 Reserving her description: EP to OR, 1 May 1933.

p. 109 Olga's "day in London": OR to EP, 2 May 1933.

p. 110 "most shatteringly beautiful": OR to EP, 11 Apr 1933.

p. 110 "On the broad pavement": W. B. Yeats, in Diliberto, *Hadley*, 144.

p. 111 "laboratory, specializing in works": Schafer, ed., *Ezra Pound and Music*, 322–23.

p. 111 "the problem of Rapallo": EP to Münch, 13 Sept 1936, EPC / YCAL.

p. 111 "Fanned by his unflagging enthusiasm": Desmond Chute, review of Rapallo concerts in *The Listener*, 5 Jan 1956; *see also* MdR, *Discretions*, 121.

p. 111 "The American violinist": *Il Mare*, "Musical Triumph in Rapallo" (June 1933); other reviews of Rapallo concerts, Box 143 ORP8 / YCAL.

p. 111 "My only interest": EP to T. Serly, [nd] June 1933, EPC / YCAL.

p. 112 "I could not have carried": OR, *I Ching* notebooks.

p. 112 Count Guido Chigi Saracini: Profile, *New Yorker*, 3 Sept 1960; see also *Time*, 31 July 1950, Box 132, ORP6 / YCAL.

p. 113 "Siena seems very pleasant": OR to EP, 5 or 6 July 1933.

p. 113 "If she stuck in Siena": EP to OR, 4 July 1933.

p. 113 "What is needed": EP to OR, 6 July 1933.

p. 113 "[One of] the best walks": OR to EP, 14 Aug 1933.

p. 113 Dinner with the Count: OR to EP, postcard ca. 20 Aug 1933.

p. 114 "Music without cuore": GCS, *New Yorker* Profile, 3 Sept 1960.

p. 114 "It would keep you occupied": EP to OR, 5 July 1933.

p. 114 "I beehaved vurry nicely": EP to OR, 13 Aug 1933.

p. 114 "His Nibs has presented her a place": OR to EP, 14 Aug 1933 (for history of the Palio, *see* Torriti, *Siena*).

p. 115 "Her figlia has comported herself": EP to OR, 4 Sept 1933.

p. 115 "I cannot accept": HP to OR, 10 Sept 1933.

p. 115 "behaving exceedingly well": OR to EP, 10 Sept 1933.

p. 115 First full season of concerts (beginning 10 Oct 1933): Schafer, ed., *Ezra Pound and Music*, 336–40)

p. 116 "not too conspicuous": Polignac to EP, 11 Nov 1933, EPAnnex/YCAL.

p. 116 "no-one but Olga": EP to G. Münch, [nd] Oct or Nov 1933, EPAnnex/YCAL.

p. 116 He took the collection home: Dorothy Pound interview, in Schafer, ed., *Ezra Pound and Music*, 325.

p. 117 "That's what all of the peasant women": MdR, *Discretions*, 120.

p. 117 "an English fambly Xmas": OR to EP, 22 Dec 1933.

p. 117 "feeling very solitary": EP to OR, 24 Dec 1933.

p. 117 "the spare parts of William Young": EP to OR, 15 Dec 1933.

p. 118 "lying there in the bank": EP to OR, 8 Feb 1934.

p. 118 "It all very noble": OR to EP, 6 Feb 1934.

p. 118 "All he thinks": EP to OR, 3 Feb 1934.

p. 118 Invoice dated 20 Feb 1934: 1996 addition, ORP/YCAL.

p. 118 "Awfully pleased": Shaw-Paige to OR, 8 Jan 1934, ORP2/YCAL.

p. 118 The Count was "very down": OR to EP, 9 Apr 1934.

p. 118 "DEE-lighted wiff concert": EP to OR, [nd] June 1934.

p. 118 Diary for 1931: Box 106, ORP4/YCAL.

p. 119 James Laughlin: *Time*, 21 Nov 1938.

p. 120 "the U.S.A. guest": Music review, ORP8/YCAL; *see also* OR to EP, 1 Dec 1934.

p. 120 A royal wedding: OR to EP, 4 Dec 1934.

p. 120 "at a local gathering": OR to EP, 28 Nov 1934.

p. 120 "didn't blow 10 pounds": OR to EP, 10 Dec 1934.

p. 120 "He wd/ like": EP to OR, 22 Dec 1934.

p. 120 "amusing, 'modern' flat": OR to EP, 28 Dec 1934.

p. 120 "He is very fond": EP to OR, 30 Dec 1934.

p. 121 "twenty minutes from the nearest": OR to EP, 3 Jan 1935.

p. 121 "expect mostly lies": EP to OR, [nd] Jan 1935.

p. 121 "Wot's Frankie going to say": EP to OR, 4 Jan 1935.

p. 121 "His voice sounded awful": OR to EP, 5 Jan 1935.

p. 121 "Your dear father": K. Rudge to OR, 6 Apr 1935, ORP2 / YCAL.

p. 122 "I am sending you": KDJ to OR, 14 Sept 1935, ORP2 / YCAL.

p. 122 "On the 7th": EP, *Il Mare* (Rapallo), Music review.

p. 122 "the earth seems": OR to EP, [nd] May 1935.

p. 122 "has been nearly off his head": EP to OR, 5 May 1935.

p. 122 Motor trip to Wörgl: Laughlin, *Ez as Wuz*, 12.

p. 122 "Everyone seems very cross": OR to EP, 22 Sept 1935.

p. 123 "I mean he wuz": EP to OR, 3 Oct 1935.

p. 123 Christmas gift and documents for Mary: OR to EP, 18 Dec 1935.

p. 123 "These Brits are incredible": OR to EP, 20 Dec 1935.

p. 123 "Baldwin has got a vote": EP to OR, 22 Dec 1935.

p. 123 "More celebrations": OR to EP, 1 Jan 1936.

p. 123 "Pride is one of the seven": OR, *I Ching* notebooks.

p. 123 Another winter concert season: *see* "An Ezra Pound Letter from Rapallo," in *Ezra Pound in Japan*, ed. Kodama, 158.

p. 124 "I am so glad": KDJ to EP, enclosure in EP to OR, 16 Jan 1936.

p. 124 "Thank God the King": OR to EP, 25 Jan 1936.

p. 124 Olga was feeling revived: OR to EP, 22 Jan 1936.

p. 124 "full of fuss and food": OR to EP, [nd] Jan 1936.

p. 124 "At least there iz one place": EP to OR, 5 Jan 1936.

p. 125 "She all *for* going": OR to EP, [nd] Jan 1936.

p. 125 "We often speak of you": E. Glover to OR, 16 June 1937, ORP2 / YCAL.

p. 125 Treasures discovered at Cambridge: OR to EP, 15 Dec 1935.

9 THE RED PRIEST OF VENICE (1936–1939)
   Principal source: OR–EP Correspondence, ORP1 / YCAL.

p. 126 "O prophetic apostle": GCS to OR, 9 Jan 1943 (trans. from Italian by M. Byrne), Accademia Chigiana.

p. 126 "ran an opera company": EP letter from Rapallo, *Japan Times Weekly,* 7 Jan 1940, in Kodama, ed., *Ezra Pound in Japan.*

p. 126 "The idea of celibacy": EP to H. Swabey, [nd] 1938, EPC / YCAL.

p. 127 OR's Vivaldi research in Turin: OR to EP, 9 Nov 1936; *I Ching* notebooks, Box 147, 1980.

p. 127 "Ricordi has printed": EP to OR, [nd] Oct 1936.

p. 127 "She is feeling rather stuffed": OR to EP, 30 Oct 1936.

p. 127 "My own private opinion": OR to EP, 9 Nov 1936.

p. 128 "A 'specially beautiful bunch": OR to EP, 7 Nov 1936.

p. 128 "his pa and ma": [nd] Dec 1936.

p. 128 OR's relationship with the Count: Author interview, Guido Burchi, Siena, July 1993; see also *Time*, profile of Count Chigi, 3 Sept 1950.

p. 128 "The last time I saw her": OR, *I Ching* notebooks, ORP3 / YCAL.

p. 129 "two ignoti, a pekinese": D. Watts to OR, 12 Mar 1937.

p. 129 "no material possessions": Bowen, *Drawn from Life*, 145.

p. 129 Letter from Antheil: GA to EP, [nd] May 1937, EPAnnex / YCAL.

p. 129 Opening session in Siena: OR to EP, 24 July 1937.

p. 129 "She regrets a misspent youth": OR to EP, 12 Nov 1936.

p. 130 Referred EP to the Reverend Mother: OR to EP, 11 Oct 1937.

p. 130 "She can tell his darter": EP to OR, [nd] Oct 1937.

p. 130 "Nixon trying hard": OR to EP, 26 Oct 1937.

p. 130 Vivaldi Society: OR to EP, 23 Oct 1937; EP to OR, 24 Oct 1937.

p. 130 Mary Rudge's first trimester report: Enclosure in OR to EP, 29 Dec 1937.

p. 130 "It's cold work": OR to EP, 27 Dec 1937.

p. 130 "NOT to waste": EP to OR, 11 Feb 1938.

p. 131 "set up a whole concert": EP to Polignac, 18 Jan 1938.

p. 131 "a stomach upset"; "All the ugly modern houses": OR to EP, 7 Mar 1938.

p. 131 "The atmosphere too Brit": OR to EP, 17 Mar 1938.

p. 131 Aldington, "another awful novel": OR to EP, 16 Mar 1938.

p. 131 "nothing against H.D.": Hilda Doolittle, Pound's first love and later Aldington's wife, was then living with her lesbian lover, Bryher (Winifred Ellerman).

p. 131 "If she doesn't hear": OR to EP, 24 Mar 1938.

p. 132 "Miss Olga Rudge, the American violinist": Ruth Sterling Frost, *New York Herald* (Paris), 18 Apr 1938.

p. 132 Palazzo Capoquadri: First mentioned in EP to OR, 24 July 1937 (later in *Guide to Kulchur*, 9, and in EP to OR, 4 Sept 1948, as one of EP's happiest memories).

p. 132 Leoncina's thirteenth birthday: OR to EP, 2 July 1938.

p. 132 "reprovin' me": EP to OR, 9 July 1938.

p. 132 Robert Browning poems Ezra sent: MdR to OR, 13 Nov 1938, ORP2 / YCAL.

p. 132 "She did not whine": OR to EP, [nd] Sept 1938.

p. 133 "If they fight": EP to OR, 17 Sept 1938.

p. 133 "everyone gibbering": OR postcard to EP, 29 Sept 1938.

p. 133 "Rothschild started buying": EP to OR, 8 Oct 1938.

p. 133 "the most charming woman in London": Olivia Shakespear, mistress of Yeats in the late 1890s, was twenty-one years older than EP when they met in 1909; he courted and married her daughter, Dorothy, 20 Apr 1914.

p. 133 "don't think it humanly possible": EP to OR, 24 & 28 Oct 1938.

p. 133 "She don't like it": OR to EP, 31 Oct 1938.

p. 133 "her li'l bro. Ted": EP to OR, 31 Oct 1938.

p. 134 "She gathers He getting tired": OR to EP, 2 Nov 1938.

p. 134 "he ain't lookin' ": EP to OR, 9 Nov 1938.

p. 134 "joy of my life": EP to T. S. Eliot, [nd] Jan 1939, Paige Carbons (#1732), YCAL.

p. 134 The Uffizi Gallery with Mary: OR to EP, late Oct 1938.

p. 134 *"Please do not* disillusion": OR to EP, 21 Nov 1938.

10 OVERTURE TO WAR (1939–1940)
    Primary source: OR–EP Correspondence, ORP1 / YCAL.

p. 135 "she hates being": OR to EP, 24 May 1939.

p. 135 "Glad you have come": Polignac to EP, 19 Apr 1939.

p. 135 "a prophet who taught": *New York Herald Tribune,* May 1939, ORP7 / YCAL.

p. 135 "that bearded wanderer": *New York Sun,* 26 May 1939, ORP7 / YCAL.

p. 135 "only inhabitable American city": EP to OR, 22, 27, & 29 May 1939.

p. 136 "Uncle Jorje" Tinkham: EP to OR, 3 May 1939.

p. 136 "seen more senators": EP to HP, 10 May 1939, EPC / YCAL.

p. 136 "A joke on me & FDR": EP to OR, 9 May 1939.

p. 136 "2 1/2 hours in an airless room": EP to OR, 17 May 1939.

p. 136 "He wants to come home": EP to OR, 23 May 1939.

p. 136 "to some college cutie": OR to EP, 26 May 1939.

p. 136 "She suffering": OR to EP, 7 & 9 June 1939.

p. 136 "She wuz walking": OR to EP, 30 May 1939.

p. 137 Hamilton College: Program of 127th Commencement, enclosure in EP to OR, 27 June 1939.

p. 137 "Waal, he iz been degreed": EP to OR, 13 June 1939.

p. 137 "He come bak": EP to OR, 27 June 1939.

p. 137 He had consulted an attorney: EP to J. H. Cochran, 16 May 1939, in Torrey, *Ezra Pound,* 312.

p. 137 "He has put her off": OR to EP, 4 July 1939.

p. 137 "I have no intention": OR to EP, 23 July 1939.

p. 138 "You are the LIMIT": EP to OR, ca. 6 Aug 1939.

p. 138 "everyone seems to think": OR to EP, ca. 1 Sept 1939.

p. 138 "Mebbe still some chance": EP to OR, 1 Sept 1939.

p. 138 Dorothea Watts of Newport: Newspaper clipping, enclosure in EP to OR, 12 July 1939.

p. 138 "Hitler apparently intends": EP to OR, 3 Sept 1939.

p. 138 "All the Brits running": OR to EP, [nd] Nov 1939.

p. 138 Entry on Vivaldi in Grove's *Dictionary:* Box 114, ORP4/YCAL.

p. 138 Vivaldi Week at the Accademia: Among OR's memorabilia (1996 addition, ORP/YCAL) was a program signed by GCS, "Alla Signora Olga Rudge, alla mia segretaria e collaboratrice preziosa nell'Accademia Musicale Chigiana, con riconoscenza sincera, commossa, vivissima, del suo devote Presidente, Fondatore, Guido Chigi Saracini, Settembre 1939."

p. 139 "Every activity, everbuddy settin' waitin'": EP to OR, 28 Apr 1940.

p. 139 "Eddie appointed Governor": EP to OR, 10 July 1940.

p. 139 "It may be all right": OR to EP, 21 July 1940.

p. 139 "If His legitime": OR to EP, 25 July 1940.

p. 139 No Palio that summer: OR to EP, 27 July 1940.

p. 139 "If she wants to worrit": EP to OR, 28 Aug 1940.

p. 140 "She has discovered": OR to EP, 7 Aug 1940.

p. 140 "Waaal, mebbe papa": EP to OR, 22 Aug 1940.

p. 140 "Leoncina all right": OR to EP, 29 Aug 1940.

p. 140 "a concert every night": OR to EP, 2 Sept 1940.

p. 140 "What wardrobe she things he requires?": EP to OR, 4 Sept 1940.

p. 140 "She 'spose He doesn't": OR to EP, 5 Sept 1940.

p. 140 Vivaldi's oratorio, *Juditha Triumphans:* Norman MacAfee to author, 12 Aug 1999.

p. 141 "a musical whoop in two parts": Transcript of Rome Radio broadcast in *If This Be Treason* (1949).

p. 141 "slumped into conventional Gais mentality": OR to EP, 30 July 1940.

p. 141 "cashed his last postal money order": EP to Kitasono, 29 Oct 1940, in Kodama, ed., *Ezra Pound in Japan,* 99.

p. 141 Delayed returning to America: Tim Redman, "Repatriation of Pound, 1939–42," *Paideuma* (winter 1979).

p. 142 "niente sino a 14 novembre": EP to OR, 12 Oct 1940.

p. 142 "She . . . don't want to go": OR to EP, 14 Oct 1940.

p. 142 "He don't want 'em": EP to OR, 11 Oct 1940.

p. 142 "Thank gawd thazz over": EP to OR, 14 Oct 1940.

p. 142 "She get her fiddle goin'": EP to OR, 15 Oct 1940.

11 THE SUBJECT IS—WARTIME (1941–1945)
   Principal sources: OR–EP correspondence, ORP1/YCAL; wartime
   Sant'Ambrogio, OR's 1943 diary, Box 106, ORP4/YCAL; OR to GCS,
   archives of Accademia Chigiana, Siena.

p. 143 "made 2 discs yesterday": EP to OR, 23 Jan 1941.

p. 143 Composed a poem: EP to Kitasono, 16 Feb 1941, in Kodama, ed., *Ezra
   Pound in Japan*, 110.

p. 144 "a bit older"; "exchanged yarns": EP to OR, 21 Feb 1941.

p. 144 "A bistecca broke a leg": OR to EP, 14 Jan 1941.

p. 144 "glad you are sticking to it": Barney to EP, 14 July 1941, ORP2/
   YCAL.

p. 144 "three [broadcasts] in a row": EP to OR, 19 July 1941.

p. 144 Permission to return: EP to OR, 29 July 1941.

p. 144 "I am all right": MdR to OR, 9 Oct 1941, ORP2/YCAL.

p. 144 "considering a flat": EP to OR, 4 Dec 1941.

p. 144 "to seek wisdom": Doob, ed., *"Ezra Pound Speaking,"* 23–27.

p. 145 "retired to continue his study": *Time,* 26 Jan 1942.

p. 145 "Because I stopped speaking": EP to OR, 7 May 1942. (From EP's correspondence with Joyce during the late 1930s: "'nother note from Joyce
   (haw-haw), longer than the other," 15 July 1938, EPC/YCAL.)

p. 145 "Rome Radio, acting in accordance": Stock, *Life of Ezra Pound*, 393.

p. 145 "sitting on the floor": Recalled in OR to RD, [nd] 1986, ORP2/YCAL.

p. 145 "Fifty kilos of tomatoes": OR to EP, 9 Sept 1942.

p. 145 "Il tuo nonno": MdR, *Discretions,* 153.

p. 145 The *American Hour*: EP to OR, 8 May 1942.

p. 146 "I have not been very well": OR to GCS, 9 July 1942.

p. 146 "They ain't even a cinema": OR to EP, 27 Jan 1943.

p. 146 "dunno if for convenience": OR to EP, 3 Feb 1943.

p. 146 252, calle Querini sequestered: OR to EP, 20 Jan 1943.

p. 146 Her "priest, the little pig": GCS to OR, 9 Jan 1942.

p. 147 "gettin' romanized": EP to OR, 12 May 1943 (*see also* 7, 9, 13 May 1943).

p. 147 Mary remembered that Allied bombers: MdR, *Discretions,* 164.

p. 147 "There ain't no zucchini": OR to EP, 22 June 1943.

p. 147 Sant'Ambrogio, that wartime summer: OR's 1943 diary, ORP4/YCAL.

p. 149 EP's indictment for treason: *New York Times,* 27 July 1943; *see also* Redman, *Ezra Pound and Italian Fascism.*

p. 149 "I have not spoken": EP to Francis Biddle, 4 Aug 1943, ORP4/YCAL.

p. 150 EP set off on foot: Carpenter, *A Serious Character,* 623–28.

p. 150 EP with Mary at Gais: MdR, *Discretions,* 186.

p. 150 "great folly to have destroyed": EP to OR, from Villa Chiara, 13 Jan 1974, copy in Research notebooks, ORP3 / YCAL.

p. 150 "At the end of this . . . year": GCS to OR, 5 Sept 1943.

p. 151 "These terrible days"; "the Poet is well": OR to GCS, 20 Sept 1943.

p. 151 Brioches at the cafés; "Beerbohm's cook"; "dry writers" in literature: OR's 1943 diary, ORP4 / YCAL.

p. 151 "I have had no news": GCS to OR, 20 Dec 1943.

p. 152 "wittiest woman in Europe": Maurice Baring, 10 Jan 1944, note in *I Ching* notebooks, 1976, ORP3 / YCAL.

p. 152 "It doesn't seem possible": OR to GCS, 11 Jan 1944.

p. 152 "My Vivaldi mania": GCS to OR, 12 Mar 1944.

p. 152 "How it hurts": OR to GCS, 1 Mar 1944.

p. 153 "the complete absence": GCS to OR, 24 Apr 1944.

p. 153 Ezra and Dorothy forced to move: *I Ching* notebooks, 12–13 Jan 1976, ORP3 / YCAL.

p. 153 Pound himself carried: OR, *I Ching* notebooks, 1980.

p. 154 "Baccin will be at the steps": OR, note to EP, [nd] May 1944.

p. 154 "I had made [the room] as comfortable": OR, *I Ching* notebooks, June 1977, ORP3 / YCAL.

p. 154 "We spent a year": DP to JL, 9 Aug 1945, EPC / YCAL.

p. 154 "We were all civilized": OR, 1983 interview, in Carpenter, *A Serious Character*, 636.

p. 154 "a somewhat Henry Jamesian attitude": MdR, *Discretions*, 258.

p. 155 "The impression she gave": Aldington, "Nobody's Baby," in *Soft Answers*, 160. (OR acknowledged that Aldington's version is close to the truth.)

p. 155 Ezra's excess energy: Author interview with James Laughlin, Norfolk, Conn., Nov 1992.

p. 155 "One solid year": OR, 1945 letterbook (Box 114), ORP4 / YCAL.

p. 155 "Whatever the civilized appearances": MdR, *Discretions*, 258. *See also* Kenneth Arnold's play in three acts, *The House of Bedlam*, unpublished ms. (1977), about which OR consulted Covington & Burling, a Washington, D.C., law firm. A thinly disguised sixty-year-old poet, Simon Moore, and his wife Catherine (a "fragile English beauty") share a house with Simon's American mistress, Vida ("dark and strikingly beautiful"), and Helen, Simon's eighteen-year-old daughter. Arnold wrote that his play "does not pretend to biography, though based on similar events in which the poet Ezra Pound found himself at the conclusion of World War II" (f. 2864, Box 117, ORP4 / YCAL).

p. 156 "one up and two to go": *New York Times*, 6 June 1944.

12 THE ROAD TO HELL (1945)

Principal sources: OR–EP correspondence, ORP1 / YCAL; Research notebooks, ORP3 / YCAL (EP in Pisa [1945], Box 101); OR–DP correspondence, ORP2 / YCAL.

p. 157 "not in a spirit": Pound's recollection of his arrest and transfer to the detention camp in Pisa, EP to MdR (from Villa Chiara), 13 Jan 1974, copy in OR's Research notebook.

p. 158 "in haste to give you": OR to MdR, 30 Apr 1945. OR's account of the events from 27 Apr to 7 May 1945, in Research notebooks, Box 101.

p. 163 "They thought I was dangerous": Torrey, in Carpenter, *A Serious Character,* 658.

p. 164 "Due to his age": Report of Capt. Walter H. Baer, DTC psychiatrist, 14 June 1945, in Carpenter, *A Serious Character,* 664.

p. 164 "He [Amprim] appreciates": John Drummond to OR, [nd] July 1945, ORP2 / YCAL.

p. 164 "Please see that Olga": EP to DP, 7 June 1945, ORP2 / YCAL.

p. 164 "I am enclosing": DP to OR, 7 June 1945.

p. 164 "That trip to Genoa": OR to DP, 2 June 1945.

p. 165 "the home-baked loaf": DP to OR, 14 June 1945.

p. 165 "very upset by your telegram": MdR to OR, 21 Aug 1945.

p. 165 "some nice Hawayan boys": MdR to OR, 2 Aug 1945, ORP2 / YCAL.

p. 165 "Mary is safe": DP to OR, 4 Aug 1945.

p. 166 "He looks wonderfully well": DP to OR, [nd] Sept 1945.

p. 166 "I just had a letter": OR to John Drummond, [nd] Sept 1945.

p. 166 "It's hard writing": OR to EP, 9 Oct 1945.

p. 166 "I felt it the best thing": OR to EP, 11 Nov 1945.

p. 166 With no library: EP's only reference works in the detention center were *Analects of Confucius,* tr. James Legg; a Chinese dictionary; Morris Speare's anthology, *Pocket Book of Verse* ("found on the jo-house seat"); and the Holy Bible (U.S. Army issue).

p. 167 "So this was Omar": MdR, *Discretions,* 260.

p. 167 "I'm very glad": OR to John Drummond, 19 Oct 1945, ORP2 / YCAL.

p. 167 "Mary and I saw EP": OR to JL, 11 Nov 1945, ORP2 / YCAL.

p. 167 "grizzled and red-eyed": MdR, *Discretions,* 256.

p. 167 "I wouldn't have undertaken": OR to GCS, 16 Nov 1945, Accademia Chigiana.

p. 168 "E's position is very different": OR to B. Somers-Cocks, 16 Oct 1945, ORP2 / YCAL.

p. 168 "By chance, I had gone": OR to EP, 23 Nov 1945.

p. 168 "Dearest child: tell your mother": EP to OR, [nd] Dec 1945.

p. 169 "Poor E's predicament": JL to OR, 4 Jan 1946, ORP2/YCAL.

13 WHAT THOU LOVEST WELL REMAINS (1946–1949) .
Principal sources: OR to GCS, Accademia Chigiana archives; OR to EP,
ORP1/YCAL; OR to MdR, ORP2/YCAL; OR to RD, Harry Ransom
Humanities Research Center (HRHRC/Tex).

p. 170 "We will take up our work": GCS to OR, 25 Mar 1946.

p. 170 "I am now convinced": MdR to EP, ca. Apr 1945.

p. 170 "the *only* thing she left": OR, *I Ching* notebooks, 1980, ORP3/YCAL;
quotation from Act II, Sc. 5, *Merchant of Venice.*

p. 171 Easter week: MdR to OR, 27 Apr 1946.

p. 171 "Work in the fields" MdR to OR, 26 Mar 1946.

p. 171 "all seem much the same": OR to EP, 3 May 1946.

p. 171 "If you have some advice": MdR to OR, 16 Apr 1946.

p. 171 "I took B. there"; "Why Mary *Rudge?*": MdR to OR, 27 June 1946.

p. 172 "the room a young man": OR to EP, 19 Oct 1946.

p. 172 "minor follies, provincial taste": EP to OR, 21 Oct 1946.

p. 172 "I will be so bold": GCS to OR, 2 Oct 1946.

p. 173 "the wedding would be very beautiful": MdR to OR, 22 June 1946.

p. 173 "Boris and I walked": MdR, *Discretions,* 275.

p. 173 "This whole affair started": OR to EP, 11 Nov 1946.

p. 173 "Waal, she has done all": EP to OR, 31 Oct 1946.

p. 173 "the Center's intelligent and hard-working Secretary": Pinzauti, *L'Accademia Musicale Chigiana.*

p. 174 "if the Poet counsels": GCS to OR, 2 Oct 1946.

p. 174 "I can't understand": OR to EP, 20 Aug 1946.

p. 174 "Yes, he wd/ be pleez": EP to OR, 14 Oct 1946.

p. 174 "beautiful Sienese country": OR to EP, [nd] Dec 1946.

p. 174 "can't bother to wait": OR to EP, 14 Dec 1946.

p. 174 The Count's "annual feed": OR to EP, 31 Dec 1946.

p. 175 "an amusing Mickey Mouse": OR to EP, 28 Dec 1946.

p. 175 Calle Querini house: Report from Controller of Property, Box 125,
ORP5/YCAL.

p. 175 "I take it that": OR to Major G. K. Cavanaugh, 6 July 1945,
ORP5/YCAL.

p. 175 "The new regime"; "economia is the order": OR to EP, 2 Jan 1947.

p. 176 "the idea of anybody": EP to OR, Feb 1947.

p. 176 "She does not doubt": OR to EP, 10 Mar 1947.

p. 177 Pound's mother would be an asset: OR to EP, 10 Feb 1947.

p. 177 "did not feel secure": IP to EP, 23 Aug 1946, EPC/YCAL.

p. 177 "While I lay waiting": MdR to OR, 10 Apr 1947.

p. 177 "a continuous state of bliss": MdR to OR, 10 Apr 1947.

p. 177 "I found a difficult situation": OR to GCS, 6 June 1947.

p. 178 "cost as much or more": OR to EP, 23 June 1947.

p. 178 "how the Old Lady recounted": OR to EP, 23 June 1947.

p. 178 "I regret you do not know": IP to EP, 7 July 1947, EPC/YCAL.

p. 178 "Sunday, His Nibs": OR to EP, 11 Aug 1947.

p. 178 *If This Be Treason . . . :* Box 115, ORP4/YCAL.

p. 178 "I chose talks": OR to Cornell, 16 Feb 1948, ORP2/YCAL.

p. 179 "I had not seen Ezra": Cornell to JL, 29 June 1948 (copy to OR).

p. 179 "You don't grasp the facts": JL to OR, [nd] Jan 1948, ORP2/YCAL.

p. 179 "Ezra has expressed": JL to OR, 14 Apr 1948.

p. 179 "is terribly intense": JL to OR, 23 Aug 1948.

p. 179 "The absolute refusal": OR to RD, 10 May 1948.

p. 179 "The reason she would like": OR to EP, 1 Feb 1948.

p. 179 "I have always suspected": RD to OR, 15 May 1948.

p. 180 "We both came to the conclusion": RD to John Drummond, 24 May 1948, HRHRC/Tex.

p. 180 "do as little as posble/": EP to OR, 13 Mar 1948.

p. 180 "in a truly magnificent uniform": OR to EP, 14 Feb 1948.

p. 180 "the child did some good ones": OR to EP, 1 Feb 1948.

p. 180 "nonna gravissima": MdR to OR, 3 Feb 1948.

p. 180 "glad I went up": OR to EP, 14 Feb 1948.

p. 181 "You've been a brick": DC to OR, 12 Feb 1948, ORP2/YCAL.

p. 181 "There is no money": OR to EP, 2 & 5 Mar 1948.

p. 181 "I feel sure Mary": DC to OR, 15 May 1948.

p. 181 "I told her not": OR to EP, 3 May 1948.

p. 182 "You were right": OR to EP, 10 May 1948.

p. 182 "It is Mr. Pound's mental quirk": Samuel A. Silk to OR, 4 May 1948, ORP2/YCAL.

p. 182 "I am afraid": Cornell to JL, 29 June 1948 (copy to OR in ORP2/YCAL).

p. 183 "I do *not* intend": OR to JL, [nd] July 1948, ORP2/YCAL.

p. 183 "complete hardhearted ignoring": OR to EP, 22 May 1948.

p. 183 "Summer is best": EP to OR, 2 June 1948.

p. 183 "She is xxxceedingly triste": OR to EP, 1 July 1948.

p. 183 "As for leading the orchestra": OR to EP, 6 July 1948.

p. 183 Huxley "very sympathetic": OR to EP 26 July 1948.

p. 183 Berenson "asking $20,000": OR to EP, 5 May 1948. (Mrs. Robert Woods Bliss, Mrs. Truxtun Beale, and Mrs. Robert Lowe Bacon were grandes dames of Washington in the 1940s.)

p. 184 "someone threw a bomb": OR to EP, 23 July 1948.

p. 184 "very hard to concentrate": OR to EP, 12 July 1948.

p. 184 "well calculated to shock": Russell, *The Independent* (London), 25 Mar 1996.

p. 184 "a nice young man": OR to EP, 18 Aug 1948.

p. 184 "My own problems": OR to EP, 30 Aug 1948.

p. 184 "the flurry in Siena": EP to OR, 6 Sept 1948.

p. 185 "The Indienne is": OR to EP, 11 Sept 1948.

p. 185 The head in the Saracini coat-of-arms: A moor's head with coiled serpent projecting from its mouth, symbolic of the infidels during the Crusades.

p. 185 "desire to escape": OR to EP, 29 Sept 1948.

p. 185 "a great relief"; "Finito la Settimana!"; excursion to San Gimignano: OR to EP, 29 Sept 1948.

p. 186 Olga arrived in Rapallo: OR to EP, 28 Oct 1948.

p. 186 "clergy, doctors, bank cashiers": OR to Peter Russell: 28 Oct 1948; Petition in Box 107, ORP4/YCAL.

p. 186 "she let Mr. Pea down": OR to EP, 10 Oct 1948.

p. 186 "[Mary] apparently feels": OR to EP, 11 Nov 1948.

p. 187 "I suppose I shall"; "choice specimens": OR to EP, 15 Nov 1948.

p. 187 "still laffin' over the election": EP to OR, 8 Nov 1948.

p. 187 "Ezra for the moment": JL to OR, 30 Nov 1948, ORP2/YCAL.

p. 187 "She minds being locked *out*": OR to EP, 17 Dec 1948.

p. 187 "literary chicken . . . musicologist": EP to OR, 7 Jan 1949.

p. 187 "[He] says we may have to wait": OR to Peter Russell, 19 Jan 1949.

p. 188 Bollingen Prize controversy: McGuire, *Bollingen*, 308–17.

p. 188 "But will he come back": OR to EP, 5 Feb 1949.

p. 189 "Be prepared": OR to Peter Russell, 10 Mar 1949.

p. 189 "I saw him in October": Barnard to OR, 5 Jan 1950.

p. 189 Dorothy Pound at St. Elizabeth's: Barnard, *Assault on Mt. Helicon*, 255.

p. 189 "Mary Barnard took": OR to T. S. Eliot, 25 May 1949, ORP2/YCAL.

p. 189 Paige's intrusion on OR's privacy: *I Ching* notebooks, ORP3/YCAL.

p. 189 Paige and carbon copies: Gallup to OR, 24 Jan 1978, ORP2/YCAL.

p. 190 "I am still not convinced": OR to T. S. Eliot, 25 May 1949, ORP2/YCAL.

p. 190 "I like a simple and quiet home": MdR to OR, 29 Sept 1949.

p. 190 "a show of spirit": EP to OR, 21 Oct 1949.

p. 190 "She doesn't want": OR to EP, 24 Oct 1949.

p. 190 "ARRANGE indeed": EP to OR, 31 Oct 1949.

p. 191 "lying in the portineria": OR to EP, 20 Dec 1949.

14 A VISITOR TO ST. ELIZABETH'S (1950–1955)
   Principal sources: OR–EP correspondence, ORP1/YCAL; OR–MdR
   correspondence, ORP2/YCAL; *I Ching* notebooks, ORP3/YCAL.

p. 192 "Banzai!" EP to OR, 8 Mar 1950.

p. 192 "Just received, in a confidential whisper": EP to OR, 28 Jan 1950.

p. 193 Letter from Hemingway: Ernest Hemingway to OR, 20 Mar 1950,
   ORP2/YCAL.

p. 193 "Sounds like a hangover": OR to EP, 7 Apr 1950.

p. 193 "Fotos rec'd": EP to OR, 24 Mar 1950.

p. 193 "Moidile looking very well"; "Them children . . . in Paradiso": OR to
   EP, 10 Apr 1950.

p. 194 A donkey for the children: OR to EP, 18 Jan 1950.

p. 194 "The most sensible man": MdR to OR, 13 July 1950, ORP2/YCAL.

p. 194 The same intrigues: OR to EP, 22 May 1950.

p. 194 "if Chigi knows": EP to OR, 28 May 1950.

p. 194 "fearing disappointment": OR to EP, 21 June 1950.

p. 194 Third International Congress of Music Librarians: Box 164,
   ORP8/YCAL; *see also I Ching* notebooks, 1979.

p. 195 Reunion with Don Arturo: Arturo Brown to OR, 25 June 1950,
   ORP2/YCAL.

p. 195 "bought meself a hat": OR to EP, 21 June 1950.

p. 196 Olga went on to London; family reunion with Teddy: OR to EP, 29 June
   1950.

p. 196 "A country doctor": EP to OR, 9 July 1950.

p. 196 Mabel "died last month": OR to EP, 8 July 1950.

p. 196 "completely demoralized": OR to EP, 7 Aug 1950.

p. 197 "Specimen Day" at the Accademia: OR to EP, 8 Aug 1950.

p. 198 "I had heard of the extreme poverty": OR, *I Ching* notebooks, 1981.

p. 198 Concert of Musica Contemporanea Americana; Teatro dei Rinnovati
   "hasn't been spoiled": OR to EP, 12 Sept 1950.

p. 198 "The view from the back"; Mary was "much more sensible": OR to EP,
   13 Nov 1950.

p. 199 "Why should He want photos?": OR to EP, 16 Dec 1950.

p. 199 "Nothing has turned up": MdR to OR, [nd] Jan 1951.

p. 199 "motoring all over England": EP to OR, 4 Feb 1951.

p. 199 "I think she is": OR to EP, 22 Feb 1951.

p. 199 Damage claim documents: Box 125, ORP5 / YCAL.

p. 200 "We always get on well": OR to EP, 17 Mar 1951.

p. 200 Claim turned over to Boris: OR, *I Ching* notebooks.

p. 200 "calculated to destroy": OR to EP, 10 Mar 1951.

p. 200 "I tried to reach you": K. Rudge to OR, 27 Feb 1949 and 2 Dec 1951, ORP2 / YCAL.

p. 201 "For a man who has": OR to EP, 10 Mar 1951.

p. 201 "Female Gabe a remarkable specimen": OR to EP, 30 May 1951.

p. 201 "He wouldn't recognize": OR to EP, 26 May 1951.

p. 202 "not very interesting young men": Conover, *Caresse Crosby*, 101.

p. 202 "so many Chigianist names": OR to GCS, 11 Nov 1951.

p. 202 Prince Sigismundo Chigi: OR to GCS, 15 Nov 1951.

p. 202 News of the Accademia: GCS to OR, 18 Nov 1951.

p. 202 Despair and loneliness: OR to EP, 2 Feb 1951.

p. 202 Eliot and Laughlin opposed: OR, *I Ching* notebooks, 1985.

p. 203 "She ain't occupying the bridal suite": OR to EP, 31 Mar 1952.

p. 203 "O.K., you bin put on": EP to OR, [nd] Mar 1952.

p. 204 "You feel that you've got": OR interview with Christopher Winner, Venice, 1977.

p. 204 "all them past glories": OR to Gloria French, [nd] May 1952, ORP2 / YCAL.

p. 204 "He forgive her for argyfying": OR to EP, 7 May 1952.

p. 204 John Kasper at St. Elizabeth's: Carpenter, *A Serious Character*, 799–801.

p. 204 "This one, who expected": OR to EP, 13 May 1952.

p. 205 "muddled up matters": OR to EP, 26 May 1952.

p. 205 "writing on an ornamental concrete bench": OR to EP, 21 June 1952.

p. 205 "The only reason": OR to EP, 31 Dec 1952.

p. 205 Saint Cecilia's Day; "He seems to think": OR to EP, 23 Nov 1952.

p. 206 "Spent whole afternoon": MdR to OR, 12 Mar 1953.

p. 206 William McNaughton: "Secret History of St. Elizabeth's," unpublished paper, Ezra Pound Conference at Brunnenburg, July 1997.

p. 206 "At social occasions": MdR, *Discretions*, 292.

p. 206 Caresse's book signing: MdR to OR, 31 Mar 1953.

p. 207 "This place is a Paradiso": OR to EP, 19 Feb 1953.

p. 207 Blanche Somers-Cocks, "great help with the children": OR to EP, 4 May 1953; *I Ching* notebooks, 1978.

p. 207 "I am all for formal politeness": OR to EP, 6 Aug 1953.

p. 207 "Have kept out of any Rapallian": OR to EP, 24 Dec 1953.

p. 207 "I was in Siena": JL to EP, 3 Jan 1954, EPAnnex / YCAL.

p. 208 "She is very tense": Barnard, *Assault on Mt. Helicon*, 254.

p. 208 She invited Clare Boothe Luce: OR to Luce, 12 July 1954.

p. 208 Olga was still waiting to see: OR to EP, 2 Apr 1955.

p. 209 "a day of great clarity": MdR, *Discretions*, 301.

p. 209 "a real rumpus is needed": B. Somers-Cocks to OR, in OR to EP, 22 May 1955.

p. 209 "I had not lived in the States": OR, *I Ching* notebooks.

p. 209 "the beard no longer": D. G. Bridson, 1956 interview at St. Elizabeth's while recording EP reading his poetry.

p. 210 Sheri Martinelli: author interview, Washington, D.C., Aug 1995; EP to Sheri Martinelli, 1 May 1957, collage on envelope to JL (31 Mar 1984), author's collection; *see also* McNaughton, "The Secret of St. Elizabeth's"; David Rattray, "Weekend with Ezra Pound," *Nation*, 16 Nov 1957.

p. 211 "If Dorothy had not told": OR, *I Ching* notebooks, 1978.

p. 211 "I can't see how"; MdR to OR, 21 July 1955.

p. 211 "Your best weapon": MdR to OR, 25 May 1955.

p. 211 "Sheri acquitted": EP to A. MacLeish, 17 Jan 1956, in Carpenter, *A Serious Character*, 819–20.

p. 212 "I wonder what I have done": Louise Birt Baynes to EMR, 14 Aug 1936; ORP2 / YCAL.

15 A PIECE OF GINGER (1956–1962)
   Principal sources: OR–EP correspondence, ORP1 / YCAL; OR–RD–EP correspondence, HRHRC / Tex; Accademia Musicale Chigiana, *see* Pinzauti, *L'Accademia Musicale Chigiana*.

p. 213 "Bear no grudge": OR to EP, 1 Jan 1957.

p. 215 Robert Frost in Washington; petition for Pound's release: Francis Sweeney, *New York Times*, 15 Dec 1972; Carpenter, *A Serious Character*, 826–40; McNaughton, "Secret History of St. Elizabeth's," 34–37.

p. 215 "Committee for Ezra Pound": Quoted from Thurman Arnold's motion for dismissal of the indictment for treason, in O'Conner and Stone, *A Casebook on Ezra Pound*, 130.

p. 216 "hailed his adopted nation": Tom Kelly, *Washington Star*, 30 Apr 1958; *see also New York Times*, 10 July 1958.

p. 216 "For how many years": MdR, *Discretions*, 304.

p. 216 Letter from her brother Teddy: EMR to OR, 18 Jan 1958.

p. 216 "Cousin Louise's . . . condition": Esther Heacock to OR, 20 June 1958, ORP2 / YCAL.

p. 216 Estate of Louise Birt Baynes: Box 125, ORP5 / YCAL.

p. 217 "Auntie Lou's legacy": OR to E. Heacock, 3 Mar 1959.

p. 217 persuaded to make recordings: EP to JL, 20 Dec 1958, Paige Carbons #1044, YCAL.

p. 217 "The Rapallo rumour": JL to OR, 3 Oct 1959, ORP2 / YCAL.

p. 217 "The family had been trained": MdR, *Discretions,* 305.

p. 218 "Thanks for the silence": EP to OR, 19 Feb 1959.

p. 218 "feeling like Jiménez": EP to OR, 27 Feb 1959.

p. 218 "Don't know if a mother": OR to EP, [nd], late 1959.

p. 218 "I told Mary": OR to EP, 3 May 1959.

p. 219 "Such things mean a lot": OR to EP, 7 June 1959.

p. 219 "Smitty" died: OR, *I Ching* notebooks, ORP3 / YCAL.

p. 219 "I envy you": KRD to OR, 4 Mar 1959, ORP2 / YCAL.

p. 219 "The Noh elements": Hesse to OR, [nd] May 1959, ORP2 / YCAL.

p. 220 "Vanni sent in Mauberly"; "monstres sacrés": OR to EP, 2 Oct 1959.

p. 220 "I grew jealous": MdR, *Discretions,* 305.

p. 220 "Where has He got this idea": OR to EP, 29 Oct 1959.

p. 220 "DEEspair the Possum says": EP to OR, 31 Oct 1959.

p. 221 "Is it possible EP remembers me?": Littlefield to OR, 19 Mar 1960, ORP2 / YCAL.

p. 221 "a tiny cottage": OR to E. Heacock, 20 Mar 1960, ORP2 / YCAL.

p. 221 "Perfectly monstrous Christmas": EP to OR, 3 Jan 1961.

p. 221 "I found the Christmas tree": MdR, *Discretions,* 306.

p. 221 "Why couldn't I have come to you": EP to OR, 3 Jan 1961.

p. 221 "His eyes were watery": Donald Hall interview, quoted in Carpenter, *A Serious Character,* 863.

p. 222 "as near the atmosphere": OR interview, *Ezra Pound: An American Odyssey* (film), May–June 1981.

p. 223 "Thanks to the Drummonds"; "He curled up": OR to RD, 3 Sept 1961.

p. 223 "I thought the end had come"; Walter had brought ginger: OR to RD, 3 Sept 1961; *see also* OR to Littlefield, 4 Aug 1961.

p. 223 "He *can* get well": OR to RD, 24 Oct 1961.

p. 223 "I telephoned Mary": OR to RD, 3 Sept 1961.

p. 223 "he was commencing to walk": OR to RD, 18 Nov 1961.

p. 223 "Even if I would": OR to RD, 24 Nov 1961.

p. 223 "Two things stand out": RD to EP, 6 Nov 1961.

p. 223 "An expensive orchestra": OR to EP, 9 Feb 1961.

p. 224 "spend a little time doodling": OR to EP, 19 Oct 1961.

p. 224 *"Please go on":* OR to EP, 10 Oct 1961.

p. 224 "President Kennedy doing something": OR to EP, 28 Nov 1961.

p. 224 "a heavenly sound": OR to EP, 10 Dec 1961.

p. 224 "Still waiting for news": OR to EP, 22 Jan 1962.

p. 225 "E . . . had a bad spell": OR to RD, 14 Feb 1962.

p. 225 "You deserve ten years": EP to OR, [nd] Feb 1962.

p. 225 "since Casella conducted": OR to EP, 21 Mar 1962.

p. 225 No news from Alto Adige: OR to EP, 22 Mar 1962.

p. 226 "I would be ready": OR to EP, 2 Mar 1962.

p. 226 "in haste—am painting": OR to RD, 7 Apr 1962.

p. 226 "EP motors from Tirolo": OR, *I Ching* notebooks, 1977, ORP3 / YCAL.

p. 226 "I gave up my job": OR interview, *Ezra Pound: An American Odyssey*.

p. 226 "a long illness": MdR, *Discretions*, 307.

16 THE LAST TEN YEARS (1962–1972)

Principal sources: OR–EP daily activities not cited elsewhere are in OR, *I Ching* notebooks, ORP3 / YCAL; OR–DP and OR–Littlefield correspondence, ORP2 / YCAL; OR–RD correspondence, HRHRC / Tex; OR–Caresse Crosby correspondence, Morris / SIU; JL–Noel Stock, WMCC / Toledo (Ohio).

p. 227 "I made a fire": OR to RD, 29 May 1962.

p. 227 She kept a daily log: OR, Research notebooks, 27 Apr 1962.

p. 228 "my bestial idiocy" (in EP's hand): *I Ching* notebooks, 1966.

p. 228 "Take a taxi": OR to DP, 30 May 1962.

p. 228 "paid purely formal visits": OR, Research notebooks, 1962, ORP3 / YCAL.

p. 228 "He has been doing well": OR to RD, 24 June 1962.

p. 229 "I hope now they will leave": DP to OR, [nd] July 1962.

p. 229 "No money is supposed to be his own": DP to OR, 11 Oct 1962.

p. 229 "Dorothy was responsible": OR, *I Ching* notebooks, 1976.

p. 230 Pablo Casals and his wife: Ibid.

p. 230 "packages, books everywhere": MdR to OR, 10 Feb 1963, ORP2 / YCAL.

p. 230 "a large crowd": OR to Caresse Crosby, 10 Feb 1963.

p. 230 "There were more causes than I realized": OR, *I Ching* notebooks, 1978.

p. 230 "gave Pope Pius some six . . . years": Littlefield to OR, 23 Aug 1963.

p. 230 "I found E. red-faced": Box 101, Research notebooks, ORP3 / YCAL.

p. 230 "Did you know when": DP to OR, 4 Dec 1965.

p. 231 "trim, gray-haired woman": M. J. Phillips-Matz, "Muse Who Was Ezra's Eyes," *The Guardian* (Manchester), 6 Apr 1996.

p. 231 "Did you know, Matz asked": Charles A. Matz, "Menotti and Pound," *Opera News*, 20 Nov 1965.

p. 232 T. S. Eliot's memorial service: *New York Times,* 31 Jan 1965; visit to Ireland, *Agenda* 21, 294.

p. 232 Dante Commemorazione: Box 101, Research notebooks, ORP3/YCAL.

p. 232 "would bring us to you": OR to Caresse Crosby, 14 June 1965.

p. 232 "Ezra Pound in Spoleto": OR, Box 115, Personal papers, ORP4/YCAL; *see also Rome Daily American,* 16 July 1965.

p. 234 The castle was cold: Conover, *Caresse Crosby,* 199.

p. 235 "I said truthfully": Caresse Crosby to OR, 2 Oct 1965.

p. 235 "We have had a German TV crew": OR to Caresse Crosby, 31 July 1965.

p. 235 "They ring my bell": Carpenter, *A Serious Character,* 897.

p. 235 Ezra's eightieth birthday, 1965 visit to Paris: OR, Personal papers, ORP4/YCAL.

p. 235 "C'est moi dans la poubelle": OR interview, *Ezra Pound: An American Odyssey* (film), May–June 1981.

p. 235 Ezra "saw no-one but Greek friends": OR, *I Ching* notebooks, 1980.

p. 236 *I Ching* notebooks, 1966–86, in Boxes 93–99, ORP3/YCAL.

p. 237 "The patient was": Medical report of Prof. Cornelio Fazio, 1966, in Carpenter, *A Serious Character,* 891.

p. 237 Read "most beautifully": OR to E. Heacock, 21 Aug 1966.

p. 237 "He is greatly missed": OR to P. Heacock, 23 Aug 1966.

p. 237 "But the most striking thing": OR to Bridson, 6 Dec 1966, ORP2/YCAL.

p. 238 Dr. Poldinger prescribed antidepressant drugs: Letter to OR, 8 Mar 1967.

p. 238 "The other graves": OR, *I Ching* notebooks, 1967.

p. 238 "For mercy's sake": DP to OR, 31 Jan 1967.

p. 238 "rather like leading 'round a . . . bear": DP to OR, 30 May 1967.

p. 238 Ginsberg at Spoleto: Personal papers, Box 117, ORP4/YCAL.

p. 238 Ginsberg in Sant'Ambrogio: Ginsberg, "Allen Verbatim."

p. 238 "Thank you for your sweetness": Allen Ginsberg to OR, 7 Nov 1967, ORP2/YCAL.

p. 239 Olga defended Ezra: OR to Connolly, [nd] Nov 1967, ORP2/YCAL.

p. 239 "Miss Rudge was clearly the sea": Richard Stern, "A Memory or Two of Mr. Pound," *Paideuma* (winter 1972).

p. 239 "Why is it, in old age?": OR, *I Ching* notebooks.

p. 239 Their daily lives; Ezra's comments: *I Ching* notebooks.

p. 240 "I do not foresee": OR to Hammond, 26 June 1969, ORP2/YCAL.

p. 240 Ezra's dreams: *I Ching* notebooks, Box 101.

p. 242 "Remember the Hill?": OR to KRD, 28 Jan 1969, ORP2/YCAL.

p. 243 "May I say how much I admire": V. Eliot to OR, 2 May 1969, ORP2/YCAL.

p. 243 OR and EP's 1969 visit to the States: *I Ching* notebooks, F.2482, Box 93.

p. 244 "Because they thought"; "Each day Olga worked out": Laughlin's account of EP and OR's visit to the U.S., JL to Noel Stock, 2 July 1969, WMCCenter / Toledo.

p. 244 "She has evidently cared for him": Claire Warren to E. Heacock, 3 Oct 1968, author's collection (from Caroline Warren).

p. 246 *Apollo 11* drama on television: *I Ching* notebooks, 1984.

p. 246 "The soapstone posts": Connolly, "Pound in Venice" (autographed galley), *Arts Front*, Personal papers, Box 117, ORP4 / YCAL.

p. 247 "When I got to 'Merciles Beaute'": M. J. Phillips-Matz, *The Guardian*, 6 Apr 1996.

p. 247 "I would be delighted to see him": Shaw to OR, 23 June 1970, ORP2 / YCAL.

p. 247 "I never cease to be amazed": Omar Pound to OR, 7 Feb 1970, ORP2 / YCAL.

p. 248 "If there was a trace of beauty": *I Ching* notebooks (in EP's hand), 1970.

p. 248 "Rapallo is now quite unpleasant": DP to OR, 23 June 1970.

p. 248 Petition for Order to Make Monthly Payment: Personal papers, ORP4 / YCAL.

p. 249 "*the* greatest living American poet": Connolly to OR & EP, 17 Apr 1970, ORP2 / YCAL.

p. 249 "We hibernated in Venice": OR to V. Eliot, 18 Aug 1970.

p. 249 Noel Stock book: *The Life of Ezra Pound*. Stock (from Hobart, Tasmania), then a professor at the University of Toledo (Ohio), began corresponding with EP in 1953.

p. 250 "It . . . looks like a triumph": JL to Stock, 1 July 1970.

p. 250 "Ezra has not *seen* him": OR to JL, 7 July 1970.

p. 250 "hogs after truffles": MdR, *Discretions*, 267.

p. 251 "A good letter from Mary": JL to Stock, 3 Dec 1970.

p. 252 "inaccuracies" in MdR's *Discretions:* OR to du Santoy, [nd] 197l, draft in Research notebooks, 1975, ORP3 / YCAL.

p. 252 Hughes at the Hidden Nest, 1971: Author interview, Oakland, Calif., Mar 1992.

p. 252 "The hardest thing": Author interview with C. Cooley, Venice, July 1993.

p. 252 Death of Stravinsky: OR interview with Christopher Winner, Venice, 1977.

p. 253 Ezra's last year: 31 Dec 1971–31 Oct 1972, in red "agenda," Research notebooks, ORP3 / YCAL.

p. 254 Academy of Arts and Sciences, Emerson-Thoreau Medal controversy: *see* JL to Stock, 5 Sept 1972.

p. 254 "Omar has 'parked' me": DP to OR, 26 Oct 1972.

p. 255 "a rather undiplomatic thing": JL to Stock, 5 Oct 1972.

p. 255 Pound's dream; Ezra at Pensione Cici: *I Ching* notebooks, Box 101, 1970–72.

p. 256 "He was like Oedipus at Colonnus": W. de Rachewiltz (quoted by Caroline Warren).

p. 256 EP's last day: "Ezra Pound Died in His Sleep," by OR, Box 116, ORP4/YCAL.

17 OLGA TRIUMPHANT (1972–1996)

Principal sources: Personal papers, ORP4/YCAL: EP's funeral (Box 110); OR's eyewitness account of EP's death and the *camera ardente* (Box 116); OR–Cyril Connolly, DP–OR correspondence, ORP2/YCAL; JL–Noel Stock correspondence, WMCC/Toledo. All quotations not cited elsewhere are (in chronological order) from *I Ching* notebooks, ORP3/YCAL.

p. 261 Olga had gone ahead with the funeral: JL to Stock, 16 Nov 1972.

p. 261 "all discussion about family matters": JL to Stock, 16 Nov 1972.

p. 261 "I regret that the funeral": DP to OR, 12 Nov 1972.

p. 262 Olga vented her anger: Personal papers, ORP4/YCAL.

p. 262 "How deeply felt": Phillips-Matz to OR, 21 Nov 1972, ORP2/YCAL.

p. 263 "deep sympathy . . . and appreciation": Bullock to OR, 11 Dec 1972, ORP2/YCAL.

p. 263 "petite and white-haired": Heymann, *The Last Rower*.

p. 264 Lester Littlefield's death: Personal papers, Box 107, ORP4/YCAL; OR to JL, 17 Feb 1973; OR to Connolly, [nd] Feb 1973.

p. 264 "I am 60 today": Littlefield to OR, 28 Jan 1973, ORP2/YCAL.

p. 264 "Lester was a thoughtful . . . friend": OR to Connolly, 11 Mar 1973.

p. 264 "Joan lent it to you": Elizabeth Gardner to OR, 30 May 1973, ORP2/YCAL.

p. 265 "like a gossipy Irish village": *The Guardian* (Manchester), [nd] 1980, ORP6/YCAL.

p. 266 "From these earnings": JL to Stock, 17 July 1973.

p. 266 "The Trustees have far too much power": (draft), *I Ching* notebooks, 1973.

p. 266 "is hedged about with . . . restrictions": JL to Stock, 17 July 1973.

p. 270 Patrizia de Rachewiltz's wedding: Author interview with William McNaughton, Hong Kong, Jan 1994.

p. 271 OR interview with Christopher Winner, Venice, 1977.

p. 271 Olga had just finished reading: A few of the eclectic mix of books on the shelves at Casa 131 that Olga listed: Montaigne's *Essays; Mao Tse-Tung,* with an introduction by Alberto Moravia; Jean Cocteau's *Orphée;* Colette's *Ces Plaisirs* (Olga noted "from 2 rue Chamfort"); *Guida a Keynes,* di Malcolm Muggeridge [Ital. translation] (OR's note: "no mention of Orage, Douglas, etc."); *King Lear* (Penguin edition); *Dante in Siena,* by Bartolomeo Aquarone (1889 ed.); W. B. Yeats' *Selected Prose;* the *Penguin Book of Animal Verse; Life with Picasso,* by Françoise Gilot (with marginal notes by EP); the complete works of Arthur Conan Doyle (with notes by OR).

p. 272 "Get slower and slower": OR to V. Eliot, 1 Jan 1978, ORP2 / YCAL.

p. 274 "It was a great event": OR to Szasz, 20 Mar 1979, 1996 addition, ORP / YCAL.

p. 276 "ten glorious days": OR to Noguchi, draft in Research notebooks, [nd] 1980, ORP3 / YCAL.

p. 276 "*C'est toujours le beau monde*": Paraphrasing a line from "A Visiting Car," tr. John Drummond (Rome, 1942), in *I Ching* notebooks.

p. 277 "To me darlin', the Irish harper": OR postcard to Pitkethly, 10 June 1982, 1996 addition ORP / YCAL.

p. 277 Baptism of Michael Ezra: MdR to Noel Stock, 23 June 1982, WMCC / Toledo.

p. 279 "translucent, perfect skin": Hughes, author interview, Oakland, Calif., Mar 1992.

p. 279 *Le Testament de Villon* in San Francisco: Program and addenda from author's collection; unpublished paper presented by author at Fifteenth International Ezra Pound Conference, Brantôme, France (July 1995).

p. 280 "She was lugging . . . an old raincoat": M. J. Phillips-Matz, "Muse Who Was Ezra's Eyes," *The Guardian,* 6 Apr 1996.

p. 281 "Toward the end": R. Vas Dias, *Times Literary Supplement,* 25 Nov 1983, 1996 addition, ORP / YCAL.

p. 282 The *convegno* to commemorate the centenary of Pound's birth: *Il Gazzettino,* 24 Feb 1984; *I Ching* notebooks, 1 June 1984.

p. 283 *Pommeriggio per* Ezra Pound: A. Pantano to OR, 20 Jan 1985, ORP2 / YCAL.

p. 283 Adelaide Ristori Prize: *I Ching* notebooks; unattributed clipping from Rome newspaper, 1996 addition, ORP / YCAL.

p. 284 "She traveled on her own": A. D. Moody, "Outlook," *The Guardian* (Manchester), 30 Mar 1996.

p. 284 *The Women of Trachis,* by Sophocles, tr. Ezra Pound, New Directions, 1957.

p. 284 Ezra Pound Memorial Trust: (draft) in Jane Rylands to OR, 28 Sept 1985, 1996 addition, ORP / YCAL.

p. 285 "skulduggery, the gondolieri": McNaughton, author interview, Hong Kong, Jan 1994.

p. 285 Centennial celebration in Idaho: Ardinger, ed., *"What Thou Lovest Well Remains,"* 1–3; *see also* Hailey, Idaho, *Sun Times,* 20 Oct 1985.

p. 286 "pushed through all of us": C. Terrell, *Paideuma,* 1989.

p. 287 "Olga, you are growing old gracefully": *I Ching* notebooks.

CODA: IT ALL COHERES

p. 289 "My memory isn't so good": OR, author interview, Oct 1992.

p. 289 Last day of her life: MdR to author, Apr 1996.

p. 290 "her constancy towards Pound": A. D. Moody, "Outlook," *The Guardian,* 30 Mar 1996.

p. 290 "I think of my dead": *I Ching* notebooks, 13 May 1980.

Secondary Sources

Ackroyd, Peter. *Ezra Pound*. London, Thames & Hudson, 1980.

Agenda 21, William Cookson, ed. (Ezra Pound Special Issue), 1979.

Aldington, Richard. *Life for Life's Sake*. New York, Viking, 1941.

——. *Soft Answers*. Carbondale, Southern Illinois University Press, 1967 ("Nobody's Baby," 88–129).

Anderson, Margaret. *My Thirty Years' War: The Autobiography*. New York, Horizon, 1969.

Antheil, George. *The Bad Boy of Music*. Garden City, N.Y., Doubleday Doran, 1945.

Ardinger, Richard, ed. *"What Thou Lovest Well Remains": 100 Years of Ezra Pound*. Boise, Idaho, Limberlost Press, 1986.

Bacigalupo, Massimo. *The Formèd Trace: The Later Poetry of Ezra Pound*. New York, Columbia University Press, 1980.

——, ed. *Ezra Pound: Un Poeta a Rapallo*. Genoa, Edicione San Marco dei Giustiniani, 1985.

Baldauf-Berdes, Jane L. *Women Musicians of Venice: Musical Foundations, 1525–1855*. Oxford, Clarendon Press, 1995.

Barnard, Mary. *Assault on Mount Helicon: A Literary Memoir*. Berkeley, University of California Press, 1934.

Beach, Sylvia. *Shakespeare & Company*. New York, Harcourt, Brace, 1959.

Bornstein, George, ed. *Ezra Pound Among the Poets*. Chicago, University of Chicago Press, 1985.

Bowen, Stella. *Drawn from Life*. London, Virago, 1984.

Brodsky, Joseph. *Watermark*. New York, Farrar, Straus & Giroux, 1992.

Carpenter, Humphrey. *A Serious Character: The Life of Ezra Pound*. New York, Dell Publishing (by arrangement with Houghton-Mifflin), 1990.

——. *Geniuses Together: American Writers in Paris in the 1920s*. London: Faber & Faber, 1988.

Chigiana: Rassegna Annuale di Studi Musicologici, XLI, Nuova Serie 21. Firenze, Leo S. Olschki Editore, 1989.

Chute, Desmond. "Poets in Paradise," *The Listener*, 5 Jan 1956.

Cody, William J. T. "Ezra Pound: The Paris Years." Unpublished paper, Conference on Creativity and Madness (Paris), 23 Sept 1990.

Conover, Anne. *Caresse Crosby: From Black Sun to Roccasinibalda*. Santa Barbara, Calif., Capra, 1989.

——. "Her Name Was Courage: Olga Rudge, Pound's Muse and the 'Circe/Aphrodite' of the Cantos." *Paideuma*, Spring 1995.

——. "The Young Olga." *Paideuma*, Spring 1997.

Cornell, Julien. *The Trial of Ezra Pound: A Documented Account of the Treason Case by the Defendant's Lawyer*. New York, John Day, 1966.

Cory, Daniel. "Ezra Pound, a Memoir." *Encounter*, May 1968.

Diggins, John P. *Mussolini and Fascism: The View from America*. Princeton, Princeton University Press, 1972. (See 246–47, 437–38, for EP's Rome Radio broadcasts and view of Fascism.)

Diliberto, Gioia, *Hadley*. New York, Ticknor & Fields, 1992.

Dixon, Vladimir. "Letters of Ezra Pound and Vladimir Dixon." *James Joyce Quarterly*, Spring 1992.

Doob, Leonard, ed. *"Ezra Pound Speaking": Radio Speeches of World War II*. Westport, Conn., Greenwood, 1978.

Doolittle, Hilda. *End to Torment: A Memoir of Ezra Pound*, ed. Norman Holmes Pearson. New York, New Directions, 1979.

Douglas, Norman. *South Wind*. New York, Macmillan, 1929.

Duncan, Ronald. *All Men Are Islands*. London, Rupert Hart-Davis, 1964.

Ede, Harold Stanley. *Savage Messiah: Gaudier-Brzeska*. New York, A. A. Knopf, 1931.

Elkin, Robert. *Queen's Hall, 1893–1914*. London, 1944.

Fisher, Clive. *Cyril Connolly: The Life and Times of England's Most Controversial Literary Critic*. New York, St. Martin's, 1995.

Fitch, Noel Riley. *Sylvia Beach and the Lost Generation*. New York, W. W. Norton, 1983.

Flory, Wendy Stallard. *The American Ezra Pound*. New Haven, Yale University Press, 1989.

——. *Ezra Pound and the Cantos: A Record of Struggle*. New Haven, Yale University Press, 1980.

Ford, Hugh. *Four Lives in Paris*. San Francisco, North Point, 1987.

Gallup, Donald C. *Ezra Pound: A Bibliography*, 2d ed. Charlottesville, University of Virginia Press, 1983.

——. *T. S. Eliot and Ezra Pound: Collaborators in Letters*. New Haven, Conn., Wenning / Stonehill, 1970.

——. *What Mad Pursuits! More Memories of a Yale Librarian*. New Haven, Beinecke Rare Book & Manuscript Library, Yale University, 1998.

Ginsberg, Allen. "Allen Verbatim." *Paideuma*, Fall 1974.

Gordon, David M., ed. *Ezra Pound and James Laughlin: Selected Letters*. New York, W. W. Norton, 1994.

Gourmont, Rémy de. *The Natural Philosophy of Love*, with translator's postscript by Ezra Pound. New York, Boni & Liveright, 1922.

Guggenheim, Peggy. *Out of This Century*. New York, Doubleday, 1980.

Hall, Donald. *Remembering Poets*. New York, Harper & Row, 1978.

——. "Ezra Pound, An Interview." *Paris Review* 28, 1962.

Hemingway, Ernest. *A Moveable Feast*. New York, Charles Scribner's Sons, 1964.

——. *Selected Letters, 1917–1961*, ed. Carlos Baker. New York, Charles Scribner's Sons, 1981.

Heymann, C. David. *Ezra Pound: The Last Rower*. New York, Viking, 1976.

Huddleston, Sisley. *In and About Paris*. London, Methuen, 1927.

Kenner, Hugh. *The Pound Era*. Berkeley, University of California Press, 1972.

Kirchberger, Joe H. *The First World War: An Eye Witness History*. New York, Facts on File, 1992.

Kodama, Sanehide, ed. *Ezra Pound in Japan: Letters and Essays*. Redding Ridge, Conn., Black Swan, 1987.

Laughlin, James. *Ez as Wuz*. Port Townsend, Wash., Graywolf, 1987.

Levy, Alan. *Ezra Pound, the Voice of Silence*. New York, Permanent Press, 1988.

Lindberg-Seyersted, Brita, ed. *Pound / Ford: The Story of a Literary Friendship*. New York, New Directions, 1982.

Littlewood, Ian. *Paris: A Literary Companion*. New York, Franklin Watts, 1988.

McAlmon, Robert. *Being Geniuses Together, 1920–1930*, rev. and enlarged ed., with Kay Boyle. San Francisco, North Point, 1968.

McDougal, Stuart Y. *Ezra Pound and the Troubadour Tradition*. Princeton, Princeton University Press, 1972.

McGuire, William. *Bollingen: An Adventure in Collecting the Past*. Princeton, Princeton University Press (Bollingen Series), 1982.

Mackenzie, Compton. *Extraordinary Women: Theme and Variations*. New York, Vanguard, 1928.

——. *My Life and Times: Octave Five (1915–1923)*. London, Chatto & Windus, 1966.

Mackenzie, Faith Compton. *As Much As I Dare*. London, Collins, 1938.

MacLeish, Archibald, with R. H. Winnick. *An American Life*. New York, Houghton-Mifflin, 1992.

McNaughton, William. "The Secret History of St. Elizabeth's." Unpublished paper, Ezra Pound International Conference at Brunnenburg, July 1997.

Meacham, Harry M. *The Caged Panther: Ezra Pound at St. Elizabeth's*. New York, Twayne, 1967.

Menuhin, Yehudi. *The Compleat Violinist: Thoughts, Exercises, and Reflections of an Itinerant Violinist*, ed. Christopher Hope. New York, Summit Books, 1986.

Meyers, Jeffrey. *The Enemy: A Biography of Wyndham Lewis*. London, Routledge Kegan-Paul, 1980.

Mullins, Eustace. *This Difficult Individual, Ezra Pound*. New York, Fleet, 1961.

Norman, Charles. *Ezra Pound*. New York, Macmillan, 1960.

O'Connor, William Van, and Edward Stone, eds. *A Casebook on Ezra Pound*. New York, Crowell, 1959.

O'Grady, Desmond. "Ezra Pound, a Personal Memoir." *Agenda* 17, 1979.

Paige, D. D., ed. *The Letters of Ezra Pound, 1907–1941*. New York, Harcourt Brace, 1950.

Paideuma: A Journal Devoted to Ezra Pound Scholarship, ed. Carroll F. Terrell. Orono, Maine.

Painter, George. *Marcel Proust: A Biography*. New York, Random House, 1989.

Perloff, Marjorie. "The Contemporary of Our Grandchildren: Pound's Influence," in *Ezra Pound Among the Poets*, ed. George Bornstein. Chicago, University of Chicago Press, 1985.

Pitkethly, Lawrence, ed. *Ezra Pound: An American Odyssey* (film). Unpublished interviews with Olga Rudge and Mary de Rachewiltz, New York Center for Visual History, 1981–82.

Pinzauti, Leonardo, *L'Accademia Musicale Chigiana: Da Boito a Boulez*. Milan, Editoriale Electra, 1982.

Pound, Ezra. *Antheil and the Treatise on Harmony*. Paris, Three Mountains Press, 1924.

——. *The Cantos of Ezra Pound*. New York, New Directions, 1989.

——. *Guide to Kulchur*. London, Faber & Faber, 1934.

——. *Spirit of Romance*. London, J. M. Dent, 1910.

Pound, Omar, and Robert Spoo, eds. *Ezra and Dorothy Pound: Letters in Captivity, 1945–1946*. New York, Oxford University Press, 1999.

Putnam, Samuel. *Paris Was Our Mistress*. New York, Viking, 1947.

Rachewiltz, Mary de. *Discretions*. Boston, Little Brown / Atlantic Monthly, 1971.

——. "Pound as Son: Letters Home." *Yale Review*, Spring 1986.

Raffel, Burton. *Ezra Pound: Prime Minister of Poetry*. Hamden, Conn., Archon, 1984.

Rattray, David. "Weekend with Ezra Pound." *Nation*, 16 Nov 1957.

Reck, Michael. *Ezra Pound: A Close-up*. New York, McGraw-Hill, 1967.

Redman, Tim. *Ezra Pound and Italian Fascism*. Cambridge, Cambridge University Press (Cambridge Studies in American Literature), 1991.

Rudge, Olga. *Facsimile di un Autografo di Antonio Vivaldi*. Siena, Ticci Editore Libraio, 1947.

Sarde, Michele. *Colette: A Biography*, tr. Richard Miller. New York, William Morrow, 1980.

Schafer, R. Murray, ed. *Ezra Pound and Music: The Complete Criticism*. New York, New Directions, 1977.

Secrest, Meryle. *Between Me and Life: A Biography of Romaine Brooks*. New York, Doubleday, 1974.

Sieburth, Richard. *Instigations: Ezra Pound and Rémy de Gourmont*. Cambridge, Harvard University Press, 1978.

Simpson, Eileen. *Poets in Their Youth: A Memoir*. New York, Random House, 1982.

Simpson, Louis. *Three on the Tower: The Lives and Works of Ezra Pound, T. S. Eliot, and William Carlos Williams*. New York, William Morrow, 1975.

Stead, C. K. *Pound, Yeats, Eliot, and the Modernist Movement*. London, Macmillan, 1986.

Stock, Noel. *The Life of Ezra Pound*. New York, Pantheon, 1970.

——. *Ezra Pound: Perspectives*. Chicago, Henry Regnery, 1965.

Szasz, Thomas S. *Law, Liberty, and Psychiatry*. New York, Macmillan, 1963.

Terrell, Carroll F. *A Companion to the Cantos of Ezra Pound*, vols. 1 and 2. Berkeley, University of California Press, 1980, 1984.

Thomson, Virgil. *Virgil Thomson*. New York, A. A. Knopf, 1966.

Tomalin, Claire. *Katherine Mansfield: A Secret Life*. New York, A. A. Knopf, 1987.

Torrey, E. Fuller. *The Roots of Treason: Ezra Pound and the Secrets of St. Elizabeth's*. New York, McGraw-Hill, 1984.

Torriti, Piero. *Siena: The Contrade and the Palio*. Florence, Italy, Bonechi, 1988.

Tytell, John. *Ezra Pound: The Solitary Volcano*. New York, Doubleday, 1987.

Valesio, Paolo. *Gabriele d'Annunzio: The Dark Flame*. New Haven, Yale University Press, 1992.

Vannini, Armando. *L'Accademia Musicale Chigiana*. Siena, Tipografia ex-Cooperativa, ca. 1952.

Ward, Margaret. *Maud Gonne: A Biography*. New York, Harper-Collins, 1990.

Watson, Steven. *Strange Bedfellows: The First American Avant-Garde*. New York, Abbeville, 1991.

Weinberger, Eliot. "A Conversation with James Laughlin." *Poets and Writers*, May–June 1995.

West, Rebecca. *The Meaning of Treason*. New York, Viking, 1947.

Wickes, George. *Amazon of Letters: The Life and Loves of Natalie Barney*. New York, Putnam, 1976.

——. *Americans in Paris*. New York, Doubleday, 1969.

Wilhelm, J. J. *Ezra Pound in London and Paris, 1908–1925*. University Park, Pennsylvania State University Press, 1990.

Wineapple, Brenda, *Sister/Brother: Gertrude and Leo Stein*. New York, G. P. Putnam, 1996.

Witemeyer, Hugh. *The Poetry of Ezra Pound: Forms and Renewal, 1908–1920*. Berkeley, University of California Press, 1969.

——, ed. *Pound/Williams: Selected Letters of Ezra Pound and William Carlos Williams*. New York, New Directions, 1996.

Yeats, William Butler. *Autobiography*. New York, Macmillan, 1965.

——. *Letters*, ed. Allan Wade. London, Hart-Davis, 1954.

Zinnes, Harriet, ed. *Ezra Pound and the Visual Arts*. New York, New Directions, 1980.

Index